C0-ANT-548

IT'S THE LAW! *Recognizing and Handling the Legal Problems of Private and Public Construction*

ALSO BY BERNARD TOMSON

Architectural & Engineering Law,
Reinhold, 1951

Recognizing and Handling the
Legal Problems of
Private and Public Construction

IT'S THE LAW!

by Bernard Tomson
edited by Norman A. Coplan
preface by Edward D. Stone

PUBLISHED BY CHANNEL PRESS GREAT NECK, NEW YORK

LIBRARY OF CONGRESS CATALOG CARD NUMBER: 60-15697

Published by Channel Press, Inc.,
159 Northern Boulevard, Great Neck, New York.

PRINTED IN THE UNITED STATES OF AMERICA.

TABLE OF CONTENTS

PREFACE *by Edward Durell Stone*

AFTER WORLD WAR II, when I returned from the service, it was impossible to find office space in New York. I established temporary headquarters in Great Neck, and there I encountered Bernard Tomson—first as a client for a new home, and next as a legal adviser in helping me re-establish my architectural practice. We became fast friends, and Judge Tomson's advice and guidance in legal and professional matters became indispensable.

One of the dividends from this association may indeed be this book, since through our association he became aware of and interested in the architect's problems and their implications—moral, ethical and legal. This led to his research and exhaustive study in architectural law; next—fortunately for our profession—to a series of articles, "It's the Law," published monthly by *Progressive Architecture;* and later to his lecture course at Pratt Institute.

The architectural profession is profoundly indebted to Judge Tomson for his intelligent guidance in a field in which the architect, owing to pressures of his own profession, is neither properly aware nor advised—nor does the traditional architectural education provide the proper background.

Mr. Tomson's interest in these matters has transcended architectural law and dry legalities. I believe that his broad social interest includes the provision of a beautiful environment for our country. By aiding the architect, the builder and the owner, he is, in a large measure, contributing toward the enrichment of man's environment.

Most building projects today involve the expenditure of millions of dollars, and it behooves all of us entrusted with the responsibility of great sums of other people's money to be acquainted with all details of this trust. Therefore, this book will perform a great social service, mandatory for government officials, business enterprises, professionals in the arts of building, and individuals who embark on the complexities of building projects.

It is an honor for me to salute Judge Tomson as a friend, a creative professional, and as a man who accepts a social responsibility of contemporary life.

INTRODUCTION

An examination of "form" contracts used by architects, engineers, and contractors throughout the United States would indicate that the problems of the construction industry in one state resemble those in another.

An examination of construction agreements relating to Latin America and Europe—or, for that matter, an Israeli "form" agreement (which is remarkably akin to the form of the American Institute of Architects)—would indicate that the similarity of the problems faced by the industry are world wide.

What is extraordinary is the absence of communication between those affected by the same problems in different parts of the United States, not to mention the void that separates them from members of the construction industry in other parts of the world. For example, a Kansas seminar on office practice in which the author participated was reported in *Progressive Architecture,* and it was only through this medium that a surprised architect in Denmark discovered that his professional society could well organize a seminar built about the same subject matter. How much wasted motion and effort ensue because the lack of understanding of the similarity and universality of these problems causes each attempt to solve them to be instituted as if it were unique rather than common! If there were true communication in the industry throughout the United States (and perhaps the Western world), licensing laws might become universal, mechanic's lien laws might resemble each other, and better standards of responsibility for design, supervision, and construction might become the rule.

Today's problems are not unlike yesterday's. Many years ago we reviewed and revised an owner-architect agreement for Edward D. Stone. The contract was prepared on the standard form of the American Institute of Architects, but was modified in a number of important respects, with particular emphasis upon the provisions concerning compensation. For example, it was provided that a retainer would be paid, constituting the minimum fee, and to be applied against the final payment for the architect's fee. The revision also provided for periodic monthly payments to the architect during the preliminary stage. It was further provided that payments would be made based upon the architect's estimate of costs until actual cost had been ascertained. To this date, these and similar aspects of the contractual provisions relating to the architect's compensation under his contract with the owner are the subject of concern as well as debate, and the problems engendered in this field —although common to all contracts in the construction industry— are often approached without appreciation of the fact that these same problems have been dealt with by others at different times. One of the primary functions this book can perform, therefore, is to have its readers from Topeka to Timbuktu recognize that the members of the construction industry should more actively exchange information as to similar problems and work together to help in their solution on a more highly organized level.

The book is based upon a monthly column written by the author over a period of years for *Progressive Architecture,* a leading architectural magazine. Although the book furnishes legal answers to specific legal questions, its primary purpose is to furnish to the architect, engineer, and contractor, a basic appreciation of some of the more important legal problems with which they may become involved. This acquaintanceship will not be sufficient, ordinarily, to permit the solution of such problems without the assistance of expert legal advice. The book should, however, create an awareness that such problems exist, and alert the reader that he requires such advice.

For the attorney, this book will provide a beginning point to initiate his research on a specific problem with which he must deal. Since the volume is concerned with a dynamic and changing field of law, it is of importance that the practicing attorney investigate the currency and applicability of judicial determinations which are here reported.

The editor, Norman A. Coplan, has collated the columns written for *Progressive Architecture,* and arranged them into five general parts. Each part is introduced by a general summary of the subject matter of that part and is further divided into chapter headings. A further summary is provided for each topic discussed within the chapter. Where the discussion requires it, forms are to be found in the body of the book, as well as in the appendix. These forms, however, are not offered as a substitute for preparation by competent legal counsel of contracts and other important documents.

I wish to express my gratitude to Thomas H. Creighton, editor of *Progressive Architecture,* for his encouragement and assistance, and to *Progressive Architecture* for permission to reprint material that has appeared in the magazine. I also wish to thank Allan S. Botter for his invaluable aid in the preparation of the manuscript.

BERNARD TOMSON

PART ONE: *Statutes Regulating the Practice of Architecture, Engineering and Building Construction*

THE PLANNING AND CONSTRUCTION of buildings and other structures is subject to regulation and control in most states. The purpose of this legislation is "to safeguard life, health and property, and to promote the public welfare," and it is on this ground that the courts sustain such regulation under the inherent "police power" of the states.

These laws also serve to protect the public against incompetent practitioners. Eliminating the practice of architecture or engineering by the unqualified has been most successful in those states where professional societies initiate and support appropriate legislation and coordinate their efforts with law enforcement agencies.

The statutes regulating the practice of architecture and engineering generally require that a license be obtained from a board, commission or other authority whose duty is to certify the qualifications of applicants. The laws of some states merely restrict the use of the title "architect" or "engineer" to those who are duly licensed to practice those professions. The statutes of other states restrict the *practice* of architecture or engineering to those duly licensed. Corporations in most states are either barred from the practice of architecture or engineering, or are permitted to practice subject to the requirement that the principal officers of the corporation are licensed.

Corporations engaged in building construction must be concerned with the laws of all states in which they are conducting activity. A corporation which is "doing business" in a state other than that of its incorporation must secure the consent of that state and must qualify under its laws. Although casual or occasional transactions will not be deemed "doing business" requiring qualification by a corporation, construction work—even though involving only the performance of a single contract or project—is generally held to be "doing business," as it extends over an appreciable length of time.

Statutes regulating the practice of architecture and engineering may provide criminal penalties for their violation. Further, an individual or company practicing architecture or engineering in violation of the applicable licensing or registration law may forfeit any compensation under his contract with the owner. The failure of a foreign corporation to comply with the statutory requirements of a state in which it is doing business may also render such a corporation subject to criminal penalties and make its contracts void or unenforceable. The severity of these penalties makes it imperative that the architect, engineer and contractor be fully apprised of the laws and requirements of the state in which the work is being done.

CHAPTER 1: *Architectural and Engineering Registration and Licensing Laws*

Licensing requirements for the practice of architecture and engineering are in the interest of the public health, safety and welfare. Contractors who perform acts which could be construed as the practice of architecture, when they are not specifically licensed to do so, may jeopardize their right to compensation for other services offered.

IN ALMOST EVERY STATE an architect, after qualifying for a license, is required in the words of a typical statute [New York] to "display it in a conspicuous place in his principal office, place of business or employment." The requirement to display the license for all to see is based on the legislative realization found in most statutes that licensing of qualified persons is required "in order to safeguard life, health and property."

Practice of architecture by unlicensed persons is recognized as reprehensible by legislatures and by the courts. Unfortunately the lay public has not been made sufficiently aware of the significance attached to the licensing of a qualified architect. Many contractors seem similarly unaware that if they perform acts constituting the practice of architecture without a license they endanger life, health and property, perform an illegal act and *jeopardize their right to compensation for services and materials otherwise legally supplied.*

Contractors and corporations nevertheless continue to draw and enter into agreements which violate the principle of illegality carefully delineated by the courts. The obvious implication is that the general public is ignorant of the importance of the architect and that contractors knowingly or unwittingly capitalize on this ignorance.

In one case, a contractor (a corporation) entered into a contract with the owner of a restaurant to remodel it and to prepare plans, drawings and specifications therefor. The contractor corporation was not licensed but employed a licensed architect who prepared the plans, drawings and specifications. The agreement between the contractor and owner provided that the owner's vice-president, who was also a registered architect, approve the plans, which he actually did. No more than 10 percent of the work involved architectural services, and about 90 percent of the work related to materials supplied and installed, such as a bar and other usual restaurant fixtures and furniture. The restaurant owner arbitrarily refused to pay for any of the services rendered or for any of the materials supplied. It undoubtedly would come as a complete surprise to most contractors to discover that not only was the contractor denied recovery for its fee for the preparation of plans, drawings and specifications, but was also not permitted to recover for *any* of the work done. The court decided that the illegal nature of that portion of the agreement of the unlicensed corporation to furnish architectural services so permeated the whole contract as to render the entire relationship illegal. The court therefore said it would not enforce payment even for the services rendered which the contractor could otherwise legally perform since they had been contaminated by the illegal agreement to perform architectural services.

The foregoing decision was by Mr. Justice Rosenman in the case of *American Store Equipment Const. Corp. v. Jack Dempsey's Punch Bowl Inc.* (174 Misc. 436 21 N.Y.S. 2d 117), affirmed by the New York Appellate Division (258 A.D. 794, 16 N.Y.S. 2d 702) and then by the Court of Appeals (283 N.Y. 601, 28 N.E. (2d) 23), the highest court in New York State. Although some would consider the result a harsh one, it seems justified by the purpose of the licensing statutes as expressed by Judge Rosenman in his decision:

> To sustain the legality of the balance of the agreement would lead to widespread disregard of the licensing statutes. It would be easy for any construction contractor to thwart the purposes for which the licensing of architects was enacted, by merely providing in his contract that architectural services would be given gratis, so long as the contractor were awarded the contract itself.

It should be a matter of concern to the architectural profession that the purpose served by the decision in the case quoted above would be obviated by a simple expedient. *When a contracting company employs a licensed architect, the licensing statutes can be satisfied by drawing two agreements—one for the contracting services rendered in which the contractor is the principal, and another for the architectural service rendered in which the licensed architect is the principal.*

Two cases determined in 1947 in New York State illustrate the prevalence of the misconception of the law. In one of these cases, although the contractor's president was a licensed engineer, it was summarily refused a judgment sought in the sum of $6,000 (6 percent of a $100,000 project) where the *corporation* had agreed to perform engineering services (*Industrial Installation Corp. v. Rosenblatt,* 74 N.Y.S. 2d 197). In the second case the court recognized the principle stated above, but decided that in this particular situation the contract was "severable" and permitted recovery. That the contractor was attempting to recover a sum in excess of $32,000 for work actually performed and materials actually furnished, and that the architectural services had been paid for by earlier payments, undoubtedly played a large part in inducing the court to seek a solution on the particular facts which would avoid what it felt was an unconscionable result. (*Industrial Installations Corp. v. Sparer,* 74 N.Y.S. 2d 198).

In view of the cases discussed, it can safely be said that *an unlicensed person or corporation may not legally perform any architectural or engineering services without jeopardizing its right to reimbursement for the cost of the whole project.* It is immaterial whether the constituent members of the company or corporation are licensed and actually perform the services. The controlling question is, "Is the principal entering into the contract licensed?" It is also immaterial whether the architectural or engineering services performed a small or major part of the agreement. In Appendix A there will be found listed cases throughout the country that discuss the essential principle involved.

It must be remembered that the licensing statutes are double-edged swords. They perform the salutary function of striking down the unqualified who attempt to deprive the licensed architect or engineer of his practice. They should also serve as a warning beacon to the architect who is careless about the letter of the law.

For example, the architect licensed to practice in one state who does not properly qualify when performing services in another state is in no better position than any other unlicensed person, and could easily be denied compensation for his labors. There should be available to every architect whose practice embraces projects in more than one state a digest of the relevant provisions of the law applicable to architectural practice in each state.

Generally speaking it will be found that states fall into one of three categories in this respect: (a) there will be no registration or licensing requirements; (b) the states restrict use of the *title,* "architect"; or (c) the states restrict actual practice of architecture to those licensed.

It should also be noted that architects often slip up on technical compliance with the licensing laws in their own states. *Steps to renew licenses should be taken before they expire so that no hiatus exists. The architect who is resuming his practice after a lapse would do well to make certain that his license is still effective.* This is no imaginary danger; it is necessary so that unscrupulous clients with knowledge of the principles of law discussed above may not seize an excuse for avoiding payment of fees for services rendered.

For the qualified, compliance with the necessary statutes may seem an unnecessary nuisance. This attitude is particularly unfortunate when *unqualified* persons and corporations, in the face of the cases discussed and existing statutes, contract with impunity to perform architectural services. The matter is obviously one that must concern the architect, and arouse him to action singly and in groups. Contractors must be educated to understand that when they agree to render architectural services they commit a crime; the public must be educated to know that to participate in such an agreement is equally reprehensible.

In summary, the matters for an architect or engineer to watch carefully in order to be sure that he is technically complying with the law are these:

(1) Make certain that your license in your state has not lapsed. If it has, drop everything and have it reinstated immediately.

(2) Before engaging in a project in a state other than the one in which you are licensed, check the licensing requirements and comply with them.

(3) Do not perform your services incidental to a contracting firm's or engineering firm's agreement where the company acts as principal. Insist on making your own agreement with the client

unless the company itself is legally permitted to practice architecture.

(4) Discuss at your professional association meetings methods of combating illegal practice of architecture and for education locally and nationally of contractors and the lay public.

SPECIAL LEGAL DECISIONS

APPENDIX A (Cases)

CALIFORNIA: Baer v. Tippett, 34 Cal. App. (2d) 33, 92 P. (2d) 1025; **McDowell v. Long Beach,** 12 Cal. App. (2d) 634, 55 P. (2d) 934; **Meyer & Holler v. Bowman,** 121 Cal. App. 112, 8 P. (2d) 936; **Force v. Hart,** 209 Cal. 600, 289 P. 828; **Jones v. Wickstrom,** 92 Cal. App. 292, 288 P. 449; **Payne v. De Vaughn,** 77 Cal. App. 399, 246 P. 1069; **Fitzhugh v. Mason,** 2 Cal. App. 220, 83 Pac. 282.

GEORGIA: Brown v. Glass, 46 Ga. App. 323, 167 S.E. 722.

ILLINOIS: Keenas v. Tuma, 240 Ill. App. 448; **Haynes v. East St. Louis Council,** 258 Ill. App. 38.

KENTUCKY: Board of Education v. Elliott, 276 Ky. 790, 125 S.W. (2d) 733.

LOUISIANA: Rabinowitz v. Hurwitz-Mintz Furniture Co., 19 La. App. 811, 133 So. 498.

MICHIGAN: Bollin v. Fahl, 206 N.W. 495; **Wedgewood v. Jorgens,** 190 Mich. 620, 157 N.W. 360.

NEW JERSEY: Gionti v. Crown Motor Freight Co., 128 N.J.L. 407, 26 A (2d) 282; **Dane v. Brown,** 70 F. (2d) 164.

NEW YORK: American Store Equipment & Construction Corp. v. Jack Dempsey's Punch Bowl, 174 Misc. 436, 21 N.Y.S. (2d) 117-aff'd. 258 A.D. 794, 16 N.Y.S. (2d) 702, 283 N.Y. 601, 28 N.E. (2d) 23; **Bowen v. Schenectady,** 136 Misc. 307, 240 N.Y.S. 784 aff'd. 231 A.D. 779, 246 N.Y.S. 913; **Bintz v. Mid-City Park Corp.,** 223 A.D. 533, 229 N.Y.S. 390; **Industrial Installations Corp. v. Sparer,** 74 N.Y.S. (2d) 198; **Industrial Installations Corp. v. Rosenblatt,** 74 N.Y.S. (2d) 197; **Roth v. Hoster Realty Co. Inc.,** 119 Misc. 686, 197 N.Y.S. 220.

OHIO: Wolpa v. Hambly, 20 Ohio App. 236, 153 N.E. 135.

PENNSYLVANIA: F. F. Bollinger Co. v. Widmann Brewing Corporation, 14 A. (2d) 81.

TENNESSEE: Cantrell v. Perkins, 177 Tenn. 47, 146 S.W. (2d) 134; **State Board v. Rodgers,** 167 Tenn. 374, 69 S.W. (2d) 1093.

TEXAS: Clark v. Eads, 165 S.W. (2d) 1019.

UTAH: Smith v. American Packing & Provision Co., 102 Utah 351, 130 P. (2d) 951.

WASHINGTON: Sherwood v. Wise, 132 Wash. 295, 232 Pac. 309.

WISCONSIN: Lytle v. Godfirnon, 241 Wisc. 533, 6 N.W. (2d) 652; **Wahlstrom v. Hill,** 213 Wisc. 533, 252 N.W. 339; **Adams v. Feiges,** 206 Wisc. 183, 239 N.W. 446; **Fischer v. Landisch,** 203 Wisc. 254, 234 N.W. 498; **Hickey v. Sutton,** 191 Wisc. 313, 210 N.W. 704.

Inadequate licensing laws open the door for the practice of architecture and engineering by the unqualified and incompetent, to the detriment of the public interest.

Imperfect licensing requirements have a considerable effect on the practice of architecture and the income derived therefrom. In Kentucky, for example, although it is provided that ". . . no person shall practice architecture without having a license, . . . it being the purpose of this chapter to safeguard life, health, and property, and to promote public welfare," the statute also states that "Nothing . . . shall prevent *engineers, mechanics, or builders* from making plans and specifications for buildings . . ." This has had the fantastic result of permitting anyone to practice architecture. Accordingly, only a small number of architects are registered in Kentucky, while large numbers of unlicensed persons practice architecture.

In Ohio a similar situation exists. There, too, although the statute provides that no one shall practice architecture without a license, it is further provided:

> This act shall not be construed to as to prevent persons other than architects from filing applications for building permits or obtaining such permits providing the drawings for such buildings are signed by the authors with their true appellation as engineer or contractor or carpenter, et cetera, but without the use of any form of the title architect, nor shall it be construed to prevent such persons from designing buildings and supervising the construction thereof for their own use.

This provision, although not quite as broad as the Kentucky section, would permit a contractor, a carpenter, or an "et cetera," to draw plans where he files the application for a building permit.

The Ohio statute has been the subject of litigation. It is now fairly clear that in Ohio the "et ceteras" may not practice architecture generally, but are specifically permitted to practice architecture in relation to those projects which they themselves will construct. Even this result was not easily obtained. The statute was interpreted in 1949 by the Ohio Attorney General. Under the procedure followed, a public official posed a problem to the Attorney General as follows:

> J.W.L., who is skilled in drawing plans and specifications for erection of buildings, drew and furnished plans for the erection of a public building at the Guernsey County Home. J.W.L. did not contract to supervise the work of erecting the building. There was no express agreement for compensation for his services in making the plans and specifications. J.W.L. is not and has never been the holder of a certificate of qualification to practice architecture in the State of Ohio under Section 1334-9 S.C., but he is a contractor and is skilled in drawing plans and specifications for the erection of buildings. He submitted to the County Commissioners of Guernsey County, Ohio, a bid for the erection of the building in question but the contract was awarded to another contractor at a lower bid. J.W.L. has presented a bill to said County Commissioners in the amount of $600 for his said services in drawing and furnishing said plans and specifications.
>
> By authority of 380 L.A. 449, Maxfield, App. v. Bressler, it would seem that J.W.L. could collect from said Board of County Commissioners the fair and reasonable value of his services for drawing and furnishing said plans and specifications.

In his answer, the Attorney General held that the contract to pay for design (as distinguished from design plus construction) was illegal and void; and that the contractor could not, therefore, recover from the Board of County Commissioners. He cited also another section of the General Code of Ohio, which requires that a governmental building be designed by a "competent architect," which he held was a licensed architect. The language of his reasoning indicates a step forward. He said, in part:

> This section (1334-17) prohibits such practice by those other than a certificate holder. That the legislature has the right to prohibit such practice has never been seriously questioned, since such practice demands learning, skill, and integrity; and it is within the police power of a legislature to regulate such practice, because the plans and specifications are for a building which may be used by the members of the public, and as such it is a business involving the public safety and health, and therefore a matter of public policy.

This decision, however, is in strict contrast to another holding: that emergency veterans' housing was not a "public building" and therefore was not required to be designed by a licensed architect.

The law as it apparently exists in Ohio was also summarized in a case where builders, not licensed as architects, designed for an owner a house with an estimated cost of $12,800. The owner decided not to build, and the builder sued for the architectural services rendered. The Court summarized the Ohio law as follows:

> (1) An owner may employ a builder to construct a building for him without the services of a registered architect, there being no such requirement.
>
> (2) That an owner may design a building and supervise the construction thereof for his own use without being a licensed architect under the exception in Section 1334-17, General Code.
>
> (3) That a builder who is not a registered architect may contract to furnish plans and specifications for an owner, provided the plans and specifications are prepared by a registered architect.
>
> But the court is of the opinion that under the laws of the State of Ohio, a builder who is not a registered architect may not prepare complete plans and specifications for the construction of a building for another, when expert knowledge and skill are required in such preparation; and that such laws apply to persons engaging in single isolated architectural transactions as well as persons attempting to practice architecture as a business or profession. (*McGill v. Carlos,* 81 N.E. 2d 726).

The significance of the existence of statutes such as those discussed cannot be overlooked. They permit incompetent persons to practice architecture and thus to jeopardize "life," "health," "property," and "public welfare." In those states where this situation exists, the local architectural organizations must be militant to bring home to the public and to the legislators the danger inherent in such statutes remaining on the books. In other states, such as New York, where the practice of architecture is generally prohibited to those not qualified, it is equally important for the local organizations to see to it that the letter and spirit of the statutes are scrupulously obeyed. The practice of architecture by incompetents bilks the public and cuts into the livelihood of the architect, who has spent many years preparing to practice. Such a situation should not be tolerated by architects and, if properly brought home to the public, will not long be permitted to exist.

The practice of such emasculation is more widespread than is generally recognized and the process is apt to be regressive as well as progressive. A good example is Oklahoma's licensing statute which was seriously weakened by amendments in 1949, providing that the statute making it mandatory for architects to be licensed was inapplicable to:

> . . . any building, or the repairing or remodeling of any building, to be used for one family residential purposes, duplexes, or apartment houses not exceeding two (2) stories in height, Hotel, Lodge, or Fraternal or Institutional building not exceeding two (2) stories in height, nor to any schoolhouses where the reasonably estimated total cost of such building, remodeling or repairing does not exceed the sum of Ten Thousand Dollars (10,000), . . .

The practice statute of Nebraska exempts from the requirement of obtaining an architectural license:

> . . . persons, mechanics or builders from making plans, specifications for or supervising the erection, enlargement, or alteration of buildings, or any part thereof, to be constructed by themselves or their own employees for their own use.

The practice statutes of Missouri and Kansas are similar to the above quoted section. Iowa has in effect what is generally referred to as a title statute:

> Nothing contained in this chapter shall prevent any person from making plans and specifications or supervising the construction of any building or part thereof, for himself or others, *provided he does not use any form of the word or title "Architect."*

The licensing statute of Iowa further provides, however, for a "certificate," and for its revocation for:

(1) Fraud.

(2) Gross incompetency or negligence in the planning or construction of buildings.

(3) Habitual drunkenness or drug addiction.

It should be noted that there is no provision in this statute preventing an unlicensed, unethical, incompetent, negligent, and habitually drunken fraud from designing and supervising the construction of buildings. The architect, whose certificate has been revoked for any of the aforementioned reasons, is still permitted to practice the profession of architecture provided only he does not use the title "architect."

The emasculated statute of Iowa quoted above is in direct contrast to the engineers' and land surveyors' statute of the same state, which has no important exceptions:

> No person shall practice professional engineering or land surveying in the state unless he be a registered professional engineer or land surveyor as provided in this chapter . . .

The statute further provides that the requirements for the engineering license are:

(1) A four-year college engineering course and two years practical experience.

(2) A written examination.

This is a good engineers' statute. Its administration is, of course, not here considered.

Architects throughout the United States should be aggressive in dealing with the problem of weak licensing statutes that permit incompetent designers to prey upon the public. Unfortunately there is some muddled thinking even within the profession on this problem. It is sometimes stated that such a statute "protects" the architects and creates a "favored" class. Such an illogical argument would be applicable to the practice of medicine, pharmacy, law, or any other profession where licensing is necessary "for the public health, safety, and welfare." This is the test and not whether architects are benefited. When the question is squarely put—"Is it necessary for the 'public health, safety and welfare' for architects to be licensed?"—the answer is not only plain, but has already been answered in the affirmative in almost every state in the Union. The recognition of this as a fact should permit no exceptions which endanger life, health, safety, and welfare.

A coordinated movement is necessary to prevent regressive changes in registration laws and to improve the effectiveness of present statutes.

The universality of architects' problems, *vis-a-vis* the client, the public and the registration law in each state, has increasingly been impressed upon me. Particularly with respect to registration-law problems facing architects throughout the country, there is a crying need for the development of an integrated approach to the pooling of information, for the exchange of ideas, and for the development of a "uniform" statute. This should be initiated as soon as it can be arranged by a conference called to acquaint those struggling with the problem in each state that the difficulties are not local in character, but national: that the problems in California are the problems in Michigan; that the problems in Georgia are the problems in Wyoming; that the problems in Colorado are the problems in Oklahoma (*ad infinitum*).

I have spoken at state conventions in California, in Georgia, in Michigan, and at regional conferences in Oklahoma and in Colorado. In California, we discussed the necessity for a change in the California statute, the nature of the required change, and the timing. In Georgia, we discussed the legislation then pending before the legislature. In Michigan, we discussed the legislation already passed by the House and pending before the Senate—an amendment which would weaken the Michigan registration law (although permitting architects to become master builders). In Oklahoma, we discussed an amendment to the act, which had weakened a previously strong licensing act. In Colorado, we argued the merits, paragraph by paragraph, of a proposed revision of the law.

What was remarkable in each of these places was the complete absence of knowledge of the problems current in other states, or even of problems in adjoining states. It is axiomatic that at least the exchange and pooling of information would have been and would be helpful. When I addressed the architects at each of these conventions, I made this point. Looking back now I feel it cannot be urged too strongly.

What disturbs me most is that changes in the registration laws do not necessarily show progress. Indeed, they often show the reverse. Although Wyoming, for the first time, now has a registration law, it is a "title" statute (limiting only the use of the title, "Architect"); Oklahoma's statute has been weakened; Michigan's statute has been weakened; Colorado's first draft of a new law has emasculating provisions; and California is not anxious to raise the issue *now*. The only bright spot is Georgia, where a "title" statute has been replaced by a strong "practice" statute, prohibiting the *practice* of architecture to anyone other than registered architects, with no important exceptions other than "one- or two-family residences regardless of cost"—a compromise no doubt dictated by compelling necessity, and perhaps temporary.

The now superseded statute of Georgia, dealing with the registration of architects, merely restricted the use of the title, "Architect," but did not ban the practice of architecture by unqualified persons. Section 84-321 formerly read, in part, as follows:

> . . . nor shall anything contained in this Chapter prevent persons, mechanics, or builders from making plans and specifications for, or supervising the erection, enlargement, or alteration of buildings or any appurtenances thereto to be constructed by themselves or their employees: Provided, that the working drawings for such construction are signed by the authors thereof with their true appellation, as "Engineer," or "Contractor," or "Carpenter," etc., without the use in any form of the title "Architect."

The courts, when confronted by statutes of this or similar import, have held that the purpose of such law is the protection of the public from misrepresentation and deceit, and its prohibition is no greater than called for by this purpose. In these states this has had the fantastic result of permitting *anyone* to practice architecture, without regard to the public health, safety, and welfare. The practical effect of such laws upon the qualified and trained architect is to compel him to compete against those who, but for the laxity of the registration laws, would merely execute his plans and specifications.

In contrast to the above weakened and ineffectual former Georgia registration statute, the present Section 84-302, effective February 15, 1952, provides as follows:

> Certificate of Qualification to Practice Under Title of Architect: An architect within the meaning of this Act is an individual technically and legally qualified to practice achitecture and who is authorized under this Act to practice architecture who prior to the passage of this Act shall not already have been registered to practice architecture in the State shall before being entitled to be known as an architect secure from the Georgia State Board for the Examination, Qualification, and Registration of Architects a Certificate of Qualification to practice under the title of Architect as provided by this chapter and the amendments thereto. The renewal of Certificates of Registration issued to architects registered prior to the enactment of this amendment shall carry the obligations required by

this amendment to the original Act under which their previous registrations have been granted. Except as otherwise provided in this Act, *no person shall practice architecture in* the State of Georgia or use the title "architect" or "registered architect" or any words, letters, figures, or any other device indicating or intending to imply that he or she is an architect without having qualified as required by this Act. No firm, company, partnership, association, corporation, or other similar organization shall be registered as an architect. Only individuals shall be registered as architects. Firms, companies, partnerships, associations and corporations may prepare plans, drawings, and specifications for buildings and structures as defined by this Act and perform the services heretofore enumerated common to the practice of architecture, provided that at least one of the chief executive officers of such firms, companies, partnerships, associations, corporations, or similar companies, is a registered architect in the State of Georgia under this Act and provided further that the supervision of such buildings and structures shall be under the personal supervision of said registered architects and that such plans, drawings, and specifications shall be prepared under the personal direction and supervision of such registered architects and bear their individual signatures and seals.

The old law merely required as a prerequisite for registration the following "accomplishments," an examination being discretionary with the Board:

> . . . satisfactory evidence of having completed the course in a high school or the equivalent thereof, and of having subsequently thereto completed such course in mathematics, history, and language as may be approved or prescribed by the said Board.

The new law provides:

> Any citizen of the United States, being at least 21 years of age and of good moral character, may apply through the Joint-Secretary, State Examining Boards, to the State Board for the Examination, Qualification, and Registration of Architects for a certificate of registration, or for such examination as shall be requisite for such certification under this Chapter; but before receiving such certificate the applicant shall submit satisfactory evidence of having completed the course in a high school or the equivalent thereof, *in addition to a minimum of seven years experience* in an office of a registered architect, as may be

approved or prescribed by the said Board. The examination for the above academic requirements shall be held by the said Board. In lieu of such examination the said Board may accept satisfactory diplomas or certificates from institutions approved by the said Board covering the course or subject-matter prescribed for examination. Upon complying with the above requirements the applicant shall satisfactorily pass an examination in such technical and professional subjects as shall be prescribed by the said Board. The said Board may, in lieu of the examination in such technical and professional subjects, accept satisfactory evidence of any one of the qualifications set forth under subdivisions (a) and (b) of this section.

(a) A diploma of graduation or satisfactory certificate from an architectural college or school that he or she has completed a technical course approved by the American Institute of Architects, and subsequent thereto, at least three years' satisfactory experience in the office or offices of a reputable architect or architects.

(b) Registration or certification as an architect in another State or Territory where the qualifications prescribed at the time of such registration or certification were equal to those prescribed in this State at date of application.

The said Board may require applicants under these subdivisions to furnish satisfactory evidence of knowledge or professional practice. (Acts 1919, p. 192; 1931, pp. 7, 36.)

Although the above-quoted paragraphs are not ideal in their requirements, they are obviously a long step in the right direction when compared with the old law.

The Georgia accomplishment can and must be duplicated elsewhere. This is required not only for the protection of the architect, but for the protection of the public as well. Unless a *co-ordinated* movement is organized, progress will probably be slow, if made at all, and regressive changes in the registration laws may ensue. The danger is to the public, but the obligation is the architect's to lead in avoiding the danger.

The evolution of the Georgia Registration and Licensing statute is illustrative of a progressive accomplishment in the licensing field which resulted from the activities of the profession itself to obtain a more effective law.

The Georgia chapter of the American Institute of Architects has been continually working on plans to strengthen its licensing statute. Many recommendations had been sent to the board which administered the statute. In 1953, the Georgia law was further strengthened by providing an injunctive procedure. Upon the recommendation of the board, the statute was again amended in 1955, and the changes in the law included many of the recommendations of the Chapter. The statute was redrawn by the office of the Attorney General of Georgia, and many provisions clarifying and strengthening the law in respect to qualification, revocation of license, and injunctive procedure were added.

The evolution of the Georgia law is an example of what can be accomplished where the profession itself is active in pressing for action and the co-operation of public officials is obtained.

Bernard B. Rothschild, then president of the Georgia Chapter, stated in an exchange of correspondence between us:

"By and large the law is better than it has ever been and it is approaching the stage where trial and error are proving its workability. The Attorney General's office is working with the Board now to make certain that the law has sufficient teeth. The co-operation between the Board, Georgia Chapter, and the Attorney General's Office is really most gratifying."

Rothschild pointed out, however, that the Georgia statute requires further change. He said:

"Our law says a corporation cannot *practice* architecture but it can employ an architect to practice for it. This subterfuge permits contractors and others to enter into the architectural profession, with an often unprofessional attitude. I am hoping we will change the law to make firm names contain only the names of living, registered architects or engineers and that all partners, or corporate officers and directors must be registered architects and engineers."

It is a cliché to state that a law is only as effective as its enforcement. I have been informed that under the Georgia law, for example, there was no conviction for its violation during a 16-year period. The usual State Board which administers the registration and licensing law often does not have the means or power to investigate possible violations and to police the practice of architecture. Rothschild, in referring to the Georgia law, points out:

"There is one observation that must be made, however: The teeth in the law are only as good as the enforcing agencies . . . The next step that we in Georgia Chapter must take—and this is as important as the law itself—is to set up a policing agency. The Chapter is going to have to go to work to see what can be done. . . . How to create and finance the position of deputy or investigator for the Board is the problem we really have to solve. This is a real challenge."

The profession still has much to do in "selling" to the public and to the state legislatures the need for strong legislation with means of effective enforcement to eliminate the dangers inherent in the practice of architecture by the unqualified and incompetent. There is no substitute for work at the "grass roots" level. Each local chapter must continue and increase its efforts in this direction in its own state. Each state chapter should consider carefully how to become a policing arm of the state to insure effective enforcement. In many states, the pattern already set up for physicians and attorneys would indicate how enforcement could be made truly effective.

Adequate enforcement of licensing statutes is a prerequisite for the protection of the public against the practice of architecture or engineering by the unqualified.

"Passing a new law" is no substitute for lack of enforcement of an existing licensing law. Most statutes need amendments, but it can safely be said that no architectural registration law is enforced to the satisfaction of the profession. New York State, which has one of the stronger licensing statutes, is a case in point. Some years ago I learned that there were only eight investigators whose job it was to cover *all* of the state to enforce *all* of the licensing statutes (physicians, pharmacists, engineers, architects, etc.).

What should architects do under the circumstances? This problem is often posed, and I have recommended that state associations of architects play an active part in enforcement. It was recommended in New York that procedures be set up for dealing with those not licensed though practicing architecture, and for those licensed individuals who apparently were violating the canons of ethics. The suggestion was further made that the procedure applicable to the suspension or disbarment of an attorney be used as a guide and that, where necessary, enabling legislation be sought giving the state association the power to act.

Article 174, Section 7308 of the Education Law of the State of New York, entitled "Disciplinary Proceedings," sets forth the procedures to be followed for the revoking, suspending, or annulling of licenses of architects, as well as the grounds necessary for such action, as follows:

> The regents shall have power to revoke, suspend, or annul the license (which term, as used in this section, shall include a temporary permit issued under section seventy-three hundred and four) and/or registration of an architect in accordance with the following provisions and procedure in any of the following cases:
>
> a. Upon proof that the holder of such license is practicing in violation of section seventy-three hundred five of this article.
>
> b. Upon proof that such license has been obtained or that the holder thereof has obtained such license by fraud or misrepresentation.
>
> c. Upon proof that any money was paid to secure such license except fees prescribed by this article.
>
> d. Upon proof that the holder of such license is falsely impersonating a practitioner or former practitioner or is practicing under an assumed, fictitious, or corporate name.
>
> e. Upon proof that the holder of such license has been guilty of a felony.
>
> f. Upon proof that the holder of such license aided and abetted in the practice of architecture under the provisions of this article.
>
> g. Upon proof that the holder of such license is guilty of fraud, of deceit, of gross negligence, incompetency, or *misconduct* in the practice of architecture.
>
> h. Upon proof that the holder of such license permitted his seal to be affixed to any plans, specifications, or drawings that were not prepared by him or under his personal supervision by his regularly employed subordinate.

The law set forth above is similar to Section 90 of the New York Judiciary Law, which relates to the suspension from practice or removal from office of any attorney or counselor at law. The said Section 90, entitled "Admission to and Removal From Practice by Appellate Division," subdivision (2), reads as follows:

> The Supreme Court shall have power and control over attorneys and counselors-at-law and all persons practicing or assuming to practice law, and the appellate division of the

supreme court in each department is authorized to censure, suspend from practice or remove from office any attorney and counselor-at-law admitted to practice who is guilty of *professional misconduct,* malpractice, fraud, deceit, crime or misdemeanor, or any conduct prejudicial to the administration of justice; and the appellate division of the supreme court is hereby authorized to revoke such admission for any misrepresentation or suppression of any information in connection with the application for admission to practice.

Some states have, under their respective licensing statutes, provided that the board authorized to examine and license architects may revoke, suspend, or annul such license for cause, such as gross incompetency or recklessness, or for dishonest practices. The board, of course, must not exercise its power arbitrarily and must conform to the procedures and standards as prescribed by the statute, and only where the discretionary power of the board is exercised with manifest injustice will the courts interfere.

Unfortunately there is a paucity of decisions in this area, but those available indicate that the boards have strictly construed the statutes and have been reluctant to exercise their powers, except in a case involving flagrant abuses by the architect in the practice of his profession.

In Illinois, Hurd's Stat. 1911, Sec. 10, p. 87, providing for the licensing of architects and regulating the practice of architecture as a profession, contains the following:

> Any license so granted may be revoked by unanimous vote of the state board of examiners of architects for gross incompetency or recklessness in the construction of buildings, or for dishonest practices on the part of the holder thereof . . .

The Illinois Appellate Court, in *Kaeseberg v. Richer,* 177 Ill. App. 527, declared that a single dishonest act on the part of an architect did not constitute "dishonest practices" under the words of the statute authorizing revocation of a license. The generality of this Illinois statute was defended in *Klafter v. State Board of Examiners of Architects* (1913), 259 Ill. 15, 102 N.E. 193, at p. 195:

> . . . The same reasoning applies to the words "gross incompetency or recklessness in the construction of buildings." These words clearly imply that the license shall not be revoked for trivial causes. What actions or conduct of an architect will bring him within the meaning of these words must be left to the

sound discretion of the state board. It must be some act or conduct that in the common judgment would be considered grossly incompetent or reckless. It is a practical impossibility to set out in a statute, in detail, every act which would justify the revocation of a license. The requirements of the statute can only be stated in general terms and a reasonable discretion reposed in the officials charged with its enforcement. The statute in question is not void for uncertainty.

The following cases illustrate the problem in California and Wisconsin. In considering these decisions, careful note should be taken of the summary of the board's findings and the weight given these findings by the court.

In *Coffman v. California State Board of Architectural Examiners, Northern California,* 19 P. 2d 1002 (1933), the court reviewed the following complaint:

Substitutions were made in practically every phase of work on the house. The work was so slighted throughout as to cheapen the building materially. There is a question as to the actual safety of the structure.

The house vibrates in the wind, and the floors shake under ordinary tread. A substitution of wooden underpinnings was made in place of concrete foundation, as specified.

The exterior woodwork and interior trim are Oregon pine, instead of redwood.

This is warping and shrinking badly.

2 x 6 floor joists were substituted for 2 x 8.

With sufficient underpinning, floor girders were smaller than specified.

Ceiling rafters are 2 x 4 instead 2 x 6, with long spans, and are insufficient to support the ceiling. Roof rafters are light 2 x 4 size and the surface 24″ center, instead of 24 as specified.

The sheathings under the shingles are 1 x 4—4½″ space. This is very light.

Local gravel was used instead of crushed rock, as specified.

Gutters and downspouts are insufficient, and drains were not provided as specified.

Stucco is in very bad condition, and is not weatherproof, due to the fact that it was not surfaced with two coats of Government whitewash as specified.

The owner charges that no architectural supervision was given by Mr. Coffman, who has accepted his fee as supervising architect.

Mr. Coffman did not give the owner a certificate of acceptance of the work of A. J. Fisher, who was legally the contractor.

Mr. Coffman acted as contractor, throughout the erection of the building.

The court then considered the findings of the board as to these specifications:

(1) It is true that substitutions were made in various phases of the work on the house, which materially cheapen the building.

(2) It is true that there is in places considerable deflection, but there is no question as to the actual safety of the structure, although there is vibration of a portion of the floors under ordinary tread.

(3) It is true that certain substitutions were made in the underpinning of the house.

(4) It is true that the exterior woodwork and interior trim were changed from redwood to Oregon pine. It is not true that it is warping badly, but certain natural shrinkage is taking place.

(5) It is true that 2″ x 6″ floor joists were substituted for 2″ x 8″ but with the knowledge of the complainant. However, the spans are greater than an alleged agreed limit.

(6) It is true that the floor girders are smaller than those specified.

(7) It is true that the ceiling "rafters" (joists) are 2″ x 4″ instead of 2″ x 6″, but are at present sufficient to support the ceiling since additional trusses were found necessary and installed after acceptance of the building.

(8) It is true that the roof rafters are 2″ x 4″ spaced approximately at 32″ centers, but the change was made with the owner's knowledge and consent.

(9) It is true that the sheathing under the shingles and its spacing is standard for this class of work.

(10) It is true that the river gravel was used in the concrete but this was allowed as an alternate by the specifications.

(11) It is true that gutters and down-spouts as shown on the drawings, were omitted, but with the owner's knowledge.

(12) It is not true that the stucco is in bad condition and it can be considered as waterproof as that specified. The surface has been given two coats of California stucco brush coat, in lieu of Government whitewash as specified.

(13) It is not true that Mr. Coffman did not give supervising architectural service to the building. Mr. Coffman did act as architect throughout the erection of the building.

(14) It is true that the building was accepted and the acceptance recorded.

(15) It is not true that Mr. Coffman acted as contractor for the building but it is true that a contract was executed and carried out between the complainant and A. J. Fisher as contractor.

Upon these findings the board rendered the following judgment:

I. That the defendant caused to be drawn under his direction and permitted to be signed a contract which would cheapen the building below the standard set forth by the contract documents—and to the disadvantage and without the knowledge of some of the interested parties. In so doing, the defendant was derelict in his duty as an architect and he is guilty of the charge of dishonest practice.

The decision of the court was that the board's order, temporarily suspending the architect for dishonest practice, was unsupported by the findings. The court stated at page 1004:

The act does not attempt to define what constitutes dishonest practice, for the very good reason, perhaps, that such dishonest practice assumes such a wide range and variety of acts and misconduct that a definition could not embrace its many forms, but for that reason the acts complained of should be found with such definiteness and certainty that the vice of the acts complained of might be apparent to all. We fail to find such definiteness and certainty in the present proceeding.

Section 101.31 (10) of the Wisconsin statute provides for the revocation of the certificate of registration of any registrant who is found guilty of ". . . (b) any gross negligence, incompetency or misconduct in the practice of architecture or of professional engineering as a registered architect or as a registered engineer." Applying the statute in *Saunders v. Johnson* (1943), 243 Wisc. 96, 9 N.W. 2d 630, the following summarized findings were found to warrant revocation of a certificate of registration, at page 634:

From the testimony in connection with Count No. 1 (Cates) the negligence and incompetence of Mr. Kuehnel is evident from the nature of the mistakes in the plans, the failure of the basement walls, the delay in the construction of the building, the failure to secure a building permit and the misplacement of the building in reference to the lot line. Further, his actions in connection with the securing of the owner's endorsement of payment on certificates after he had knowledge of the misplacement of the building is evidence of misconduct. The owners were kept in ignorance of the true state of affairs. In connection with Count No. 3 (Jensen) the negligence and incompetence of Mr. Kuehnel is again evident from the nature of the mistakes in the plans, the planning of an impractical and dangerous stairs which could not be safely installed, the improper construction of floor joists under bathroom and the lack of foundation for pantry walls.

I strongly recommend that enforcement activities be reviewed by each state society with the end in view of increasing the governmental appropriation for enforcement. Architects in each state should determine how their societies can actively participate in enforcement. Further, this should be a major subject of discussion at regional meetings so that action can be taken in a number of states at a time.

What was it that Benjamin Franklin said about hanging together?

Successful attacks upon legislative efforts to regulate the practice of architecture and engineering indicate the need for a "uniform" licensing and registration law.

The need for a uniform licensing and registration law governing the practice of architecture is highlighted by a decision of a Colorado court declaring the registration and licensing law of that state unconsitutional (*People of the State of Colorado v. Wallace*). This was the third time that a Colorado court struck down a legislative attempt to regulate and control the licensing and registration of architects.

The law that was declared unconstitutional was adopted by the Colorado Legislature in 1955. This act was so hedged with exceptions that it had little regulatory effect in limiting the practice of architecture to licensed architects. As a matter of fact, the law contained almost no restrictions upon the right to design or supervise construction. Its most significant aspect was that it prohibited the use of the title "architect" by other than a duly licensed individual. However, even this minimum attempt to regulate was ruled invalid by the court on the ground that the statute was worded too vaguely and generally to be enforceable.

The defendant was charged with practicing architecture without a license, and with advertising and holding himself out in such a way as to indicate to the public that he was entitled to practice architecture. Despite the intervention of the Colorado Chapter of the American Institute of Architects in support of the statute, the court ruled that the definition of the practice of architecture contained in the statute was so vague as to render the statute unconstitutional. The court said:

> To say that Section 10-2-2 is verbose is to speak with restraint, but verbosity, though it may unnecessarily obscure the meaning of a legislative enactment, does not necessarily make it void. After clearing out the grammatical brush from this section of the statute, we find that the practice of architecture is defined as the offering to the general public, or the performance, of professional services consisting of the *co-ordination* of some of the processes which enter into planning, designing, erection, alteration, or enlargement of any public or private building. These processes are listed as "consultations, evaluations, investigations, preliminary studies, plans, specifications, contract documents, supervision of construction and other related service."
>
> It should be noted that it is not the performance of any or all of these processes that constitute the practice of architecture under the statute, but rather, the co-ordination of these processes, whatever that may mean. Parenthetically, it might also be pointed out that it is only the "safe, healthful, scientific, esthetic and orderly co-ordination" of these processes that constitutes the practice of architecture. Presumably one who unsafely, unhealthfully, unscientifically, or unesthetically co-ordinates the processes is not practicing architecture and requires no license. It is so difficult to conceive of a disorderly co-ordination that I hesitate to hazard an opinion as to whether or not that would constitute the practice of architecture.
>
> The activities into which the enumerated processes enter are set forth by the statute in the disjunctive, to wit: "planning, designing, erection, alteration or enlargement." It is, therefore, apparent that the co-ordination of these processes in connection with the erection of a building by a building contractor or his agent requires licensing as an architecture [sic]. This would be true of the co-ordination by a farmer of the processes entering into the erection of a barn on his farm, or even in connection with the adding on of another stall to that barn.

> It thus can be seen that the statute is very broad and affects many people. Since "co-ordination" of this type constitutes the practice of architecture, and since the practice of architecture without a license constitutes a crime under the statute, it is important to know the meaning of the word "co-ordination." We are helped little by the dictionary, however, since "to co-ordinate," according to a standard work, means "to place in harmonious or reciprocal relations; combine or adjust for action or for any end." These terms are indeed most vague, and general. Vague and fluid words of definition render criminal statutes invalid because, in the words of Mr. Justice Douglas, they may constitute "a trap for the innocent." *U.S. v. Cardiff*, 344 U S 174.

The Colorado County Court further invalidated that part of the statute which prohibited an unlicensed person from holding himself out to the public as entitled to practice architecture. The court asserted that the wording of the statute in this respect did not indicate a sufficient relationship to the public health, morals, safety, or welfare. The court ruled:

> Invalidity of that part of the statute defining the practice of architecture doubtless renders void the entire statute. That part of the statute which makes it unlawful "to advertise or put out any sign or card or other device which might indicate or lead the public to believe that such person, firm, association or corporation is entitled to practice architecture," however, is objectionable on another ground. The fact that such an advertisement *might* mislead the public is not enough to justify prohibiting it. The basis for such a prohibition is the police power, and it must have a reasonable relationship to the public health, morals, safety, or welfare. Unless the advertising reasonably could be *expected* to mislead the public, it is beyond the police power. *Chenowith v. State Board*, 57 Colo. 74.

Whatever the merits of the decision of the Court relating to the lack of clarity in the wording of the statute, it is apparent that a "uniform" statute would be of considerable aid to state groups of architects seeking an effective licensing law.

The duty to prepare standards of qualification for licensing for the practice of architecture or engineering may be delegated to a licensing board, but these standards should be established in collaboration with the professions.

Should a state registration or licensing board be guided by the profession in determining the standards for qualification of a person who seeks to become licensed as an architect? Is it lawful for a representative committee of the profession to prepare standards of qualification for licensing and otherwise to pass upon the qualifications of applicants?

The Supreme Court of the State of Utah was called upon to determine the validity and constitutionality of a statute which delegated the duty of preparing standards of qualification for licensing to representative committees of several professions (*Clayton v. Bennett, et al* (5 Utah 2d 152, 298 P. 2d 531). The court upheld the validity of the statute, ruling that it did not result in an unconstitutional delegation of legislative powers.

The plaintiff in the Utah case was a professional engineer duly licensed as such under the Utah law. He also had a degree in architecture and made application to the appropriate administrative body for a license to practice that profession. The plaintiff was given an examination which he failed to pass. He then instituted a legal action on the ground that the right to engage in a profession was a property right of which he had been deprived under an unconstitutional statute. The statute under attack provided in part as follows:

> *Sec. 58-1-5.* The functions of the Department of Registration shall be exercised by the director of registration under the supervision of the Commission . . . in collaboration with the assistance of representative committees of the several professions, trades (etc.) . . .
>
> *Section 58-1-7.* It shall be the duty of the . . . committees to submit to the director standards of qualification for their respective professions, trades . . . and methods of examination of applicants. They shall conduct examinations at the request of the director . . . (and) shall pass upon the qualifications of applicants . . . and shall submit in writing their findings and conclusions to the director.
>
> *Sec. 58-1-13.* The following functions and duties shall be . . . performed by the department of registration but only upon the action and report in writing of the appropriate representative committees:
>
> (1) Defining . . . what shall constitute a school, college (etc.), in good standing.
>
> (2) Establishing a standard of preliminary education

deemed requisite to admission to any school, college or university.

(3) Prescribing the standard of qualification requisite . . . before license shall issue.

(4) Prescribing rules governing applications for licenses. . . .

(5) Providing for a fair and wholly impartial method of examination. . . .

The court initially emphasized that it was within the police power of the state to establish reasonable standards which must be complied with as a prerequisite to engaging in a profession. The court said:

> It has been recognized since time immemorial that there are some professions and occupations which require special skill, learning and experience with respect to which the public ordinarily does not have sufficient knowledge to determine the qualifications of the practitioner. The layman should be able to request such services with some degree of assurance that those holding themselves out to perform them are qualified to do so. For the purpose of protecting the health, safety and welfare of its citizens, it is within the police power of the state to establish reasonable standards to be complied with as a prerequisite to engaging in such pursuits. Architecture is recognized as one such occupation.

The plaintiff contended, however, that even if it be conceded that it is within the police power of the state to prescribe the standards of qualification, the statute in question was unconstitutional because it provided for the appointment of committees from the professions to establish standards of qualifications and to conduct examinations. In rejecting this contention the court emphasized that the committee ultimately acted under the direction, control and supervision of the appropriate administrative body which had the final authority. The court said:

> In support of his first contention plaintiff points to the wording of the statute providing that the Department of Registration shall perform its duty, "*only* upon the action and report in writing of the appropriate representative committee" and reasons therefrom that the actual authority is reposed in the committee. A survey of the entire procedure set up by statute indicates that such is not the case. The Committee, at the request of the Director, conducts the examination, making its report of the results thereof to him. If the report is satisfactory

> and other qualifications have been met, the duty then devolves upon the director to issue the license. He is appointed by and performs his duties under the supervision of the Commission of the Department of Business Regulation, which has final authority as to the carrying out of the functions of the Department.

The court recognized the desirability of permitting each profession to collaborate with the administrative board in establishing appropriate standards.

The plaintiff also challenged the validity of the statute on the ground that it prescribed no express or definite standards. The court noted that the statute did contain certain basic qualifications relating to education, age, moral character and the requirement of satisfactorily passing an examination, and further emphasized that it would not be appropriate to require the legislature to set up something more than general standards. The court, in concluding that the matters committed to the administrative board were proper, relied upon a decision of the United States Supreme Court (*Douglas v. Noble*) in which Mr. Justice Brandeis in writing the opinion stated:

> The statute provides that the examination shall be before a board of practicing dentists; the applicant must be a graduate of a reputable dental school; and that he must be of good moral character. Thus the general standard of fitness and the character and scope of the examination are clearly indicated. Whether the applicant possesses the qualifications inherent in that standard is a question of fact. . . . The decision of that fact involves ordinarily the determination of two subsidiary questions of fact. The first, what the knowledge and skill is which fits one to practice the profession. The second, whether the applicant possesses that knowledge and skill. The latter finding is necessarily an individual one. The former is ordinarily one of general application. Hence it can be embodied in rules. The legislature itself may make this finding of the facts general application, and by embodying it in the statute make it law. When it does so, the function of the examining board is limited to determining whether the applicant complies with the requirements so declared. But the legislature need not make this general finding. To determine the subjects of which one must have knowledge in order to be fit to practice dentistry; the extent of knowledge in each subject; the degree of skill requisite; and the procedure to be followed in conducting the

examination; these are matters approximately committed to an administrative board. . . . And a legislature may, consistent with the Federal Constitution, delegate to such board the function of determining these things, as well as the functions of determining whether the applicant complies with the detailed standard of fitness.

Collaboration between the architectural profession and the administrative boards charged with the obligation of preparing standards for qualification for the practice of architecture is highly desirable. This is true not only from the viewpoint of maintaining proper and adequate standards but also from the viewpoint of the prestige and status of the architectural profession.

A licensing board may examine an applicant with respect to his abilities in design or composition, but may not withhold a license because of a disagreement on esthetics.

Q. Does a licensing body have the "right" to give an examination in design or composition?

A. Yes, if expressly or impliedly authorized to do so by the enabling statute.

Q. Can that body deny an applicant a license because its individual members disagree with him on "esthetic principles?"

A. No. If the solution of the problem would be given a passing grade by members of any generally recognized "school," then it should be deemed passing by any board. Any other result would be arbitrary, capricious, and an abuse of discretion, and subject to reversal by the courts.

It has often been repeated that the constitutional basis for professional licensing statutes is the state's police power protecting the health, welfare and safety of the populace. In upholding the constitutionality of the architectural registration laws, as a valid exercise of the state's police power, a New York Court stated (*Bowen v. City of Schenectady,* 240 N.Y.S. 784 aff'd 231 App. Div. 779):

The Legislature is invested with a wide discretion in determining whether a business or occupation should be barred to the dishonest or incompetent. Generally it is for the Legislature to determine what laws and regulations are needed to protect

> the public health * * * The practice of architecture demands learning, skill, and integrity. The Legislature has the right to prescribe the qualifications of those engaged in this important work. The object of an examination is to ascertain whether applicants possess the necessary requirements. The layman must place his trust and confidence in the architect he employs. * * * In designing, planning, and supervising the erection of large public and private structures, tragic indeed are the perilous results of incompetence and ignorance. I am convinced that this enactment should be upheld as a legitimate exercise of police power.

There are two types of registration statutes in effect today. In the first type, the issuance of an architectural license by the board is a ministerial act, as the legislature sets forth requirements the applicant must possess, and if the conditions are met the applicant is entitled to a license. Most states, in the enactment of their first licensing law, included a "grandfather clause," which clause had the effect of permitting the licensing of practitioners if they possessed certain qualifications. A Michigan court construed the powers of the board in this situation as follows (*Wair v. State Board of Registration*, 303 Mich. 360):

> The board, in our opinion, in denying registration to the appellant, nullified the effect of the provision by substituting its judgment for that of the legislature as to the requirements that an applicant for registration must possess. The legislature has prescribed that certain applicants . . . must also establish that they have had either practical experience or formal educational training, or both . . . before they can apply for examination. However, the legislative body was of the opinion that one having at least 12 years of practice as an architect was conclusively presumed to be qualified to engage in the profession without regard to educational training, ability to pass an examination propounded by the board, or the opinion of the board as to whether he was a "good" or "bad" architect.
>
> If appellant submitted a specific record of 12 years active practice, the board was bound to grant the application regardless of their personal opinions.

The second type of regulatory statute empowers the board to examine applicants upon certain subjects to ascertain their qualifications and ability to practice architecture. The subjects upon which the examination is to be based are usually included in the basic curriculum of architectural colleges. Obviously, design and composition—courses which are part of the curriculum of all architectural schools—are included. It is discretionary with the board as to the nature and substance of the examination and the method of grading to be used. The courts will not interfere with the board unless it has acted arbitrarily or discriminately.

An interesting Louisiana decision (*Sill v. Examining Board*, 129 So. 427) demonstrates the courts' attitude toward discretionary steps taken by licensing boards. The applicant received a grade of 74.3 upon his qualifying examination, and, as the passing grade was 75, he was refused a license. An appeal to the courts was taken upon two grounds: the action of the board was arbitrary, and the method of marking was unfair. Both sides agreed with the universal proposition that the examination and the method of grading were purely discretionary with the board and "mandamus will not lie to hinder, regulate, or control their [the board's] actions in regard to such matters unless it manifestly appears that their actions have been arbitrary, unjust, or discriminating."

The court surveyed the entire record and decided that there was nothing tangible in such record to conclude, as a factual matter, that the board acted arbitrarily. The court then turned its attention to the grading method of the board. There were three members of the group: one of them read the questions, another read the applicant's answers, and the third kept a record of the grades. If the answer was partly correct, the members had a consultation and fixed the grade. If they differed, all three put down the grade which was thought proper and the average of the three proposed grades was taken.

The applicant claimed that this was unfair, and that only the two highest proposed grades should be considered. The court held:

> It is purely discretionary with the board as to what method it should pursue in arriving at the proper grade or percentage an applicant should be given on his examination. The Court will not interfere and substitute its judgment for that of the board in such matters.

This decision expresses the policy of the courts not to interfere with the discretionary powers of the board concerning the matters upon which the examination is based, or upon the marking procedure followed, unless the board acts arbitrarily or unjustly. If the arbitrary action of the board offends the court's conscience, an appeal will lie. Some licensing statutes include procedures for appeal to the courts. In the absence of such a provision, the writ of mandamus is available to compel the board to act upon the application.

The problem whether a board can examine upon questions of design or composition, does not concern itself with the legal right to examine, but with the fairness of the question and the manner of grading the answers. The prejudices of individual members of an examining board must not prevent qualified applicants from becoming licensed architects. No matter what "school" the examiner belongs to—"Classic," "International," "Contemporary," or other—he must impartially examine and grade all applicants. Evidence of such bias, partiality or unfairness, as will affect either the examination or the marking of the answers, will support an appeal to the courts, which would correct inequities.

Implicit in all this discussion is the question whether architects of one school trust those of another school to pass on each other's work and qualifications. That issue, however, is not for me, but for the architects. It should be remembered that the public has a stake in the resolution of this distrust.

CHAPTER 2: *Doing Business in a Foreign State*

A construction corporation "doing business" in a foreign state must be licensed by that state. Failure to so qualify may constitute a violation of the criminal law and invalidate the construction contract.

Is your contractor incorporated in another state? If so, has he "qualified" his corporation to do business in the state in which the project is to be built? His failure to comply strictly with the laws concerning "qualification" may result in illegal, void, or unenforceable contracts or even criminal prosecution. This could not only be disastrous to him but would also seriously affect the performance of his work.

The problem of doing business in a "foreign" state without qualifying is to be distinguished from that of engaging in general contracting without securing a contractor's license as required by state law. Only a limited number of states require those who engage in contracting to procure an occupational license; but virtually every state demands that a "foreign" corporation secure the proper authorization. A "foreign" corporation is one whose charter was issued in another state.

Criminal prosecutions are infrequently instituted against corporations for failure to qualify. But they are available and states have resorted to them upon occasion. For example, some years ago Arkansas imposed a $1000 penalty on an unlicensed Mississippi corporation found to be engaged in extensive construction work in Arkansas. The construction company fought the action up to United States Supreme Court, where its appeal was dismissed.

A more serious detriment to the non-complying foreign corporation stems from the invalidation of its construction contracts performed within the state. In various states, a contract for construction entered into without complying with local conditions of doing business is rendered void either by the express terms of the statute or by statutory interpretation. Statutes in other states, while not making the contract void, expressly prohibit the maintenance of an action on it. In either case, the result is the same—the corporation is barred from presenting its case for determination to the courts, however meritorious its claim may be.

It may develop that a contract is valid in the state in which it is made but invalid and unenforceable in another state in which it is to be performed. In a Texas case, a construction company made a contract in New York to do certain work on a bridge in Texas. The company took no steps to perform the contract but brought an action in a Texas court to have the contract cancelled on the ground that the defendant had misrepresented the facts and concealed the real nature of the work in inducing the company to take the job. Again, because the company had not secured a permit to do business in Texas, the court refused to consider the merits of the case. The Texas law prevents a corporation from maintaining a suit on any demand unless it complies with the requirements for doing business. The court construed the words "any demand" as being broad enough to cover a request to cancel the contract and, therefore, dismissed the case.

It has been held that a contract made by a corporation which has not qualified remains void and unenforceable although the corporation does so qualify during the performance of the contract. In a Mississippi case, a construction company which had a contract with the state to work on a highway project secured a permit to do business after eight months and approximately two thirds of the working days allowed for the completion of the contract had elapsed. When the project was completed, the state refused to pay for extra work which it had required under the contract, and the company sued to recover such compensation. The court held that the contract was wholly void and the company could not enforce it. Compliance with the statute, the court said, cannot be made to relate back to the date when the contract was executed. "The contract was either enforceable on the date of its execution or unenforceable."

In another case, a Colorado corporation entered in a "cost plus" contract with a canal company in Colorado to construct and enlarge a canal in Wyoming. During the performance of the contract, a dispute arose between the parties regarding the work, and the canal company terminated the contract. The construction company was not permitted to recover even for the money it had expended in transporting its machinery into the state to do the work.

The court held that the claim arose out of an unlawful performance of the contract. The corporation had complied with the statute for doing business after the contract was terminated and before it brought suit. A subsequent compliance, the court stated, was of no effect. It pointed out that the rule is different where only the right of action is suspended during the period of noncompliance.

Another category of state statutes permits a corporation to sue on its contracts provided it qualifies before bringing the suit. Some of these states, in addition, require the corporation to pay a penalty before it may apply to the courts.

In those states with statutes making contracts of corporations which have not qualified absolutely unenforceable, it is immaterial what form of relief is sought. Thus, courts have refused to entertain actions to recover the balance of payment due under contracts, actions to enforce mechanic's liens, actions to recover for "extras" incurred in the performance of the work, actions to foreclose chattel mortgages on machinery sold, actions to rescind contracts induced by fraudulent misrepresentations—all by reason of the corporation's failure to secure recognition.

Listed below are the three categories of states which have enacted laws relating to the enforceability of contracts entered into by corporations chartered in states other than those in which they do business. *Obviously, this list is subject to change.* The statutes are concerned with those contracts of foreign corporations which are entered into within the state and involve intrastate activity.

(1) States in which a foreign corporation cannot enforce a contract entered into while it was unlicensed, even though the corporation is later qualified to do business:

Alabama	Mississippi	Texas
Arizona	Missouri	Utah
Arkansas	New Jersey	Vermont
Idaho	New York	Wisconsin
Iowa	South Dakota	Wyoming
Michigan	Tennessee *(by court decision)*	

(2) States in which an unlicensed corporation must first qualify before it can enforce contracts made prior to qualification:

Colorado	Montana	Oklahoma
Indiana	Nevada	Oregon
Louisiana	New Hampshire	Rhode Island
Maine	New Jersey	Virginia
Massachusetts	New Mexico	Washington
Minnesota	North Dakota	West Virginia

(3) States in which an unlicensed corporation must first qualify and pay a penalty before it can enforce contracts made prior to qualification:

California ($250)	Illinois (10% *of taxes and fees*)	Ohio ($250 *and* 15% *of fees*)
Connecticut ($250)	Maryland ($200)	Pennsylvania ($250)
Florida ($250)		

In the following states, the right of unlicensed corporations to sue is not covered by statute, but the decisions indicate that the right to sue will be granted:

Delaware	Nebraska (*late case denies right to sue*)	South Carolina (*right to sue suspended until corporation qualifies*)
Kansas	North Carolina	
Kentucky		

New Jersey merits a special note of its own. Generally, unlicensed foreign corporations may sue on contracts made in New Jersey if they first qualify to do business. However, by virtue of a retaliatory statute, corporations organized in states under Group 1 above may not enforce contracts made in New Jersey even though they subsequently qualify.

That the corporation already has a certificate from its home state, or conducts the larger portion of its business there, are immaterial facts if it steps outside the state to engage in even one project. If it carries its activities into all 50 states, then it becomes subject to the laws of each and must obtain the authority to conduct its enterprise within them. The theory behind what may appear a troublesome and unnecessary duplication of effort rests in the nature of our governmental system. Each state is accorded the rights and privileges of a sovereign and exercises full dominion within its boundaries. Recognition in one state constitutes a grant of privilege by that state to conduct business within its borders, protected by its laws. If the corporation ventures into another state, it subjects itself to a new sovereign from whom it must request similar recognition.

Not all business contacts or transactions in a foreign state require qualification. A corporation will be required to qualify only if it is "doing business" within the state. The rule is broadly stated and what situations it covers depends largely on the facts of the individual case. Generally speaking, the courts have said that an out-of-state corporation must transact a substantial part of its business within the state as distinguished from casual or occasional transactions.

A corporation which enters into one contract or one isolated business act in the state is not said to be "doing business" therein. *The courts have refused, however, to apply this general rule to a contract contemplating a construction project;* because, they say, the nature of its performance is such that it extends over an appreciable length of time and thus cannot be described as a casual or occasional transaction. As a matter of practice, a corporation which agrees to perform but a simple construction contract has been held to be "doing business" within the state, so as to require its qualification.

In one case in which a "foreign" corporation undertook a single construction project, the court held that it must qualify for the following reasons:

> The contract contemplated not a single act but a continuing project within this state for at least four months. Plaintiff's agents and employees were here to advise and do the work, employ labor and purchase materials. New obligations were incurred as the need arose. The acts which were done in this state were not a mere incident of plaintiff's corporate existence, but were the performance of the very function for which the corporation was organized. The fact that part of its capital as represented by wages, trucks, tools, etc., was not permanently invested here is of no consequence . . . The rule as to "isolated transactions" not being within the meaning of the phrase "doing business" has been limited to single transactions, such as the ordering of one machine, the selling of one machine, the holding of one corporate meeting.

A Florida court has gone so far as to require qualification of a corporation which contracts outside the state to build a railroad within the state, even though it does no part of the actual work itself but employs independent contractors for that purpose.

The question of qualification also arises in connection with agreements made by "foreign" corporations to install within the state an article shipped from without. It is held that an incidental agreement to assemble a structure sold by an out-of-state corporation does not constitute "doing business" within the state. On the other hand, if the sale of the article is merely incidental to a contract to perform labor within the state, the activity is within state control and the corporation must qualify to do business.

A contract for the sale, assembling, and erection of certain gas machines for a municipality which involved extensive construction work has been held to be a sale of equipment and apparatus merely incidental to the construction project—hence, a certificate of qualification required. The same view has been taken of a contract for the sale and installation of marble in a building under construction, and the construction of chimneys and plants containing machinery manufactured outside the state.

A contractor who is employed to construct a project for the federal government does not thereby become exempt from state laws requiring qualification. In one case in which a corporation asserted such immunity, the court found that the corporation, in using its own equipment and hiring its own employes for the work, was an independent contractor rather than an employe of the federal government, immune from state regulation. A similar conclusion has been reached in another Supreme Court case involving a contract entered into between the government and a contractor for the construction of a post office building. The court observed:

> While, of course, in a sense the contract is the means by which the United States secures the construction of its post office, certainly the contractor in this independent operation does not share any government immunity.

Despite the rigid application of state laws relative to qualification, some contractors may think these consequences can be avoided by suing in the federal courts. The United States Supreme Court has held to the contrary, on the ground that when applying state law, a remedy barred in a state court should likewise be barred in a federal court. A different rule, the court said, would be discriminatory. This means that when the law of any state makes an unlicensed corporation's contract unenforceable, that is the law that federal courts will apply—and will apply just as effectively as the state's own courts.

In summary:

(1) Most states require that "foreign" corporations "qualify" as a condition to doing business within them.

(2) A "foreign" construction company is usually "doing business" within a state when it performs but one construction project.

(3) A "foreign" corporation which does business without qualifying may subject itself to criminal penalties. It may further imperil the legality or enforceability of its contracts. Some states will permit enforcement of contracts provided the corporation qualifies before bringing the action.

(4) In performing a contract to sell and install equipment which it ships into the state, a corporation may be "doing business" if the sale is incidental to the construction job.

(5) A "foreign" corporation cannot evade state requirements to qualify by suing on its contracts in a federal court, since the federal court will apply state law as effectively as a state court.

MISCELLANEOUS DECISIONS

LICENSE LAWS FOR THE ARCHITECT, ENGINEER AND GENERAL CONTRACTOR

ARKANSAS. *Arkansas State Board of Architects* v. *Bank Building & Equipment Corp. of America,* 286 S. W. 2d 323 (1956). In a suit brought by the Arkansas State Board of Architects to enjoin a corporation from engaging in certain activities which the Board alleged to be the practice of architecture in violation of statute, it was held that where a corporation was contracting in Arkansas to furnish architectural services for constructing banks and rearranging the interiors thereof, and where it had a staff of about 200 architects to perform such services, and only the chief architect was licensed within Arkansas to practice the profession of architecture, and he worked for the corporation as an employe and detailed the inspection and supervision work to his subordinates, none of whom was licensed under the Arkansas law, and his name did not appear in the name of the corporation, the corporation was engaging in the practice of architecture in violation of statute.

CALIFORNIA. *Walter M. Ballard Corp. v. Dougherty,* 234 P. 2nd 745 (1951). Where the practice statute made the practice of architecture by an unlicensed person a misdemeanor, the Court held that an unlicensed corporation, engaged in the business of hotel decoration, was not lawfully precluded from hiring a licensed architect for the preparation of the plans and specifications pursuant to a contract between the hotel owner and the plaintiff.

Lehmann v. Dalis, 269 P. 2d 727 (1953). A licensed civil engineer performed work, labor, and services, which included the drawing of plans and sketches for the erection of a bowling alley, at the builder's request and subsequently sued for the value of his endeavors. The defense was raised that these were architectural services and that the engineer was not a licensed architect, nor had he informed the builder in writing of this fact as provided for by statute. The Court held, however, that the civil engineer was entitled to recovery, stating that the Civil Engineering Act permitted some services of an architectural nature, and that the Architectural Practice Act did not preclude recovery.

Marshall v. Von Zumwalt, 262 P. 2d 363 (1953). In an action by an owner against a contractor for monies loaned to the contractor, the Court held that, although the contractor could not sue the owner for compensation without proving that he was licensed as required by statute, the contractor could, nevertheless, when sued, assert the contract and recover the amount of his compensation which exceeded the amount which the owner sought to recover.

Shields v. Shoaff, 253 P. 2d 102 (1953). A building contractor's license was suspended by operation of law when his responsible managing employe resigned and no qualified replacement was employed as required by statute. The subsequent acceptance of license fees without disclosure of the contractor's disqualification did not reinstate the original license. Therefore, the Court held that the contractor was barred from recovery.

Palmer v. Brown, 273 P. 2d 306 (1954). Where an unlicensed member of a partnership engaged in the practice of architecture, signed without the direction or supervision of the licensed members, a certificate of payment in which he, the unlicensed member, was designated as the "architect," his action defeated the licensed partners' right to recover on the partnership contract for the rendition of the architectural services.

People v. Wright, 293 P. 2d 165 (1956). A designer was convicted of violation of a statute making it a crime for one not licensed as an architect to hold himself out to the public as an architect. The basis of the conviction was the use of the letters "AIA" after the designer's name. On appeal, it was held that under the statute authorizing designers who are not licensed architects to draw plans and specifications and render other architectural services for their employer, such designer had the right to inform the public of his membership in the American Institute of Architects and his display of the sign which contained his name, followed by "AIA," did not constitute a violation of the statute.

DISTRICT OF COLUMBIA. *Dunn v. Finlayson,* 104 A. 2d 830 (1954). Suit for the balance of compensation due was brought by a person designated in a construction contract as architect and supervising engineer. The owner counter-claimed for the amount paid under the contract on the ground that the contract was void because the architect did not have the required certificate. The Court held that the Architects Registration Act of the District of Columbia did not forfeit compensation in the absence of a certificate prior to 1950 when it had been amended and that, therefore, the architect could recover for those services he rendered prior to the 1950 amendment even though the building was not completed until after the amendment.

Holiday Homes, Inc. v. Briley, 122 A. 2d 229 (1956). Where an architect's license was erroneously renewed in 1953 because the fee forwarded was insufficient, and the architect did not renew his registration until October, 1955, it was held that he could not recover for services rendered while his license as architect had lapsed. However, the violation was applicable only to those services which were rendered under an agreement made in November of 1954 under which the architect consented to the use of existing plans and agreed to design a new house, but did not preclude his recovery of compensation under a separable agreement for the rendering of designs which, in fact, were not furnished until after the renewal of the architect's license.

GEORGIA. *Folsom v. Summer, Locatell & Co., Inc.* 83 S. E. 2d 855 (1954). In an action for architectural fees due under a contract, it was held that a corporation was not prohibited from using the title "architects and engineers" in its contracts, as the word "person" within the statute prohibiting any but qualified architects to use the title "architect" prohibits only natural persons, in view of the fact that "person" is modified by the pronouns "he" and "she."

IDAHO. *Johnson v. Delane,* 290 P. 2d 213 (1955). An engineer licensed in Washington contracted in Idaho to furnish plans and specifications for erection of a building in Idaho where he was not licensed. However, he prepared such plans and specifications in Washington. The Court held that he was not practicing engineering in Idaho within meaning of the statute barring recovery of compensation by unlicensed engineers.

ILLINOIS. *Gastaldi v. Reuterman,* 345 Ill. App. 510, 104 N.E. 2d 115 (1952). Plaintiff submitted a bid for construction of defendant's salesroom and garage based upon plans drawn by a licensed architect retained by the defendant. Defendant refused to proceed with the project after numerous conferences. The Court determined that the defendant dealt with plaintiff knowing that he was a general contractor and that the contract did not call for the rendition of architectual services by the plaintiff so as to preclude recovery for services rendered on the ground that he was not a licensed architect. The Court declared that under the act defining the practice of architecture and under Section 4 which provides that the act shall not prevent the employment of superintendents of construction, etc., it was not the intent of the legislature that supervision of construction by a licensed architect should necessarily preclude any other supervising of the construction.

On P. 117, the Court quotes an earlier Illinois case as follows:

"The object of this statute was not to protect architects merely by limiting the work to those that possessed a license. The real purpose of the statute is the protection of the public against incompetent architects, from whose services damage might result to the public by reason of dangerous and improperly constructed buildings and by badly ventilated and poorly lighted buildings."

MICHIGAN. (U.S. Dist. Ct.) *Lowery* v. *A. Rosenthal, Inc.* 104 F. Supp. 496 (1952). In an action to recover for services rendered by industrial designers in connection with the proposed modernization of defendant's store to increase the volume of business, the Court found that the services consisted of industrial design work and not architectural work within the meaning of the Michigan statutes requiring a license to engage in the practice of architecture but making such requirement inapplicable to the practice of any other legally recognized profession.

The Court cited with approval *Teague v. Graves,* 261 App. Div., 652, 27 N.Y.S. 2nd 762, which stated in part:

"Industrial Designing as a separate field of endeavor has been developed recently . . . it is now recognized by many institutions of learning . . . The graduates from the universities, institutes and schools who will have scholastic degrees as Industrial Designers doubtless will be regarded as professional men . . ."

NEBRASKA. *Downs v. Nebraska State Board of Examiners of Professional Engineers & Architects,* 139 Neb. 23, 296 N.W. 151 (1941). Plaintiff was held entitled to mandamus directing Board of Examiners to issue a certificate of registration to practice engineering without an examination where statutory provisions of residence, good character, payment of registration fee were complied with and plaintiff was a professional engineer of good standing holding two engineering degrees.

State ex.rel. Binty v. Nebraska State Board of Examiners For Professional Engineers and Architects et al., 155 Neb. 99, 50 N.W. 2d 784 (1952). The statute requires the board to examine the evidence and exercise its discretion with reference to every application for a certificate of registration as an engineer or architect that is filed. The Court held that mandamus would not lie to control the exercise of discretion vested by the board and require it to issue a certificate of registration where the board had already denied the application.

NEW YORK. *D'Luhosch v. Andros,* 200 Misc. 400, 109 N.Y.S. 2nd 491 (1951). In an action for work, labor, and services rendered in drawing plans and specifications for a dwelling which defendants had contracted to have constructed, the court held that the licensed engineer was entitled to recover for drawing the plans and specifications even though he was not a licensed architect. In view of the fact that the practice statutes make no distinctions between the services which may be legally rendered by a licensed engineer and an architect, it is not contrary to the fundamental purpose of licensing which is to protect and safeguard life, health, and property.

NORTH CAROLINA. *Tillman v.* Talbert, 93 S.E. 2d 101 (1956). In an action by an unlicensed builder-designer to recover in *quantum meruit* for services performed in drawing up plans and specifications for a residence, it was held that where the builder-designer contracted to furnish plans and specifications for a residence estimated to cost $18,000, and subsequently, at the defendant's request, altered the plans to provide for a residence estimated to cost over $20,000, the builder-designer was entitled to recover in *quantum meruit* for services rendered before the change, in spite of a statute declaring unlawful any agreement other than by licensed architects to furnish plans and specifications for any building valued over $20,000.

PENNSYLVANIA. *Baker v. Chambers,* 133 A. 2d 589 (1957). In an action by a corporation against a home owner to recover compensation for architectural services performed in the preparation of preliminary plans for remodeling of the defendant's home, it was held that the corporation could recover, even though the Pennsylvania statute provided that a corporation could not qualify for registration as an architect, and could neither hold itself out as an architect nor practice architecture. The plans and specifications in question were prepared by a registered architect employed by the corporate plaintiff, and the Court ruled that the prohibition against practicing was "not intended as prohibiting any person from doing the work usually done by an architect, but aimed at such persons as claimed to be architects, but were not or who, at least, could not or would not register and who, notwithstanding still employed the professional title."

TEXAS. *M. M. M., Inc. v. Mitchell,* 265 S.W. 2d 584 (1954). An action was instituted by an engineer to recover his compensation for services performed. The engineer had been issued a certificate under the statute regulating the practice of his profession but had failed to pay an annual renewal fee as required by statute. The Court denied a recovery because the services for which compensation was sought had been rendered during the year in which the renewal fee had not been paid.

VIRGINIA. *Clark v. Moore,* 86 S.E. 2d 37 (1955). In an action for services rendered pursuant to an oral contract, it was held that investigation, design, and cost valuation in connection with obtaining an award of contract work at a naval base constituted "engineering" services for which compensation could not be recovered by one not having first obtained a license.

PART TWO: *Organization and Business Problems of Architectural, Engineering and Construction Firms*

No matter how devoted he may be to the art of his profession, the architect or engineer cannot divorce himself from business problems which must be solved if he is to establish and maintain a practice that will be both artistically satisfying and financially remunerative. The form of business organization utilized for professional practice is often restricted by law. Since many states prohibit corporations from practicing architecture or engineering, the most common complex form of business organization for the practice of these professions is that of the partnership. This relationship is created by contract and its formulation is of primary importance, as the legal consequences flowing from such a contract affect all aspects of professional practice.

The organization of his business is but one of the many vital business problems with which the architect or engineer must cope. Securing of contracts, dealing with clients, establishment of appropriate fees, the ethics of business practices, the accumulation of savings, and provision for his family in the case of death, are but some of the essential considerations for the practicing professional.

The building contractor's business and legal problems are even more complex than those of the architect and engineer. On a contractual level, he must negotiate not only with the owner, but with his sub-contractors as well. In order to obtain contracts, he must generally prepare and submit competitive bids with the hazards attendant thereto. On a regulatory level, he must be concerned with the application and enforcement of building regulation, the supervision of the architect, and his relationship with the bonding company from which his payment and performance bonds have been obtained. Tax laws, decedent estate laws, licensing laws, anti-trust laws, codes of ethics and public work laws are but examples of the statutes and codes which affect the practice of all professions and businesses in the construction industry.

CHAPTER 3: *Partnership Agreements*

The partnership agreement should include all essential elements relating to the control and management of the business, and should define the rights and obligations of each of the partners.

Do you have or do you intend to have a partner? How are the profits and losses to be shared among the partners? Who is to control and manage the business? Is a partner entitled to a salary in the absence of profits? What happens when one of the partners retires or dies? Do the testamentary provisions in the wills of the partners conform to the partnership agreement and will the death of a partner embarrass the partnership? All these and many other questions should be expressly answered by the terms of a contract entered into by the partners at the initiation of the relationship. Lack of a written agreement, or adoption of an inadequate one, may result in a judicial determination as to the rights of the partners, which may be injurious to one or more of them.

Should you have a partner in your practice? Once having determined this question in the affirmative, the importance of a complete written agreement delineating the rights, privileges, duties, and responsibilities of the partners can not be overemphasized. Such a written agreement not only sets forth the legal relationship, but also affords an opportunity for the parties to consider serially the practical aspects of the relationship that exists or will exist.

Failure to enter into such an agreement can result in legal responsibility not contemplated by one or more of the partners. It can also result in complications arising from a failure on the part of all the partners to determine in advance what specific part each partner is to play. Although it is not the intention of this brief essay to consider all of the aspects of a partnership agreement, a discussion of some of the matters involved illustrates the pitfalls inherent in an architect's association with other architects, when no written agreement exists.

The partner's relationship is a fiduciary one: each partner is both principal and agent, trustee and beneficiary. Thus the acts of one partner in his dealings with third parties, within the scope of the partnership business, will bind all the others. As between themselves, persons associated in business will not be deemed to be partners unless it was their intention to be so associated. Under certain circumstances, persons associated in business even though they do not intend to be partners, are so considered insofar as third persons are concerned.

The partnership agreement is the structure upon which the rights, responsibilities, and liabilities of each partner is based. Any person who is capable of entering into contractual relations may become a partner. The partnership contract should set forth the length of time the partnership is to endure. In the absence of such provision it will be inferred that the partnership is terminable at will. Even with a specific clause setting forth the term of the partnership, it may be dissolved by any of the partners. However, the dissolution of a partnership by the act of one of the partners before the specified term has expired, will make him responsible for the damages suffered by the other partners for his breach of contract.

Perhaps the most important term in the partnership agreement is that provision relating to the proportion that profits and losses are to be shared by the partners. In the absence of such provision, courts called upon to construe such an agreement will infer that the profits and losses are to be shared equally among the partners. The *quid pro quo* which supports the validity of a partnership contract is the contribution of each partner of either his capital, property, or skill to the business. In many instances these contributions are not of equal value and the shares of the profits of the business are therefore not intended to be distributed equally. Sometimes it is desirable to guarantee one or more partners against losses. The partnership agreement should spell out in detail the financial relationship between the parties.

It is often the practice to provide for salaries to be paid to the partners. If the contract between the parties does not provide for compensation for services to be rendered, no compensation may be paid for such services. This is so, even if the services rendered the partners are not equal and even if one of the partners is the active manager of the business. The contract must expressly state the compensation to be received by any one of the partners. Disputes also have arisen as to whether these salaries are to be paid in the absence of profits. If the partnership agreement does not expressly cover such contingency, the courts must resort to custom and usage in order to determine this question.

There are many situations where an employer and an employee are associated in business and in lieu of wages the employee shares the profits of such business. Such associations are not partnerships. If it is the intention of the parties to create a partnership, then the profits of the business must be shared as profits and not in lieu of wages. The question as to whether it was the intent of the parties to establish a partnership relation or a mere employment relation, often arises where the contribution to the business association by one of the parties involved is that of skill only. Since this is often the situation in the association of architects, it is particularly important that the intention of the parties be clearly and validly expressed in the partnership or employment contract.

Every partnership agreement should declare the rights of each partner in the management and conduct of the business and the duties of each partner including the services to be rendered. In the absence of an express agreement, it will be assumed that each partner has an equal right of management and control and that each partner must contribute his full time to the partnership business. A limitation upon the right of equal control and management of the partnership enterprise and the freedom to participate in other businesses is often desirable. A carefully drawn agreement will avoid future disputes on this subject. Even where it is the intention of the parties to have equal control and management of the partnership, nothing should be left to inference, but the partnership contract should expressly set forth the intention of the parties.

There are other problems to be considered in relation to management and control of the business enterprise when the partnership contract is drawn. For example, in a large partnership it may be desirable to give the partners the right to expel a partner. There is no right of expulsion unless it is specifically provided in the partnership contract. It is a rule of law that where partners have an equal right of management and control, the majority view will govern.

However, where a difference of opinion is equally divided between the parties or where there are only two partners, a tie will result and the partnership activity will be stymied. It is therefore of importance that this situation be considered and a solution provided in the partnership agreement.

Each partner has the right of possession, in common with all other co-partners, of the partnership property. If considered desirable, the partnership agreement can provide exclusive control of the property in one or more of the partners. Any type of property may become partnership property. Moreover, the partnership agreement may prohibit the partnership from acquiring certain types of property. The property of the partnership consists of all property that is contributed at the formation of the contract and all that is subsequently acquired by the firm. It was the law in many states, prior to the adoption of the Uniform Partnership Act, that real property could not be held by a partnership as such. Many states today still indulge in a presumption that real property is not partnership property. In order to avoid confusion and doubt on this subject, where it is the intention of the partnership to own real property, the partnership contract should specifically so provide.

The liabilities of partners to third persons, the necessity of expressing the scope of the partnership business in the partnership contract, the consequences of a partnership dissolution or the death of one of the partners are all important phases of this subject that must be considered in the formulation of a well-drawn partnership agreement. Immediate liquidation of a business may be financially catastrophic. In the absence of a specific agreement to the contrary, however, upon the death of one partner surviving, partners must do just this. A partnership business must be liquidated upon the death of a partner even though by the terms of the partnership agreement it was to endure for a fixed term, unless the contract between the partners provides for survival of the partnership entity. Upon dissolution the surviving partners must immediately settle all accounts, collect all the property and assets of the partnership, existing at the time of its dissolution, and wind up the partnership affairs. The dissolution of a partnership by the death of one of the partners ends the mutual agency of each of the partners and the community of interest of the partners only subsists long enough to enable the survivors to settle the affairs of the business.

The effect of the death of one partner upon the financial status of the survivor was aptly illustrated in a case litigated in Arkansas.

In that case, a partnership operated a hotel business. The partnership contract had no provision relating to the death of either of the partners. Upon the death of one of the partners, his executor agreed with the surviving partner to continue the operation of the hotel business. Subsequently the executor of the deceased partner demanded that the business be liquidated. The surviving partner contended that the continued operation of the partnership business constituted a sale and assignment of the deceased partner's interest to him and that he was entitled to continue the business in his name. He further contended that the estate of the deceased partner had only a creditor's claim for the value of the deceased partner's interest in the business. The Arkansas court ruled that the partnership business could not be carried on by the surviving partner, and that the assets would have to be sold at public or private sale. The court would not consider the economic undesirability of immediate liquidation. It stated the rule as follows:

> The legal rule is fixed on this subject. If the survivors of a partnership carry on the concern, and enter into new transactions with the partnership funds, they do so at their peril, and the representative of the deceased (partner) may elect to call on them for the capital, with a share of the profits, or with interest. If no profits are made or even if a loss is incurred, they must be charged with interest on the funds they use and the whole loss will be theirs.

The importance, therefore, of the partnership agreement containing a *modus operandi* to cover the contingency of the death of one of the partners, is evident. There are many possible provisions that can be used to fill this requirement. The partnership agreement may provide that in the event of the death of one of the partners the partnership be liquidated over a period of time. This will enable the surviving partner to achieve the maximum benefits from the liquidation. The partnership contract may provide that the heirs, administrators, or executors of the deceased partner shall carry on the operation of the partnership business together with the surviving partners. Such a provision is usually binding upon the survivors but is optional with the representative. The partnership agreement may provide that the interest of the deceased partner shall continue in the partnership business and that upon the death of one of the partners the partnership need not be liquidated. Such a provision will be binding upon all of the parties.

Many partnership agreements provide that upon the death of one of the partners the surviving partner will have a preferential right to purchase the interest of the deceased partner and to carry on the business. If a workable formula determining the interest of the deceased partner is delineated in the partnership agreement, future disputes will be avoided. The value of the interest of the deceased partner may be based upon book value or upon actual value or determined by some other formula. It should be specifically provided in the partnership contract whether the good will is to be considered in determining the value of the deceased partner's interest or whether good will shall become the sole property of the surviving partner. It has often been deemed advisable for the contract of partnership to provide that mutual life insurance policies be taken out on the lives of each of the partners, in order to enable the surviving partner to have sufficient funds to purchase the deceased partner's interest, based upon a formulated value set forth in the partnership agreement. By careful and prudent planning, both the surviving partner and the estate of the deceased partner can be fully and adequately protected from a financial viewpoint upon the death of one of the partners.

There is a direct relationship between the provisions of a partnership agreement relating to the survival of the business and the provisions that should be contained in the last will and testament of each of the partners. No matter what plan is evolved in the partnership agreement to cover the contingency of the death of one of the partners, the wills of each of the partners should be in conformity with such plan.

Where the interest of the deceased partner is to be purchased by the survivor by means of insurance provided for that purpose or otherwise, the estate will be the recipient of a large cash sum. It may be desirable to provide for a testamentary trust to protect the widow and children of the deceased partner and for sound investment of such cash. If the partnership business is to be carried on by the legal representative of the deceased or if the interest of the deceased in the business is to be maintained, it will be of importance to provide in the wills of the partners for sufficient liquid assets to pay for estate taxes and administration fees. If it is the desire of the partners that the partnership continue after the death of one of them and that their legal representative continue to operate such business, the wills of the partners should contain testamentary provisions sufficiently broad to empower the executors to carry on the business with facility and without the necessity of constant application to court for authorization to perform acts in connection with the continued operation of the business.

The partnership interest may be the most important asset of the estate. Contrary to popular belief, when a man dies intestate, his assets do not go exclusively to his wife, but may be shared by other heirs. In New York, for example, if a man dies without a will, his wife is entitled to only one-third of his estate and his children are entitled to the balance. If only one child survives, widow and child share the estate equally. Only a vaild will can provide for a different result or prevent a number of heirs from exercising their divergent views on the operations of the surviving partnership. Understandably, the results in the absence of a will or with one poorly drawn, can be emotionally as well as financially disastrous.

As we have seen, the partnership agreement should contain a definitive and express provision outlining the financial arrangement between the partners and the method by which management and control is to be exercised. It is also important that the relationship of partners to third persons be considered at the time the partnership agreement is drawn and that the powers and limitations of the partners to bind the firm be delineated.

Each partner is both principal and agent in his relationship to every other partner, and consequently each partner may be legally liable for the activity of every other partner. However, the authority of a partner to act as agent for the partnership is limited to transactions within the scope of the partnership business. It is consequently desirable to set out in the partnership contract the scope of the partnership business and those express limitations considered desirable, upon the rights of the partners to bind each other.

The Uniform Partnership Act provides that all partners will be bound by the act of any one of them which is *apparently* performed in the course of the business of the partnership. Even where the activity in question is not authorized by the partnership agreement, if it is within the apparent scope of the business of the partnership, all partners will be bound. However, the Uniform Partnership Law specifically provides that unless expressly authorized, a partner has no authority to assign the partnership property in trust for creditors, dispose of all the good will of the business, confess judgment, submit a partnership claim to arbitration, or do any other act which would make it impossible to carry on the ordinary business of the partnership.

In the absence of specific provisions in the partnership agreement the courts have been called upon to consider questions dealing with the authority of partners to bind the partnership. The nature of the partnership is often decisive in these considerations. The association of architects is designated as a "non-trading partnership" in contrast to a partnership conducting a commercial business. In the case of a non-trading partnership, the presumption is made that no partner has been given the right to bind the firm by a promissory note. In the case of a commercial partnership it is presumed that a principal of the firm who borrows money or gives a note in the name of the firm is acting for authorized partnership purposes. Many partnership contracts, in order to protect each partner from indiscreet activities of any other partner, provide for the necessity of more than one signature on checks. No matter what the type of partnership, the rights, limitations and powers of the partners to bind the firm should be expressly stated.

In gross outline, a partnership agreement should set forth in detail:

(1) *The term of the partnership.*

(2) *The financial arrangements between the partners.*

(3) *How control and management of the business is to be exercised.*

(4) *A consideration of the impact on the partnership of death, withdrawal, or illness of a partner.*

(5) *The rights and limitations of the partners to bind the firm.*

The value of a practice which would otherwise be liquidated because of death can be preserved by a properly drawn will.

Although the following comments concerning wills are of general application, they should be of particular interest to architects. The chief asset of an architect is often his business. In the absence of a will, this asset must usually be immediately liquidated upon death. If the business can be continued or its value otherwise conserved by proper testamentary provision, this fact should be of extreme significance to the practicing architect.

Despite the importance of wills, intestacy (the state of dying without making a will) is more often the rule than the exception. Judge John J. Bennett, Surrogate of Nassau County, New York, has been rendering an important public service by leading a campaign to alert the public (and women particularly) to the importance of securing a proper will in order to protect the security of the decedent's family. The surrogate is the judicial officer under whose supervision estates are administered and, consequently, he is continually faced with unhappy and sometimes tragic situations which arise out of the failure of a property owner to protect his family by securing a properly drawn will. For example, in Judge Bennett's county in the year 1957, there were more than 850 estates which were administered in his court where no will was left. He notes that in New York State this was true of more than half the estates: and estimates for the United States have placed the figure as high as eighty percent. He urges each wife to know the answers to the following questions:

How will I be provided for in the event of my husband's death?

How will my children be provided for in the event of my husband's death?

What will happen to my husband's business in the event of his death?

Judge Bennett states that the refusal of wife or husband to consider these problems (because of the unpleasant and unhappy nature of the subject) is shortsighted and foolhardy.

The primary purposes of a will are:

(1) to set forth the intentions of the maker of the will concerning how he wishes his property to be distributed at the time of his death,

(2) to conserve his assets and to insure against their dissipation, and

(3) to maintain at a minimum the amount of taxes and other expenses which will be charged against his estate.

These three objectives cannot be realized in the absence of a will and can often be defeated by an inadequate will. The widow whose husband dies without a will is surprised to learn that her children receive a larger proportion of her husband's estate than she does. For example, under the law of New York, the assets of a property owner, who dies without a will, leaving a wife and children, passes one-third to the wife and two-thirds to the children: the latter two thirds *not* subject to the control of the wife even if the children are under the age of twenty-one. If it is necessary to utilize any portion of that inheritance for the maintenance or education of the children, the widow is required to seek the permission of the court for that purpose. Further, the relatively small share of her husband's estate which passes to her may be inadequate for the widow's continued and proper support. In such a situation the absence of a will providing that the entire estate is bequeathed to the widow would result in real hardship.

Perhaps even more shocking to the widow is to discover that her "in-laws" may share in her husband's estate where he dies without a will. Using New York law again, as an example, a widow without children whose husband left an estate of any size would only receive a little more than one-half of that estate if a parent, brother, sister, nephew, or niece of her husband survived him.

In many estates, the chief asset is the husband's business. In the absence of a will, the law generally requires that his business be immediately liquidated. The financial loss resulting from forced liquidation is, of course, obvious. A will can provide for the orderly disposition of the business by granting broad powers to the executors. More important, however, the business asset can be conserved by providing that the business be continued. A successful business which supported the family during the husband's lifetime can continue to do so after his death if proper provision is made. When that business must be liquidated or otherwise disposed of and the income from it thereby terminated because of the absence of a will, such result is, at best, wasteful, and at worst, tragic.

Many husbands may feel that they do not wish to burden their wives with the problems involved in running a business or that their wives do not have sufficient business experience or capability to continue their husband's business. Many husbands also worry that their wives will quickly dissipate the assets of the estate as a result of unsound advice, undue influence, or other misfortune. Again, only through a will can these worries and concerns be eliminated. In a properly drawn will, the husband can provide for the appointment of persons in whom he has trust and confidence to act as trustees to operate his business and to manage his estate. The trustees, under the supervision of the court, will pay over to the widow the income earned from the estate and she will be relieved of the responsibility involved. The widow will also be protected from unsound investments, predatory relatives, and unskillful management.

A will can also save taxes and expenses. In the absence of a will, the estate must bear the expense of surety bonds which the administrator must obtain; expenses of guardianship proceedings for children; and expenses of petitioning the court for permission to take various actions in connection with the estate. A will can eliminate the necessity of the surety bond, and—by granting broad powers to the executors—can avoid many other expenses of administration.

Even more significant is the tax burden which can be limited by a will prepared with this problem in mind. Under the Federal Inheritance Tax Law, certain exemptions from taxation are provided. One of these exemptions is commonly known as the "marital deduction." The amount of the estate which is left to the wife and the manner in which it is left determines the amount of this exemption. A good proportion of this exemption can be lost in the absence of a will or as a result of a will not prepared to treat with this tax problem.

This chapter has touched upon only a few of the more obvious problems arising under our inheritance laws. There are many other complex questions which must be considered in preparing a will which will do the job intended. Laws and circumstances continually change and, consequently, wills must periodically be reviewed. The primary fact, however, is that in the absence of any will, the husband and father has failed to justify the faith which is ordinarily reposed in him by his family.

CHAPTER 4: *Professional Practice by Corporations—Business Advantages and Disadvantages*

Corporate practice of architecture and engineering can result in substantial business benefit, but can constitute a threat to professional standards and ethics if not properly regulated.

THE TAX LAWS of the United States were modified in 1958 by a law known as the Technical Amendments Act, which permits small corporations, the stock of which is closely held, to be treated, for tax purposes, as a partnership. Under this act, small corporations can avoid high corporate tax rates and at the same time retain the benefits of corporate operation.

This act will undoubtedly give additional impetus to the debate that has been raging for many years concerning the desirability of the practice of architecture or engineering by corporations. Over thirty-five states now permit the practice by corporations of engineering. A substantially lesser number of states permit the practice of architecture by corporations. Many states prohibit the practice of architecture or engineering except by natural persons. In the final analysis, the decision as to the propriety and desirability of professional practice by a corporation must be considered and determined by the profession involved.

The history of the New York law regulating the practice of engineering is illustrative of the conflicting viewpoints on this issue. Prior to 1920 there were no licensing requirements in New York; consequently, individuals and corporations practiced both public and non-public engineering. During this period, many corporations combined nonprofessional business activities with the practice of engineering.

In 1920, the first registration law was enacted in New York. This law provided that a corporation or partnership could engage in the practice of professional engineering provided that the persons "in charge of the designing or supervision which constitutes such practice" were licensed as professional engineers. In 1921, a new section was added to the New York law distinguishing between public and nonpublic practice of engineering. This section provided in substance that employees of a manufacturer who performed engineering services which were related to the corporation's products (as distinguished from offering engineering services to the public) need not be licensed. The underlying philosophy of this change in the existing law was that engineering services rendered to a company for the purpose of design, research, etc., in connection with the company's products do not call for the same safeguards as engineering services which are rendered directly to the public.

The New York law was again amended in 1923 to provide that the practice of professional engineering "solely as an officer or employe of a corporation engaged in interstate commerce" would be exempted from the license law. In 1932 a section was adopted which excluded from the licensing provisions of the law the practice of professional engineering by an officer or employee of a public service corporation "in connection with its lines and property which are subject to supervision with respect to the safety and security thereof" by other governmental regulatory bodies.

As the result of the efforts of professional societies, New York, in 1935, amended its registration and licensing law to prohibit the public practice of engineering by corporations except for those corporations lawfully practicing prior to the enactment of the amendment. This amendment followed by approximately six years the prohibition against the practice of architecture by corporations.

The provision of law which permitted a corporation to continue practicing engineering if it was so practicing prior to the adoption of the prohibition ("grandfather" clause) was construed to require that such practice be continuous, and that the employment of a licensed engineer as a chief executive officer also be continuous. This amendment was also interpreted to apply to foreign corporations. The provision of law, however, permitting the practice of engineering by nonlicensed persons in a nonpublic area such as research in and design of manufactured products was not changed.

Although certain corporations were permitted to continue the practice of engineering under the "grandfather" clause contained in the law which prohibited the practice of engineering to all other corporations, there was no specific provision contained in this law requiring the registration of those corporations which could lawfully continue to practice. In 1952, the law was amended to require such registration. Following this amendment, a committee of corporations was formed to work toward amendment of the New York law to permit the practice of engineering by corporations. Several bills to this effect were introduced into the New York legislature between the years 1953 and 1959, but none have been adopted. The first of these bills, introduced in 1953, would permit corporate engineering practice by corporations provided the officer in charge of such engineering was a licensed engineer. This bill was opposed by the New York Society of Professional Engineers and was supported by the Committee on Engineering Laws (which consisted of a group of engineering corporations, some of whom were operating on a national scope). A second bill was introduced into the legislature not only requiring that the officer in charge of professional engineering be licensed, but further providing for disciplinary action against a corporation if the license of the executive in control of the professional service was revoked. This bill was not only opposed by the New York State Society of Professional Engineers, but was also opposed by the Medical Society and other engineering and professional groups.

In 1955, a bill sponsored by the New York State Society of Professional Engineers was introduced into the legislature providing that a corporation be permitted to practice engineering provided that all of the directors and officers of the corporation, as well as all employees rendering professional engineering services be licensed in New York. This bill was opposed by American Institute of Architects, American Institute of Consulting Engineers, Dental and Medical Societies of New York, New York Association of Consulting Engineers, and many other groups. Several other bills followed, each of which substantially provided that a corporation may practice engineering provided that the person in responsible charge, and the employees who perform professional engineering services, shall be licensed engineers. These bills, however, were not adopted, although the pressure continues for a change in the New York law.

The opponents to corporate practice contend that the life, health, and property of the public would be jeopardized by corporate professional practice, whereas the proponents of such measures contend that the business benefits of corporate practice can be obtained without jeopardizing the safety or welfare of the public.

Opponents of professional practice by corporations argue that the furnishing of professional service to the public must depend upon the integrity and responsibility of the individual practitioner. It is the basic premise of licensing laws, they contend, that the life, health, and property of the public must be safeguarded by insuring the competence of the professional and by insuring his personal responsibility for the services rendered. This is incompatible with the limited liability of the corporate entity, and would increase the difficulties in effective enforcement of the licensing and regulatory laws which have been adopted for public protection. Corporate practice is a dilution, they contend, of the safeguards implicit in licensing of natural persons, and a perversion of the relationship which should exist between the professional practitioner and client.

It is further asserted that to secure to the public the maximum safeguard of its welfare, the engineer must be in a position to act independently and that corporate practice would subvert that independence. If large corporations carry on professional pursuits, this activity would be—it is contended—subordinated to other business activities, and the independence of the engineer or architect might be compromised in respect to dealings with contractors, owners, and others.

The opponents of corporate practice see a basic inconsistency or conflict in combining the practice of a professional man (who owes a special obligation to the public) with business activities (where the responsibility of management to the stockholder is to realize the maximum profit).

The opponents of corporate practice further assert that such practice would be dangerous, particularly in relation to hazardous industries. For example, they question whether safety would be the first consideration in approving a site for chemical or atomic processes if that determination was made by corporate management rather than by an individual engineer. Professional ability and integrity are personal attributes not transferable to a corporation, contend the opponents of a corporate practice, and the public interest can only be safeguarded by those who have personally pledged themselves to the ethical and legal obligations of their profession.

The subordination of professional control to nonprofessional management is inevitable, say the opponents of corporate practice, even where the executive officers of the corporation are duly licensed. If only the executive officers in charge of professional practice in a corporation are licensed, they are subject to the control of a board of directors; if the officers and board of directors are licensed, they are subject to the control of the stockholders. If corporations were permitted professional practice, provided all of their officers, directors, and stockholders were licensed, then, it is finally argued, such corporate set-up removes the incentive against malpractice because of the limited liability of a corporation as against the unlimited liability of an individual.

On the other hand, proponents of corporate professional practice argue that only by this method can the public receive the full benefit of rapid industrial and technological expansion of our economy. The Committee on Engineering Laws, which supported various bills before the New York State legislature to permit corporate practice of engineering, made the following arguments:

(1) The corporate form of organization is the only one which permits accumulation of the capital required to maintain necessary operating, research, and specialized engineering staffs required in the undertaking of huge engineering projects for Government and private business.

(2) A corporation can undertake large and complex projects which would be impossible for an individual, because of its integrated operation; and can provide superior engineering services, as a consequence.

(3) A corporation can furnish continuous services, whereas in the case of individuals or a partnership the death of the individual or a partner would interrupt the progress of a project being developed.

(4) Corporations can offer greater security to corporate employees with such things as pension plans, because of the continuity of its existence.

The proponents of corporate professional practice argue that there is nothing wrong or undignified in this type of operation, and that to oppose it in view of the industrial advances of our society is to be unrealistic and to lack vision. They assert that only through large organizations able to accumulate capital can research be conducted, new processes developed, and complex and huge industrial projects be properly handled. If the professional services rendered by a corporation are controlled by licensed individuals, why then, ask the proponents of corporate practice, isn't the public being protected and at the same time realizing the benefits of the integrated and continuous operation of the corporate form of organization?

If control of a corporation is in the hands of licensed professionals, say the supporters of corporate practice, there is no inconsistency with such practice and the duties owed by professionals to client and public. As a matter of fact, they argue, it is possible that the public is protected more fully by the resources of a corporation than by the assets of an individual practitioner. Corporate practice with proper legislative safeguards will result, they argue, in such business advantages as continuity of operation, tax savings, capital accumulation, security to the employe, and financial responsibility to the client—and at the same time, will benefit the public. Why sacrifice these benefits, they ask, if the public is properly safeguarded?

The central and fundamental issue in this continuing debate is whether it is possible to have a corporate organization in which control of professional activities remains in the hands of professionals and is not subordinated to some objective of the corporation that may be inconsistent with the duties owed to public and client. The requirement, for example, that a majority of the board of directors of a corporation be licensed professionals may not necessarily solve this dilemma because the professionals on the board might disagree and the decision, in a particular issue in such situation, might be made by the nonprofessionals. Moreover, there does not appear to be much support or enthusiasm by organizations supporting corporate professional practice for legislation which would permit such practice only if all stockholders, directors, and officers are licensed.

The problem of proponents of professional practice by corporations, in those states where it is now prohibited, is to suggest a form of corporate organization that will protect the interests of the public and of the client by insuring that professional standards are not subordinated to business objectives. If, however, corporations are not permitted to practice architecture or engineering, is there any way that individual architects or engineers can secure some of the business benefits which could be realized with corporate operation?

One of the chief problems of the professional under our present tax structure is to accumulate savings for himself and his family. Many corporate executives are securing their future through profit-sharing plans approved by the United States Treasury Department, and under certain circumstances it may be possible for the architect or engineer also to utilize this procedure.

The spread of profit-sharing plans among medium and small corporations, where stock is closely held, is particularly evident today. Even where profits are great, the high individual and corporate tax rate make it difficult to accumulate savings; and small corporations, by utilizing a qualified profit-sharing plan, can convert part of their profits (that would otherwise go out in taxes) into capital that accumulates until the need for that capital arises. In small corporations, ownership and management are generally combined in the same few people. The stockholders who own the stock also run the corporations as officers and directors. Under profit-sharing plans authorized by the present law, a corporation may institute a profit-sharing plan of which the executives are members. The corporation agrees to contribute a certain proportion of its year's profit, if any, to the fund which is set up in proportion to a certain limited percentage of each executive's salary. Under some plans the amount contributed to the fund is discretionary. The profits placed in the fund are not subject to tax. This fund can be invested, and the income or profits realized upon these investments are also tax free. Upon their retirement, the members of the fund are paid their share, at which time said distribution is subject only to a long-term capital gains tax.

Until a member has continued his employment for a period of ten years, his rights do not become fully vested; and if he should voluntarily leave the corporation prior to this period, he forfeits part of the fund, the remaining part of which is credited to the other members. Consequently, the profit-sharing plan is an incentive for the members to continue in the employment of the company; and when employes leave without obtaining a vested right in profit-sharing fund, the owner-managers of the corporation increase their interest proportionately.

If a corporation may not practice architecture or engineering, and profit-sharing plans may only be approved for corporations, how then may a professional obtain the benefit of such a plan? One way may be to divide the architectural or engineering firm into two, separate entities. One such entity would continue, through the individual or partnership firm, furnishing exclusively architectural or engineering services, such as design and supervision of construction. The other entity would consist of a corporation formed for the purpose of furnishing drafting services only, and would be owned and operated by the individual architect or engineer or by the partners of the architectural or engineering firm. The drafting corporation, whose salaried executives would be the owners of the company, would then initiate a profit-sharing plan and could, like any other corporation, obtain the benefits of a tax-free accumulation.

The foregoing plan might be subject to challenge by state authorities in those states where corporations may not practice architecture or engineering, on the ground that the furnishing of drafting services is such practice. The line between the performing of architectural services, as distinguished from purely drafting services, is very fine. At a minimum, the drafting corporation must be set up so that it is not furnishing services to the public; the final responsibility for and approval of the work performed there must lie with the architectural or engineering firm whose members are duly licensed. The success or failure of this plan may depend on the care and competency with which the charter of the drafting corporation is drawn, and also upon the varying interpretations of the licensing laws given by the courts in different states.

If corporate practice constitutes a hazard to professional obligations and standards, and if the business benefits of such practice cannot be legally obtained by individuals or partnerships, the solution to the problem may be legislation which grants some of these benefits to the individual practitioner or to the partnership firm. This is a question which should be considered carefully by the profession.

CHAPTER 5: *Establishing Architectural or Engineering Fees*

The fixing of minimum fees by a professional society may be deemed an illegal price-fixing scheme.

HOW FAR can a professional society of architects go in fixing or recommending schedules of minimum fees for services? An answer to this question is found in the decision of the United States Supreme Court in *U.S.A.* v. *National Assn. of Real Estate Boards,* 339 U.S. 485. The Court by that decision declared illegal a schedule of minimum fees by an organization of real estate brokers on the ground that such fixing violated the Sherman Anti-Trust Act.

The government instituted this suit against the National Association of Real Estate Boards and the Washington Real Estate Board to enjoin these organizations and their members "from engaging in a price-fixing conspiracy in violation of Section 3 of the Sherman Act." The pertinent portion of Section 3 declares illegal every conspiracy *in restraint of trade.*

The code of ethics by which members of the Washington Board agreed to abide included a provision "that brokers should maintain the standard rates of commissions adopted by the Board and no business should be solicited at lower rates." The Court pointed out that the prescribed rates were used in a great majority of transactions, although lower charges were made in exceptional cases. It appeared, however, that the Washington Board had not applied sanctions against members who deviated from the established rates. On these facts the Court determined that an illegal price-fixing scheme had been established. It stated:

> Price fixing is *per se* an unreasonable restraint of trade. It is not for the courts to determine whether in particular settings price fixing serves an honorable or worthy end. An agreement, shown either by adherence to a price schedule or by proof of consensual action, fixing the minimum or uniform price, is itself illegal under the Sherman Act, no matter what end it was designed to serve. And the fact that no penalties are imposed for deviations from the price schedules is not material. Subtle influences may be just as effective as a threat or use of formal sanctions to hold people in line.

Thus it appears that the *purpose* for which a fee-fixing arrangement is designed is not material in determining whether the Act has been violated. Nor is it necessary to prove that the organization uses coercive measures to compel members to charge the standard rates. Any direct agreement by the parties to fix prices or any agreement indirectly shown by adherence to a fixed schedule is condemned.

In reaching its conclusion that a conspiracy in restraint of trade had been proved, the Court found that real estate brokers are engaged in "trade" within the meaning of the Anti-Trust Law and do not fall within the well known exception applicable to labor organizations. The Court refused to consider a real estate broker's services as falling within the typical employer-employee relationship protected by the Act, but viewed members of the Washington board as entrepreneurs, each in business on his own.

In defining real estate brokers as persons engaged in a "trade," the Court took the first step to extend the term to a sale involving personal services rather than commodities. Whether it will be further extended to include services rendered *by the professions* is not now certain. The Court, while declining to pass on this question, quoted a lower court opinion in which the practice of medicine was held to be a trade. With respect to that broad application of the term "trade," the Court remarked:

> Chief Justice Groner made an extended analysis and summary of the problem in *U.S.* v. *American Medical Ass'n.,* 110 Fed 2nd, 703, 707-711, where the Court of Appeals for the District of Columbia held that the practice of medicine in the District was a "trade" within the meaning of Section 3 of the Act. Its conclusion was that the term included "all occupations in which men are engaged for a livelihood." We do not intimate an opinion on the correctness of the application of the

> terms to the professions. We have said enough to indicate we would be contracting the scope of the concept of "trade," as used in the phrase "restraint of trade," in a precedent-breaking manner if we carved out an exemption for real estate brokers.

The Court held, however, that the National Association had not conspired with the Washington Board to fix and prescribe minimum rates. It pointed out that the provision in the National Association's code of ethics that a schedule of fees "should be observed" was somewhat ambiguous and suggested that it might be advisory only.

It would appear, then, that a society of architects which draws up a schedule of fees *advisory* in nature and intended solely as a guide for its members is not guilty of a violation of the Act.

As a result of this decision there has been considerable speculation as to whether the government will institute similar suits against organizations of professional architects and engineers. However, any statements found in professional publications to the effect that such action will be taken have not been confirmed by the Justice Department, which states that it is not its policy to advance information with regard to future actions. It has therefore declined to furnish information as to whether enforcement in the architectural and engineering fields is contemplated.

In the event that any future action is taken by the government, it will be based upon the above decision. According to the opinion, advisory schedules are permissable. Whether in any future suit the Court would accept the statement in a given schedule of charges to the effect that the fees are "recommended" or to be used as a "guide"; or whether it would receive extraneous evidence of uniform adherence to such schedules as tending to prove a price-fixing agreement, are matters which are not made clear in the opinion.

Most of the professional engineering and architectural societies have taken the position that their minimum-fee schedules are purely recommendations intended to serve as a basis for discussion and negotiation of a working agreement with the client. But there is danger in the adoption by such professional societies of rules and by-laws providing that deviation from the minimum schedule will result in disciplinary action. Societies which have adopted such rules will be advised to delete the coercive features to afford at least minimal protection against the possibility of suit by the Federal Government.

In the absence of an agreement specifying an architect or engineer's compensation, the courts may award fees substantially lower than those recommended by professional societies.

In this discussion we don our bowler hat, stroke our chin whiskers, and consider a leading case in the law of architecture decided in Louisiana at the turn of the century (*Sully v. Pratt,* 106 La. 601, 31 So. 161). A review of the judge's decision indicates that although time moves on and façades change, architects' relations with clients remain basically the same. The facts presented to the Louisiana court were as follows:

It was the intention of a theater owner to demolish his building and to erect a larger and finer one. He therefore employed the services of a company which was in the general architectural and building business. This company was a licensed corporation. (It is of interest to note at the outset that today, in most states, corporations may not practice architecture.) The company made preliminary studies and prepared plans and specifications. Based upon these plans, bids were received indicating that the cost of the building would be approximately $100,000. However, the theater owner had a change of heart and decided to abandon the new construction.

There had been (alas) no specific agreement as to the architect's compensation, and the architectural company billed the client for $3,500, based upon a fee of three and one-half percent for a $100,000 structure. The client refused to pay this bill and the company instituted legal action. The trial court awarded the architect a judgment in the magnificent sum of $700. And feeling aggrieved thereby, the plaintiff appealed.

In justification of its bill, the architect contended on appeal that the American Institute of Architects had promulgated a schedule of compensation for architectural work and that such schedule provided for a fee of three and one-half percent for preliminary studies, general drawings, details, and specifications. (Historically interesting is the full text of this schedule, which was as follows:

For full professional services (including supervision), five percent upon the whole cost of the work.

For preliminary studies, one percent.

For preliminary studies, general drawings and specifications, two and one-half percent.

For preliminary studies, general drawings, details and specifications, three and one-half percent.

For warehouses and factories, three and one-half percent, upon the cost, divided in the above ratio.

For works that cost less than $10,000, or for monumental and decorative work, and designs for furniture, a special rate in excess of the above.

For alterations and additions, an additional charge to be made for surveys and measurements.

An additional charge to be made for alterations or additions in contracts or plans, which will be valued in proportion to the additional time and services employed.

Necessary travelling expenses to be paid by the client.

Time spent by the architect in visiting for professional consultation and in the accompanying travel, whether by day or night, will be charged for, whether or not any commission, for office work or supervising work, is given.

The architect's payments are successively due as his work is completed, in the order of the above classification.

Until an actual estimate is received, the charges are based upon the actual cost.

The architect bases his professional charge upon the entire cost to the owner of the building when completed, including all the fixtures necessary to render it fit for occupation, and is entitled to a fair additional compensation for furniture or other articles designed or purchased by the architect.

If any material or work used in the construction of the building be already upon the ground, or come into possession of the owner without expense to him, the value of said material or work is to be added to the sum actually expended upon the building before the architect's commission is computed.

Drawings, as instruments of service, are the property of the architect.

The Louisiana Appellate Court refused to be bound by the AIA schedule. The court stated:

The American Institute of Architects has promulgated a schedule of prices for architectural work, and plaintiff's charges are based upon the same, one or more members of the firm being members or fellows of the Institute. But it is shown that very few architects doing business in the city of New Orleans are at this time members of the Institute, and it may not be said

> that any custom prevails there to charge for services according to the scale of the Institute. Defendant had not been apprised of this schedule, and had no knowledge of the same. Much less did he assent to it. The schedule of charges, then, of the Institute, may be useful in assisting the court to arrive at a proper estimate to be put upon plaintiffs' services, but can be given no greater weight.

Moral: Then, as now, make certain the agreement specifically covers all contingencies as to compensation.

The court further said:

> The evidence shows that the custom obtaining among architects generally is to regulate their charges according to a rule of percentages. Thus, for preliminary studies, general drawings, specifications and details, and superintendence, where the building is erected five percent appears to be the usual charge; and a less percentage, according to the work done and skill and time employed, where the building is not constructed, or the architect's employment does not include superintendence. But courts will adopt with caution a rule which binds an employer to pay a percentage on a building such as the architect sees fit to figure out, and at a price which he, or the bidders to whom he sends the plans (as in this instance), put upon its probable cost. There is in such a rule too much inducement to architects to make the plan expensive for it to be readily accepted by those called upon to sit in judgment in matters of controversy between owners and architects. (*Editor's query: Have we come a long way since*?)

In considering what was a reasonable fee, the appellate court first considered the estimated cost of the structure which was to be built. Although the evidence established such cost at $100,000, the court arbitrarily accepted a figure of $87,500.

The court then went on to determine that a fee of two and one-half percent for the plans and specifications prepared by the plaintiff was "not unreasonable." Applying this figure, which was one percent less than the schedule figure of the AIA, to the estimated cost of $87,500, the court came up with the figure of $2187.50. However it was still reluctant to grant this sum to the plaintiff and awarded it, as its full compensation for services rendered, $1750, apparently feeling that an architect is not entitled to what he has earned.

Of course, since the determination of this case, the architects' situation vis-a-vis the law has improved considerably. A fairly comprehensive review of the licensing statutes indicates that in 1900 there were no legal impediments, in any of the states, to anyone calling himself an architect or practicing architecture, whether or not he was qualified. The New York statute, which is certainly one of the oldest, was enacted in its first form in 1910. Since 1900, the American Institute of Architects has helped advance the architects' position considerably. For many years it has made available its guides to ethical principles, its forms of agreements and "general conditions," and other aids which have been of substantial benefit to the profession generally and to the individual architect.

If a proper public relations program is initiated and conducted throughout the country, if the organizations representing architects keep pace with the times, if the individual architect also does, the next 50 years will find the architect assuming his proper place and his proper share of responsibility in the development of our country. Only then will the architectural profession be properly rewarded for its labor and credited with its contribution to our civilization.

CHAPTER 6: *Dealing with the Government*

Fees for professional services on governmental projects can be unfairly minimized if they are based upon an arbitrary cost instead of the actual cost of construction.

THERE IS SOMETHING MORE THAN a suspicion that an increasing tendency exists on the part of some agencies—by one device or another—to reduce architects' net fees on governmental projects.

One expedient is to use an arbitrary pricing period (pre-Korea, for example) based upon which costs are to be estimated. Under contracts which base the architect's fee on a fixed percentage of the estimated cost, arbitrary choice of such a low-cost period will cut the architect's fee considerably. It is reasonable to assume that when general construction costs rise, the architect's own expenses rise correspondingly. At a time when such costs are at their highest levels, arbitrary selection of any earlier period for determining the estimated cost of a project will result in a marked disparity in the ratio between the architect's outlay and his financial return. While the architect's compensation lags behind the price trend, his expenses rise with every increase in cost of labor and materials.

The situation prevailing in one of the largest states illustrates this inequity from the architect's point of view. Roughly described, one form of contract used in that state for substantial building projects stipulates as the architect's fee a certain percentage of the estimated cost of construction. The contract provides that the architect's estimates shall be based upon the prevailing rate of pay and materials costs in effect June 1, 1958 in the area of the proposed construction. Thus, an architect employed in 1960 will have to contend with 1960 prices in paying the expenses he incurs in carrying out the project—but his compensation will depend upon costs prevailing in June 1958. No economic data are required to establish the fact that prices have risen sharply since June 1958; and that anyone who must face a 1960 overhead while his earning capacity remains at the June 1958 level will find himself at an unhappy disadvantage.

The above-described form of contract is similar to one employed by the state for projects undertaken at the end of the war. In the earlier contract, however, the estimated cost of construction was based upon 1940 prices, increased by 50%. Again, this arbitrarily selected period bore no substantial relation to construction costs prevailing in the years 1947-1950. Yet, owing to the disparity in costs, architects employed under this form of contract were compelled to accept less than the usual and customary return for their services obtained under private contracts.

The schedule of fees set forth in the earlier contract was as follows (no supervision required by the architect):

Estimated Construction Cost	Fee	Estimated Construction Cost	Fee
Under —$ 70,000	6.0%	$300,001—$350,000	4.9%
$ 70,001— 90,000	5.9%	350,001— 400,000	4.8%
90,001— 110,000	5.8%	400,001— 450,000	4.7%
110,001— 130,000	5.7%	450,001— 500,000	4.6%
130,001— 150,000	5.6%	500,001— 550,000	4.5%
150,001— 170,000	5.5%	550,001— 600,000	4.4%
170,001— 190,000	5.4%	600,001— 650,000	4.3%
190,001— 210,000	5.3%	650,001— 700,000	4.2%
210,001— 230,000	5.2%	700,001— 750,000	4.1%
230,001— 250,000	5.1%	Over — 750,000	4.0%
250,001— 300,000	5.0%		

The schedule of fees set forth in the 1951 contract is the same as above, until the $750,000 estimated cost level is reached. For projects with estimated costs in excess of this sum, the new contract provides a further gradual reduction of fees. The schedule continues as follows:

Estimated Construction Cost	Fee	Estimated Construction Cost	Fee
$ 750,001—$1,000,000	4.0%	$3,500,001—$4,000,000	3.4%
1,000,001— 1,500,000	3.9%	4,000,001— 4,500,000	3.3%
1,500,001— 2,000,000	3.8%	4,500,001— 5,000,000	3.2%
2,000,001— 2,500,000	3.7%	5,000,001— 5,500,000	3.1%
2,500,001— 3,000,000	3.6%	Over — 5,500,000	3.0%
3,000,001— 3,500,000	3.5%		

Thus, for projects where the estimated cost is anywhere between $1,000,000 and $5,500,000, the architect's percentage fee is further reduced in inverse proportion to the cost of the project. The difference in payment for a project to the architect under the two sets of schedules above set forth may be considerable. On a project estimated to cost $6,000,000 under the earlier contract, computing his fee at 4.0% of the estimated cost, the architect will be paid $240,000; under the contract in current use, computing his fee at 3.0% of the estimated cost, he will receive $180,000—a difference of $60,000. Actually the difference may be greater because of the "estimated cost" formula.

Even the somewhat higher percentages referred to in the earlier contract will suffer by comparison with the percentages recommended by individual American Institute of Architects chapters. It should be noted that the AIA schedules are based upon complete architectural services, while the contracts above considered exclude supervision of the actual work of construction.

The schedules devised by the individual AIA groups provide different rates of compensation for different types of structures, the rates varying with the complexity of the type and the degree of care and skill required in their design.

One AIA chapter, for comparable structures, has the following schedule:

Building Cost	Rate (with supervision)
$ 25,000	7.00%
50,000	6.75%
100,000	6.50%
200,000	6.00%
500,000	6.00%
1,000,000	6.00%
2,000,000	6.00%
5,000,000	6.00%

Another chapter, for similar structures, has the following schedule (includes supervision):

Cost of work up to:	
$ 300,000	8.00%
500,000	7.75%
1,000,000	7.50%
2,000,000	7.25%
3,000,000	7.00%
4,000,000	6.75%
5,000,000	6.50%

The schedule of minimum rates adopted by a third chapter provides a fee of 7.0% for similar buildings. After making the necessary adjustment for supervision, the architect still finds that his fee is far below these "minimums" because the "estimated costs" are not current costs and the percentage itself is substantially lower.

Another type of contract which bears critical analysis from the architect's viewpoint is a sort presently in use by one of our largest cities. The architect's undertaking under this contract also does not include supervision of construction. The contract provides for payment of a lump sum fee to the architect for his entire services. The fee paid is arrived at after negotiation. As a basis for negotiation, however, the "estimated cost" of the project is used. This means the cost of construction estimated by the agency at the time of the execution of the contract with the architect. The fee is then adjusted upon a sliding scale depending upon the size of the project.

It should be noted, however, that the agency is under no obligation to estimate the cost of the project on the basis of prevailing market prices. The contract, while providing that the "preliminary estimated cost" and the "final estimated cost" are to be estimated by the architect on the basis of the prevailing market price of construction work and materials, entirely omits any criterion for arriving at the "estimated cost," which is set in advance. The architect is thus deprived of any objective measurement by which his compensation is to be determined. There will be a natural tendency on the part of the contracting officer to *under*estimate the cost. Should the proposed structure be of a type which the municipality has not erected for a number of years, the difficulty of correctly estimating the cost of any such project will be magnified. Add to this the factor of sharply rising costs, with which all persons in any way connected with the building industry must contend, and the final cost of the contemplated structure will in all probability (if recent experience is any criterion) far exceed the modest estimate of the municipality.

As we pointed out above, it is valid to assume that the architect's expenses for labor and materials will also be directly affected by the prevailing price trend. Yet the contract specifically prohibits any adjustment of the architect's fee should the "estimated cost" be revised upward. The net result is that all contractors and suppliers are paid at current price levels. The architect is paid at an arbitrary, anachronistic price level.

The three forms of contracts which we have just discussed illustrate some of the techniques by which municipal and state agencies can effectively reduce an architect's fee below the amount to which he is entitled, according to the customary fees charged by the architectural profession for projects of similar scope. This situation affects not only those directly concerned in government projects but the entire profession, since such contracts also serve as yardsticks for private structures.

In dealing with government agencies, an architect, engineer or contractor is required to know all the terms of the public works contract and to follow its provisions exactly.

The United States Court of Claims decided a case (*John J. Hart Co. v. United States,* 117 Ct. Cl. 309), in which were described the trials and tribulations of one architect's dealings with the United States Government. It should serve as an object lesson and as a danger signal to all others similarly situated. Perhaps a question and answer period, using quotations from the case, is in order:

Question: Does the following constitute duress?

"Upon arrival at Memphis, Mr. H. [the architect] went to the office of Colonel G. W. Miller, Executive Assistant to the District Engineer. After waiting in the outer office for two days Mr. H. was allowed to see the Colonel who met him with severely critical language and threatened to throw him off the job. Mr. H. was then handed a contract purporting to cover the fixed fee for the new work and was told by the Colonel, 'You can take it or leave it. That is it.' He took it voluntarily, as we have found, but was doubtless motivated in so doing by the prospect of loss of work, impairment of credit, and the unnecessarily overbearing conduct of the Colonel."

Answer: No.
"We do not find that this amounted to duress upon the plaintiff." (*By the Court*)

Question: ". . . the contract reads in its parts pertinent here, as follows: . . . All disputes arising under this contract shall be decided by the Contracting Officer whose decision shall be in writing subject to written appeal by the Architect-Engineer within thirty (30) days to the Secretary of War or his duly authorized representative, whose decision shall be final and conclusive upon the parties hereto . . ."

The architect waits thirty-four (34) days before appealing. What rights does the architect have to recover his just fees where the Court finds that "many of the facts are in the plaintiff's [architect's] favor?"

Answer: None

"As we see it, there is no necessity to go into any of these questions except one because the tragedy of the plaintiff's situation is that it has failed to exhaust its administrative remedy before coming to this Court . . . It follows that when a contractor (*or architect*) chooses without due cause to ignore the provisions of Article 15 he destroys his right to sue for damages in the Court of Claims. That court is then obliged to outlaw his claims, whatever may be their equity. To do otherwise is to rewrite the contract." (*By the Court.*)

The full story revealed in the opinion has all the fascination of a horrible example.

The architect, in 1942, accepted a letter contract offered by a United States District Engineer and thereafter entered into a cost-plus-fixed-fee architect-engineer contract in connection with the construction of a bombardment station in Tennessee to cost $2,466,750. For the designing, Mr. H. agreed to a fee of $10,650, and to a fee of $7,100 for supervision. (As I figure, this is less than 1%.)

Shortly after completion of the design, the United States Government decided to change the type of installation being built. The cost of the new project was now estimated at $5,647,950. Upon the issuance of the new directive effectuating this change, the architect was instructed to perform the necessary redesigning, which he did. Unknown to Mr. H., the District Engineer's office at Memphis obtained approval for its own rough layout for the new project, and let contracts on the basis of this inadequate plan—all while H. was laboring on the new drawings. This made his new drawings as useless as his old ones.

As might be expected, because of the inadequacy of the District Engineer's drawings upon which the contracts had been let, serious difficulties arose in the execution of the plans and the performance of the work. It became necessary for Mr. H. to redesign much of the work.

Mr. H. claimed further compensation because of the additional necessary designing, the unwarranted interferences in the performance of his work putting him to great extra cost and expense beyond what would ordinarily be encountered in contracts of this sort, and for extra work done for which he was not requested in writing to do. He also claimed that he signed the changed contract under duress.

On February 14, 1945, the contracting officer made findings of fact in which he determined that he was without authority to decide the matter of duress in connection with the signing of the changed order and in findings on the other matters—and disallowed the architect's claims.

On March 20, 1945 (thirty-four days after the contracting officer's decision), Mr. H. appealed to the Secretary of War. The War Department Board of Contract Appeals dismissed the appeal because it had not been taken within the prescribed time stated in the contract. Upon this disallowance the architect brought an action in the Court of Claims which, as stated, denied him any recovery.

To summarize:

(1) Do not permit yourself to be stampeded into anything just because you are dealing with a public officer.

(2) When you execute a public works contract, know its terms and *follow the letter of its provisions.*

CHAPTER 7: *Standards of Professional Practice*

Solicitation of work by non-professionals on behalf of an architect or engineer, and the splitting of fees, involve both ethical and legal considerations.

"I can swing this job to you for 10 percent. Is it a deal?"

"Can you swing this job to us for a percentage of the fee?"

"Our firm of architects is engaging you to solicit commissions for us. Even though you are not an architect, you must conform to the Standards of Professional Practice in urging our special abilities. Your compensation will be an appropriate percentage of our fee. Are you agreeable to this arrangement?"

If any of these questions are answered in the affirmative, will the resulting agreement be illegal or unethical?

Unquestionably psychoanalysts would say that the problem exemplified by these questions has been gnawing at the subconscious of many an architect (not necessarily in the form in which they have been put above). However, whether the language is more or less genteel or the situation any one of the other variants which human ingenuity can devise, it is unquestionably a situation which should be faced squarely by the profession. The individual architect is troubled whether to engage a layman to solicit commissions. He also is faced by the corollary of the problem, when other members of the profession decide to use laymen for that purpose.

It would be presumptuous of the writer to attempt to determine here this question of ethics. This the profession must do. But here it can be stated that every architect is entitled to a definitive guide which can determine his own answer to this question and which will serve to police those who are inclined to stray from principles clearly and definitely set forth by the profession. No such set of ethical principles determining this question is available.

A start towards answering the legal question is appropriate here. In each case the state statute and the court decisions interpreting the state statute would control. Unfortunately there is a paucity of the latter.

In the interest of getting a fairly comprehensive guide, the writer addressed a communication presenting this problem to the Executive Secretary of Professional Conduct of the New York State Education Department, since the New York law has served as a model for those of many other states. In the absence of a specific prohibition against solicitation, or specific approval of the practice, the question resolves itself into whether solicitation constitutes the practice of architecture. If it does, the practice is illegal; if it does not, there is no violation of law. Accordingly my letter read in part as follows:

"The Education Law (McKinney's Cons. Laws of N. Y., Book 16, Sec. 7309) provides that it shall be a misdemeanor for any person to practice or offer to practice or hold himself out as entitled to practice architecture unless duly licensed. In relation to this and other companion provisions, I would like to know, (1) Whether there is any restriction upon the solicitation of a commission by an architect (2) If there is no such restriction, is it illegal for a layman to solicit such commissions for an architect (3) If such activity is permissible, may a solicitor be paid by the architect a fee based upon the business which is solicited, or must the compensation of the solicitor be unrelated to the business he acquires for the architect.

"I believe a definitive answer to these questions would greatly aid the profession."

In reply the Executive Secretary stated:

"In response to your letter of May 23, 1949, I can now inform you that none of the situations which you posed in your letter can be considered a violation of the laws pertaining to the practice of Architecture in this state. I do not see any prohibition against an architect employing a solicitor, nor do I see any violation if the solicitor is paid a fee based upon the business which was solicited."

Thus it would appear that the solicitation of business and the acceptance of fees for such solicitation probably does not constitute the practice of architecture and is therefore lawful. If such conduct is lawful, the next question presented is whether such conduct is ethical. The Standards of Professional Practice established by the AIA and set forth in Document No. 330 do not refer to the problem of solicitation or of splitting of fees. Paragraph 7 refers to publicity and advertising but not to direct solicitation of business, as follows:

> An architect shall avoid exaggerated, misleading or paid publicity. He shall not take part, nor give assistance, in obtaining advertisements or other support toward meeting the expense of any publication illustrating his works, nor shall he permit others to solicit such advertising or other support in his name.

In interpreting this section, the Executive Committee of the Board of Directors of the AIA determined that the use of paid advertising was unethical but that it was not improper to hire public relations counsel. Although related, this standard and its interpretation does not resolve the problem as to the propriety of solicitation of business and the making of payments to solicitors by the architect, based upon the amount of business obtained.

The architect, of course, is permitted by the Standards of Professional Practice to offer his services to anyone provided "that he rigidly maintains his professional integrity, disinterestedness and freedom to act." The architect is further required to be absolutely disinterested in his advice to his client and if he acts in a judicial capacity as between client and contractor, he must act with entire impartiality. "His honesty of purpose must be above suspicion."

It is possible that solicitation of business by a contractor for an architect would result in a divided allegiance of the architect between the client and contractor. If this were the case, the acceptance of such solicitation would undoubtedly be considered an unethical practice. On the other hand, solicitation of business by a third party may not have any relationship to the fidelity of service of the architect to his client and therefore the ethical principles which have been referred to heretofore would have no application. Such solicitation may as a matter of fact be desirable from the viewpoint of free competition by architects and the advantages to the public and profession that result from such competition. The conflict and confusion at present in the profession is aptly illustrated by the Code of Ethics adopted by the Georgia Chapter of the AIA. One provision of this code provides that "An architect may introduce to a possible client the service which he is able to perform." This provision would seem to approve solicitation. However, in the same code, the following quotation from Marcus Vitruvius, architect in the reign of Augustus Caesar, is included:

"An architect should be high-minded, not arrogant but faithful, just and easy to deal with; without avarice. Let him not be mercenary nor let his mind be preoccupied with his remunerations. Let him preserve his good name with dignity. At the request of others, not at his own, should he undertake a task."

Thus ethical judgment of this Roman architect would seem to disapprove of solicitation. In any event, nothing in the Georgia Code refers to solicitation by a third party on behalf of the architect.

Nothing here discussed should be construed as any indication of this writer's opinion as to solicitation of commissions by laymen. The problem is one that has been faced by every profession with startlingly different results. Among physicians, "fee-splitting" even among members of the profession, is held anathema. Among lawyers, fee splitting is a respectable procedure, if "splitter" and "splittee" are each duly licensed to practice, and if services are shared. In other professions, there is no restriction on the division of fees.

What should be the rule for architects is something that the profession itself should determine; but it is unquestionably important that rules for the guidance of the individual architect with relation to the specific problem be set up.

The line of demarcation between the practice of architecture and the practice of engineering is difficult of definition, resulting in an encroachment by one profession upon the other.

What, if anything, is to be done by architects about the practice of architecture by engineers? What are the differences between the professions of architecture and engineering? When may it be said that the latter is encroaching upon the area of activity of the former? What are the bounds, if any, as prescribed by law?

The distinction between the professions is generally recognized to be of considerable importance, but the relative success in maintaining two distinct categories has largely been dependent upon the type of legislation in effect and its construction by the state courts.

For example, in *Clark* v. *Eads,* 165 S.W. 2d 1019 (1942), a Texas court denied recovery for architectural services rendered by an engineer who represented himself as an architect, and who was not licensed as an architect. It is important to note that there are several such jurisdictions which have in effect title statutes where anyone may pursue the practice of architecture, provided that he does not use the title "architect" and represent himself as an architect. Apparently the result would have been different if the engineer had not represented himself as an architect.

A licensed engineer, who was not licensed as an architect, was denied recovery for architectural services in *Gionti* v. *Crown Motor Freight Co.,* 128 N.J.L. 407, 26A.2d 282 (1942), despite the overlapping of the two professions. The statutes distinguished the two professions and the court held that a license to practice in one did not carry the right to practice in both. The court declared, on page 285:

> It is argued that as a result of the progress made in the professions of the practice of architecture and engineering, many "overlapping functions and activities" have arisen between them, that the result has been that all "distinctions" between them have "passed away," that they "differ in name only," and, therefore, we should construe the respective statutes relating to these professions accordingly. However interrelated the professions and the statutes relating to them may be, the legislature has made and maintained a marked cleavage between them. It is beyond our power to thwart that clear legislative cleavage.

A New York case, *D'Luhosch* v. *Andros,* 200 Misc. 400, 109 N.Y.S. 2d 491 (1951), in construing the wording of the definitions of architect and engineer, found them to be substantially the same, except for the inclusion in the definition of an architect of the phrase including "esthetic and structural design" and the further statement that his professional service "requires the application of the art and science of construction based upon the principles of mathematics, esthetics, and the physical sciences." No engineer drafting plans and specifications for any dwelling would knowingly and seriously avoid using this art, reasoned the court, and therefore recovery was granted to a licensed engineer for services rendered in drawing plans and specifications, even though he was not a licensed architect. The reasoning of the Court is interesting and is therefore appended.[1]

[1] "(1, 2) Both articles define a person practicing professional engineering, Sec. 7201, and architecture, Sec. 7301. The wording of the two definitions are substantially the same except for the fact that the definition of an architect uses the word esthetic. However, both definitions specifically provide that both an engineer and an architect may plan, design, and supervise the construction of buildings both private and public. Both articles are similar with respect to the educational qualifications required of licensees, disciplinary proceedings, penalties, prosecutions for violations, etc. Moreover, both articles provide that nothing contained in either statute shall be construed so as to effect or prevent the practice of the other profession by one duly licensed thereunder, the only prohibition being that an engineer shall not use the designation or hold himself out as being an architect nor the latter as an enginer. Secs. 7208, 7307, I cannot find that there is any statutory distinction between the services which may be legally rendered by a licensed engineer and that by an architect. True it is, that historically at least, an architect has always been classified as one associated with the arts. Young v. Bohn, C. C., 141 F. 471, 472, which does not appear to be so with respect to the engineer. This undoubtedly accounts for the inclusion in the definition of an architect of the phrase including 'esthetic and structural design' and the further statement that his professional service 'requires the application of the art and science of construction based upon the principles of mathematics, esthetics, and the physical sciences.' However, it can scarcely be contended successfully that the principles of mathematics and the physical sciences are not and have not always been utilized by the engineer, and to some extent at least, the art of esthetics. Certainly no engineer drafting plans and specifications for any dwelling would knowingly and seriously avoid using this art. Moreover, there is further evidence within the article defining architecture readily indicating that the licensed professional engineer is placed on an equal footing with the architect. The same educational qualifications are required by the State as hereinbefore noted. Moreover, Sections 7203 and 7302 dealing with public works specifically indicate that either or both may be employed to prepare plans, specifications, and construction. In the past undoubtedly, so far as construction itself was concerned, the architect frequently required the services of the engineer. Today, however, the architect appears to possess at least equal qualifications, and a statute authorizing his sole employment in preparing plans and specifications for the erection and construction of multiple dwellings in the City of New York, has been held constitutional. Goldschlag v. Deegan, 135 Misc. 535, 238 N.Y.S. 3, affirmed 254 N.Y. 545, 173 N.E. 859. It is significant that the lower court in his opinion stated that, 135 Misc. 536, 537, 238 N.Y.S. 4, 5, 'the architect of the future will probably be more of engineer than of what was formerly known as an architect' but that 'speaking of today, there are many elements of service in the preparation of plans for the construction of a building of whatever type, and the superintendence of construction, that may be more properly left to what

A similar result was reached in *Smith* v. *American Packing and Provision Co.,* 102 Utah 351, 130 P. 2d 951 (1942), wherein a licensed engineer was permitted to recover for services which covered an area common to the field of architecture. The court declared that the real criterion for determining if a licensed professional engineer must also have a license as an architect, is not whether some service he performs might be lawfully performed by an architect, but whether such functions are necessarily embraced within the scope of engineering covered by his license.

See also, *Rabinowitz* v. *Hurwitz-Mintz Furniture Co.,* 19 La. App. Rep. 811, 133 So. 498 (1938), where a licensed engineer recovered for services rendered under a contract drawn on a printed form for architects. Use of the printed form was not enough to subject him to the architect's licensing statute, nor did it amount to a holding out that he was an architect. The court defined an architect as one "who, skilled in the art of architecture, designs buildings, determining the disposition of both their interior and exterior space, together with structural embellishments of each and generally supervises their construction," while a civil engineer is one "whose field is that of structures, particularly foundations, and who designs and supervises construction of bridges, great buildings, etc. One judge, in a vigorous dissent, sets forth the contrary view in succinct fashion.[2]

---

we now know as an architect than to what we now know as an engineer.' Of course, it must be borne in mind that the court in rendering the foregoing decision was passing upon a statute which involved a new type of dwelling in the designing and planning of which I think it is only fair to say, an architect would be more properly trained than an engineer. Only to a limited degree, if at all, may this be said to be true of a dwelling house as in the case at bar.

(3) It must also be remembered that neither statute prohibits the practice of the other's profession, but on the contrary as already pointed out, specifically excepts the other profession from the statute under consideration. Fundamentally as stated in the statutes, the purpose of licensing both engineers and architects is to protect and safeguard life, health, and property."

[2] "Janvier, J. (dissenting). Plaintiff Rabinowitz admits that he is not a licensed architect. Thus he is prohibited by Act No. 231 of 1910 from undertaking architectural work.

That the work which he here undertook and for which he now seeks remuneration is architectural is best evidenced by the fact that the contract under which he obtained the employment was executed on a standard form of the American Institute of Architects, prepared for use where a contract is entered into between an owner and 'an architect.'

I am well convinced that one who prepares plans for and supervises the

Finally, the wording of several of the practice statutes has, in some instances, all but erased the distinctions between the two professions. A typical example of this is the Kentucky statute providing that ". . . no person shall practice architecture without having a license . . ." but adding that "nothing . . . shall prevent engineers, mechanics, or builders from making plans and specifications for buildings . . ."

Shall anything be done about it?

II

Correspondence commenting on our consideration of the legal implications in the practice of architecture by engineers included a letter from O. Clarke Mann, a structural engineer and a member of a state legislative committee in Tennessee. The court's opinion, mentioned in the letter, is so stimulating and is of such universal interest that I want to take several quotations from it:

> The bill was filed in this cause by the complainant who is a licensed engineer, against the members of the State Board of Architectural and Engineering Examiners, praying, among other things, for a declaratory judgment and decree defining the rights of complainant as a registered engineer under the terms of the Act.
>
> Intervening petitions were filed on behalf of the Tennessee Chapter of the American Institute of Architects and on behalf of the Tennessee Society of Professional Engineers . . .
>
> Proof was taken by complainant and defendants, as well as the intervenors, which proof included the depositions of board members, as well as other eminent architects and engineers.

---

remodeling of the entire front of a store building thus undertakes architectural work. That is what Rabinowitz did here.

The fact that the plans required certain structural steel work to be done did not deprive the whole work of its architectural character. In the organization of a corporation, a notarial charter is necessary. Does this fact render the work of organizing and advising the corporation notarial rather than legal? Or does it give to one who is a notary and not an attorney the right to give legal advice to the corporation?

It cannot be denied that considerable difficulty was encountered in the carrying out of the work. It was to eliminate as far as possible just such difficulties that the statute of 1910 was enacted.

Architectural work should be done by architects, and it is a plain violation of the statute for a civil engineer to undertake it. His styling himself a 'civil engineer' does not change the character of the work."

The statute appears in Williams Annotated Code at Sections 7098-7112, and provides among other things (7098): *"In order to safeguard life, health and property and promote public welfare, by requiring that only properly qualified persons shall practice architecture and engineering in this state . . ."* and further requiring that a person seeking to practice architecture or engineering shall submit evidence that he is qualified and must be registered, and making it unlawful for persons to practice architecture or engineering unless duly registered, etc.

A definition of *architect* used by some of the Courts, quoted from Webster's Dictionary, is "one skilled in practical architecture; one whose profession it is to devise the plans and ornamentations of buildings or other structures and direct their construction." The definition found in the American College Dictionary is "one whose profession it is to design buildings and to superintend their construction." While the same dictionary defines *engineer* as "one versed in the design, construction and use of engines or machines, or in any of the various branches of engineering: one trained in engineering work: *one who plans, constructs, or manages as an engineer:* one who arranges, manages or carries through by skillful or artful contrivance."

"Engineering" is defined as "the art or science of making a practical application of the knowledge of pure science such as physics, chemistry, biology, etc.: the action, work, or profession of an engineer." In the deposition of N. W. Doughetry (pp. 74, 75, 76) this appears: . . .

"This Committee has made a very careful study of definitions of 'architect,' 'architecture,' 'engineer,' and 'engineering,' but it was found that any definition of 'engineering' would be so general as to include too much, or too specific to be sufficiently general, or too voluminous to be suitable to incorporate in a law. Some have endeavored to include in a definition of 'engineering practice' all sorts and kinds of construction work, but engineering includes investigations as well as plans and no catalogue can well be prepared sufficiently detailed to include all sort of engineering activities. Both architecture and engineering are broad terms involving construction and necessarily there can be no sharply drawn distinction. Architects in the broadest sense are engineers even if usually architecture is associated with ideas of artistic or decorative features. Architects are eligible to membership in the American Society of Civil Engineers and several architects are members.'

From the definitions given by the witnesses, as well as those hereinbefore quoted, and from this record as a whole, it appears as a fact that cannot be seriously questioned that the functions of these two professions, viz., architecture and engineering, so overlap that there is no practical way to draw a clear line of demarcation between the two.

As applied to the field of building construction, it seems perfectly clear from the proof and the record as a whole, as well as from facts of which the Court might take judicial knowledge, that an architect, in order to successfully pursue his profession must be trained in certain branches of engineering, while, on the other hand, an engineer trained in the field of construction might be able to design many types of buildings and many of the components of various buildings with as much scientific skill as an architect, even though the engineer might not be trained in the art of making buildings artistically beautiful.

The proof discloses that the great TVA organization, which has built many types of structures, including dams, power plants, administrative offices, residences, and buildings of all kinds, has a large staff of engineers (about 550 in number) and a small staff of architects (about 30). (See Dep. Tour p. 97.)

Significantly, the head of the whole division that supervises the design and construction of all of their buildings, dams, etc., is an engineer, and has been through the history of the great Federal authority. (Tour pp. 103-105) Tour testified that the chief design engineer of TVA is R. A. Munroe, a civil engineer . . .

All the foregoing is by way of saying that it is the judgment of this Court that it cannot define and delineate the functions of architects and engineers in such way as to draw a line of demarcation between them which could be successfully applied in practice. This is emphasized in the record since it appears that the architects and engineers themselves could not agree on such a definition and division of functions.

The statute involved herein is a regulatory measure. The Tennesee Legislature, as hereinabove stated, has not attempted to define and delineate the practice of architecture and engineering as separate fields for purposes of regulation, and unless and until the Legislature makes such a definition and lays down the requirements of practice in those fields the Court will not undertake to invade this field of legislation.

From all of the above it thus follows that the prayer for a declaratory judgment defining and delineating the practice of architects and engineers must be denied. [*End of quotation*]

A number of definitions have been adopted by legislatures and courts in allocating to each profession its particular function. Although the duties incidental to one profession may overlap with those in another, the fundamental distinction between them is carefully maintained, and any unwarranted excursion into a related, controlled occupation is prohibited.

An *architect* has been defined as one who makes it his occupation to form or devise plans and designs and draw up specifications for buildings or structures and to superintend their construction. . . .

A *professional engineer* has been defined as one who, by reason of his knowledge of mathematics, the physical sciences, and the principles of engineering, is qualified to engage in the practice of engineering. The term engineering includes any professional services, such as consultation, investigation, evaluation, planning, design, or responsible supervision of construction or operation in connection with public utilities, structures, buildings, machines, equipment, etc., wherever the public welfare is concerned, when such service requires the application of engineering principles or data. . . .

While it may be difficult, if not impossible, to compartmentalize the activities of the architect and the engineer, a recognition of the distinction is of considerable importance in view of the fact that courts are unwilling to accept the whole area of activity of the one as completely within the particular province of the other.

The difficulties encountered in maintaining the separateness of the professions can be illustrated by referring to the experience of one state which may be typical.

Under the laws of the state in question, it is provided that "any person who shall pursue the practice of architecture . . . or shall engage in the business of preparing plans, specifications and preliminary data for the erection or alteration of any building . . . or shall advertise or use any title, sign, card, or device to indicate that such person is an architect without a certificate thereof . . ." is in violation of the law. Excepted from this provision, however, are buildings "designed by licensed professional engineers incidental or supplemental to engineering projects."

The laws of this state further provide that no department in the state and no department in the municipality which was created for the purpose of filing plans and specifications for buildings shall receive or file any plans or specifications unless they bear the seal of a licensed architect. This law was amended to provide that no official was to receive or file any plans and specifications for buildings unless they bore "the seal of a *licensed professional engineer* or a licensed architect."

It was contended that this amendment in permitting the filing and planning of specifications which bore the seal of a licensed engineer, as well as the seal of a licensed architect, in effect authorized the practice of architecture by licensed, professional engineers. The attorney general of the state, however, ruled that this was not the intent of the amendment, stating:

> These laws do not broaden the scope of professional activities which may be performed by licensed professional engineers and the sole purpose of the two laws is to substitute a seal of a licensed professional engineer on plans and specifications for buildings designed by such engineer incidental and supplemental to engineering projects for the affidavit now required of a professional engineer.

Thereafter the question was presented to the attorney general as to whether a building inspector or state official who was presented plans and specifications for filing, having the seal of an architect or engineer affixed thereon, could refuse to accept them if the official believed that the plans submitted constituted illegal practice of architecture by an engineer or vice versa. The attorney general answered this question in the negative, stating:

> Where the plans and specifications offered for filing bear the seal of either a licensed architect or a licensed engineer of this State, they meet the requirements of the quoted statutes. The municipal building inspector or the State Official to whom the plans are submitted for filing must so recognize them. It is not his function to determine whether plans which bear the seal of a licensed engineer indicate that there has been a violation of R. S. 45:3-10 prohibiting the unlicensed practice of architecture nor whether the plans which bear the seal of a licensed architect indicate that there has been a violation of R. S. 45:8-27 and 28 as amended, prohibiting the unlicensed practice of engineering.

The attorney general might have reached the opposite conclusion with some justification. If prior to the amendment a building official had no power to accept plans and specifications for a building without an architect's seal, and if the only purpose of the amendment (as stated by the attorney general) was to permit engineers to file plans and specifications for buildings which were incidental to an engineering project, it would be a consistent interpretation of the amendment to conclude that plans or specifications which had an engineering seal, but which were *not* "incidental to an engineering project," could be refused acceptance by the building official.

The attorney general suggested that there were other penal provisions in the law which could be utilized to protect the architectural profession from the practice of that profession by unauthorized persons. However, if the law had been so written or so interpreted as to grant power to the building official to reject plans and specifications which, at least on their face, constituted an illegal practice of architecture by engineers, such a power would have furnished a forceful, direct and effective means of requiring compliance with the architectural practice law.

It is of interest to note that in this same state a special board consisting of five members had been established for the purpose of holding hearings on the complaint of any board or other persons against a licensed engineer for the alleged illegal practice of architecture and against a licensed architect for the alleged illegal practice of enginering. Membership on the board, as provided by statute, included a member of the professional society of architects and a member of the professional society of engineers. The statute also provided that upon receipt of a complaint of unlawful practice of architecture or engineering, the special board would hold a hearing, and would take into consideration in making its determination "all of the facts involved, any inter-professional code of ethics applicable to the alleged violation and all statutory provisions pertaining to the alleged violation."

Despite the fact that both the architectural and engineering professional societies are represented on the board, and the board is empowered to hear complaints made and filed by any person, this procedure has seldom been utilized by either the members of the architectural or engineering professions, to assist in the protection of their respective spheres.

The practice of architecture and engineering has been traditionally considered by the courts and legislatures as distinct and separate professions. There has been, nevertheless, judicial and legislative recognition that the functions of the architect and the engineer overlap. In determining, however, the permissible area in which either may practice, the judicial decisions are often inconsistent. Further, some courts have viewed this area of overlapping function as the basis for a conclusion that there is no distinction between the areas included in the professional competence of architects and engineers.

The elimination of a distinction between the practice of architecture and the practice of engineering, by legislative enactment or by judicial fiat, should be a matter of great concern to the architectural profession. If this distinction is to be maintained, the architectural profession must consider what steps can and should be taken to protect itself and the general public.

CHAPTER 8: *Construction Bids*

Contracts for public works must be awarded to the lowest bidder provided that he is qualified and responsible.

CONTRACTS FOR PUBLIC WORKS NEED NOT necessarily be awarded to the lowest bidder. To award the contract to anyone else is, however, an open invitation to litigation by disappointed contractors. Therefore, great care should be exercised before the lowest bid is rejected. The contractor to whom the contract is awarded, when he is not the lowest bidder, should review the situation carefully, particularly where there is a threat of a law suit. It has been held that the contractor himself, under some circumstances, may not be able to recover for the work done if the courts determine that his contract was illegally awarded.

Statutes and ordinances which control the award of public contracts generally call for competitive bidding. The language used is to the effect that the contract is to be awarded to the "lowest bidder," the "lowest responsible bidder," the "lowest and best bidder," or something similar. The lowest bidder in terms of dollars and cents may not be the "lowest responsible bidder," or the "lowest and best bidder," and thus much discretion is left in the hands of public officials selecting the bidder to whom the contract will be awarded. The term "responsible," as used in the term "lowest responsible bidder," does not refer merely to financial responsibility alone but also, among other qualifications, to skill, business judgment, honesty, and fidelity to purpose. The reputation of the contractor, his performance under prior contracts and the quality of his past work may be considered in determining responsibility. If the public authorities in exercising their discretion have not acted arbitrarily, the courts will not ordinarily interefere with their selection of a competing contractor, even though such a competitor did not submit the lowest bid.

In evaluating bids the public officials who are in charge of awarding the contract generally consider the adaptability of materials or workmanship to the purpose contemplated. For example, Arlington County, Virginia, accepted competitive bids on a municipal incinerator. Specifications provided for two types of plants. One set of specifications was drawn for hand-stoked incinerators and a second set of specifications was drawn for mechanically-stoked incinerators. The provisions under which the contract was to be awarded provided that the county board could accept that proposal which in its judgment best served the interests of the county. The county board decided to award the contract to a bidder who proposed to construct the hand-stoked incinerator. One of the contractors who had based his bid on the mechanically-stoked incinerator brought legal action to compel the county board to reverse its decision. His contention was that the bids had not been properly evaluated and that the contract had been arbitrarily and improperly awarded.

The evidence revealed that the mechanical unit which was to be used for the mechanically-stoked plant had been in operation for only three months. The court held that the county board had not been arbitrary in determining that the mechanical unit was in an experimental stage and that it therefore was in the best interests of the county to approve the bid for a hand-stoked incinerator, even though this bid was not the lowest dollar bid. The court, therefore, refused to interfere in the exercise of discretion by the local county board.

On the other hand, in a decision in New York state, where a town board had granted the contract to the highest bidder, a court set aside the award on the ground that such award was arbitrary in nature. The Town Law of New York provides that the local town board "shall determine the lowest responsible bidder. . . ." In the case at issue three contractors were approved by the town board in identical language as being "responsible bidders," but the board did not award the contract to the lowest bidder of the three. The court stated:

> The court recognizes that the Board has proper discretion in determining the qualifications of bidders, but after fully

qualifying all bidders, it cannot arbitrarily ignore its obligations imposed by law to award the contract to the lowest responsible bidder.

The court further held that the chosen contractor could not recover for the work which he had performed. The court stated that:

> . . . Under such circumstances the relator's contract was illegal and void, and that he cannot recover for his work is settled beyond controversy by the authorities . . . (*Brady v. Mayor,* &c., 20 N.Y., 312, *McDonald v. Mayor,* &c. 68 id., 23; *Dickinson v. City of Poughkeepsie,* 75 id., 65).

Relative to the various statutes and ordinances which require competitive bidding in public contracts, a serious problem arises when the municipality wishes to use materials or processes which have been patented. Specifications which call for a patented article or process often eliminate free competition in the bidding. Therefore, a conflict arises between the desire of the government body to receive the benefits of the patented article and the proscription of law which requires competitive bidding. For example, the code of Iowa City provides that public work shall be let to the lowest responsible bidder. The same code further provides that the city council in authorizing street improvements shall state the kind of material to be used. The city council in its advertisement for bids specified certain patented pavement. The contention was made that this specification was illegal in that it restricted free competition in the award of the public contract. The Supreme Court of Iowa in determining that the advertised specifications were not unlawful held that the requirement of competitive bidding meant that "there must be competition where competition is possible." The weight of authority is in agreement with the Iowa Court to the effect that municipal authorities are entitled to specify or designate a patented material without violating the law of competitive bidding on public contracts *if it is not the purpose of such designation to restrict competitive bidding.*

A Connecticut court, in also rejecting the contention that it was not lawful for municipal authorities to specify a patented article in advertising bids on a public contract, stated that any other rule would prevent the municipality from availing itself of new inventions.

> This is offensive to the fundamental principles of a sound public policy, and would require the city to "travel in the same paths

in which the predecessors trod," without benefit from any new discoveries of science, or any new advances in matters of work applicable to public use.

There are legal decisions in some jurisdictions which have held that the specification of patented or monopolized materials by public officials in advertising bids for public contracts is unlawful as a violation of the statute which calls for competitive bidding. In an effort to obtain the advantages resulting from the use of patented articles, and at the same time to maintain the advantages which result from competitive bidding, some municipalities obtain agreements from the owner of a patented article or process to permit its use on equal terms by all bidders. A few jurisdictions require as a prerequisite to bidding that all competing contractors be permitted to use the patented article or process by the owner of the same, so that there may be a fair and reasonable opportunity for competition.

In summary, it may be stated with respect to contracts for public works:

(1) The lowest bidder is not necessarily the successful bidder.

(2) Before the lowest bid is rejected, however, care should be exercised that the rejection of the bid is not arbitrary.

(3) Most courts hold that public officials may provide specifications calling for a patented article or process.

(4) Under such circumstances, however, it is, in most cases, best to stipulate that the contractor owning such patent should agree to permit its use on equal terms by all bidders.

II

As we have seen, it is not unusual for a state statute to provide that a contract for public work shall be awarded to the "lowest responsible bidder." For example, the New York Appellate Division (*Kaelber v. Sahm,* 281 App. Div. 980) considered the grievance of a low bidder who was not awarded a contract even though he was financially responsible, had previously done satisfactory work, had a substantial engineering and construction business, and had submitted a bid which was $30,000 less than the bid of the successful bidder.

The contract involved the construction and installation of incinerator equipment in an incinerator. Although the unsuccessful bidder had previously constructed and installed incinerator equipment at other times and places, he had never previously installed or constructed incinerator equipment involving a mechanical stoker. The successful bidder had patented one and installed many. The low bidder's plans for the mechanical stoker were rejected by the town board as "experimental."

In upholding the board's determination that the low bidder was not "responsible," the Court said:

> The issue is not whether the determination of the town board is wise, but whether there was a reasonable and plausible basis for such determination . . .
>
> The duty devolved upon the town board (*Town Law* Sec. 197) to award contracts to the lowest responsible formal bidder requires consideration not only of the price bid, but also of the qualifications of the bidders to perfrom the work proposed . . .
>
> In the absence of any finding of fraud on the part of the members of the town board, it is to be presumed that they honestly determined that there was risk in letting the contract to the petitioner . . .
>
> It cannot be said as a matter of law that the board should have been satisfied that the apparatus proposed to be installed by the petitioner, which had never been put to actual test, could do that which was to be done in the incinerator. In the absence of any proof that fraud or other misconduct on the part of the board motivated the rejection of petitioner's bid, it cannot be said that the board acted arbitrarily. The findings that the mechanical stoker was an insignificant part of the equipment, that the board acted arbitrarily, and that the petitioner was the lowest responsible formal bidder are reversed and contrary findings made.

In an earlier case, the Court of Appeals in *Tuller Construction Co. v. Lyon,* 257 N.Y. 206, 177 N.E. 421, declared that the commissioners had been justified in finding that the bid of the petitioner was not a desirable one to accept because its financial statement "did not impress the commissioners favorably."

Subsequent decisions clearly indicated that "responsible" apparently meant more than financial responsibility. In *Picone* v. *City of New York,* 176 Misc. 967, 29 N.Y.S. 2d 539 (1941), it was said to encompass moral worth as well. The Court upheld a finding that the plaintiffs who had submitted the lowest bid on a municipal contract constituted a "front" for a certain person and his corporations, whose activities in connection with public construction contracts were such as to bring them into frequent conflict with the criminal law.

The Court stated that the phrase "lowest responsible bidder" implied "skill, judgment, and integrity as well as sufficient financial resources."

Similarly, in the matter of *Kniska v. Splain,* 201 Misc. 729, 110 N.Y.S. 2d 267 (1952), an administrative determination was upheld which stated that petitioner was "not qualified by equipment, working space, personnel, or standard of work product to meet the requirements of the said contract."

The term "responsible" has come to mean "ability to do the job," as was stated in *Martin Epstein Co. v. City of New York,* 100 N.Y.S. 2d 326 (1950). Unless the public authorities abuse their discretion by acting in an arbitrary fashion, the courts will not interfere with their selection even though the lowest bid is rejected, provided that the board determines that the lowest bidder is not such a responsible bidder so as to entitle him to the award of the contract.

Though the cited cases trace the development of the law in New York, other states have adopted similar rules, as is clearly indicated in 63 C.J.S. 834-836:

> A statute, charter, or ordinance requiring a municipal contract for a public improvement to be awarded to the lowest responsible bidder or to the lowest and best bidder does not mean that the award must be made to the lowest bidder . . . since price is not the only element to be considered. On the other hand, an award of the contract to a person who is not the lowest bidder is not justified unless supported by good and sufficient reasons . . . The proper municipal authorities have a wide discretion which will not be controlled by the courts except for arbitrary exercise, manifest abuse . . .

When a board or other governmental body has determined that it will not award the bid to the lowest bidder, the architect should see to it that the reasons for the decision are clearly stated in writing in the minutes of the meeting. This would make it clear, in the event of suit, that the action taken was not capricious or arbitrary, but rather that the discretion of the governmental agency was properly exercised.

Whether a contractor's bid may be withdrawn on the grounds of mistake is dependent upon such various factors as negligence on the part of the bidder and the prejudicial effect of the error upon the party receiving the bid.

When may a contractor withdraw his bid? Errors as to material facts urged as justifying such a withdrawal include: errors in computing a group of figures, errors in estimates of materials, or labor costs, of omissions of materials, or clerical errors in transposing figures. Such mistakes have put bidders in the unenviable position of being faced with the problem of construction of a project, at a price far below actual cost or the forfeiture of their bonds and deposits.

The courts of the United States have considered many cases dealing with this problem and the decisions of the various jurisdictions are by no means uniform. The problem is further complicated by legislation in some states controlling the procedures to be followed in connection with public works construction bids, at all governmental levels.

These cases arise when a bidder attempts to recover the deposit (which accompanies his bid) and, by way of equitable relief, seeks to have the agreement rescinded and the bid withdrawn.

Although there is no uniformity of opinion, patterns of judicial inquiry may be ascertained from the opinions of the courts. Equity courts have historically placed a great deal of importance upon the actions of the parties before the court. Therefore, in deciding whether the bidder may rescind his agreement due to error in his bid, the courts have sought for the following elements of conduct:

(1) Was there a reasonable excuse for the error by bidder?

(2) Was the error in regard to a material fact?

(3) Did the party receiving the bid have actual or constructive knowledge of the mistake?

(4) Was the party receiving the bid prejudiced?

(5) Was there prompt notice of the error by the bidder?

(6) Was there any negligence or carelessness by the bidder?

In discussing those elements the court, in *Conduit & Foundation Corporation v. Atlantic City*, 2 N.J.Super. 442, 64 A. 2d 382, 385, (1949), stated:

> The essential conditions to such relief by way of rescission for mistake are (1) the mistake must be of so great a consequence that to enforce the contract as actually made would be unconscionable; (2) the matter as to which the mistake was made must relate to the material feature of the contract; (3) the mistake must have occurred notwithstanding the exercise of reasonable care by the party making the mistake, and (4) it

must be able to get relief by way of rescission without serious prejudice to the other party, except for loss of his bargain.

Where the previously listed questions were answered adversely to the bidder, the courts have held the bidder not entitled to rescind and withdraw his bid. In *Steinmeyer v. Schroepel,* 226 Ill. 9 (1907), the Supreme Court of Illinois held:

> A mistake which will justify relief in equity must affect the substance of the contract, and not a mere incident or the inducement for entering into it. The mistake of the appellants did not relate to the subject matter of the contract, its location, identity, or amount, and there was neither belief in the existence of a fact which did not exist, nor ignorance of any fact material to the contract which did not exist. The contract was exactly what each party understood it to be, and it expressed what was intended by each. If it can be set aside on account of the error in adding up the amounts representing the selling price, it could be set aside for a mistake in computing the percentage of profits which appellants intended to make, or on account of a mistake in the cost of the lumber to them, or any other miscalculation on their part. If equity would relieve on account of such a mistake, there would be no stability in contracts; and we think the appellate court was right in concluding that the mistake was not of such a character as to entitle the appellants to the relief prayed for.

The Court of Civil Appeals of Texas, in *Brown v. Levy,* 29 Tex. Civ. App. 389, 69 S.W. 255 (1902), refused to permit a contractor to withdraw an accepted bid where there was an error of over $10,000 contained in a bid for the erection of a building, stating:

> The first count in the petition shows that the plaintiff made a proposition to erect the building for the gross sum of $64,000 and that the defendant accepted that proposition. This shows a consummated agreement, constituting a binding contract, unless the mistake made by the plaintiff in procuring data for his bid should be held sufficient to release him from the contract. That it should not be given that effect is, we think, quite clear. The petition fails to show that the defendant was in any wise responsible for the mistake referred to. When the plaintiff offered to build the house for a specified sum, and the defendant accepted the offer, a binding contract was made, and it was of no consequence, in so far as the validity of the contract was concerned, that the plaintiff had made a mistake in forming his preliminary estimates.

In another Illinois case, *Douglas v. Grant* 12 Ill. App. 273, the court refused equitable relief to a bidder who had erred in the price of a certain brick and who had not discovered the error until after the work was begun.

The rules of law, as applied to public construction are, in the absence of statutory enactments, similar to those applicable to private construction. Where the bidder was negligent, or where the person receiving the bid would be prejudiced, or where there was a failure to give prompt notice by the bidder of his error, the courts have refused to allow the bidder to withdraw.

In *John J. Bowes Co. v. Inhabitants of Town of Milton,* 255 Mass. 200, 151 N.E. 116, 118 (1926), the court refused to allow a bidder to rescind, although it was claimed that there was an error of over $10,000 in his bid. The court stated as follows:

> The principal ground upon which the plaintiff contends that it is not bound by the proposal and acceptance is that the amount finally bid of $184,020 was due to a miscalculation of the sum for which it would construct the building. It is well settled that where a contract has been entered into under a mutual mistake concerning a material fact a court of equity will grant relief. It is equally well settled in this commonwealth that a mistake of but one of the parties to a contract is not a ground for relief either in law or equity.
>
> There was no mistake on the part of the members of the committee who acted for the town; they acted in good faith without any knowledge that the plaintiff had made any mistake in the submission of its bid. The mistake was wholly its own; it was not induced in any way by the defendant or its agents. The committee accepted the bid as finally made, and had a right to assume that the plaintiff would carry out its agreement. In these circumstances the plaintiff must be held bound by its preliminary contract.

The rationale of the opinion was the fact that, subsequent to the submission of the bid, discussions were held between the parties, at which time the error could have and perhaps should have been discovered. In *Crilly v. Board of Education,* 54 Ill. App. 371, the Illinois court held that a clerical error of $3000 in a bid could easily have been avoided by the exercise of ordinary care and diligence. Therefore, the mistake was not such as would entitle him to relief in equity.

In *City of Hattiesburg v. Cobb Bros. Const. Co.,* 183 Miss. 482,

184 So. 630 (1938), the Supreme Court of Mississippi refused to allow a bidder to withdraw due to his failure to give prompt and detailed notice concerning the error contained in the bid. The Court stated:

> The letting of public contracts by competitive bidding is for the protection of the public, and the public authorities are without the right to permit a bid for the contract to be withdrawn in the absence of circumstance that would render it inequitable not to permit its withdrawal. The inequitable circumstance here claimed is an honest mistake in determining the amount of the bid. Unless the mistake was in fact made, and honestly made, no right of withdrawal would appear. In determining whether to permit the withdrawal of this bid, the Mayor and Commissioners were under the duty to the public to ascertain whether a mistake affecting the amount of the bid had in fact been made. In order to do this, it was necessary for them to be advised of the character of the claimed mistake so that they might consider it in connection with the bid and the advertisement therefor. The mere claim that a bidder has 'made a mistake' or 'found some error' in his bid neither gives him the right to withdraw his bid nor impose on the public authorities any duty to examine the bid in order to ascertain whether a mistake appears therein. Another reason for requiring the character of the mistake made to be set forth in a notice of withdrawal of a bid is that, in an action to rescind the contract made by the acceptance of the bid and to recover a benefit conferred by the bidder on the other party to the contract, the bidder may be confined to the particular mistake claimed to have been made when the notice of withdrawal was given.
>
> But, the appellee says that this rule does not apply here for two reasons: (1) The appellant waived the failure of the notice to set forth the character of the claimed mistake in the appellee's bid by not requesting the appellee, when the notice was given, to then disclose the character of the mistake claimed to have been made; and (2) it appears from the evidence that the appellant, prior to the giving of the written notice of the mistake, had been verbally informed of the character of the mistake.
>
> The appellant's duty was to act on the notice as given, and it was under no duty to advise the appellee what the notice should contain in order to be effective. There is some evidence that prior to the day on which this notice was given the two Cobbs conferred with the appellant's officers and engineer as to the appellee's bid, but it does not appear therefrom what mistake, if any, in the bid was then claimed.

Where the court has found the presence of one or more of the elements previously discussed, they have been inclined to grant to the bidder the relief he has requested. The result of these holdings have been to relieve a bidder, who has incorporated some error into his bid, from the onerous position of forfeiting his deposit or performance of the contract at a substantial loss. In *Kemper Const. v. City of Los Angeles*, 37 Cal. 2d 696, 235 P. 2d 7 (1951), the Supreme Court of California had before it for determination a claim of a bidder for cancellation of his bond, on the grounds of mistake in fact. The plaintiff had been preparing his bid until 2:00 a.m. of the last night prior to the deadline and during the preparation an error in excess of $300,000 was made. The bidder notified the city within hours after the bids were opened and prior to any award being made. In granting the relief requested, the Court stated:

> The type of error here involved is one which will sometimes occur in the conduct of reasonable and cautious businessmen, and, under all the circumstances, we cannot say as a matter of law that it constituted a neglect of legal duty such as would bar the right to equitable relief.
>
> The evidence clearly supports the conclusion that it would be unconscionable to hold the company to its bid at the mistaken figure. The city had knowledge before the bid was accepted that the company had made a clerical error which resulted in the omission of an item amounting to nearly one-third of the amount intended to be bid, and, under all the circumstances, it appears that it would be unjust and unfair to permit the city to take advantage of the company's mistake. There is no reason for denying relief on the ground that the city cannot be restored to status quo. It had ample time in which to award the contract without readvertising, the contract was actually awarded to the next lowest bidder, and the city will not be heard to complain that it cannot be placed in status quo because it will not have the benefit of an inequitable bargain. Finally, the company gave notice promptly upon discovering the facts entitling it to rescind, and no offer of restoration was necessary because it had received nothing of value which it could restore. See *Rosemead Co. v. Shipley Co.*, 207 Cal. 414, 420-422, 278 P. 1038. We are satisfied that all the requirements for rescission have been met.

In *School District of Scottsbluff v. Olson Contstr. Co.*, 153 Neb. 451 45 N.W. 2d 164 (1950), the Supreme Court of Nebraska considered the error so fundamental that the municipality receiving the bid must have been aware of the mistake when the bid was considered. The court further found no negligence on the part of the bidder and reasonable notice on his part. The Court stated:

> The record establishes that the claimed error of $23,600 in the amount of the bid was a clerical mistake in tabulating and computing the bid. It was not an error of judgment in computing the quantity or cost of materials and labor. The mistake was unilateral, there being no allegations or evidence of mutual mistake. The school district contends that under such circumstances a bidder may not be relieved of his bid except where it is shown that the party receiving the bid knew or ought to have known, because of the amount of the bid or otherwise, that the bidder had made a mistake. While we think it could be said that the difference in the bids on the vocational agriculture and grandstand building was such as to indicate to the school district that a mistake had been made and thereby bring it within the rules applicable to mutual mistake, the bidder has the right under the facts shown by the record to withdraw its bid even though it was the result of unilateral error.
>
> The rule under such circumstances is: When the mistake is so fundamental in character that the minds of the parties have not, in fact, met, or where an unconscionable advantage has been gained by mere mistake, equity will intervene to prevent intolerable injustice where there has been no failure to exercise reasonable care on the part of the bidder and where no intervening rights have accrued. In the case before us the mistake was discovered and notice thereof given to the school district within four days after the opening of the sealed bids. It was a fundamental mistake as distinguished from an incidental one. While the bid of the Olson Construction Company had been accepted and the contract awarded to it, no contract had been entered into; it was wholly executory. Failure to use reasonable care on the part of the Olson Construction Company is not shown and rights of third persons had not intervened. The parties could have been placed in status quo at the time of the withdrawal of the bid.

The Supreme Court of Oregon, in *Rushlight Automatic Sprinkler Co. v. City of Portland,* 189 Ore. 268, 219 P. 2d 732 (1950), also allowed a bidder to withdraw, where his error was the omission of the cost of steel for a construction project. The Court was of the opinion that the error was not due to any negligence on the part of the bidder and that he had given timely notice of error to the municipality. Furthermore, the court felt the error was such as to appraise the municipality of the fact that a mistake had been made. The court said:

> One who considers in the cloistered calm of appellate court chambers the mistake which the plaintiff made is prone to indict. Tranquil repose magnifies mistakes made by those who work under stress and strain. It is even inclined to condemn alacrity and insist upon such methodical care that error will be virtually eliminated. Courts, however, cannot create a Utopia and must deal with the realities of life. Contractors who compute estimates do not work under ideal conditions. The record shows that those who computed the plaintiff's bid were compelled to cope with conditions which afforded error opportunity to steal in. The trial judge who saw the witnesses, and who himself questioned some of them, recited in his findings that the mistake was excusable and not culpable. We know of no reason for rejecting that finding; we think that the evidence warrants it.
>
> We believe that it is manifest from the evidence that the difference between the plaintiff's bid and the next higher was so large that all of those concerned with the undertaking were rendered uneasy. The plaintiff's officers at once returned to their work sheets, fearing that they must have committed a mistake. The City Engineer, according to his own words, found the variation so great that it "scared us to death." A member of the Board of Engineers, who seemingly expressed himself in wary words, described the plaintiff's bid as "a very low" one and termed the difference between it and the City's estimate "a very decided difference." The bid aroused suspicion in all minds. We think that the difference apprised the City that a mistake had probably occurred.

Knowledge of the error by the receiver of the bid is one element given a great deal of weight. The Supreme Court of Illinois distinguished earlier cases (discussed previously) and held the bidder entitled to rescission where there was actual knowledge of the error on the part of the city. The court stated in *R. O Bromagin & Co. v. City of Bloomington*, 234 Ill. 114, 84 N.E. 700 (1908), as follows:

> The bid submitted showed by one item thereof that appellees proposed to furnish and lay 6,020 feet of 16-inch pipe for a sum therein designated. This sum was less than they could purchase this pipe for, leaving out of consideration the expense of laying the same. The City Engineer, who was a member of the board of local improvements, observed this fact, and acquainted the

other members of the board therewith. It seems apparent, therefore, that the board of local improvements accepted the bid knowing that this mistake had been made. It is suggested that the board could not know but that appellees may have fixed this sum at less than its actual cost and fixed other items at a correspondingly high price so that upon the whole they would be able to realize a profit from doing the work at the total of the bid.

Statutes have been enacted to govern the conduct of the parties with regard to errors in bids for public construction. Such legislation in effect codified the existing rules of law with regard to this problem. They set forth the procedures to be followed with regard to the withdrawal of a bid, due to a mistake of fact.

The case of *Krasin v. Village of Almond,* 233 Wisc. 513, 290 N.W. 152 (1940), was decided, upon a statute then in force, regulating the procedure in the withdrawal of a bid. The statute[1] required im-

[1] Sec. 66.29 '(5) Corrections of errors in bids. Whenever any person shall submit a bid or proposal for the performance of public work under any public contract to be let by the municipality, board, public body, or officer thereof, who shall claim mistake, omission, or error in preparing his bid, the said person shall, before the bids are opened, make known the fact that he has made an error, omission, or mistake, and in such case his bid shall be returned to him unopened and the said person shall not be entitled to bid upon the contract at hand unless the same is readvertised and relet upon such advertisement. In case any such person shall make an error or omission or mistake and shall discover the same after the bids are opened, he shall immediately and without delay give written notice and make known the fact of such mistake, omission, or error which has been committed and submit to the municipality, board, public body, or officers thereof, clear and satisfactory evidence of such mistake, omission, or error and that the same was not caused by any careless act or omission on his part in the exercise of ordinary care in examining the plans, specifications, and conforming with the provisions of this section, and in case of forfeiture shall not be entitled to recover the moneys or certified check forfeited as liquidated damages unless he shall prove before a court of competent jurisdiction in an action brought for the recovery of the amount forfeited, that in making the mistake, error, or omission, he was free from carelessness, negligence, or inexcusable neglect.

'(7) On all contracts the bidder shall incorporate and make a part of his proposal for the doing of any work or labor or the furnishing of any material in or about any public work or contract of the municipality, a sworn statement that he has examined and carefully prepared his bid from the plans and specifications and has checked the same in detail before submitting the said proposal or bid to the municipality, board, department, or officer charged with the letting of bids, and also at the same time as a part of such said proposal, submit a full and complete list of all the subcontractors and the class of work to be performed by each.'

mediate notice of error upon its discovery and the filing of proof that the error was not due to any negligence. The Court held that the bidder, having complied with the terms of the statute, could recover his deposit. The court stated:

> The plaintiff furnished such evidence of complying with the statute as thus far stated by showing to the Village Board his final estimate sheet, which showed on its face that his mistake was in wrongly setting down thereon an "O" for a "6" in the thousand space of the total of a column of figures representing the cost of materials required for the work. This estimate sheet also showed on its face that this total was one of the items that made up the amount of the bid. The plaintiff on the day of the opening of the bids explained his mistake in detail to the Board. None of his statements in this respect was disputed. In showing just how his mistake occurred the plaintiff showed that it did not result from any carelessness in examining the plan and specifications or in conforming to the statute as thus far stated. The trial court considered, and so do we, that the plaintiff fully complied with the statute up to this point.
>
> The defendant also claims that the plaintiff cannot recover because of the closing part of subsec. (5) which reads: "and in the case of forfeiture (the bidder) shall not be entitled to recover the moneys or certified check forfeited as liquidated damages unless he shall prove before a court of competent jurisdiction, in an action brought for the recovery of the amount forfeited, that in making the mistake, error or omission he was free from carelessness, negligence or inexcusable neglect." The three terms last above appearing as applied to the instant facts are synonymous. "Carelessness" consists of the doing of some act or omitting to do some act. So as to negligence. The "carelessness" or "negligence" here involved, if any there was, consists of an omission to do some act. The "neglect" involved, if any there was, consists of that same omission. The "carelessness" or "negligence" if any, was thus only "neglect." The only neglect that under the statute visits the penalty of forfeiture is "inexcusable neglect." Assuming that the legislature has power by its mere fiat to create a forfeiture by calling a penalty liquidated damages, a point which we do not here consider, unless the plaintiff's "neglect," if any there was, was "inexcusable" there was no forfeiture under the language of subsec. (5) relied on as creating a forfeiture, and if such neglect did not create a forfeiture because it was excusable, neither did carelessness or negligence which consisted of the same thing as neglect.

The court was of the opinion that under the facts of this case, the bid, as corrected, should have been allowed to stand. The court stated:

> Subsecs. (5) and (7) of the statute on which the defendant relies, so far as here material, are set out in the margin. Subsec. (5) is headed "Corrections of Errors in Bids." This heading manifestly contemplates that corrections of errors may be made in proper cases, and this would seem to imply that a bid when properly corrected may stand as a bid. Under this concept of the purpose of the statute, the Village should, under the facts found by the trial court, which are well supported by the evidence, have permitted substitution of the correct amount in the bid.

CHAPTER 9: *Payment and Performance Bonds*

The scope of coverage of a construction bond is limited by the contractual obligations of the owner and contractor as defined in the construction contract. Performance and payment bonds must be checked to insure the broadest coverage possible for the protection of all parties.

ARCHITECTS AND OTHERS CONCERNED with the problem should realize that all bonds are not the same in scope or coverage. A bond is a contract made with an insurance company or similar organization and is enforceable only according to its terms. It is therefore important to look at the terms to determine whether the owner is properly covered. Sometimes matters outside the apparent expressed language of the bond determine the coverage of the bond. Of paramount importance in considering a performance bond is the construction contract itself. If the performance bond guarantees performance in accordance with the terms of the construction contract, it is obvious that an inadequate construction contract will make inadequate the performance bond.

Bonds and insurance have been and remain essential provisions in construction contracts to protect the owner against liability. In public construction, legislative bodies have enacted laws making it mandatory for most governmental bodies to require construction bonds when entering into any building contract.[1] Some jurisdictions

[1] A typical statute to this effect is:

"Any person, or persons, entering into a formal contract with the State of Florida, any county of said State, or any city in said State, or any political

have gone so far as to require private construction to be covered by such construction bonds.[2]

The law with regard to the construction and application of construction bonds generally, is governed by the law of suretyship. Here we will confine ourselves to a discussion of problems faced by architects, engineers, contractors, and owners.

---

subdivision thereof, or other public authority, for the construction of any public building, or the prosecution and completion of any public work or for repairs upon any public building, or public work, shall be required, before commencing such work to execute the usual penal bond, with good and sufficient sureties, with the additional obligations that such contractor, or contractors shall promptly make payments to all persons supplying him, or them, labor, materials and supplies, used directly or indirectly by the said contractor, contractors, sub-contractor or sub-contractors in the prosecution of the work provided for in said contract; and any person, or persons, making application therefor, and furnishing affidavit to the Treasurer of the said State of Florida, or any city, or county, or political subdivision, or other public authority, having charge of said work, that labor, material or supplies for the prosecution of such work has been supplied by him or them, and payment for which has not been made, shall be furnished with certified copy of said contract and bond, upon which, said person, or persons, supplying such labor, material or supplies shall have a right of action, and shall be authorized to bring suit in the name of the State of Florida, or the city, county, or political subdivision, prosecuting said work for his, or their use and benefit, against said contractor, and sureties, and to prosecute the same to final judgment and execution: Provided, that such action, and its prosecution, shall not involve the State of Florida, any county, city or other political subdivision, in any expense. (Ch. 6867, Acts 1915, #1; Ch. 10035, Acts 1925, #1.)" (Comp. Gen. Laws of Fla., 1927 Ann., Sec. 5397).

[2] "The owner of such work shall require of such undertaker, contractor, master-mechanic, or engineer, a bond with good and solvent surety as follows: For all contracts not exceeding ten thousand dollars ($10,000) the amount of the bond shall be the amount of the contract. If the contract is over ten thousand dollars ($10,000), but does not exceed one hundred thousand dollars ($100,000), the bond shall be not less than fifty per cent of the amount of the contract but not less than ten thousand dollars ($10,000) in any event, if the contract is over one hundred thousand dollars ($100,000) but does not exceed one million dollars, the bond shall be not less than thirty-three and one-third per cent of the amount of the contract; and if the contract exceeds one million dollars, the bond shall be not less than twenty-five per cent of the amount of the contract. The bond shall be attached to and recorded with the contract in the office of the clerk of court or recorder of mortgages, as above set forth, and the condition of the bond shall be the true and faithful performance of the contract and the payment of all subcontractors, journeymen, cartmen, workmen, laborers, mechanics, and furnishers of material, machinery, or fixtures jointly as their interest may rise." (Louisiana Gen. Stats. 2, Sec. 5107.)

PERFORMANCE BONDS

The problem which usually arises in connection with such construction bonds is an inspection and interpretation of the bond, so as to determine whether or not a given claim may be recovered against the surety. It is fundamental law that a surety cannot be held for any claim beyond his obligation, as set forth in the written agreement of suretyship. Thus, the courts of the various states have been frequently called upon to determine the extent of the surety's liability upon a given bond.

It should be stated at the outset that it is to the best interests of the architect, owner, contractor and the parties dealing with them, to have the terms of the bond (coverage) as broad as possible. This, however, is not possible if the construction contract be ineffectually drawn. It is the provisions of the construction contract which determine the degree of protection afforded an owner (and the parties dealing with him) under a performance bond. That which is omitted from the construction contract is automatically omitted from the coverage of a performance bond. It is therefore of paramount importance that construction contracts be completely and carefully prepared so as to express all of the contractual obligations of the owner and contractor. Even a casual inspection of various parts of a performance bond form shows the incorporation of the construction contract into the terms of the bond, and the limits beyond which a surety may not be held liable.

> WHEREAS, Contractor has by written agreement date . . . . entered into a contract with Owner for . . . in accordance with drawings and specifications prepared by . . . which contract is by reference made a part hereof, and is hereinafter referred to as the CONTRACT.
>
> NOW, THEREFORE, THE CONDITION OF THIS OBLIGATION is such that, if Contractor shall promptly and faithfully perform said CONTRACT, then this obligation shall be null and void; otherwise it shall remain in full force and effect.
>
> Whenever Contractor shall be, and declared by Owner to be in default under the CONTRACT, the Owner having performed Owner's obligations thereunder, the Surety may promptly remedy the default, or shall promptly:
>
> (1) Complete the CONTRACT in accordance with its terms and conditions, or
>
> (2) Obtain a bid or bids for submission to Owner for completing the CONTRACT in accordance with its terms and condi-

tions, and upon determination by Owner and Surety of the lowest responsible bidder, arrange for a contract between such bidder and Owner and make available as work progresses (even though there should be a default or a succession of defaults under the contract or contracts of completion arranged under this paragraph) sufficient funds to pay the cost of completion less the balance of the contract price; but not exceeding, including other costs and damages for which the Surety may be liable hereunder, the amount set forth in the first paragraph hereof. The term "balance of the contract price," as used in this paragraph, shall mean the total amount payable by Owner to Contractor under the CONTRACT and any amendments thereto, less the amount properly paid by Owner to Contractor.

LABOR AND MATERIALS PAYMENT BONDS

The problems presented under a labor and materials payment bond are somewhat similar to those of a performance bond. Here, however, the type of bond purchased (some types of bonds afford greater coverage and protection) is an important factor. In performance bonds, the surety merely insures performance of the construction contract by the contractor, whereas under a labor and materials bond, the surety may guarantee payment of all claims or of enumerated claims arising from and dealing with the particular construction job. The coverage provisions of a desirable labor and materials payment bond are as follows:

> WHEREAS, Principal has by written agreement dated . . . entered into a contract with Owner for . . . in accordance with drawings and specifications prepared by . . . which contract is by reference made a part hereof, and is hereafter referred to as the CONTRACT.
>
> NOW, THEREFORE, THE CONDITION OF THIS OBLIGATION is such that if the Principal shall promptly make payment to all claimants as hereinafter defined, for all labor and material used or reasonably required for use in the performance of the CONTRACT, then this obligation shall be void; otherwise it shall remain in full force and effect, subject, however, to the following conditions:
>
> 1. A claimant is defined as one having a direct contract with the Principal or with a sub-contractor of the Principal for labor, material or both, used or reasonably required for use in the performance of the contract, labor, and material being construed to include that part of water, gas, power, light, heat, oil,

gasoline, telephone service, or rental of equipment directly applicable to the contract.

2. The above named Principal, and Surety hereby jointly and severally agree with the Owner that every claimant as herein defined, who has not been paid in full before the expiration of a period of ninety (90) days after the date on which the last of such claimant's work or labor was done or performed, or materials were furnished by such claimant may sue on this bond for the use of such claimant in the name of the Owner, prosecute the suit to final judgment for such sum or sums as may be justly due claimant, and have execution thereon, provided, however, that the Owner shall not be liable for the payment of any costs or expenses of any such suit.

As a general rule the terms "labor" and "materials" have been held to mean that the labor and materials necessary for the construction under the terms of the construction contract. Where just the above quoted items of "labor and materials" are used in the coverage of the bond, some courts have refused to extend the liability of the surety to those claims arising from the rental of machines and equipment by the contractor. In *Southern Surety Co. v. Municipal Excavator Co.,* 160 Pac. 617, the court refused to hold the surety liable for the rental of trenching machines used in the construction of a public sewer project. The court stated:

It cannot be said that the excavator company furnished either labor or material for the public works, or that it sustained any contract relation to such public works. It merely furnished tow machines to the contractor that he employed in the construction of this public work. It is true that the excavator company furnished the skilled operator and retained the right in its contract to furnish an engineer and fireman, but it expressly stipulated that such employes should be the employes of the contractor, and should be paid for by him. It therefore performed no labor in connection with the operation of the machine. Its claim is only for a stipulated rental for the use of the machine. Such a claim was not within the letter or spirit of the bond and was not protected thereby.

The Oregon Supreme Court, in *School Dist. No. 6 of Wallowa County v. B. E. Smith, et al.* 127 Pac. 797, held that material furnished to a partner of the contractor, and which material was used in the construction job, was not covered by the bond, which was given to the contractor in his name alone. The court, in its opinion, stated:

> The conditions of the bond are for the individual liability of Smith, and not for the liability of a firm of which Smith was a member. The bond, being statutory, should be strictly construed, and sureties thereon have a right to demand that plaintiff shall bring itself fairly within its terms.

Other jurisdictions, in dealing with the same problems, have held to the contrary. It cannot be overemphasized that the determining feature in all coverage litigation is the specific language of the bond.

In the *United States Fidelity & Guaranty Co. v. R. S. Armstrong & Bro.*, 142 So. 576, the Supreme Court of Alabama, in discussing whether or not the rentals of equipment were included in the coverage of a construction bond, made this curt statement: "Claims for rentals of machinery and equipment are within the coverage of such bonds."

The owner under a labor and materials bond has little difficulty establishing his right of action. The problems arise in situations wherein the bond itself is limited to some degree in its scope and coverage, and persons furnishing materials or labor, who are not specifically mentioned in the bond, present claims.

The questions to be answered in each instance are:

(1) Does the bond contain a specific provision for the protection of the claimant?

(2) If there is no specific clause, was such claimant intended to be protected by the parties to the bond or agreement?

Prior to the twentieth century it was not possible (save in isolated instances) for a person to recover on a contract to which he was not a party. The modern legal principle of "third party beneficiary" in force in many jurisdictions today, permits a party who is a stranger to an agreement, but yet the one to whom the benefits of the agreement run, to enforce the contract. It is under this concept of "third party beneficiary" that laborers and materialmen are able to institute actions, as against the surety on the bond, though not specifically mentioned in the bond.

To answer question "(1)" above, one must examine the bond to ascertain whether adequate coverage is afforded persons furnishing labor and materials. A sample provision contained in bonds, which provides adequate coverage, reads as follows:

> 1. A claimant is defined as one having a direct contract with the Principal or with a subcontractor of the Principal for labor, material or both, used or reasonably required for use in the per-

> formance of the contract, labor, and material being construed to include that part of water, gas, power, light, heat, oil, gasoline, telephone service, or rental of equipment directly applicable to the contract.

Under this or similar clauses, laborers, and materialmen, having been specifically enumerated as persons protected by the bond, have little difficulty when instituting actions against the surety.

The answer to question "(2)" above is more complex, as the courts in our various jurisdictions are not in complete harmony. It is well settled that the intention of the parties to a contractor's bond is the controlling factor in the determination of the rights of laborers and materialmen to recover on a bond. The Court, in *Algonite Stone Mfg. Co. v. Fidelity & Deposit Co.*, 163 P. 1076, stated this principle as follows:

> It may be conceded that it was competent for the parties to agree that the church society would be satisfied, provided the building was turned over completed according to the plans and specifications and free from all liability on the part of the owner for any claims on account of material or labor. Plainly, the intent of the parties to the contract of suretyship is the controlling question. In arriving at the intention it is reasonable to take into consideration the fact that it is seldom an owner of residence property would be satisfied to live in a home erected of material or by labor which would never be paid for. The church organization which made the contract for the erection of the building intended the edifice to be used for religious services, and was careful to insert in the contract a provision that no work upon it should be performed on a church holiday. It is fair to assume that the organization had no intention of securing a building to be used for religious worship upon which claims for labor or material might remain unpaid.

Beyond this point of intention, some courts have required that there must be some form of agreement or "contract" between the owner and the person making claim upon the bond. Courts espousing this point of view have expressed their position in the following manner:

> And the question comes to this: Where, in a contract between two persons one promises the other to do something for the benefit of a stranger to the contract, and the promisee has no relation to the thing to be done nor to the stranger to be benefited, can such stranger bring an action to enforce the promise.

In some of the text-books and decisions it is stated generally "that, where one person makes a promise to another for the benefit of a third person, that third person may maintain an action upon it." But we do not think there is a case to be found in which such an action upon contract can be maintained only where there is privity of contract between the parties.

Without undertaking to lay down a general rule defining when a stranger to a promise between others may sue to enforce it, we are prepared to say that, where there is nothing but the promise, no consideration from such stranger, and no duty or obligation to him on the part of the promisee, he cannot sue upon it. Such is this case.

Order affirmed. (*Jefferson et al. v. Asch, et al.*, 55 N.Y. 604, 605.)

Other jurisdictions adhering to the principle of "third party beneficiary" do not require a contractual relationship between the owner and the claimant. It is sufficient, if it was the intention of the parties to the bond that the claimant was of a group to be benefited thereby. The Court, in *Royal Indemnity Co.* v. *Northern Ohio Granite & Stone Co.* 126 N.E. 405-406, stated this position, as follows:

Where contracts for improvements are entered into between an owner and a surety, who receives a premium for its engagement of fidelity, terms may be employed which fairly contemplate the financial protection of subcontractors, who employ labor and furnish material for the structure contemplated in the bond. That labor and materialmen may eventually perfect liens against a structure would be a sufficient consideration for immunity of the owner upon the part of the surety.

While under our statute our mechanic's lien law may not have provided for liens on this particular structure, because of its public nature, the city, in this case, knowing that fact, may have had in contemplation the protection of mechanics and materialmen who could not obtain a valid lien upon this structure. Unlike an ordinary private surety, a surety of the character here involved, which accepts money consideration has the power to and does fix the amount of its premium so as to cover its financial responsibility. This class of suretyships, thereof, is not regarded as "a favorite of the law." Bryant v. American Bonding Co., 77 Ohio St. 90,99,82 N.E. 960,961. And if the terms of the surety contract are susceptible of two constructions, that one should be adopted, if consistent with the purpose to be accomplished, which is most favorable to the beneficiary.

Due to the conflict existing in this field, various states have enacted legislation requiring *private* contractors to execute bonds specifically naming laborers and materialmen as beneficiaries. The Louisiana statute (which is typical), after setting forth many of the requirements of the bonds, states:

> The bond shall be attached to and recorded with the contract in the office of the clerk of court or recorder of mortgages, as above set forth, and the condition of the bond shall be the true and faithful performance of the contract and the payment of all subcontractors, journeymen, cartmen, workmen, laborers, mechanics and furnishers of material, machinery or fixtures jointly as their interest may arise.

In the field of *public* construction, legislation has been enacted by almost all municipalities requiring bonds to be executed covering possible claims discussed in this article.

In summary:

(1) A labor and materials bond should contain specific clauses naming laborers and materialmen as beneficiaries.

(2) The coverage of the bond should be no less than that required by statute.

II

Is the purpose of a payment bond given by a subcontractor to a general contractor primarily for the protection of the general contractor or for the protection of unpaid materialmen?

In a New York case, *Morris Co., Inc. v. Glens Falls Indemnity Co., et al.*, 283 App. Div. 504, a materialman who furnished materials to a subcontractor sued the surety company under a payment bond furnished by the subcontractor to the general contractor. The subcontractor had been required under its contract to furnish a payment bond which covered 20 percent of the contract price and a performance bond which covered 20 percent of the contract price. The issue before the court was whether the materialman had a right to sue as a third-party beneficiary, or whether the payment bond had been given for the sole benefit of the general contractor.

The court conceded that undoubtedly the bond had been obtained by the general contractor primarily for its own protection, but further ruled that it was not the motive in securing the undertaking that determined the issue, but rather the intent of the parties as to who was to be benefited by the furnishing of such bond. The court stated that such intent was to be ascertained from the terms of the bond, plus the provisions of the building contract considered in the light of the surrounding circumstances.

In determining the intent of the parties, the court was influenced by the fact that both a performance and payment bond had been furnished by the subcontractor to the contractor. The court stated that, since there was no question that the purpose of the performance bond was to protect the general contractor from damages in the event of the failure of the subcontractor to perform, the object of the payment bond must have been to secure some other protection not afforded by the performance bond. The surety company, however, argued that the performance bond covered only 20 percent of the contract price, and that, in view of the large amounts of mechanic's liens which had been filed, it might well be that the general contractor would need a sum in excess of 20 percent in order to be adequately protected.

The court, in reaching the conclusion that the materialman could recover from the surety as a third-party beneficiary, reasoned as follows:

> If there were no payment bond in existence, and an unpaid materialman of a subcontractor placed a lien on the job, he would only be able to recover against the general contractor to the extent that the said contractor had moneys in his possession to which the subcontractor might have recourse. In the absence of such fund, any lien filed by any materialman or laborer would be ineffective as against the general contractor. The claimant would be relegated to an action against the subcontractor. It would seem, therefore, that the purpose of the payment bond between the subcontractor and the general contractor would involve more than indemnifying the latter as to the risks of mechanics' liens and related litigation. It was designed to assure the general contractor that the materialmen and laborers would in fact be paid by the principal or the surety. Such payment would be in the direct interest of and inure to the benefit of the general contractor. The condition, therefore, would evidence an intent to benefit the third parties referred to . . .

One judge in a dissenting opinion pointed out that the materialman was not named in the bond, nor was he expressly given the right to sue, and that, in the absence of a clear showing that the parties entered into the undertaking with the intention of benefiting him, the materialmen had no right to sue under the bond. The dissent emphasized that, while a materialman's lien against the general contractor is limited to the moneys of the subcontractor in the possession of the general contractor, no such restriction applies to a lien which may be asserted against the property itself. The dissenting opinion points out that it is common practice for owners to withhold payments to the general contractor in the event a lien is asserted, and that it was, therefore, probably that the general contractor insisted on both a performance and payment bond to guard against this contingency.

A Pennsylvania court has denied recovery to a materialman against a surety on a subcontractor's bond which covered both payment and performance (*Dravo-Doyle Co. v. Royal Indemnity Co.* 372 Pa. 64, 92 A. 2d 554). The contract between the subcontractor and the general contractor provided that the former would pay or provide security to his materialmen for the payment of any obligation they might have "in aid of the enforcement of which a lien or right of any kind is established." The materialman involved in this case had not been paid, but he had not asserted a lien.

The court held that a materialman who could not assert a lien could not recover against the surety on the bond as a third-party beneficiary. The court differentiated between the liability of a surety who guarantees the performance of a contract by a contractor who has promised the owner to pay those furnishing labor and materials from the liability of a surety who guarantees the performance of a contractor who merely agrees to complete the work free of liens. This is a rather technical distinction, but was sufficient to defeat the claim of the materialman in this case.

The foregoing cases and many similar ones emphasize the importance of clearly stating the intention of the parties in payment of performance bonds. The mere securing of a bond does not guarantee adequate protection. The bond must be so written as to clearly set forth the nature, extent, and type of coverage desired.

CHAPTER 10: *Compensation of General Contractor*

When a contractor's fee is measured by the cost of construction, the manner of determining such cost should be defined in the construction contract.

WHEN CONPENSATION under a construction contract is to be measured by a determination of costs, disputes are often engendered by terminology which permits of conflicting interpretations. A decision of the New York Court of Appeals (*Bethlehem Steel v. Turner Construction Company and Mutual Life Insurance Company,* 2 N.Y. 2d 456) involves a unique situation, but is illustrative of the problems that may arise in this area. Although this case involved the construction of an "escalator" clause contained in a "fixed fee" construction subcontract, the issues involved are pertinent to "cost plus" contracts as well.

In the New York case, the contractor entered into a subcontract with a steel company for the furnishing, fabrication, and erection of the structural steel for a 20-story office building in New York. The subcontract provided that the contractor was to pay $182.00 per net ton for the steel, subject to a price adjustment, or "escalator" clause. This clause provided:

> The price or prices herein stated are based on prices for component materials, labor rates applicable to the fabrication and erection thereof and freight rates, in effect as of the date of this proposal. If, at any time prior to completion of performance of the work to be performed hereunder, any of said ma-

terial prices, labor rates and/or freight rates shall be increased or decreased, then in respect of any of said work performed thereafter there shall be a corresponding increase or decrease in the prices herein stated.

The fabrication and erection division of the steel company purchased the steel to be used for the building from the parent company. When, subsequent to the making of the subcontract, the company increased its price for steel to its own erection and fabrication division, as well as to all of its customers, it demanded an increase in its fee under the subcontract as provided by the "escalator" clause. It was established in the litigation that the steel company, prior to the increase in price to its customers, had charged uniform and regular prices to all purchasers, including its own fabrication and erection division.

It was the contention of the subcontractor that the plain steel which it sold to its own division for fabrication and erection of the structural steel for the office building was a "component material" within the meaning of that term as used in the "escalator" clause. The contractor and the owner, however, contended that the term "component materials" referred only to those materials from which the plain steel was produced, and that only an increase in price to the steel company of those raw materials, could justify the application of the "escalator" clause.

The New York Court of Appeals, in a divided opinion, found in favor of the steel company, ruling that the "escalator" clause was unambiguous, and that it clearly provided that an increase in the price of steel which was to be used for fabrication and erection (as distinguished from an increase in the price of raw materials from which the steel was produced), would entitle the subcontractor to an increase in the subcontract price. The majority opinion was based in part upon the fact that the price-adjustment clause although referring to an increase in labor rates applicable to the fabrication and erection of the structural steel, did not include any mention of labor costs at the mill. The Court stated:

> The basic issue, then, is the meaning of the term "prices for component materials" as used in the price adjustment clause of the contract. . . . If "component materials" means raw materials used in the production of steel, escalation on account of labor rates would not be limited to those specifically mentioned in connection with design, fabrication, and erection, but would have included labor costs at the mill as well. However, it does

not. The formula employed referred to the computation of "prices for component materials, labor rates applicable to the fabrication and erection thereof and freight rates." A normal and reasonable meaning of that clause has the word "thereof" referring to the term "component materials" so that component materials signify the materials that Bethlehem contracted to provide in performing the work "furnishing, delivering, erecting and painting all structural steel work in accordance with Class A material AISC Code of Standard Practice," &c.

In answer to the argument that the steel company had an unrestricted and unilateral power to increase the prices it was to receive under its subcontract, by increasing its own price for steel, the court held:

> Appellants argue that unless the escalation clause has the meaning attributed to it by them, Bethlehem has an arbitrary unilateral power to change the price terms of the Bethlehem-Turner contract. In other words, appellants are saying that the contract lacks requisite mutuality and that an escalation clause, in order to be valid, must be based on some extrinsic standard by which escalation can be determined. However, this escalation provided for increases or decreases in accordance with changes in Bethlehem's regular prices to all purchasers of plain steel products and such a provision does not give Bethlehem undue power of determination of the contract price.

The dissenting judges in their opinion, stated that the interpretation urged by the subcontractor sought "to impress technical and uncommon meanings upon general, every-day words." The minority opinion concluded that the "escalator" clause was ambiguous, and that it was susceptible of the interpretation that "component materials" refers only to the raw materials from which the plain steel was produced. The minority stated:

> As the appellants point out, the usual purpose of an escalation clause is to *preserve,* substantially, the benefit of a bargain. Such a clause is intended to protect against unanticipated or unpredictable changes which might render the bargain unduly harsh. An escalation clause is not ordinarily intended to enable one party to render the bargain more profitable to himself. It seems to me that the words "prices for component materials" taken in their ordinary meaning can reasonably be understood to refer to the additional prices which Bethlehem would be required to pay in order to obtain and furnish the materials

necessary for the performance of the contract work. In other words, those words could reasonably mean that the contract price was to be increased pursuant to the escalation clause, if Bethlehem's costs and expenses increased.

As in all legal relationships, the more skillfully a construction contract is drafted, the more likely that it will be interpreted to reflect the intentions of the parties making it. Under contracts where the rights and liabilities of both parties are dependent upon the calculation of cost, the manner in which this term is described and defined is particularly important.

CHAPTER 11: *Building Codes*

Many local building codes are outmoded and contain obsolete and unnecessary provisions. Statewide building codes have been urged as a correction of this situation.

THE DRIVE TO MODIFY, correct, and enlarge outmoded building codes that have been throttling construction has resulted in affirmative action in at least two states, Massachusetts and New York. The anxiety and interest of business (as well as that of the public generally) concerning this problem was reflected some years ago in an article in *The Wall Street Journal,* where it was stated:

> Tradition-conscious Massachusetts is quietly usurping the traditional right of its cities and towns to regulate building within their limits.
>
> Here and there through the state are now appearing homes which do not fully comply with local building codes. The first Lustron steel home erected in Boston has been sold, for example, though Boston's building code specifically bans homes made of metal. Down in South Weymouth, Carl Wolsey has completed 70 houses with walls of two-by-three inch studs, covered with plywood outside and inside, which fail to meet the local code's requirement of two-by-four studs.
>
> Such snubbing of local building codes is the result of the Yankee commonwealth's determination to do something drastic about its housing shortage. The state's legislators couldn't do much about such early postwar obstacles to home building as material shortages. But when they learned building codes were holding up the production of many homes the solons ground out a couple of laws to override local codes.

> These laws seem to represent the boldest solution any state has yet attempted for the national problem of what to do about local building codes. Massachusetts building authorities do not consider their system final and perfect, and some local officials claim it involves dangerous seizure of municipal powers. Yet the Massachusetts legislation and its administration undeniably represent a more radical experiment than is being attempted, for instance, by New York State. There Governor Dewey has signed a bill passed by the last legislature, providing for a five-man commission to promulgate a state-wide building code. The catch is that no municipality needs to heed it; New York City, for instance, is expected to ignore it.

Initially, Massachusetts adopted a law which gave authority to local boards of appeal to grant variances from local building and zoning laws. The statute further provided that if a local board failed or refused to take advantage of this authority, the builder could appeal to a state commission. Many appeals have been taken to this commission and variances granted. Most of these variances are concerned with conversions where, for example, the commission has permitted one-family houses to be converted to apartment dwellings. Another type of variance which was granted permitted a builder to construct a single apartment house containing a certain number of units where, under the local building code, this type of multiple dwelling was restricted in area and it would have been necessary to construct three separate buildings to obtain an equal number of units.

The Massachusetts law of 1946 was a piecemeal approach to the general problem of restrictive building codes. In 1947 the Massachusetts legislature enacted a statute providing for a Board of Standards with the power to draw up a building code giving builders an alternative to local building codes in methods of construction and materials to be used. Under this code, prefabricated houses of different types have been authorized. For example, builders are permitted to use gypsum sheathing on the exteriors of their houses and to construct metal-pipe chimneys instead of brick. But many local building inspectors in Massachusetts contend that the statute permitted the municipality to reject the alternatives set forth in the state-wide code. This contention will undoubtedly be resolved by litigation in the Massachusetts courts.

The State of New York has adopted a program which substantially is a compromise between groups that believe a statewide agency should promulgate building codes superseding local codes and those that believe the operation of such a central board to be an infringement upon the local regulatory powers of municipalities. The Governor of New York has appointed a committee made up of contractors, architects, engineers, labor representatives of the building trades, and officials of banks and insurance companies to study this problem and make recommendations. Their function is to promote a program that will lead to increased construction at lower cost and they have five major duties: (a) to develop methods and materials in construction that will decrease building costs; (b) to increase the opportunities for the training and hiring of apprentices within the building trades, and to make recommendations for the stabilization of employment conditions in the building trades; (c) to survey housing needs in all localities, and determine the possibility of private builders satisfying such needs; (d) to stimulate interest in the development of cooperative housing projects; and (e) most important, to determine the effects of local building codes on construction costs and make recommendations relative to the adoption of a state-wide uniform building code, which is to be prepared by a commission pursuant to statute.

The State Building Code Law of New York which was adopted by the 1949 Legislature provides for a commission to draw up a State Building Construction Code which shall provide for uniform standards for construction and materials. The purpose of the code is to permit, to the fullest extent possible, the use of modern technical methods and improvements which will reduce the cost of construction. It is provided that the state code shall be so designed as to encourage the standardization of techniques, equipment and materials and to eliminate restrictive, obsolete and unnecessary building requirements. This statute, however, differs from the Massachusetts law in that a municipality need not be bound by this central code but may adopt or enact its own building regulations. The New York law, therefore, hesitates to encroach upon the philosophy of local home rule.

The Governor of New York, in approving the State Building Construction Code Law, criticized the failure of localities to modernize their building codes. He stated that there are many obsolete, unnecessary, and costly practices in the building of homes which are aided and abetted by ancient and tradition-frozen provisions which exist in local building codes. The Governor stated:

The simple fact is that our localities for many decades have had the power to provide modern building codes. The science, the resources, and the enterprise of our people long ago placed within our grasp the building of low-cost homes for all. This boon has eluded our grasp. Had parallel restrictions, outmoded approaches, and group inspired controls enmeshed the production of the automobile, it would still be the luxury plaything of the very rich. Strangely enough, the individual, so far as his health, well-being, and comfort are concerned, would probably have foregone the low-cost automobile if he could have had the low-cost home in its place.

There is little doubt that many of the provisions in local building codes are obsolete and unnecessary. Housing shortages and the high cost of construction have spotlighted this fact. Few governing bodies on the local level have amended or altered their building codes in order to utilize to the maximum the new methods and techniques of construction and the new types of materials. The efforts of state legislative bodies to meet this problem are handicapped by the assertion of the prerogatives of local home rule and in some states by restrictive constitutional provisions. On the other hand, the efforts of the American Institute of Architects and other interested groups in support of statewide building codes, as alternatives to local codes, are being steadily increased.

If the solution or a substantial part of it lies in the direction taken by Massachusetts and New York, it is obvious that the steps taken by these two states are only tentative and timid. It is to be hoped that all governmental bodies directly concerned will heed the admonitions of the architectural profession and proceed more boldly towards the solution of the problem.

MISCELLANEOUS DECISIONS

COMPENSATION OF GENERAL CONTRACTOR

UNITED STATES. *Herlihy Mid-Continent Co. v. Northern Indiana Public Service Co.,* 245 F. 2d 440 (C. A. 7th 1957). Under a cost-plus construction contract which defined the "net cost" as including "all expenses incurred by contractor which are *directly chargeable to work,*" including federal, state and local taxes, it was held, in an action by the contractor against the owner for reimbursement of a state tax on gross income, that the contractor was entitled to reimbursement of amounts paid by it on income attributable to monies received from the owner under the construction contract.

MISSOURI. *Tatez v. Groff,* 253 S.W. 2d 824 (1953). In a suit based on a contract which provided that compensation would be based on a percentage of the building cost, the court held that the many changes and additions which were made and which increased the final cost did not effect abandonment of the original contract on the part of the owners. The contractor had based his suit, not on the contract, but on the theory of recovering for the reasonable value of services rendered. The court said that the contractor's recovery could not exceed the contract price. Furthermore, where the contractor obtained certain items at wholesale he was not entitled to a percentage above the reasonable market value of the items, but was restricted to the actual cost to him as the basis of computing his compensation.

NEBRASKA. *Grothe v. Erickson,* 95 N.W. 2d 368 (1953). In an action to foreclose a mechanic's lien for the balance allegedly due under a cost plus contract to construct a dwelling, the court held that the contractor was not entitled to commission on the cost of lumber purchased by the owner, for which the contractor incurred no financial liability. The court further held that the contractor was not entitled to charge as costs upon which to calculate his commissions the cost of making a penciled plan of changes in floor plans furnished by the owner, the cost of services of the contractor's accountant in preparing statements to be submitted to the owner, nor for wages plus ten percent thereof for time spent on the job, in addition to ten percent commissions under the cost plus contract.

OHIO. *Charles A. Burton, Inc. v. Durkee,* 106 N.E. 2d 313 (1951). A contractor sued for the unpaid balance of a construction contract which he claimed was to be on a cost-plus-fee basis. The owners claimed that compensation was to be on a fixed fee basis only. The court held that the evidence indicated a cost plus basis but that the owners were entitled to offset against such costs the damages suffered by them by reason of any malfeasance, extravagance, wastefulness, or negligence in the execution of the work.

Dougherty v. Iredale, 108 N.E. 2d 754 (1952). In an action by the guardian of an incompetent against the Building Contractor, the court held that where the construction contract called for work to be done on a time and materials basis, the contractor was excluded from charging any overhead expenses and from adding any percentage of profits, as is customary in a cost plus contract.

PART THREE: *Architect, Engineer, Contractor and Owner—The Employment Relation*

CONSTRUCTION is one of our largest industries; commitments in it run in the billions of dollars annually. The obligations and rights of building contractors, sub-contractors, architects, and engineers, in relation to each other, involve highly complex problems and considerations. Yet this industry pays insufficient attention to the legal relationships created at the time of the employment by the builder or owner of the architect, engineer or contractor.

Contracts of this magnitude in other business areas are artfully prepared by competent and expert legal counsel, and carefully reviewed by the parties concerned. In the construction field, however, there has been too often the practice of relying merely upon forms or, in some instances, only upon the good faith of the parties concerned.

A well-prepared contract serves several functions. It informs the contracting parties of their precise duties and obligations, and thereby avoids later surprise or chagrin. It constitutes an unequivocal acceptance by both parties of the terms of the contract. It defines the manner of performance and establishes standards for that performance. It limits the area of potential future disputes and often provides a procedure for the speedy determination of such disputes. It is oriented to cover the particular problems indigenous to the particular construction project involved, and it is prerequisite to the maintenance of a healthy and cordial relationship between the parties.

This is not to say that form contracts have not served and do not serve a useful and important function. The American Institute of Architects has published standard contract documents covering the employment relationship between owner, architect, engineer and contractor. These forms have great prestige and are very useful tools. But these documents—indeed, any other forms—cannot be used by rote; they must be adapted to meet particular and special conditions for each project.

Form contracts should be revised periodically. The law is not static, and experience often dictates the desirability of contract changes. The American Institute of Architects issued a revised edition of its standard contract forms in 1959. Many articles in this Part relate to the standard documents of the American Institute of Architects prior to their 1959 revision. Some of the criticisms contained in these articles still apply to the revised forms; others apply only to a limited extent. In any event, it is the theme of these articles that if forms must be used, let us use better ones. Implicit in this theme is a need for continuous reexamination of such forms to achieve progressive improvement.

CHAPTER 12: *Agreements Between Architect or Engineer and Owner*

An architect or engineer who agrees to render services without a written agreement which adequately defines the terms and conditions under which he is retained may sustain substantial monetary loss.

THE ARCHITECT best serves his client who first puts his own house in order. Architects are planners—they design and plan homes for others to live in efficiently; commercial buildings for others to work in efficiently; recreation areas for others to play in efficiently. Most members of the profession, however, will agree that they seldom take the time to plan so that their own businesses operate efficiently, economically, and profitably. Members of no other business or profession will as casually and unknowingly risk the monetary fruits of their labor. Most architects approach the problem of entering into a definitive agreement with a client with great timidity. The result is that very often no understanding at all exists or the agreement is so vague and indefinite as to be unenforceable.

An architect who embarks upon a project without a well-defined agreement may incur minor or major monetary loss. Every member of the profession has been the victim of the owner of property who has the architect spend several mornings or afternoons at a site, for no other apparent purpose than to have him approve in general terms the owner's vague ideas and affirm his exclamation, "Ain't it a beauty." This situation may only involve a minor monetary loss, although the architect has only his time, ability, and experience as his stock in trade. Far more serious consequences

from proceeding beyond this "advice" stage with a
agreement or no agreement at all. The architect is
that he has worked himself into a position where he
adequate or no compensation. The truly unfortunate
f this type of architect-client dealing, however, is that
rendered to the client as well as to the architect. The architect may fail to get a just return for his efforts. At the same time the client may become dissatisfied, because he has proceeded in ignorance of the expenses and costs for which he is obligated.

The very nature of the architect-client relationship makes it morally the duty of the architect to define the terms and conditions under which he is retained at the inception of the relationship. Only then can the architect proceed freely to solve the problem for which he was retained, with reasonable assurance of having a satisfied client.

What form should the agreement take? Should it be a contract drawn for the particular situation or will a printed form suffice? Although it may be advisable to rely upon the AIA forms primarily as a basis for negotiation, they should be modified to fit the particular case. Experience will indicate those changes or additions which will adapt standard forms to the particular operation of the user. Let us examine some of the modifications that might be made in such standard printed forms as those developed by the American Institute of Architects.

It is suggested that there be a clause providing for a retainer fee payable at the time the agreement is signed. This is particularly advantageous since it guarantees a minimum fee, and indicates at the outset to the client that the architect's time is valuable and that reimbursement is expected therefore—an elementary principle but one very often overlooked. The architect too often feels that to require the payment of a retainer will result in his losing the client. If such is the case, he should also realize that he is better off. A client who does not expect to pay fees is not a desirable client.

In most cases it is probably desirable to provide for periodic payments not only during the progress of the building operations, but also during the preparation of preliminary studies and working drawings. The architect should know at the beginning, just as the client should, when the client is required to make additional payments. The architect is not a banker and should not be required to finance the client.

Another clause that might be desirable, for self-evident reasons, would provide that the architect's estimates are to be binding for the purpose of determining the amount of the respective payments, until actual costs are finally determined.

Since each case must be considered in the light of its own peculiar facts, there can be no blanket preference for one type of contract over another, though there is an increasing preference for the "three times drafting costs" arrangement.[1] This contract has serious limitations, however, when the architect's own services in the particular case are out of proportion to the time usually spent by him. The percentage contract, on the other hand, has obvious limitations where the work required is out of proportion to the net return. At times a combination of the cost-plus and percentage contract will be found most appropriate.

Where preliminary studies will require an inordinate amount of time and effort, it is probably advisable to use a cost-plus basis for the preliminary studies and a reduced percentage basis to cover the balance of the project. This arrangement recognizes the fact that the architect's preliminary studies make the greatest call on his imagination, and guarantees reasonable recompense at this stage.

How best can the architect avoid pitfalls in planning his business—in other matters as well as the contract provisions we have considered? Probably the most important single thing is to recognize the fact that running an office efficiently and profitably requires planning and competent advice. A profession that knows how important it is for a client to obtain the advice of an architect when building is contemplated should appreciate the function of professional advice from an attorney and accountant when legal problems and books of account are involved. It is earnestly suggested that you discuss at length the general nature of your practice with your attorney and accountant. Have them present at periodic office meetings so that they will have the proper background of knowledge of your current problems to advise you properly. *Submit to your attorney each and every contract to which you are a party. Follow the advice of the experts with whom you consult in the same fashion as you expect your expert advice to be followed.*

The benefits that flow from following this procedure are immedi-

[1] In the cost-plus-fee contract, the architect's fee—the amount paid him in excess of his costs—may be determined by one of three methods: negotiation, a percentage of the construction cost, or a ratio to the technical salaries. It is this third method that is referred to.

ate and important. Records, proper from a legal and accounting standpoint, mean security from "wages and hours" claims, "social security" errors, unnecessary tax liability, and a host of other evils. They will accurately reflect the financial story for the client who is a party to a cost-plus arrangement. They will satisfy tax requirements. And, above all, the architect will personally benefit from plans carefully conceived, legally sound, and properly executed. Such plans can be evolved at regular office meetings attended by the architect-attorney-accountant team. They will pay dividends and will accomplish what every architect has a right to expect: a fair and profitable return for his efforts.

In summary, the matters for an architect to watch carefully, and the steps to take to insure a good business practice, include these:

(1) Don't be timid about proposing a contract for your services.

(2) Make clear the duties and responsibilities of both architect and client.

(3) Modify the standard contract forms as necessary for each job.

(4) Consider the advisability of a retainer fee.

(5) Provide clearly for periodic payments through ALL STAGES of your work.

(6) Make your estimates binding for fee purposes until actual costs are known.

(7) Consider the cost-plus method of payment, at least for preliminary studies.

(8) Secure competent legal and accounting advice.

(9) Hold regular meetings with your attorney and accountant present.

II

Faith is a wonderful thing, but experience dictates that a written agreement between owner and architect, defining their relationship, is the only satisfactory method of operation for each. If a project is abandoned and the architect has completed his preliminaries or even the working drawings, his compensation can be jeopardized by the absence of a written agreement. This is illustrated once again by a Federal case in Delaware (*Abramson vs. Delrose, Inc.,* 132 Fed. Supp. 440).

In the Abramson case, the defendant owned property upon which it intended to erect an apartment house. The plaintiff was retained

to prepare plans and specifications but no formal written ag
was made between the parties. The architect prepared plans
specifications and actually obtained bids. However, as the result
difficulty in financing the project, the apartment house was never
built and the project was abandoned. The owner attempted to sell the land, together with the architect's plans, as a "package deal," but this attempt was not successful.

The architect, who had not been paid his fee, instituted action against the owner, contending that there had been an oral understanding that he was to receive as his compensation five percent of the cost of the construction. As a defense to this suit, the owner pleaded the "Statute of Frauds." This statute, which has been adopted by most states, requires that certain contracts be in writing in order to be enforceable. One such is a contract which is not to be performed within one year. The services of the architect in the Abramson case were held to be furnished over a period of more than one year, and consequently, the owner argued, the alleged contract could not be enforced as it was not in writing.

The architect contended that the application of the "Statute of Frauds" would be unjust and unconscionable and that the defendant should be estopped from relying on it. The Court, however, rejected the architect's position, stating:

> The plaintiff contends that 75% of the architect's services were rendered in preparing the plans and obtaining bids or estimates and that these services continued over a long period of time. He contends that the action of the defendants in allowing the plaintiff to continue his activities to such an extent would make it unjust and unconscionable to say that the contract was not in writing as provided by the Statute. . . . This is not a case where one party had fully and completely performed his contract and nothing remained but the payment of money by the other party. No fraud with reference to the nature of the contract has been alleged or shown and no misrepresentation at the inception of the contract. While circumstances may exist making the pleading of the Statute of Frauds inequitable, no such facts are here apparent. . . .
>
> The defendants, under the facts here present, are not estopped from pleading the Statute. Any other result would necessarily imply that any party to an oral contract, not concerning the sale of lands, who had performed a large portion of his contractual obligation was immune from the operation of the Statute of Frauds.

hitect further contended that there were several
the owner which, when considered together,
nstitute a written memorandum, thereby making
uds" inapplicable. One of these papers was an
owner to a prospective mortgagee in which it
hitect's payment as being deferred. A second
er which accompanied the mortgage application
ed how the architect's fee for supervision was
to be paid. The third writing was a written contract between the owner and a subcontractor which indicated that the plaintiff was the architect and stated that the plans and specifications were the property of the architect. The court, however, refused to consider these three writings as sufficient to avoid the application of the "Statute of Frauds," stating:

> I am of the opinion that the three writings taken individually or collectively do not comply sufficiently with the Statute of Frauds. In writings "A" and "B" no mention is made of any particular architect or engineer and unless writing "C" is read in connection with the others, the architect is not named. There is not shown in any of the writings any internal or direct connection of the three writings as among themselves, or with the alleged contract between the parties to the action. There is no mention of any particular service to be rendered by the plaintiff or the extent of such services; there is no indication of any price, consideration or amount involved and no terms of the contract are set out. These seem to be required by all the authorities.

The architect, failing to enforce the specific oral agreement which he alleged, then sought to recover from the owner compensation for his services based upon their reasonable value. This is termed in law "quantum meruit." The owner, however, defended against this cause of action by urging that the suit had not been instituted within the time required under Delaware law, which provided that a suit based on "quantum meruit" be instituted within three years of the time the debt arose. The defendant argued that the plaintiff completed his plans in 1950 and that all services had been fully completed by February of 1951, which was the date of the abandonment of the project. The plaintiff, on the other hand, argued that he performed services within the three year period relative to the "package deal" which the owner sought to transact after he had abandoned the project.

The court ruled in favor of the architect on this theory, holding that the architect's right to compensation did not, under the alleged contract, arise until the building was constructed or until the project was abandoned, and it was the Court's opinion that this abandonment did not occur until the failure of the consummation of the "package deal." It is significant to emphasize in this connection that if the owner had merely abandoned the project and had not attempted to sell the property and the architect's plans, the architect would have been unable to recover *any* compensation under *any* theory.

Although the facts in the Abramson case are unusual, disputes between owner and architect in the absence of an adequate written agreement are not. A good relationship between architect and owner will not be affected by insistence upon a written agreement; rather, such an agreement will be instrumental in preserving their relationship. Again, and perhaps *ad nauseum,* it must be stated that not any agreement will do, but only one that properly protects the architect as well as the owner.

Adequate contract documents will not only protect the rights of the architect or engineer, and inform the client as to the extent of his commitment, but can be of assistance in educating the public as to the true value and importance of the architect's and engineer's function.

On occasion this writer has stated that the American Institute of Architects contract documents relating to the architect-client relationship require modification and amendment. Some of the difficulties that have been encountered in the use of the present forms have, indeed, been previously discussed.

It has been pointed out that there is no clause providing for a retainer fee payable at the time of the making of the agreement. There is no provision for adequate periodic payments during the preparation of preliminary studies and working drawings. The present provision of the percentage of cost agreement, that the percentage is to be computed "upon a reasonable estimated cost," should, it has been urged, provide that for this purpose the architect's estimates are to be binding until actual costs are finally determined. The advisability of a clause protecting the architect against claims based on alleged underestimates and the inadequacy of the provision relating to arbitration will be discussed.

This is by no means an all-inclusive recital of areas for amending the present form. The subjects recited are merely illustrative and sufficient to point out that the present forms could, like anything else, be improved. The present forms, therefore, place the architect on the horns of a dilemma. If he attempts to use the printed form he must strike out, modify, and insert to the point of mutilation, and thereby take the risk of placing the client on guard. If he does not use the printed form, he thereby loses a psychological advantage and ordinarily will rely on a simple letter which often results in a vague, indefinite, inadequate, or unenforceable "agreement."

It seems fairly obvious that the profession urgently needs:

(1) A simple short form of architect-client contract which could be used without significant alterations.

(2) A separate, comprehensive set of terms, conditions, and general rules which could be "incorporated by reference" into the short form.

(3) A brochure in simple, lay language for the client which will indicate in detail the probable extent of his commitment.

The need for these stems from the fact that, strangely enough, the general public has only a vague conception of what constitutes an architect's services. It knows the value and duties of a lawyer and doctor; everyone understands the financial worth of design (as distinguished from tailoring) in women's clothes; all appreciate that an inventor is entitled to a monetary return for a novel idea or design embodied in a patent. But for reasons unknown, the architect is not properly regarded as one whose ideas for design embodied in sketches and working drawings are compensable. Put another way, many people, including those who certainly should know better, think of an architect principally in terms of supervision of construction and as one closely related to what the architect would designate "a clerk of the works." Those who understand the true function of an architect in building form a very small minority. This is one of the basic problems facing the profession. Just as no one should think in terms of disease, actual or potential, without also thinking of a doctor, so no one should think of the problems affecting construction without also thinking of an architect. This is a problem in public relations which requires the continuing attention of all organizations of architects everywhere.

This difficulty is obviously one with which the architect wi.. have to live for some time. Until this problem is resolved, and as long as the public and the profession can meet on no common ground of understanding, the subject of architect-client contracts and relationships will continue to create in the architect a reaction of embarrassment, timidity, and bewilderment. In the meantime it is vital that the architect provide himself with a psychologically advantageous method of entering into the contractual relationship with his client. In order to reassure the client and to protect the architect, it is necessary to have adopted by local chapters or local groups of architects a document incorporating such general conditions as apply to the usual architect-client relationship. These conditions should be such as could readily be referred to as "incorporated by reference" in the short form of agreement to be signed by the architect and client. The fact that these conditions are drawn by the profession as a whole would make it easy to have them accepted by the client. The short printed form of contract officially adopted by the profession locally would also serve the two-fold purpose of permitting the client to know exactly what his commitment is and would again indicate that the compensation sought by the architect was fair and reasonable. A brochure telling the client what his potential responsibility was at the *inception of the relationship* would have educational value and avoid further difficulties stemming from ignorance.

If the profession is to meet the challenge presented by the tremendous building program that lies ahead, it must also see to it that it is integrally associated with the planning of its every phase. No building project, no alteration, no construction should be envisaged by anyone anywhere in the United States without the employment of an architect. Since that concept is not yet part of the thinking of the American public, it is essential that the architect have available contract documents designed to cope with the problem that springs from this lack of comprehension. It is, therefore, suggested that each local organization face this problem and decide:

A) Are the "contract documents" now used inadequate?

B) Should an immediate study be made to formulate appropriate revisions?

The employment agreement between owner and architect or engineer should provide for adequate compensation in the event the project is terminated during the preliminary stage of services.

What with fickle owners and fluctuating costs, an architect with a substantial project may find it evaporating into thin air prior to the time preliminary sketches or even the program are agreed upon. What compensation is he entitled to in such event?

This situation is covered by the standard AIA contract employed when a multiple of the technical personnel costs forms the basis of payment for professional services. When the agreement is terminated prematurely, the following clause applies:

> Upon such termination the Architect will be entitled to the payments due or incurred on account of the provisions of this agreement up to the date of such termination.

The provisions of the contract, to which the above clause refers, state the basis of payment as follows:

> The Owner agrees to pay the Architect for such (Professional) services,
>
> (a) A sum equal to . . . times the Technical Personnel Costs, as stated in Article 2 hereinafter set forth, paid or incurred by the Architect for work performed in connection with this project by the Architect's personnel.
>
> (b) Reimbursements (for the Architect's costs) as stated in Article 4 hereinafter set forth.
>
> (c) The cost for the time actually spent by the Architect (or any partner thereof) on this work, which cost is hereby fixed at the rate of $ . . . per hour of time so spent.

However, most owner-architect agreements (including the standard AIA agreement) provide a definite basis for computing the architect's fee only after the preliminary sketches have been completed. Before that stage is reached, a substantial amount of time and effort will be expended in preliminary work. The amount of the architect's compensation, should the project be abandoned at this point, is not easily determined unless additional explicit provisions are inserted in the agreement.

In the AIA contract which provides for a "fee plus cost" payment for architectural services, the following clause governs the architect's right to compensation on the abandonment of a construction program:

> In the case of the abandonment or suspension of the work or of any part or parts thereof, the Architect is to be paid in proportion to the services rendered on account of it up to the time of its abandonment or suspension, such proportion being 20% upon completion of preliminary sketches and 75% upon completion of working drawings and specifications.

The AIA "percentage of the total cost" form of fee arrangement contains the following provision:

> If any work designed or specified by the Architect is abandoned or suspended, the Architect is to be paid for the services rendered on account of it.

Since the reported cases on this subject have dealt with projects terminated at some point following the completion of preliminary sketches, the courts have found little difficulty in computing payment on the basis of percentages due, as set forth in the contract.

If the contract specifies no method for determining compensation in the event it is terminated before completion, the architect, in order to recover for work already performed, must base his claim on the "reasonable value" of his services. This would seem to apply not only to contracts which make no provision for percentage payments at certain stages, but also to the situation here under consideration, where there is no stipulation for a fee for services rendered prior to the submission of preliminary studies in the event of abandonment. The burden then devolves on the architect to prove the "reasonable value" of his services.

Under one architect-owner contract, stipulating a given percentage of the cost of the work as the architect's fee, the architect had not supervised the construction of a portion of the building for which he had prepared plans and specifications. For his services in preparing the plans for that portion, the architect sued in *quantum meruit,* that is, for the "reasonable value" of the services he had rendered. The court held that this was a proper basis for recovery since the contract provided no means or data by which the relative value of the plans, as distinguished from the value of supervision of the work, could be ascertained. The architect in that case was

nitted to establish his claim by producing competent witnesses
estify concerning the "reasonable value" of such services.

Vhere a percentage of the cost agreement is entered into, payments to the architect are usually computed on the reasonable cost estimated by the architect, or if bids have been received, on the lowest bona fide bids, if the contract is abandoned. However, even such provisions cannot be given effect if the work is stopped at a point where no price can be estimated and no bids received. Here again, the architect will be required to produce independent proof of "value" of his services.

The above illustrations amply point out the desirability of inserting some clause in the contract which will relieve the architect of the difficult burden of proving the "reasonable value" of his services at the trial, and which may well avoid litigation concerning his right to recover for preliminary services. Three bases upon which his fee could be computed in the event of a premature abandonment of the contract will be suggested here.

1

The first is a fixed retainer which would constitute the minimum payment to the architect for his services prior to the completion of preliminary studies. If the provision does not clearly state that it is applicable *only in the event that the work is stopped before preliminary studies are completed,* it is in danger of being construed as applying to an abandonment at a more advanced stage in the execution of the contract. Thus, under a given contract where the architect was to be paid 3½% of the contract price on the awarding of the contract, and 1½% on the completion and acceptance of the building —but in the event the employer failed to erect the building within a certain time, the architect should receive $250 "for preliminary services rendered in connection with his contract,"—the court held that the contract provided for payment on one basis if a contract was awarded for construction, but on the basis prescribed by the proviso if the building was not erected. Therefore, since the employer had abandoned the project without having let a contract for construction, the architect's recovery was limited to $250 although he had prepared not only preliminary plans but complete working drawings and specifications as well.

2

A second method for computing the architect's compensation is on a *cost plus basis* prior to completion of preliminary studies. This envisages payment to the architect of (a) all actual expenses incurred by him in connection with the preliminary work and (b) in addition, a stipulated amount. It is analogous to the standard contract form providing for a cost plus fee method of computing the architect's compensation for full professional services.

A third possible stipulation might provide for payment on the basis of the amount of time the *principal* spends on the preliminary work. This method, of course, contemplates that the principal will spend substantial time on the preliminary details, and payment should be made for his time rather than that of a draftsman.

The clauses suggested above do not preclude a consideration of other types. No one formula will prove suitable to all types of contract. In addition to the cost plus and percentage of the cost contracts already mentioned, other types—such as contracts stipulating a lump sum fee for professional services, contracts under which the architect is paid a salary, and others—will demand special clauses.

Today, more than ever, the architect should adequately protect himself against the adverse effects of a possible premature termination of his contract by inserting a clause in his contract which will provide specifically his exact compensation in that event.

Consider the incorporation of one or more clauses reading somewhat as follows:

> (1) A retainer fee of $ . . . shall be due and payable upon the signing of this Agreement and shall constitute the minimum fee payable hereunder. The said sum shall be retained by the Architect and shall be applied on account of the final payment for the Architect's fees.
>
> (2) Services rendered pursuant to Article (insert number of article referring to abandonment of work) shall be billed by the Architect and paid for by the Owner at the rate of "drafting" costs plus . . .%
>
> (3) In the event of an abandonment of the contract, prior to the completion of preliminary sketches, the Owner agrees to pay the Architect for services rendered:
>
> (a) A sum equal to . . . times the Technical Personnel Costs, as stated in Article . . . hereinafter set forth, paid or incurred by the Architect for work performed in connection with this project by the Architect's personnel.
>
> (b) Reimbursements as stated in Article . . . hereinafter set forth.
>
> (c) The cost for the time spent by the Architect or any partner thereof, on this work, which cost is hereby fixed at the rate of $ . . . per hour of time so spent. [a, b, & c are taken from the "multiple of technical personnel costs" (AIA contract.)]

II

Volatile building costs and other business hazards, actual and potential, cause us to consider again the still-born project and the architect-owner contract. It was previously pointed out that the contract should contain some provision for the architect's compensation in the event that a contemplated project is abandoned *before* completion of preliminary studies.

An architect's right to a fee based on "estimated cost" is not assured even if his preliminary studies have been approved or his working drawings and specifications completed before the work is abandoned.

The highest court in Michigan has held that where the American Institute of Architects "percentage of cost" contract is employed, the architect may not be entitled to this fee unless a contract for construction is let. Under this contract, the architect's compensation is a certain percentage of the "cost of the work." If no contract is let, says this court, there is no "cost" by which to measure his compensation.

The Michigan case illustrates the financial loss which the architect may suffer in the event of premature termination of the contract. In *Loyal Order of Moose v. Faulhaber*, 327 Mich. 244, 41 N.W. 2d 535, an architect had entered into a contract for the remodeling of a building under which he was to be paid 10% of the cost of the work. The contract included a provision for periodic payments, which, on completion of the working drawings and specifications, were to equal 75% of the basic rate (10%).

Two bids for $35,000 and $29,414, respectively, were submitted for the work. The owner did not carry out the improvements as originally planned because he could not raise the necessary funds. Instead, he spent $6,800 on remodeling the building under other plans. Whether the latter plans were a modification of those submitted by the architect does not clearly appear.

The architect (who had completed the working drawings and specifications) brought suit to recover 75% of the basic rate (10%) on the lesser of the two bids received. The court refused to accept this view of the case stating:

> The contract between the parties, as written, is not free from ambiguities . . . If defendant is correct in his claim as to the interpretation of his agreement with the plaintiff, the conclusion

would necessarily follow that he would be entitled to a fee based either on estimated cost of the improvement under plans and specifications prepared by him, or on the basis of the lowest bona fide bid received for the doing of the work contemplated thereby, without reference to the amount of the estimate, or the bid, or the letting of any contract. It may not be assumed that the parties intended such a possible result. Doubtless they thought at the time the agreement was made, all parties acting in good faith, that a contract might be made with a responsible contractor under which the improvement would be accomplished. In such event defendant's fee was to be based on the cost of the work to the plaintiff. The agreement may not be construed as meaning that the defendant was to receive his fee regardless of whether any work was done in the remodeling of plaintiff's building. Such result would mean the practical elimination, so far as this case is concerned, of the clause of the contract prescribing the basic rate for the determination of the architect's fee.

The trial court had allowed the architect 10% of the actual cost of the remodeling done. According to the Supreme Court, this award was apparently based on the theory that the work actually done on the building was in accordance with the architect's plans and specifications, although much less in scope. This award was not questioned by the owner and the Supreme Court let it stand.

The above result was predicated upon the decision in a previous case, *Wetzel v. Roberts,* 295 N.W. 580, in which the facts were substantially similar, but here the architect was denied any fee whatsoever.

Here again, the court held that the architect's right to his fee depended upon the letting of a contract for the work. It stated:

In spite of obscurity and contradiction, it appears that the architect's fees are based upon a percentage, to be computed upon the cost of the work; and the cost of the work is to be based on the amount specified in the executed construction contract.

In this case no contract for the construction work was ever executed. When Roberts received the bid on the plans prepared by plaintiff, it amounted to $28,000. This was so much greater than the amount that he had planned upon, and so in excess of the limitation of expense which was communicated by Heartt to Wetzel, that Roberts refused to go ahead with the proposition. He later remodeled the building according to another plan. Plaintiff sued for 60 percent of a fee based upon 10 percent of the bid of $28,000, claiming that such sum was due him under the contract.

There is nothing in the terms of the contract which provides that the total fee of the architect would be 10 percent of the amount of a bid. The fee depends upon the letting of a contract. The architectural fees were based upon the total amount that it would cost to do the work, according to the terms of the construction contract. Apparently the form of contract here used was drafted to cover a case where the owner actually let a building contract; but it did not cover the case before us, where no building contract was ever executed. To sustain the claim of the plaintiff it would be necessary to hold that no matter how large the bid for doing the work, Roberts would have been obligated to pay an architectural fee based upon the amount of such a bid. The contract does not so provide, and Roberts did not so agree.

The court then stated that since the action had not been brought to recover "reasonable value," no recovery of any kind could be granted the architect.

The courts in both cases quoted from the contract a stipulation to the effect that on abandonment or suspension of any part of the work, the architect was to be paid for the services rendered on account of it. Despite this provision, the courts remarked that the contract as written was not free from "ambiguities" and "contradiction." They resolved these ambiguities by concluding that if no building contract was executed the plaintiff could not receive compensation based on "cost."

In both contracts provision was also made for periodic payments to the architect on the basis of the estimated cost of the work. The *Wetzel* opinion did not discuss this provision, while the court in the *Faulhaber* case stated that no estimate had been made by the architect and added that under the contract the parties could not have intended that the architect should be entitled to a fee based on the estimated cost of the improvement under the specifications prepared by him.

The decisions are not all in accord in denying the architect compensation if no contract is entered into for construction. Other cases have held that the architect's estimated cost is the proper basis for determining his compensation. Where the employer abandoned the contract because of the increased cost of labor and materials due to the first World War, the court permitted recovery for architectural services on the basis of the cost estimated by the architects themselves. It appeared in this case that the architects' estimate of the cost was considerably less than that shown by the rejected bids.

In view of the conflicting decisions on this point, architects who enter into percentage of cost contracts will be well advised to make some definite provision for compensation in the event the owner for any reason fails to proceed with the work. A stipulation that the architect's estimated cost of the work shall be final and conclusive as to the cost of the work in the event no contract is let would appear to protect the architect against the kind of decision found in the *Faulhaber* and *Wetzel* cases.

Such a stipulation may not afford full protection to the architect if he has not furnished an estimate before the project is terminated. In the absence of such estimate, the architect may be required to prove the reasonable value of his services.

This problem arose in a case where the contract provided that periodic payments were to be computed upon a reasonable cost estimated by the architect, or if bids had been received, then upon the lowest bona fide bid. The court found no cost price, since the building was not erected, and no estimated price had been furnished. Accordingly, the court could not enforce the covenant as written. It determined, however, that the architects were entitled to prove, by competent witnesses, the reasonable value of their services.

To sum up, architects rendering services pursuant to "percentage of the cost" contracts should consider the following:

(1) Include in the contract a provision reading somewhat as follows: "The Architect's estimate of costs shall be conclusive in determining payments to the Architect whether or not the project is completed. When actual costs are finally ascertained upon completion of the work, an adjustment will be made based upon such actual costs."

(2) In view of the rising cost of labor and materials, keep the owner advised as to revised estimates of the cost of the work at all stages prior to the letting of a contract.

An employment agreement which requires the architect or engineer to prepare the contract between owner and contractor may be construed as constituting the illegal practice of law.

Architects misunderstand the effect of a Michigan case (*Sheill v. Howard*) where a lower court refused to permit an architect to recover for services rendered his client, "for the reason that it is based upon a written contract between the plaintiff and the defendant wherein the plaintiff agrees to do certain work which constitutes the practice of law, and since the plaintiff is not an attorney licensed to practice law in Michigan, such work is illegal and the contract is void."

The contract referred to was the American Institute of Architects' *Owner-Architect Agreement Form,* which contained the following paragraph:

> 1. The Architect's Services.—The Architect's professional services consist of the necessary conferences, the preparation of preliminary studies, working drawings, specifications, large scale and full size detail drawings; *the drafting of forms of proposals and contracts;* the issuance of certificates of payment and the keeping of accounts, the general administration of the business and preparation of the work.

There were services rendered pursuant to this contract in *Sheill v. Howard.* Some payments were made. A disagreement then arose between the architect and owner as to the balance due, and the architect sued.

In a preliminary motion before answering the complaint, the owner took the position that the AIA Owner-Architect Agreement Form provided for the performance by the architect of legal services, and since the architect was not licensed to practice law in Michigan, the contract provided for the performance of unlawful acts, which in turn rendered the entire contract illegal and void. The court found:

> It being and appearing to this Court that the plaintiff is not a licensed attorney, and that he did draw the contract between the defendant and the contractor, *and that the drawing of contracts is the practice of law, and that such part of the contract between the plaintiff and defendant is therefore illegal, the entire contract is therefore void.*

Whether the court's original decision was correct; whether on reargument it will be changed; whether it ultimately will be sustained by a higher court in Michigan,—these are all matters secondary to the important issue.

The primary difficulty is that the issue, once having been raised, may be raised again in any one or more of the 50 states. If the highest court in Michigan determines that the AIA standard form is valid and not illegal, the determination will be persuasive, but not controlling, in other states.

The determination as to what amounts to the practice of law is a complicated and involved question. It is practically impossible to frame a comprehensive definition which could serve as a readily ascertainable standard for all cases, and the determination of the question must be left to the facts in each particular case. Yet the phrase "practice of law" does have a sufficiently definite meaning to enable courts when called upon to give it effect.

Contrary to wide belief, the practice of law is not confined to practice in the courts. It extends to the giving of legal advice and counsel and the preparation of legal instruments and contracts involving legal rights, although these matters may not be pending in court. It has been said to include the giving of advice or rendition of service when use of any degree of legal knowledge or skill is required.

One of the most common ways in which the layman may be practicing law is in drawing *for others* papers conferring or involving legal rights. It is not always easy to determine when the drawing of a document amounts to such unauthorized practice. Efforts have been made to distinguish between the mere filling in of blank forms upon so-called simple instruments and the preparation of complex instruments. This distinction of itself is difficult to apply in particular instances, and many courts have refused it as an unsatisfactory test. Since the licensing requirement has been enacted for the protection of the public it would seem that written instruments drawn for others when calling for more legal knowledge than the average layman may be deemed to possess, readily fall into a category requiring expert legal attention.

How complicated the issue is and how difficult of solution is exemplified by a case decided by the highest court in New York State. This case involved the question whether the Title Guaranty Trust Company (which was authorized to guarantee bonds, mortgages and titles to real estate) engaged illegally in the practice of law by preparing *on a single occasion,* a bill of sale and chattel mortgage. The court held by a four to three vote that it did not, but there were four separate opinions written by members of the court upholding on different grounds the legality of the particular activity. There was also a dissenting opinion by Judge Cardozo in which it was stated that the acts were illegal. In this opinion, two additional judges joined. These separate expressions of opinion indicate that the problem is not easy of solution. The decisions will vary according to the facts of a particular situation, and even where the facts are the same, the courts of different states may hold conflicting views.

In spite of the complexity of the issue, it is a practical necessity for the architect to reach some important immediate conclusions:

(1) The architect is at perfect liberty to draw his own contract with the owner, or use the AIA or any other architect-owner form. The Sheill case has no application to any agreement which the architect makes with his own client. It applies only to such agreements as are made with third persons by the architect acting for the client-owner.

(2) If the AIA Owner-Architect or similar Agreement Form is used, the safest procedure is:

(a) to strike out the reference to the drafting of contracts, and if a substitute phrase is inserted, the duty to draw contracts and other "legal" papers should be placed on the owner;[1]

(b) to use an attorney in the drafting of any contracts between the owner and persons other than the architect even where forms are employed.

This does not in any way prevent, prohibit, or inhibit the architect from supplying the necessary technical information to be inserted in the contract, or from passing on the matters contained in the contract with respect to their accuracy or sufficiency, from the architect's point of view.

More simply stated, the necessary conclusions are:

(1) You may draw your own contract with the owner.

(2) The duty to draw other contracts should, in express language, be placed on the owner.

(3) All contracts other than the architect-owner contract should be drawn by a lawyer, although technical architectural matters should be supplied by the architect.

The effectiveness of an arbitration procedure provided by the employment contract is dependent upon the skill with which this provision is formulated.

[1] Note: Since this was written, the AIA Owner-Architect Form was revised to provide that the architect shall furnish "*assistance* in the drafting of forms of proposals and contracts."

Are any of the arbitration clauses in AIA contracts recognized by law in your state? Will an arbitration provision actually avert prolonged litigation? Do you specify the types of dispute covered? Can a contractor who agrees to arbitration also file a lien?

Each standard form contract of the American Institute of Architects contains a clause relating to arbitration. This would indicate the importance that is generally attached to arbitration as a means of settling disputes.

Arbitration furnishes a simple, clear-cut, informal, and effective procedure. It avoids protracted and expensive litigation by providing for an adjudication by arbitrators specially qualified in the profession, trade, or business in which the issues are raised.

Once it is determined that a clause providing for arbitration should be inserted in a contract, it is elementary that the best possible clause should be used. The American Institute of Architects' forms should be examined with this criterion in mind.

Any arbitration clause which makes up one of the provisions of an existing primary contract should be formulated so that it is legally effective, comprehensive enough to cover all possible future disputes which the parties wish to have arbitrated, and sufficiently detailed to afford at least some guide to the procedures and rules which should be followed in the arbitration.

Since arbitration in one sense pre-empts the jurisdiction of legally constituted courts, it must be realized at the outset that in the absence of special statutory provisions, an agreement to arbitrate may not be recognized and enforced. There are approximately fifteen states which have enacted legislation providing for the judicial recognition and enforcement of arbitration provisions. However, in those jurisdictions where there are no enforcing statutes, an executory agreement to arbitrate will not prevent a party to such agreement from commencing legal action. As a second requisite of legal effectiveness, arbitration must conform to the prescription of any applicable statute which has been adopted to regulate such activity.

The New York State arbitration law affords legal enforceability to agreements to arbitrate and was the first statute of its type. It has been used as a model by other states adopting similar statutes. This law provides for the entering of a judgment based upon an arbitration award if the requirements of the statute are met. For example, the statute provides that a contract to arbitrate a possible future controversy must be in writing. Further, the statute contains provisions as to notice, hearings, oaths of arbitrators, etc.

In order to give legal effectiveness to an agreement to arbitrate, the court enforcing the agreement must be able to obtain jurisdiction over a recalcitrant party. For example, the courts of New York have held that the service of papers to compel arbitration upon a nonresident by registered mail will be insufficient to confer jurisdiction unless there is a provision in the contract permitting such service. Therefore, in a contract between residents of different states it may be of importance to designate specifically the manner in which notice must be given, in order to comply with the jurisdictional requirements of the state in which the agreement will be enforced. If this is not done, the effectiveness of the arbitration agreement will depend upon the good faith of both parties in voluntarily complying with it.

From the viewpoint of legal effectiveness, it also may be of importance to designate, in the agreement to arbitrate, the state in which the arbitration is to be held and the law which is to govern the contract. This would be important, for example, where the contract in question is made in a state which does not have an enforcing arbitration statute. In such a situation, it would be desirable in most instances to provide that the arbitration be conducted in and pursuant to the laws of a state which has such a statute. Many (although not all) of the states which do not have an arbitration statute will nevertheless not assume jurisdiction of a legal action where there is an agreement to arbitrate in a foreign state which does have such a statute. Thus, indirectly, the agreement to arbitrate is enforced. Similarly, where the actual contract in question is between a citizen of the United States and a citizen of a foreign country, the arbitration agreement should provide the place and the law under which the arbitration should be conducted.

An arbitration clause which is well drawn will clearly set forth what disputes are subject to arbitration. On this point, the architect-owner form contract of AIA merely provides: "All questions in dispute under this agreement shall be submitted to arbitration at the choice of either party."

The arbitration clause in the AIA form for Small Construction Contracts (Owner-Contractor) provides in part as follows:

> Any disagreement arising out of this contract or from the breach thereof shall be submitted to arbitration and this agreement shall be specifically enforceable under the prevailing arbitration law, and judgment upon the award rendered may be entered in the highest court of the forum, state or federal,

> having jurisdiction. It is mutually agreed that the decision of the arbitrators shall be a condition precedent to any right of legal action that either party may have against the other.
>
> . . . At the written request of either party, at any time prior to the complete appointment of arbitrators, as provided above, or in the event of any default or lapse in the proceeding, the arbitration shall be held under the Standard Form of Arbitration Procedure of The American Institute of Architects or of the Rules of the American Arbitration Association.

These clauses differ in respect to a description of the disputes that are to be covered by the contract in that the latter provision includes the words *or from the breach thereof.* Thus it could be asserted by a party seeking to avoid arbitration that the disputes covered by the first above-quoted provision are only those disputes which involve an *interpretation* of the contract as distinguished from a *breach* of the contract. There have been legal adjudications concerning this very point.

The purpose of arbitration is to avoid protracted litigation. Where the arbitration clause does not provide an adequate guide for the procedures which are to be followed and the rules by which the arbitration is to be conducted, the clause is self-defeating. If the arbitration agreement does not provide a method for selecting the arbitrators, holding the hearings, affording notice, etc., the parties to the agreement will find it necessary to go to court to resolve these questions if they cannot mutually agree. The parties run the further risk that the methods and procedures which they follow by agreement may not comply with the requirements of the state arbitration statute, if such a statute exists. On the other hand it is impractical to provide in the arbitration agreement all the necessary rules pursuant to which the arbitration should be conducted.

To resolve this problem, many commercial contracts have incorporated the standard form of arbitration clause provided by the American Arbitration Association. This clause provides:

> Any controversy or claim arising out of or relating to this contract or the breach thereof, shall be settled by arbitration, in accordance with the rules then obtaining of the American Arbitration Association and judgment upon the award rendered may be entered in any court having jurisdiction thereof.

The rules of the American Arbitration Association have been so drawn that there will be compliance with the arbitration statutes when these rules are followed. Furthermore, these rules provide a standard procedure under which impartial arbitrators are selected, a fair hearing is conducted, and the technical requirements of notice, oaths, etc., are complied with. In utilizing a standard procedure, the parties to an architectural contract are thereby insuring, so far as possible, that the arbitration procedure will be effective and that resort to the courts will be unnecessary.

The arbitration clause in the AIA form in the General Conditions of the "Contract for the Construction of Buildings," provides in part as follows:

> All disputes, claims, or questions subject to arbitration under this contract shall be submitted to arbitration in accordance with the provisions, then obtaining, of the Standard Form of Arbitration Procedure of the American Institute of Architects, and this agreement shall be specifically enforceable under the prevailing arbitration law, and judgment upon the award rendered may be entered in the highest court of the forum, state or federal, having jurisdiction. It is mutually agreed that the decision of the arbitrators shall be a condition precedent to any right of legal action that either party may have against the other . . .
>
> Notice of the demand for arbitration of a dispute shall be filed in writing with the architect and the other party to the contract. If the arbitration is an appeal from the architect's decision, the demand therefor shall be made within ten days of its receipt; in any other case the demand for arbitration shall be made within a reasonable time after the dispute has arisen; in no case, however, shall the demand be made later than the time of final payment, except as otherwise expressly stipulated in the contract.

It will be noted that this clause, unlike the one found in the AIA form for architect-owner contracts quoted above, incorporates by reference the standard arbitration procedure of the AIA.

In the absence of such reference the parties to an agreement have no agreed procedure pursuant to which the arbitrators will be selected and the arbitration hearing conducted. Their only remedy would be to resort to legal action and have the court fill in the gaps which exist in their contract. The AIA arbitration clause which is included in the Small Construction Contract previously quoted also refers to the standard procedure of the AIA and the rules of the American Arbitration Association. This clause provides a *modus operandi* for proceeding with the arbitration where there is a disagreement between the parties. Incorporating by reference into your arbitration agreement a standard procedure which has successfully met the test of legal interpretation and adjudication is a practical and safe way to insure the benefits sought through the agreement.

There are a few jurisdictions in which the right of an architect to apply a mechanic's lien where he is unpaid for his services may be lost if he resorts to arbitration. Certain states have held that the submission of a dispute to arbitration constitutes a waiver of the right of the arbitrating party to a mechanic's lien. The courts of Illinois, however, have held that resort to arbitration does not constitute a waiver of the right to a mechanic's lien and that such right is a cumulative remedy. The majority of opinions agree with this view. The law in New York on this subject is somewhat in a state of flux. Early decisions contained language which indicated that an arbitration award constituted a waiver of a lien asserted by the plaintiff. A later decision seemingly reversed this rule in part. This decision was to the effect that an arbitration award did not eliminate the right of the plaintiff to go into court in order to foreclose a lien; but, the arbitration award would not afford the basis for such foreclosure. It would be necessary for the contractor in an independent legal action to establish his right to a judgment against the property.

Parenthetically, there is a related problem which also should be considered. A few jurisdictions have held that the filing of a lien is a waiver by the contractor of his right to enforce an arbitration agreement. The theory underlying this rule is based upon the assumption that the filing of a mechanic's lien indicates an attempt by the contractor to abandon his right to arbitrate. This assumption is, of course, not warranted, and therefore many states have adopted legislation reversing this rule. In the lien law of New York, for example, it is specifically provided that the filing of a notice of lien does not constitute a waiver of any right of arbitration. This law further provides that in any arbitration in which the value of labor or materials furnished is determined, such value will be conclusive between the parties to the arbitration in any action to foreclose a lien. It is thus important for a contractor to examine the applicable law of the state to determine the relationship between his right to a lien and his right to arbitrate.

In summary, a properly formulated arbitration clause should contain:

(1) A provision that "any agreement arising out of this contract *or from the breach thereof* shall be submitted to arbitration."

(2) A reference to a standard procedure pursuant to which the arbitration is to be conducted.

(3) A specific provision that all notices may be served by registered mail.

(4) The designation of a state which has adopted an arbitration statute as the place where and pursuant to whose laws the arbitration will be conducted.

II

Can one of two associated architects require arbitration, under the AIA form contract, of a dispute arising between him and the owner, despite the passive and active opposition of the other associated architect? This is the question involved in a case argued before the New York Court of Appeals, the highest court of New York (*Baker v. Board of Education,* 309 N.Y. 551).

The case before the Court of Appeals involved architectural services for the construction of a school building. In 1951 an architect (who will be called Architect "A") negotiated with a Board of Education in respect to furnishing services on a proposed school building. He was interested only in performing the design and supervision phases of the work, and it was necessary for the Board to retain a second architect (who will be called Architect "B") to furnish working drawings and specifications.

The Board of Education entered into a single contract with Architects "A" and "B" in association, the contract designating them as "the Architect." The contract was the AIA standard form of agreement between owner and architect, and provided that "all questions in dispute under this agreement should be submitted to arbitration at the choice of either party."

On the same day that Architects "A" and "B" entered into the agreement with the Board of Education, they also entered into an agreement of association between themselves, incorporating by reference the provisions of the contract between owner and architect. The terms of the agreement of association provided for the division of work and for a 50-50 division of fees. Architect "A" was an individual practitioner and Architect "B" was a partnership consisting of two partners.

Construction of the school was commenced in 1953 under supervision of Architect "A" as provided in the agreement of association. One of the services of Architect "A" was, of course, to issue certificates of payment to the contractor. It was contended before the Court by Architect "A" that as construction progressed he was of the opinion that a request for payment of a certain requisition by the contractor was excessive and that the progress of the construction was such that the contractor might not be able to complete the same within the construction contract price. Architect "A" thus required, he stated, a further justification by the contractor of his requisition before he, the architect, would issue a certificate of payment.

The contractor threatened to terminate his contract and to stop the work and, in fact, he reduced the number of workmen on the project. Further, the contractor filed a claim for damages against the owner, the Board of Education. The Board, in order to avoid delay in the completion of the job by the contractor, made a substantial payment to him and discharged Architect "A."

Architect "A" then filed a claim against the Board of Education for the balance of his fee, as provided by the contract, and for disbursements which he had made. This claim was rejected. Architect "A" then requested Architect "B" to join in a demand for arbitration, but Architect "B" did not reply to this request. Architect "A" then demanded arbitration against the owner in his own name and in his demand for arbitration he requested that the arbitrator determine whether the Board was justified in depriving him of his right to supervise the job and whether he was entitled to be paid his full share of the contract price for architectural services performed under the contract with the Board.

The demand for arbitration further requested that the arbitration be held pursuant to the rules of the American Institute of Architects, even though the provision for arbitration in the AIA form contract did not provide for such procedure and, in fact, provided for no standard procedure at all.

The Board of Education and Architect "B" commenced legal action to stay the demand for arbitration and the Board opposed such demand on the ground (among others) that the arbitration clause contained in the form AIA contract did not permit arbitration of any dispute in respect to the interpretation of the contract, or in respect to its breach. The lower New York court denied the right of Architect "A" to demand arbitration and held that the questions raised by Architect "A" did not relate to a dispute between "owner" and "architect" under the owner-architect contract, but that Architect "A" would be required to sue the owner for damages for any tortious act on the part of the owner claimed by Architect "A."

Architect "A" then filed a new demand for arbitration in the joint names of Architect "A" and "B." Again, the Board of Education and Architect "B" opposed this demand. The lower New York court again held that arbitration was not appropriate. The court pointed out that Architect "B" was a partnership consisting of two partners, whereas Architect "A" was a single individual, and, therefore, the court concluded, the partners of Architect "B" constituted a majority of all partners.

Both of the decisions of the lower court were eventually appealed to the New York Court of Appeals and that Court reversed in each instance. The Court held that any differences between Architect "A" and the contractor, or between Architect "A" and his associate, Architect "B," arose out of performance of Architect "A's" duties under the contract and that, therefore, any dispute between Architect "A" and the owner as to the propriety of their acts was subject to arbitration under the arbitration clause. The Court further concluded that Architect "A" could require arbitration without the acquiescence of Architect "B." The Court pointed out that the associated partnership consisted of two members, Architect "A," an individual, and Architect "B," a partnership. The commissions were to be paid one-half to Architect "A" and one-half to Architect "B." The association contract was executed by the partners of Architect "B" not as individuals, but as members of a partnership which is one entity. The Court concluded:

> Under such conditions, one of two members of a partnership may demand arbitration without consent of the other partner, as such partner is an agent of the partnership. . . . We do not decide whether one of three equal partners may compel arbitration of a dispute arising out of a contract to which the partnership is a party.

This case illustrates:

(1) The importance and necessity of the preparation or review

of agreements of association between architects and between owner and architect by competent legal counsel;

(2) That form contracts, whether AIA or otherwise, must be adapted to each particular situation;

(3) That an arbitration clause must be written sufficiently broad to include all questions and disputes of whatsoever nature that may arise and to provide for a workable, standard, arbitration procedure; and

(4) That the relationship of associated architects between themselves and to the owner must be clearly defined to avoid further disputes.

The standard contract documents of the American Institute of Architects fill a vital need in providing the profession with forms which have earned wide acceptance. However, these standard documents can be improved and should be periodically revised.

Previous statements in these pages critical of the American Institute of Architects' contract documents have perhaps not made it sufficiently clear that the documents have served an extremely useful purpose in providing the profession with forms approved by a nationally recognized organization. Everything that has been stated in these pages about the need which the architect has for similar forms applies, in principle, to the AIA documents. It is, therefore, unfortunate if an attitude has been adopted that the forms are sacrosanct and inviolate and must not be altered. Such an attitude will destroy their usefulness.

The importance of the AIA standard documents and their unique position in the field of this particular type of contract may be judged from the fact that *Williston on Contracts* sets them out in full, together with the AIA's *Notes on the Standard Documents.* Williston's work is considered the leading one in its field. The documents and notes may be found in Volume 7 devoted to forms, at page 5918. It is significant and typical that this prominent authority on the law of contracts at this point makes the following observation: "These notes are not sponsored by the author. From a strictly legal view some of the comments are not technically accurate."

Like all documents composed by mortals, the AIA forms were not perfect when drawn and even if they were, would, as time went on, require revision. Ths law of contracts has been deeply affected by the changes in economic conditions and the increasing complexity of our industrial society. Some of the fundamental tenets of contract law are under re-examination by the courts and by the state and federal governments. Many common law doctrines have been modified by statute or by court interpretation. These doctrines have been adapted and altered by the courts and legislatures to meet the problems of our economic and social system. Many of the most fundamental principles of contract law, such as the need for consideration, the effect of mistake, the problem of the illegal and void contract, etc., are still developing concepts. The law moves rapidly and it is just as necessary for the technician who draws legal documents to keep up with this change as it is for the physician to keep informed on new developments in medicine.

The failure on the part of those responsible for the AIA documents to recognize this fact will have the unfortunate consequence of abandonment of their use by the profession. This will be unfortunate for the individual architect who feels the need for these standard documents and unfortunate for the profession as a whole which has the need for uniformity in practice. There is an increasing number of architects who feel that some of the present forms have outlived their usefulness and who have abandoned them in part, or altogether. There are others who are sincerely troubled by the problem. That the problem exists is something which the committees responsible for the contract documents should recognize and move to solve.

The solution attempted should consist not merely of a line by line examination of the documents as they now exist. The analysis made should first consider what kind of documents would best serve the architect. In previous essays there was urged the necessity for (a) a simple short form of architect-client contract which could be used without significant alterations; (b) a separate comprehensive set of terms and conditions and general rules which could be "incorporated by reference" into the short form; (c) a brochure in simple lay language for the client which will indicate in detail the probable extent of his commitment. This, of course, will require an approach *de novo* for the architect-client agreement. A similar approach should be made to the other documents. Only after the general nature of the documents is determined, should there be considered what the contents of each form should be. This would require a comprehensive review of the present contract documents, paragraph by paragraph, and a further consideration as to whether additional matters should be added.

A further problem to be considered was well stated by William Stanley Parker, chairman of the AIA Committee on Contract Documents, as follows: "A standard clause must try to fit all states as accurately as possible, but in certain matters it may be necessary for the local Chapters to develop standard additions or amendments to conform to local controlling statutes."

Ideally, this would mean that there should be prepared by the AIA a comprehensive revision of the contract documents which could be used in those states where the chapters do not further amend or modify the documents issued by the national organization. In those states where the local chapter is able to devote the necessary attention to the problem, the documents put forth by the AIA should be treated as a set of recommendations which can be revised to conform to local needs. This would permit such local chapters as do make revisions to publish forms for the particular state in question.

Again it is emphasized that the question should be squarely put to the profession as to whether the standard documents are satisfactory in their present form. If not, what revisions are required? Obviously, the answer to the second question would require a comprehensive study on the part of a committee adequately advised so that the result of its deliberation would be "strictly legal" and not subject to Williston's criticism quoted above.

II

It is my position that *any* form is too static to cope with the combinations and permutations that result from the individual differences found in the relationships of the architect, the client, the project, the contractor, the municipality, the dynamic society we live in, and so on, *ad infinitum*. But if there must be forms, let them be better, rather than worse ones.

The Office Practice Committee of AIA has recognized the need for the revision of the forms and prepared a revision of the form for use where a percentage of the cost of the work is used as a basis of determining the fees to be paid to the architect. Many of the changes are highly desirable and long overdue. Some of the changes appear to put additional burdens upon the architect, or do not go far enough in protecting the architect's interests. It is important that the members of the profession analyze the changes, to determine whether additional improvement in the forms is required.

The Office Practice Committee, in commenting on its changes, pointed out that the only practical way to improve the architect's status in relation to the client, is to include in the form contracts those items which will establish a favorable position for the architect whether common practice or not. The Committee stated:

> Since it is almost impossible to add an item favorable to the architect in a printed agreement the Committee felt that generally all items possible should be included. Any stipulation can be omitted as a concession to the Client simply by striking it out. Upgrading the Architect's treatment by Clients must come by making it possible to include items in the agrement not now entirely common practice.

The approach of the Committee in this respect is sound, and the revised forms should be analyzed with this goal in mind.

Perhaps the most important part of the agreement between client and architect (at least from the architect's viewpoint) relates to those provisions which deal with the architect's compensation. One essay in which I discussed this subject emphasized the desirability of (1) a retainer fee payable at the time the agreement is signed and constituting a minimum fee; (2) periodic payments during all stages of the work; and (3) a provision in percentage of cost contracts that the architect's estimates are to be binding for the purpose of determining the amount of the respective payments until actual costs are finally determined. Does the revised form adequately protect the architect in respect to his compensation?

The unrevised AIA form did not provide for a retainer, nor for periodic payments during all stages, nor for the architect's estimates to be binding for the purposes of determining the amount of periodic payments. In the absence of such provisions, the architect can often be placed in the dangerous position of financing the client.

The revision in the present form contract is a substantial improvement. It provides for a retainer of 10% of the total fee to be paid in advance. However, some of the value of this provision is lost as the retainer is to be applied against the first phase of the architect's services ("schematic phase") rather than the final payment of the architect's fee. Further, it is not provided that the retainer shall be the minimum compensation under the contract. This would be of

particular importance if the owner should abandon the proje
terminate the architect's services in a very early stage after ut
a substantial amount of the architect's time. A suggested
would be as follows:

> A retainer fee of ——— shall be due and payable upon the signing of this agreement and shall constitute the minimum fee payable hereunder. The said sum shall be retained by the architect and shall be applied on account of the final payment for the architect's fees.

The revision provides for monthly payments in all stages of the architect's services in proportion to the value of the services rendered. This, again, is an improvement over the previous form. However, the value of monthly payments, at least during the preliminary stages, must be based on an estimate of cost. The revision is silent as to how this estimate is to be made. The architect would be best protected if his estimate of cost was binding until actual costs were ascertained, at which time his fee would be adjusted. A suggested clause is as follows:

> Where the Architect's fee is determined by a percentage of cost, his estimate of such cost is made for that purpose only and such estimate shall be conclusive in determining payments to the Architect until costs are finally ascertained upon completion of the Project, at which time an adjustment will be made based upon actual cost.

In a contract where the architect's fee is measured by the cost of the work, the definition of "cost" is extremely important. The Committee has changed that definition in its revision by adding the following language: "It shall be the lowest bona fide bid if bids have been taken or shall be based on estimate of cost for the work as submitted by the Architect."

This language may in some instances have the effect of reducing the architect's fee, as the actual cost of the work may exceed the lowest bona fide bid. In this respect, the desirability of this change is questionable. However, that part of the additional language which provides for the cost of the work to be based on estimate of the architect in the event bids have not been taken is a definite improvement of the original clause. It would be even more effective if it provided that such estimate is conclusive.

Provisions relating to the compensation of the architect for the performance of extra services have also been revised by the AIA Committee. The unrevised AIA form provided that the architect is to be "equitably paid" for extra drafting or other expense "due to changes ordered by the Owner, or due to the delinquency or insolvency of the Owner or Contractor, or as a result of damage by fire." No formula for payment is included. The revised form provides:

> Extra expense is caused for the Architect if the Client orders revisions in drawings previously approved, if construction work is awarded on other than a single lump-sum basis, if construction contract time is extended by more than 25%, or if other extra services are required. Payment therefor shall be as provided in Article VI.
>
> VI. PAYMENTS TO THE ARCHITECT
>
> Payments for Extra Services of the Architect—Payment for work included under Article II shall be made monthly in addition to the basic fee as follows:
>
> 1.———% of the cost of work let separately from the general contract or on a cost-plus basis.
>
> 2.——— times the Direct Personnel Expense incurred by the Architect in rendering other extra services.

Although the above quoted clause could be more broadly formulated to protect the architect's right to compensation for extra services, the establishment of an express formula (a multiple of direct personnel expense) for calculating the architect's compensation is a marked improvement in the form.

Under the revised form the architect's services are divided into four phases: "schematic design," "basic design," "construction document," and "construction phase." The Committee points out that a large proportion of the AIA membership thought that the statement of services in the form contract was inadequate. However, revision has not only detailed the architect's services, but also has increased his obligations. For example, in respect to the cost of the work, the architect is required under the schematic design phase to acquaint the client with the probable cost of the work. Under the basic design phase, he is required to acquaint the client "with any indicated adjustment in the probable cost of the work" and, when authorized, to "obtain a semidetailed estimate of the cost of the work." Under the construction document phase of the services, the architect is required to "advise the client of any indicated adjustment in previous estimates of cost due to known market fluctuations or changes in scope or requirements, and, when client so authorizes, obtain a detailed estimate of cost of the work."

The revised form further provides:

> Estimates of probable Cost of the Work made by the Architect will be square and cubic foot or other computations at current costs based on what the Architect believes are similar projects in the area.
>
> Preliminary estimates shall be in semidetailed form computed on complete wall, floor, or other units of work in place.
>
> Detailed estimates shall be detailed take-offs of the material, labor, and equipment rental, and with current costs applied thereto, to which factors for overhead and profit shall be added.

Even though the form provides that the architect does not guarantee his estimate of cost, the placing of this responsibility upon the architect can be dangerous. Loss of compensation or a legal suit for damages, or both, may be the consequence of an architect's misjudging the cost of a proposed structure. The revised form although increasing the architect's responsibilities in respect to estimating of cost, does not adequately protect the architect from possible litigious clients.

The theory of the AIA Committee in comprehensively detailing the architect's services, was stated by it as follows: "A definite statement of services should protect the legitimate Architect from the marginal operator and service cutter. The detailed statement is much better public relations."

It is questionable whether the inclusion of a comprehensive and detailed list of the architect's services in a form contract is desirable. The services to be rendered vary with the project and there is no reason why a form contract cannot be used in which the architect's services can be especially expressed in a blank space provided for that purpose. In this way, rigidity in respect to the architect's services can be avoided.

The changes in the provisions of the architect-owner agreement relating to reimbursements to the architect specifies, in greater detail than the original, the items which are to be reimbursed. Both the old clause and the revision provide that the architect is to be reimbursed the cost of special consultants when authorized to retain the same by the client. However, if an owner fails to pay the fee of the special consultant because of dissatisfaction with his services or other reason, the architect may find himself as a party defendant in a law suit instituted by the special consultant to recover his fee. A form contract could provide that the architect, in retaining the special consultants, only acts as agent for the owner and that any expenses or damages incurred in defending the owner's interests shall be compensated by the owner.

The revised form states that in the event of abandonment or suspension of the work "the Architect shall be paid the earned portion of the fee, reimbursements then due, and reasonable terminable expenses." It is often difficult to determine the appropriate compensation for an architect when the abandonment or suspension occurs during the preliminary stage of the work. It is generally during this stage that the principal has spent substantial time on the project. It may be desirable to provide that, if the abandonment of the project occurs during the preliminary stage, the fee to be paid the architect shall be based upon a multiple of direct personnel cost including the cost for the time spent by the architect or any partner at a rate fixed in the contract.

The responsibilities of the client are set forth in the revised form. However, there is no provision to the effect that the owner will bear the costs of any audit of the contractor's books and records. Such an audit may be of great assistance to the architect in supervising both the project and the contractor. The cost of such an audit should be clearly stated as one of the owner's responsibilities.

The revised form provides for arbitration of any dispute under the standard procedure of the American Institute of Architects "and the laws of the state in which the project is located." This clause does not improve the defects contained in the unrevised form contract. Further, by providing that the laws of the state in which the project is located shall govern, arbitration will be defeated if the project is located in a state which does not accept or enforce arbitration.

III

The most desirable type of form would be one that aided in the standardizing of provisions which are advantageous to the architect, but that permitted flexibility in respect to individual situations and problems.

One such form could be made up of two parts. One part would consist of a series of first sheets, each setting forth a different method of compensation, such as percentage of cost, cost-plus, fixed-fee, fixed-fee plus percentage, fixed-fee plus cost, etc. This part of the form would contain a page entitled, "The Project and the Architect's Professional Services," which would be blank. On this page a description of the project and of the services to be performed by the Architect would have to be expressly set forth for each separate contract. The second part of such form would consist of a set of General Conditions applicable to any type of owner-architect agreement and would be attached to the applicable first sheet.

An example of Sheet One of the form for use where the architect's compensation is based on the percentage of cost follows. (*It should be noted that this form is written to avoid the implication that the contract is severable and can be terminated by the owner at the end of any particular stage.*)

THIS AGREEMENT made the .... day of ...., 19.., by and between ...., hereinafter called the Owner, and ...., hereinafter called the Architect.

The Owner hereby engages the Architect to perform all such professional services as are hereinafter provided and the Architect agrees to perform said services.

METHOD OF PAYMENT

The Owner agrees to pay the Architect his compensation in the following manner:

(a) A retainer fee of $...... shall be due and payable upon the signing of this Agreement and shall constitute the minimum fee payable hereunder. The said sum shall be retained by the Architect and shall be applied on account of the final payment for the Architect's fees.

(b) The Owner shall pay the Architect ....% of the cost of the Project.

25% of the fee shall be paid during the preliminary stage and shall be billed and payable monthly in proportion to the amount of services completed therefor.

An additional 55% of the fee shall be paid during the general working drawings and specifications stage and shall be billed and payable monthly in proportion to the amount of services completed therefor.

An additional 20% of the fee shall be paid during the supervision stage and shall be billed and payable monthly in proportion to the amount of services completed therefor.

(c) In addition to the foregoing, the Architect is to be reimbursed for his expenses, as hereinafter provided.

Another example of the Sheet One of the form for use where the architect's compensation is based on cost plus is as follows:

THIS AGREEMENT made the .... day of ...., 19.., by and between ...., hereinafter called the Owner, and ...., hereinafter called the Architect.

The Owner hereby engages the Architect to perform all such professional services as are hereinafter provided and the Architect agrees to perform said services.

The Owner agrees to pay the Architect the following compensation for his services:

(a) A retainer fee of $...... shall be due and payable upon the signing of the Agreement and shall constitute the minimum fee payable hereunder. The said sum shall be retained by the Architect and shall be applied on account of the final payments for the Architect's fees.

(b) The Owner shall reimburse the Architect for the cost of technical employes' salaries employed on the Project and said cost shall be billed and payable monthly.

(c) The Owner is to pay the Architect an additional sum equal to 200% of Parargraph (b) above for overhead and fee. Said sum shall be billed and payable monthly.

(d) In addition to the foregoing, the Architect is to be reimbursed for his expenses, as hereinafter provided.

Another example, applicable where the architect's compensation is based on cost plus for preliminaries and percentage of cost for the balance of services is as follows:

THIS AGREEMENT made the .... day of ...., 19.., by and between ...., hereinafter called the Owner, and ...., hereinafter called the Architect.

It is agreed between the parties as follows:

The Owner hereby engages the Architect to perform professional services, as hereinafter provided, and the Architect agrees to perform said services.

METHOD OF PAYMENT

The Owner agrees to pay the Architect the following compensation for his services:

(a) A retainer fee of $...... shall be due and payable upon the signing of this Agreement and shall constitute the minimum fee payable hereunder. The said sum shall be retained by the

Architect and shall be applied on account of the final payment for the Architect's fees.

(b) During the preliminary stage of the Architect's services, the Owner shall pay the Architect as follows:

(1) The Owner shall reimburse the Architect for the cost of technical employes' salaries employed on the Project and said cost shall be billed and payable monthly.

(2) The Owner is to pay the Architect an additional sum equal to 200% of sub-paragraph (1) of this Paragraph (b) above for overhead and fee, and said cost shall be billed and payable monthly.

(c) During the balance of the services called for under "The Project and Services of the Architect," the Owner shall pay the Architect ....% of the cost of the Project. Said fee shall be billed and payable monthly in proportion to the amount of services completed therefor. ....% of this fee shall be paid during the supervision stage.

(d) In addition to the foregoing, the Architect is to be reimbursed for his expenses as hereinafter provided.

Another example of Sheet One of the form for use where the architect's compensation is based upon a fixed fee is as follows:

THIS AGREEMENT made the .... day of ...., 19.., by and between ...., hereinafter called the Owner, and ...., hereinafter called the Architect.

The Owner hereby engages the Architect to perform all such professional services as are hereinafter provided and the Architect agrees to perform said services.

The Owner agrees to pay the Architect as compensation for professional services rendered, the sum of $......, to be paid as follows:

$...... shall be paid upon the signing of this contract and shall constitute the minimum fee payable hereunder;

The balance of the fee shall be paid as follows: ....
In addition to the foregoing, the Architect is to be reimbursed for his expenses, as hereinafter provided.

A further example of a form for use where the architect's compensation is based upon a fixed fee for preliminaries, plus a percentage of cost for the balance of his services, is as follows:

THIS AGREEMENT made the .... day of ...., 19.., by and between ...., hereinafter called the Owner, and ...., hereinafter called the Architect.

The Owner hereby engages the Architect to perform all such professional services as are hereinafter provided and the Architect agrees to perform said services.

METHOD OF PAYMENT

The Owner agrees to pay the Architect his compensation in the following manner:

(a) A retainer fee of $...... shall be due and payable upon the signing of this Agreement and shall constitute the minimum fee payable hereunder. The said sum shall be retained by the Architect and shall be applied on account of the final payment for the Architect's fees.

(b) During the preliminary stage of the Architect's services, the Owner shall pay the Architect the sum of $......; said sum shall be billed and payable monthly in proportion to the amount of services completed therefor.

(c) During the balance of services called for under "The Project and the Architect's Professional Services," the Owner shall pay the Architect ......% of the cost of the Project. Said fee shall be billed and payable monthly in proportion to the amount of services completed therefor. ....% of this fee shall be paid during the supervision stage.

(d) In addition to the foregoing, the Architect is to be reimbursed for his expenses as hereinafter provided.

An example of a set of General Conditions which can be used in conjunction with a form that sets forth the method of compensation of the architect, a description of the project, and the architect's services, is as follows. (*Where the AIA clause is to be used, the same is noted.*)

The Owner and Architect further agree as follows:

1. *Reimbursable Expenses*—The Owner shall reimburse the Architect for the following expenses:

(a) All out-of-pocket expenses for work on the project, including but not by way of limitation, costs of blueprinting, reproducing drawings, printing or mimeographing of specifications, models, telegrams, long-distance telephone calls, expressage, and the costs of living and transportation incurred by the Architect or his employees while traveling in discharge of duties connected with the work.

(b) In addition to any other compensation, a per diem fee of

$ . . . . for each day, or part thereof, spent by a partner of the firm outside of the metropolitan area of . . . ., in connection with the Project shall be paid by the Owner to the Architect.

(c) The Architect shall maintain an efficient and accurate record as to all costs and expenses incurred by him in connection with the subject of this agreement and his accounts, at all reasonable times, shall be open to the inspection of the Owner or his authorized representative. Reimbursable expenses shall be billed and paid monthly.

2. *Construction Contracts*—It is the Owner's intention to let the work under a single General Construction contract. If, however, the work is let under a General Construction contract, but a portion of said work is excluded therefrom and separately let, the compensation to be paid the Architect by the Owner, for that portion of the work so separately let, shall be increased in the amount of . . . .% of the cost of construction. If there is no General Construction contract, the additional compensation of . . . .% of the cost of construction shall apply to the entire work.

3. *Legal and Accounting Service*—The Architect shall have no obligation to prepare contracts and forms of proposals, such preparation being the responsibility of the Owner. The Architect, however, shall furnish such information and shall attend such conferences as are necessary for the drafting of contracts and forms of proposals. Upon authorization by the Owner, the Architect shall secure legal services in connection with the Project and the Owner will pay the reasonable cost of such services.

The cost of any audit of the Contractor's books and records shall be paid by the Owner, and the Owner shall furnish appropriate personnel to conduct such audit.

4. *Consultants*—If the Owner authorizes or directs the Architect to retain consultants and/or engineers whose services are not elsewhere covered by this agreement, the Architect, in retaining such consultants and/or engineers, acts as agent for the Owner and the Owner shall reimburse the Architect for any sums advanced to such consultants or engineers. The Owner shall hold the Architect harmless against any claim by any such consultant or engineer for payment for his services or otherwise.

5. *Supervision of Project*—(AIA Form.)

6. *Preliminary Estimates*—If requested by the Owner, the Architect will furnish preliminary estimates as to the cost of the Project. However, such estimates are not to be construed in any way as a representation, warranty, or agreement on the part

of the Architect of the accuracy of such estimate or that the Project can be constructed for the amount thereof. The Architect's compensation under this contract shall in no way be affected by the correctness of such estimates.

Where the Architect's fee is determined by a percentage of cost, his estimate of such cost is made for that purpose only and such estimate shall be conclusive in determining payments to the Architect until costs are finally ascertained upon completion of the Project, at which time an adjustment will be made based upon actual cost.

7. *Extra Services*—If the Architect furnishes extra or unanticipated services because of any changes or additions to the Project requested or authorized by the Owner, or because the scope or extent of the Project is changed, or because of any delay, default or action of the Owner or of the Contractor, or as a result of fire or other casualty, or for any reason not the Architect's fault, then the Owner shall pay the Architect as compensation for such extra or unanticipated services: (a) the cost of technical employes' salaries employed on the Project and for the time expended by partners on the Project, plus (b) ....% of (a) for overhead and fee. Partner's time under (a) shall be calculated at the rate of $.... per hour.

8. *Abandonment and Suspension of the Project*—If the Owner abandons or suspends the Project, the Architect is to be compensated in proportion to the services performed under the contract. If such abandonment occurs prior to the completion of the preliminary stage of the Architect's services, the Owner shall pay to the Architect as his compensation, in addition to the minimum fee payable hereunder, (a) the Architects' cost of technical employes' salaries employed on the Project and for the time expended by partners on the Project, plus (b) ....% of (a) for overhead and fee. Partner's time under (a) shall be calculated at the rate of $...... per hour. In the event of abandonment or suspension of the Project, the Architect is to be reimbursed by the Owner for all expenses incurred or for which he is committed, including the cost of mechanical and structural engineers and other engineers or consultants.

9. *Survey, Boring, and Tests*—(AIA Form.)

10. *Ownership of Documents*—All studies, sketches, drawings, plans, details, and specifications, being instruments of service, are and shall remain the property of the Architect whether the Project for which they are made be executed or not. Any publication of the Project shall be under the control of the Architect.

11. *Transfer of Interest*—(AIA Form.)

12. *Arbitration*—Any dispute arising between the parties to this Agreement, or involving the interpretation of the terms of this agreement, or any breach thereof, shall be submitted to and determined by arbitration before the American Arbitration Association in the City of ————, in accordance with the rules then obtaining of said association and the laws of the State of ————. All notices with respect to the demand for arbitration, the conduct of the arbitration and the enforcement of the arbitration award shall be deemed sufficient if served by registered mail addressed by one party to the other at the addresses heretofore set forth.

So much for forms. The pessimism I once felt about architects not protecting their pocketbooks has yielded to a cautious optimism, as more and more I see architects realizing that good practice of the profession carries with it the prior necessity of proper protection as to their compensation. An architect with relative financial security in his contractual arrangement with his client does better work. Architects should recognize this as a maxim.

CHAPTER 13: *Agreements Between Contractor and Owner*

The architect may run a grave risk when issuing certificates of payment without an audit of the contractor's disbursements. The standard documents of the American Institute of Architects should be revised to provide for a more effective supervision of construction by the architect.

"Supervision by architect required."
. . . supervision of what?
. . . supervision of construction?
. . . supervision of the contractor?
. . . or supervision of both?

What do I mean by "supervision of the contractor?" I mean the architect's control over and audit of those monies paid to the contractor which the contract requires him to distribute: *i.e.* where in effect he is acting as a fiscal agent of the owner. Among other things, this would require a proper audit to determine whether the contractor's requisitions properly reflect requisitions of sub-contractors, material men, and the like, and that payments to the contractor are disbursed in accordance with contractual obligations. For example, *Article* 37 of the General Terms and Conditions of the AIA General Construction Contract requires him to pay sub-contractors proportionately as he is paid. How many architects, even on very large projects, actually "supervise the contractor" as well as construction? The very language of the General Terms and Conditions indicates that the answer is few, if any. The terms and conditions, themselves (*Article 24*), in considering the contractor's application for payment, call for receipts or vouchers only "if required." The contractual provisions, of course, are silent as to any periodic audit.

In respect to the architect's function as a "supervisor of construction," the General Terms and Conditions and the carefully written specifications on each project state quite explicitly the architect's function. The attitude of the architect, the contractor, and even the bonding company, indicate quite clearly that this is the apparent primary function of the architect in supervision.

But is "supervision of construction," alone, what the owner expects and the General Terms and Conditions require? As to the owner, the answer is an emphatic no! As to the General Terms and Conditions, the answer is again, no—but in muddied language.

I doubt whether the financial end of any operation in any other field, involving the large amounts of monies that are spent in construction, is as loosely run as the usual construction operation. If this is continued, the consequences could be disastrous, given any kind of general or even local economic recession or disturbance, temporary, or otherwise, affecting prices or materials. Even in the absence of any economic disturbance, the consequences could be equally unfortunate in individual situations.

Let me illustrate by an example that could be typical: The contractor, instead of making payments to his sub-contractors, as required by *Article 37*, shades these amounts. As the job draws to a close he finds himself seriously in arrears to a number of subs. He feels secure because of the 10% retained by the owner and hopes to stall the subs until the receipt of that amount. The owner and the architect apparently have felt secure because of the 10% retention fund.

As a practical matter, however, this is a sham, a snare, and a delusion. The 10% is intended to cover possible claims for defective work. The defective work can be so serious as to absorb that entire fund. In addition, there may be claims for inexcusable delay which may run into substantial sums, where time is of the essence. If the claims of the subs turn out to be so substantial that, when added to the owner's claims for defective work, the 10% becomes grossly inadequate and the contractor is unable to meet his payments, the owner is in the position of paying far more for the job than the contract price. Reliance on the contractor's bond may, for reasons not necessary to discuss here, also be illusory.

I do not mean to imply here that contractors are dishonest or that they cynically disregard their contractual obligations. When large amounts are expended, it is not only prudent but routine to require regular audits. The owner and the architect should feel that the contractor engaged is honest, reliable, ethical, and financially responsible. Employes of banks and officers handling public funds are certainly so regarded, yet audits there are routine, expected, and are not considered insulting. A wise man once told me that it is unfair to put unnecessary temptation before an honest man. Routinely in construction this is done because of a generic failure to require the contractor to adhere rigidly to his contractual requirements as to disbursements of funds.

The problem, therefore, is extremely important, but may be very simply stated:

(1) Should the contractor's books and records be audited periodically?

(2) If so, who shall pay for or provide the necessary accounting services—the architect, the owner, or the bonding company?

(3) How do the General Terms and Conditions now deal with these and related problems?

(4) How should the General Terms and Conditions be amended so as to clarify the respective responsibilities of the architect, the contractor, and the owner?

I have emphasized the importance of a periodic audit of the contractor's books and records in order to provide the owner and architect with the security to which they are entitled. The cost of furnishing accounting and auditing services, as between architect and owner, should be borne by the owner. It is not within the ordinary contemplation of owner or architect that such services be furnished by the architect—and no compensation therefore is provided. It is in the interest of the owner that he obtain the security which periodic audits would furnish him; therefore the expense and cost of such service are properly his. If there is a bonding company which has an interest in proper performance by the contractor, then that bonding company should share in the expense of a periodic audit.

II

What are the provisions of the General Conditions which pertain to payment to the contractor? Initially, it should be pointed out that the Conditions do not contain any provision for audits of the contractor's books and records. In *Article 24* is the chief provision relating to payment to the contractor. This article provides in substance that the contractor shall submit to the architect an application for each payment and that *if required* by the architect, he is to furnish receipts or other vouchers showing payments for material and labor and payments to sub-contractors. This article further provides that if payments are made, based on valuation of work done, the contractor is to submit to the architect a schedule of values on the various parts of the work and, *if required,* support such schedule by such evidence as the architect may direct.

For the protection of the owner, *Article 24* should not make the requirement to furnish evidence optional with the architect. Before a Certificate of Payment is issued, the architect should have sufficient evidence in his hands to make a sound determination. In this respect, receipts and vouchers are not sufficient. The contractor should be required to furnish to the architect the requisitions of his sub-contractors and other supporting papers upon which the contractor's own application for payment is based. The architect then is in a position thereafter to check against such sub-contractor's requisitions to ascertain if they have been paid pursuant to *Article 37* of the General Conditions. This check could be made by an audit of the contractor's books and records, if the General Conditions were amended to provide for such procedure.

Article 37 of the General Conditions covers the relations of concontractor and sub-contractor. It provides that the sub-contractor submit to the contractor application for payment, in order to enable the contractor to apply for payment under *Article 24.* The contractor agrees to pay the sub-contractor:

(1) The amount allowed to the contractor on account of the subcontractor's work under the schedule of values described in *Article 24;* or

(2) To pay the sub-contractor upon payment of Architect's Certificate, so that at all times such payments shall be in proportion to the value of the work done by the sub-contractor; or

(3) To pay the sub-contractor in the manner provided by the contract documents, or the sub-contract, if these provide for earlier or larger payments than "(1)" or "(2)" above; and

(4) To pay the sub-contractor on demand at the time the Architect's Certificate should issue, even though it has not been issued for any cause not the fault of the sub-contractor.

No method is provided for the owner, under *Article 37,* to determine as a matter of course whether *Article 37* has been complied with. Noncompliance can result in such unfortunate consequences as the imposition of mechanic's liens, disputes delaying completion or interrupting the job, insolvency, or bankruptcy of the contractor, and other situations which can follow a contractor's neglect or failure to treat such funds in the same manner as trust funds. Regular audits of the contractor's books and records, to ascertain if payments have been made for labor and material and if the subcontractors have been paid under *Article 37*, will afford a more orderly and controlled method for the supervision of the contractor by the architect.

Article 26 of the General Conditions is concerned with payments withheld. It provides that the architect may withhold or nullify a Certificate of Payment to protect the owner from loss because of (a) "defective work not remedied"; (b) "claims filed or reasonable evidence indicating probable filing of claims"; (c) "failure of the Contractor to make payments properly to sub-contractors or for material or labor"; (d) "a reasonable doubt that the contract can be completed for the balance unpaid"; and (e) "damage to another Contractor." This again emphasizes the need to empower the Architect or owner to check and audit the contractor's books and records to determine whether payment should be withheld.

Article 32 of the General Conditions, which refers to final payment to the contractor, provides that neither the final payment, nor any part of the retained percentage shall become due until the contractor, *if required,* shall deliver a complete release of all liens arising out of the contract, *or* receipts in full for all labor and material. It further provides that *if required* the contractor will furnish an affidavit that the releases and receipts include all labor and material for which a lien could be filed.

For obvious reasons it would be better if *Article 32* provided that the final payment or the payment of a retained percentage should be based upon proof of payment for all labor and material and upon the furnishing of release of liens by the contractor. Further, the owner and not the architect should have the option of waiving this requirement.

The provisions of the General Conditions, which relate to payment of the contractor and sub-contractor, are not satisfactory from either the owner's or architect's point of view. In making optional the contractor's duty to furnish proof, it may be implied that the architect is to require the submission of such proof only when he has reason to believe, because of extraneous facts, that the application or requisition of the contractor is improper. The owner, however, should be satisfied with nothing less than a binding requirement that proof be furnished as a matter of regular course and practice before a Certificate of Payment is issued. Further, it is obviously in both the owner's and architect's interest that the proof furnished be sufficient so that the architect's determination is not based on surmise.

The General Conditions, as presently drawn, afford the architect no sure and certain method by which he can execute his responsibility with a minimum of risk. In recommending that the General Conditions contain a provision making the books and records of the Contractor subject to audit, I do not mean to imply that the final responsibility for the issuance of a Certificate of Payment should be shifted from the architect to the owner. The costs of any audit and the personnel to conduct the same should be borne and furnished by the owner, but the responsibility for the issuance or withholding of a Certificate should continue in the architect. The General Conditions of the Contract require amendment to properly protect both owner and architect in their relations with the contractor. The inadequacies of the General Conditions, as discussed previously, can be summarized as follows:

(1) The supporting papers to be submitted by the contractor to justify his application for payment are insufficient.

(2) The furnishing of proofs is made optional.

(3) No provision is made for an audit of the contractor's books and records to insure that proper payments have been made for labor and material furnished on the project, and that sub-contractors have been appropriately paid in accordance with the contract and the General Conditions.

III

The application of the contractor for payment is based in part upon the requisitions of sub-contractors for payment. If the money paid by the owner pursuant to the issuance of a Certificate of Payment by the architect is not utilized in turn by the contractor to pay the sub-contractors, the position of the owner can be seriously jeopardized. A quick and certain method of checking payments to sub-contractors should be provided. In other fields, periodic audits have furnished the answer and the same solution is called for in the construction field. The General Conditions should include a clause in which the contractor agrees to subject his books and records to audit and his plant to inspection. A suggested provision reads as follows:

> The Contractor agrees that its books and records shall at all reasonable times be subject to audit and its plant subject to inspection, by the Owner or Architect, or by their authorized representatives. Compliance with this article shall constitute a condition precedent to the issuance of a certificate of payment by the Architect.

Article 24 of the General Conditions provides for applications for payments by the contractor. The amendment required by this article is to eliminate the optional aspect of the furnishing of proofs by the contractor and to provide adequate proofs. This Article might be amended in the following manner (*words in parentheses are to be eliminated from the article and italicized words are to be added):*

> Art. 24. Applications for Payments—The Contractor shall submit to the Architect an application for each payment, and (if required) receipts or other vouchers, showing his payments for materials and labor, including payment to Sub-contractors as required by Art. 37. *In addition thereto, the Contractor shall submit to the Architect the requisitions of his Sub-contractors and such other supporting papers as the Architect may require upon which the Contractor's application for payment is based.*
>
> If payments are made on valuation of work done, such application shall be submitted at least ten days before each payment falls due, and (if required) the Contractor shall, before the first application, submit to the Architect a schedule of values of the various parts of the work, including quantities aggregating the total sum of the contract divided so as to facilitate the payments to Sub-contractors in accordance with Art. 37 (e), made out in such form as the Architect and the Contractor may agree upon, and (if required) supported by such evidence as to its correctness as the Architect may direct. This schedule, when approved by the Architect, shall be used as a basis for certificates of payment, unless it be found to be in error. In applying for payments, the Contractor shall submit a statement based upon this schedule, and (if required) itemized in such form and supported by such evidence as the Architect may direct, showing his right to the payment claimed. *Included in such itemization and evidence to be submitted to the Architect shall be a description of the extent and amount of each Sub-contrac-*

tor's interest in the Contractor's application for payment, together with the requisitions of his Sub-contractors for payment, and any other supporting papers as the Architect may require upon which the Contractor's interest in the Contractor's application for payment is based.

If payments are made on account of materials delivered and suitably stored at the site, but not incorporated in the work, they shall (if required by the Architect) be conditional upon submission by the Contractor of bills of sale or such other procedure as will establish the Owner's title to such material, or otherwise adequately protect the Owner's interest. *Such payments shall be held by the Contractor in trust until the Architect shall certify that the Owner's title to the materials has been properly established.*

Article 32 of the General Conditions, which provides when final payment or the retained percentage shall be paid, is also inadequate, in that the proofs required are insufficient and their furnishing is made optional with the architect. This article might be amended as follows (*words in parentheses are to be eliminated from the article and italicized words are to be added*):

Art. 32. Liens—neither the final payment nor any port of the retained percentage shall become due until the Contractor (if required) shall deliver to the Owner a complete release of all liens arising out of this contract, (or) *and* receipts in full (in lieu thereof) *for all the labor and material furnished on the project,* and (if required in either case) an affidavit that so far as he has knowledge or information the releases and receipts include all the labor and material for which a lien could be filed; but the Contractor may, if any Sub-contractor refuses to furnish a release or a receipt in full, furnish a bond satisfactory to the Owner, to indemnify him against any lien. If any lien remains unsatisfied after all payments are made, the Contractor shall refund to the Owner all monies that the (latter) *Architect determines the Owner* may be compelled to pay in discharging such a lien, including all costs and a reasonable attorney's fee.

Control of the contractor's disposition of payments received from the owner by the audit of the contractor's books and records requires personnel to conduct the audit—and this will incur costs. It should be understood between owner and architect that, although the responsibility for the issuance of the Certificates of Payment remains in the architect, the cost of auditing the contractor's books and records shall be borne by the owner and he shall furnish appropriate personnel for that purpose. If the contract between owner and contractor provides for audit of the contractor's books, the contract between owner and architect should provide as follows: "The cost of any audit of the Contractor's books and records shall be paid by the Owner, and the Owner shall furnish appropriate personnel to conduct such audit."

Consideration by architects, individually and by their societies, of the suggestions contained in this and the preceding material would result in substantial benefit to the entire building industry, as well as the profession.

The architect, as an arbitrator of disputes between owner and contractor, exercises a limited function under the standard documents of the American Institute of Architects.

The role of an architect as arbiter under the AIA form provisions was critically examined by the Appellate Division of the Supreme Court of New York in the case, *Gold Plastering Co., Inc. v. 200 East End Ave. Corp.*, 282 App. Div. 1073.

The contractor had entered into an agreement to lath and plaster a building then under construction. The AIA General Conditions were incorporated by reference and made a part of the specifications. An action was subsequently commenced by the contractor to recovered damages for breach of contract and for the reasonable value of labor and materials furnished.

The owner relied heavily upon a decision rendered in its favor by the architect to whom it had submitted the dispute for determination pursuant to the General Conditions of the AIA, Article 39, of the standard form of the American Institute of Architects, which provides, in part:

> The Architect shall, within a reasonable time, make decisions on all claims of the Owner or Contractor and on all other matters relating to the execution and progress of the work or the interpretation of the contract documents.
>
> The Architect's decisions, in matters relating to artistic effect, shall be final, if within the terms of the contract documents.

> Except as above, or as otherwise expressly provided in the Contract Documents, all the Architect's decisions are subject to arbitration.

Article 40 pertaining to arbitration contains the following clause: "It is mutually agreed that the decision of the arbitrators shall be a condition precedent to any right of legal action that either party may have against the other."

The Appellate Division, in affirming a judgment for the contractor, denied that the architect's decision had any binding effect upon the parties, particularly since the owner had failed to move to compel arbitration *or* to stay the proceedings in the instant suit. Thus, by its very participation in the action, the owner had waived any right it might otherwise have had to rely on the architect's decision.

The owner had urged vigorously that Article 39 vested jurisdiction of the dispute in the architect; and that, by reason of plaintiff's failure to appeal from the architect's determination and employ the arbitration provisions of Article 40, made the architect's award a final one.

Without so much as an oblique reference to Article 40, which makes the arbitrator's decision a "condition precedent" to a law suit, the court implied that it was apparently unnecessary to resort to arbitration after the decision of an architect because the architect himself was an "arbitrator." The court stated:

> While the architect is not referred to as an "arbitrator" in the "General Conditions" and his decisions made subject to "arbitration" thereby, it is our opinion that the proceedings before the architect contemplated by Article 39 of the "General Conditions" are part of a general scheme for arbitration of disputes, and that such proceedings constitute "arbitration" within the meaning of Article 84, Civil Practice Act . . .

The owner's contention that the architect had jurisdiction to decide the suit was likewise denied. Said the court:

> However, we agree with the trial court that the dispute involved here, as to breach of contract, was not one which the parties had agreed by incorporation of the General Conditions to submit to the architect for determination. In our opinion, the "claims of the owner or contractor" which the architect was authorized to determine under Article 39 of the General Conditions must be construed in view of other provisions of those

conditions to refer only to claims "relating to the execution and progress of the work" and not to claims arising out of alleged breach of contract.

The AIA General Conditions having been made a part of the "specifications" rather than of the whole contract, the architect could not hear disputes that did not relate to the work (specifications) to be done under the contract. Since the dispute did not concern the "execution and progress of the work," but a "claim arising out of alleged breach of contract," any decision of the architect had no binding effect.

Finally, the court rejected as well the defendant's contention that the architect's decision was final. Said the court:

> . . . it is also our opinion that in any event a decision of the architect, standing alone, was not intended to be final or to provide a basis for the entry of judgment, except insofar as it might relate to artistic matters.

This decision points up again the necessity of reconsidering the AIA General Conditions, particularly with respect to the ethical and legal status of the architect as an "arbiter."

II

When is a dispute a proper subject for arbitration under the General Conditions (Articles 39 and 40 of the standard form building contract issued by the American Institute of Architects)? This was the issue before the Appellate Division of the Supreme Court of New York in the *Matter of Board of Education Union Free School District No. 3, Town of Islip, Suffolk County, New York,* 283 App. Div. 880.

A general contractor had entered into a contract with the Board of Education for general construction work for alterations and additions to the East Islip School. The contractor was required, under the contract, to do certain excavation work, including the excavation for footings and foundations, as well as to perform certain concrete work, including the construction of the footings and foundations.

Article 6 of said contract provided in part as follows:

> The Contract Documents—The General Conditions of the Contract, the Specifications and the Drawings, together with this agreement, form the contract, and they are as fully a part of the contract as if hereto attached or herein repeated.

The general instructions and information with regard to the excavations for footings and foundations and for the construction of the footings and foundations were contained in the specifications furnished the general contractor. Drawing No. 3 gave detailed dimensions and measurements for the depth of the excavation for the footings and foundations. The drawing specified that the excavations for the footings and foundations were to be carried to a depth of 1′-10½″.

A notation on Drawing No. 1 read as follows: "All footings to bear on undisturbed soil of minimum two ton per square foot bearing capacity."

Pursuant to the provisions of the specifications, the contractor notified the architect when the footing excavation was carried to the 1′-10½″ level. After an inspection, the architect disapproved of the soil conditions, at the 1′-10½″ level because of roots in the soil and directed the contractor to carry the footings down so that they rested on 2 ton per square foot bearing soil.

The contractor claimed an extra for the additional work and was notified by the architect that the matter of compensation would be adjudicated at a later time. When no further remuneration was forthcoming, the contractor filed a demand for arbitration, which proceedings were stayed on motion of the Board of Education and appealed to the Appellate Division, after a lower court held that this was a proper case for arbitration.

On appeal the Board maintained that there was no bona fide dispute within the meaning of the contract. The Board cited as controlling the note to Drawing No. 1, as well as other sections, one of which provided as follows: "Concrete and cement work footings and foundations: Pour only on undisturbed earth. Where ground has been disturbed, carry footings down lower than as shown on the drawings, at no additional cost to the owner."

Under the Board's theory, therefore, the contractor could not be excused from his contract because of unforeseen difficulty, soil conditions, or unusual or unexpected expenses and, consequently, was not entitled to extra compensation. Thus, as there was no bona fide dispute within the meaning of the contract, the contractor had no right to arbitration.

The contractor contended that there was a bona fide dispute between the parties as to the construction of the contract provisions and rejected the Board's reference to Drawing 3, which showed the 1′-10½″ dimensions as "only typical," as in no way binding. As the contractor stated in its brief:

> A typical detail in the building industry does not signify something indefinite like the "typical woman." A typical architectural detail establishes the exact size, shape, quantities, etc., for specially located work and for all other similar work.

This, claimed the contractor, was clearly a controversy subject to arbitration under the arbitration agreement.

The Appellate Division reviewed the AIA arbitration provisions incorporated in the contract, which provided, in part:

> The Architect shall . . . make decisions on all claims . . . relating to the execution and progress of the work on the interpretation of the Contract Documents"; that ". . . all the architect's decisions are subject to arbitration"; and that "the decision of the arbitrators shall be a condition precedent to any right of legal action . . ."

The court determined that the dispute as to whether or not certain work constituted an extra was properly a subject for arbitration by the architect.

In conclusion, the court declared: "The language of the arbitration provisions of the contract is sufficiently broad to express an intention of the parties to submit a dispute such as the one herein to arbitration."

It is to be noted that the merits of the controversy were not considered by the court, which merely passed upon the presence or absence of a bona fide arbitrable dispute.

It is also important to note that this is not a discussion of the arbitration clauses in the "Architect-Owner" AIA form. The court decisions only emphasize the importance of amending that particular arbitration clause so as to insure that an arbitration tribunal and not a court, will decide disputes between an architect and his client.

A performance bond can be an effective tool in the supervision of the contractor.

Certain changes in the General Conditions have been recommended in the preceding pages in order to accomplish a more effective supervision of the contract and to furnish both architect and owner with greater protection. In this connection, I was recently asked by an architect to outline the role he should play in the contractor's furnishing a performance bond. I pointed out that a suitable performance bond furnished by a responsible bonding company is one of the most effective aids in assuring proper performance on the part of the contractor. I also stated that both owner and architect have a vital interest in the selection of a proper bonding company, represented by an able broker or agent.

Article 30 of the AIA General Conditions reads as follows (the emphasis is mine):

> Guaranty Bonds.—The *Owner shall have the right* prior to the signing of the Contract *to require the Contractor to furnish bond* covering the faithful performance of the Contract and the payment of all obligations arising thereunder, *in such forms as the Owner may prescribe and with such sureties as he may approve.* If such bond is required by instructions given previous to the submission of bids, the premium shall be paid by the Contractor; if subsequent thereto, it shall be paid by the Owner.

Generally the owner's "right" is *not* exercised. His interest is usually confined to the amount of the bond alone. In some instances, the owner may be lulled into feeling secure that the contractor is able to perform because he believes that the contractor has been thoroughly investigated by the bonding company when, as a matter of fact, the bonding company—doubtful of the contractor's reliability—may have insisted on guarantees from others. This information, of course, is not made known to the owner.

The choice of the broker or agent, through whom the bond is written, is also a matter of some importance since he can be of substantial value in keeping a wavering contractor in line, in getting the bonding company to give assistance to a contractor temporarily financially embarrassed, or in prodding the bonding company to take over the project with the least amount of delay, inconvenience, and financial loss to the owner.

It is good business for the owner to insist on exercising his right to approve the bonding company and the terms of the bond. The bond is for the protection of the owner (*not the contractor*) and paid for by the *owner* directly or indirectly (and not by the contractor). The interests of the owner and of the contractor in respect to the choice of bonding company are *not* similar; indeed, they are in many respects conflicting. The accompanying table outlines the divergent motivations of the owner and contractor in the selection of a bonding company and an agent or broker to write the bond.

RESPECTIVE INTERESTS OF OWNER AND CONTRACTOR IN SELECTING BONDING COMPANY AND AGENT OR BROKER

Criteria for owner:	*Contractor's motivation:*
(1) A bonding company which will require the contractor to furnish maximum financial, personnel experience, and other necessary data to assure contractor's responsibility and ability to perform.	(1) A bonding company which will require the contractor to furnish minimum financial, personnel experience, and other data.
(2) A bonding company which will give maximum supervision to and interest in the operations of the contractor to insure proper performance on his part and to minimize claims.	(2) Minimum "interference" and interest by the bonding company in the contractor's operations.
(3) A bonding company which will intervene at the earliest possible moment to aid the contractor financially, or take over the job, if required.	(3) Intervention by bonding company at last possible moment, if contractor is not applying funds according to contract, or job otherwise goes sour.
(4) A bonding company which has the highest financial rating.	(4) No interest in bonding company's financial rating.
(5) A bonding company which has an excellent record for the assumption of responsibility when contractor fails to perform in whole or in part, and a company which does not have a litigious history based upon its efforts to avoid responsibility.	(5) No interest in bonding company's history in accepting responsibility.
(6) A broker or agent* who shall be in an influential position to act on the owner's behalf, and who will be in a position to exercise sufficient supervision over the contractor's performance to protect the bonding company's and the owner's interest.	(6) An agent or broker who will exercise a minimum of supervision and "interference" in the contractor's performance.
(7) A broker or agent whose ability and experience in the contractor-surety field is extensive, and whose status, ability, and experience is affirmatively recognized by the bonding company.	(7) Interest in broker or agent is confined to ability of broker or agent to use influence in *contractor's* behalf.

* Broker must write bond through the agent or company while agent issues bonds immediately in company's name.

What role should the architect play in all of this? The answer is implicit in the foregoing. He should call the substance of this discussion to the owner's attention, and if required by the owner, he should see to it that a proper bond is written through an appropriate broker or agent.

CHAPTER 14: *The Architect's Status Under Building Contracts*

Disputes between owner and contractor can best and most speedily be determined by an arbitrator who has specialized knowledge in the construction field. Either the architect's function as an arbitrator should be expanded under the building contract, or panels of architects should be available from whom arbitrators can be selected.

WHO SHOULD ARBITRATE DISPUTES between owner and contractor, and what procedure should be followed in the conduct of such arbitration?

Is the architect the most qualified and logical person to determine and solve such disputes?

Would it be in the interest of all to expand the architect's function as arbitrator and make his decision final?

Or, if a standard procedure for arbitration is provided in the contract between owner and contractor under which some "outsider" determines issues in dispute, should that procedure mandatorily require the utilization of an arbitrator or an arbitration tribunal that will have the proper orientation, qualification, and lack of bias?

These are questions which need consideration when reviewing the adequacy of the provisions on arbitration of the form contracts of the American Institute of Architects.

Under the Owner-Contractor agreements issued by the American Institute of Architects, the role of architect as arbitrator is severely limited. The American Institute of Architects' Short Form for Small Construction provides that "any disagreement arising out of this contract or from the breach thereof shall be submitted to arbitration" and "the arbitration shall be held under the standard form of arbitration procedure of the American Institute of Architects or under the rules of the American Arbitration Association." This means all decisions of the architect are subject to further arbitration.

The General Conditions of the Contract of the American Institute of Architects provide that "the Architect's decision relating to *artistic effect* shall be final, if within the terms of the contract documents" and that *all other decisions* of the architect are subject to arbitration under the standard procedure of the American Institute of Architects.

The courts have held that the General Conditions of the Contract do not permit architects to determine questions of law, nor to determine whether the contract has been breached. No factual decision is final, except relating to artistic effect, and even in that respect the General Conditions are ambiguous as to when this decision would be final. The General Conditions make no provision in the event the architect is disabled, dies, or is replaced by the owner.

The architect is certainly in the most knowledgeable position to determine questions of the extent of the contractor's obligations under the contract; whether work performed constitutes an extra; if, when, and how much the contractor should be paid; whether the contractor is properly paying the sub-contractors, etc. If the architect's decisions relating to performance under the contract were final, disputes would be quickly resolved and the architect would have an effective and vital weapon to assist him in his function as supervisor of the project and of the contractor.

If it is considered advisable to exclude certain disputes or disagreements from the decision of the architect, and to submit them to arbitration by some other person or body, then the procedure for such arbitration should be realistic and effective. The AIA General Conditions provide for arbitration under the standard procedure of the American Institute of Architects. This is, in fact, merely an agreement to agree.

The standard arbitration procedure of the American Institute of Architects provides that the parties to a dispute "agree upon and jointly designate either a single arbitrator or three arbitrators." The procedure further provides that, "if the parties fail to agree and designate the Arbitrator or Arbitrators . . . The American Arbitration Association shall designate one or three arbitrators at its discretion, and the arbitration shall be administered by the Association." No special qualifications or standards are required for the arbitrator or the members of an arbitration tribunal.

An agreement to agree is without legal effect and is substantially meaningless. Under the AIA procedure, if there is no agreement, the entire arbitration is "dumped in the lap" of the American Arbitration Association. In this event, the standard procedure is not that of AIA, but of the American Arbitration Association.

Is the American Arbitration Association the best and most appropriate organization to determine disputes in the construction industry? Are the arbitration panels of that Association made up of qualified members for the consideration and determination of questions which are peculiar to this industry? Do any of the members of the arbitration panels of the American Arbitration Association have a leaning or bias which would favor the contractor over the owner, or vice versa? Would it not be a better procedure for the American Institute of Architects to provide arbitration panels consisting of architects from which to select the arbitrator or arbitration tribunal? These are the questions which should be considered by the profession in determining whether the standard arbitration procedure of the American Institute of Architects requires revision. If the answer to these questions is "yes," the AIA forms do require revision.

II

The General Conditions of the contract of the AIA provide that the architect shall make a decision on all claims of the owner or contractor "relating to the execution and progress of the work or the interpretation of the contract documents." It is further provided that all of the architect's decisions, except those relating to artistic effect, are subject to arbitration. Due to the fact that the courts, in construing the General Conditions of the AIA contract have held that the architect's right to make decisions in respect to disputes between owner and contractor is confined to a narrow area, a revision intended to expand the architect's function as arbitrator must be broadly written. If the architect's decisions are to be conclusive and final, any further arbitration must be excluded from the contract. The following clauses are suggested in order to accomplish these purposes:

> Any dispute, claim, or question concerning the execution of and the performance under this contract, including, but not limited to, any matters relating to quantity, quality and artistic effect, extras, and payments to the contractor or sub-contractors, shall be submitted to the Architect for arbitration and his decision shall be final, binding and conclusive.
>
> Any dispute, claim or question concerning the interpretation, construction or meaning of the contract documents, the plans or specifications, or concerning a breach of the contract, shall be submitted to the Architect for arbitration and his decision shall be final, binding and conclusive.

If the architect's role as arbitrator is expanded and his decisions made final, it is certainly of importance that a procedure be provided in the event that the architect no longer furnishes services to the project because of incapacitation, discharge, or other reason. The General Conditions do not provide for this contingency. If the architect is discharged by the owner and a new one selected, it would be manifestly unfair to permit the new architect to substitute as arbitrator, as the reason for the removal of the original architect may have been related to a dispute between owner and contractor. If, on the other hand, a new architect has been designated by his predecessor, then there is no reason why he should not have the same status. The following suggested clause is drawn to provide for these contingencies:

> In the case of the termination of the employment of the Architect, the Owner shall appoint a capable and reputable Architect, whose status under the contract shall be that of the former Architect, except that in the event of such termination, any dispute, claim, or question which is subject to the arbitration of the former Architect as heretofore provided shall be submitted for arbitration to the American Arbitration Association, pursuant to the rules of said Association then obtaining and the laws of the State of ——————. The foregoing exception, however, shall not apply to a successor of the Architect created or designated by him, or to an assignee of the Architect. Such successor or assignee shall have the same status under the contract as the named architect herein.

In the event that it is considered advisable to submit certain disputes between owner and contractor to arbitration by some person or body other than the architect, the question again must be asked: "Would it not be a better procedure for the American Institute of

Architects to provide arbitration panels consisting of architects from which to select the arbitrator or arbitration tribunal?"

As pointed out, the standard procedure of the AIA is neither realistic nor effective, as it requires the parties to a dispute to agree upon an arbitrator. Failing such agreement the arbitration is to be conducted by the American Arbitration Association. However, the arbitration panels of the American Arbitration Association contain many members who would not be particularly qualified to determine disputes arising between owner and contractor. Of perhaps more importance, they also contain attorneys and members of the construction industry who because of their background might be biased in favor of one party or the other.

The architect knows the problems of both owner and contractor. He is an expert in the field in which the dispute arises and is certainly the most competent and qualified person to determine disputes between contractor and owner. There is no reason why the American Institute of Architects cannot under its standard procedure provide an arbitration panel consisting of architects, from which the parties to a dispute are required to select the arbitrator or arbitration tribunal.

A suggested procedure is for the Institute to furnish both parties to a dispute with a list of architects from which the arbitrator must be selected. Each party would select three names from said list. If there was any agreement in the selection, the Institute would appoint that architect as the arbitrator. If no agreement, the Institute would appoint an arbitrator from the panel.

A standard arbitration procedure such as this is desirable from the viewpoint of both the owner and contractor as it would insure competent and unbiased determination of disputes. Further, from the architect's point of view it would be desirable as a factor in aiding the architect to achieve the role of leader in the construction industry, which is his appropriate status.

Government construction contracts which provide that the contracting officer's determination of any dispute between the government and the contractor shall be "final and conclusive" are valid, and such determination may apply to both questions of fact and law.

In *U.S. v. Moorman,* 338 U.S. 457, the U.S. Supreme Court decided a case of considerable importance to architects, engineers, and contractors. The precise question presented to the court was the effect of the "disputes" clause[1] found in contracts with the federal government. This clause empowers the contracting officer to decide questions arising under the contract, with a right of appeal to the head of the department *whose decision is stated as being final.* In deciding that the clause was valid and that on questions of law, as well as fact the decision of the head of the department is final, the court incidentally discussed the familiar contractual provision found in building contracts that the amount, classification, sufficiency, completion, etc., of work done under a building or construction contract by the contractor shall be determined by an architect, engineer, superintendent, or other person. The Supreme Court stated that these provisions were valid in every state (except Indiana) and held that such provisions were valid and binding.

In this case the contractor, Moorman, had entered into the usual government contract to grade a plant site. The controversy arose as to whether the contract required the contractor to grade a particular portion of the site. Moorman did the grading and then filed a claim for extra compensation. It was rejected by the government engineer. An appeal was taken to the Secretary of War whose authorized representative also considered the facts and denied the claim. This was, under the specifications, "final and binding" upon the parties.[2] Moorman then brought an action in the Court of

[1] "Disputes.—Except as otherwise specifically provided in this contract, all disputes concerning questions of fact arising under this contract shall be decided by the contracting officer subject to written appeal by the contractor within 30 days to the head of the department concerned or his duly authorized representative, whose decision shall be final and conclusive upon the parties thereto. In the meantime the contractor shall diligently proceed with the work as directed." Article 15 of the contract.

[2] "If the contractor considers any work demanded of him to be outside the requirements of the contract or if he considers any action or ruling of the contracting officer or of the inspectors to be unfair, the contractor shall without undue delay, upon such demand, action, or ruling, submit his protest thereto in writing to the contracting officer, stating clearly and in detail the basis of his objections. The contracting officer shall thereupon promptly investigate the complaint and furnish the contractor his decision, in writing thereon. If the contractor is not satisfied with the decision of the contracting officer, he may, within thirty days, appeal in writing to the Secretary of War, whose decision or that of his duly authorized representative shall be final and binding upon the parties to the contract. . . ." Paragraph 2-16 of the specifications.

Claims contending that he had a right to challenge the findings of the Secretary of War as "questions of law" because one of the provisions of the contract stated that determinations on "questions of fact" were final and conclusive on the parties. The Court of Claims considered the facts, made new findings, overturned the Administration decision and entered a money judgment for Moorman. The U.S. Supreme Court reversed the Court of Claims and held:

> First. Contractual provisions such as these have long been used by the Government. No Congressional enactment condemns their creation or enforcement . . . In upholding the conclusions of the engineer the Court emphasized the duty of trial courts to recognize the right of parties to make and rely on such mutual agreements. Findings of such a contractually designated agent, even where employed by one of the parties, were held "conclusive, unless impeached on the ground of fraud, or such gross mistake as necessarily implied bad faith."
>
> The holdings of the foregoing cases have never been departed from by this Court. They stand for the principle that parties competent to make contracts are also competent to make such agreements.

The court then went on to discuss a case involving a contract provision that "the decision of the Supervising Architect as to the proper interpretation of the drawings and specifications shall be final." About such a provision the court said:

> Similar agreements have been held enforceable in almost every state. See cases collected in Note, 54 A.L.R. 1255, et seq. In one state, Indiana, the courts do seem to hold differently, on the ground that permitting engineers or other persons to make final determinations of contractual disputes would wrongfully deprive the parties of a right to have their controversies decided in the courts. See cases collected in Note, 54 A.L.R. 1270-1271. In the McShain case we rejected a contention that this Court should adopt a rule like Indiana's and we reject it now. It is true that the intention of parties to submit their contractual disputes to final determination outside the courts should be made manifest by plain language. Mercantile Trust Co. v. Hensey, 205 U.S. 298, 309. But this does not mean that hostility to such provisions can justify blindness to a plain intent of parties to adopt this method for settlement of their disputes. Nor should such an agreement of parties be frustrated by judicial "interpretation" of contracts. If parties competent to decide for themselves are to be deprived of the privilege of making such

anticipatory provisions for settlement of disputes, this deprivation should come from the legislative branch of government.

The Supreme Court then determined that the contract did show an intent to authorize final determinations by the Secretary of War and stated that his determination was final, whether it was one of fact or of law. In conclusion the court stated:

> The oft-repeated conclusion of the Court of Claims that questions of "interpretation" are not questions of fact is ample reason why the parties to the contract should provide for final determination of such disputes by a method wholly separate from the fact-limited provisions of Sec. 15. To hold that the parties did not so "intend" would be a distortion of the interpretative process. The language of Sec. 2-16 is clear. No ambiguities can be injected into it by supportable reasoning. It states in language as plain as draftsmen could use that findings of the Secretary of War in disputes of the type here involved shall be "final and binding." In reconsidering the questions decided by the designated agent of the parties, the Court of Claims was in error. Its judgment cannot stand.

The importance of this case justifies the extensive quotations taken from the body of the opinion. The impact that it will have on prospective contracts with the government cannot be overemphasized. In the future the Court of Claims will, in this type of situation, as a practical matter, be deprived of jurisdiction, unless the form of contract is changed to deny the power of determining questions of law to the contracting officer. In the absence of considerable pressure placed on the government it is doubtful whether this result can be accomplished. The problem should be squarely faced by those directly concerned and an appropriate course of conduct determined on.

No further discussion is necessary with respect to that portion of the decision which holds that contractual provisions relating to the finality of an architect's or engineer's certificate or decision are valid, if the language is plain in the contract and if no fraud, bad faith or dishonest judgment is present. These clauses now can therefore be properly said to have been sustained by the state courts everywhere (except in Indiana) and by the Supreme Court of the United States.

II

A clause makes the "contracting officer's" decision in a government construction contract "final and conclusive." His decision is found by the Court of Claims to have been "arbitrary," "capricious," and "grossly erroneous."

Question: Would the United States Supreme Court permit such a decision to stand?

Answer: Yes! By a vote of six to three (with blistering language in the minority opinions), the United States Supreme Court in *United States v. Wunderlich,* 342 U.S. 98, refused to void an "arbitrary," "capricious," and "grossly erroneous" determination by a government official acting under a "final and conclusive" clause.

In essence, the Court found that only fraud, alleged and proved, would permit such a determination to be set aside; and, the Court stated, "By fraud we mean conscious wrongdoing, and intention to cheat or be dishonest." The implications of this decision are important, not only for the entire building industry but also for that increasingly large number of industrial plants which depend more and more on government contracts.

What does this decision mean for the architect, engineer, the contractor, and other professionals and the businesses affiliated with the building industry? Some answers are apparent and will be discussed here. First, a discussion of the case itself is necessary.

The facts in issue were as follows: A controversy arose between the contractor and the government, due to a change order authorized by the terms of a standard-form government construction contract. The dispute related to the amount of equitable adjustment allowable because of the change order. The contractor was dissatisfied with the resolution of the dispute by the Secretary of Interior, and brought action in the Court of Claims. Both parties agreed that the question decided by the department head was a question of fact. The Government contended that the decision of the Secretary of the Interior was final under Article 15, the Disputes clause of the contract. This clause reads as follows:

> Except as otherwise specifically provided in this contract, all disputes concerning questions of fact arising under this contract shall be decided by the contracting officer subject to written appeal by the contractor within 30 days to the head of the department concerned or his duly authorized representative, whose decision shall be final and conclusive upon the parties thereto.

The Court of Claims reviewed the contentions of the parties and set aside the decision of the department head on the ground that his decision was "arbitrary," "capricious," and "grossly erroneous." The Government appealed to the United States Supreme Court on the ground that even though the decision of the Secretary of the Interior was "arbitrary," "capricious," and "grossly erroneous," it was not fraudulent and was therefore "final and conclusive" under Article 15, and not reviewable by the courts.

Some of the questions and remarks made before the court during oral argument, brought into focus the divergent views of the judges. Mr. Justice Jackson pointedly asked:

> Can you call it arbitration when a man decides his own case?
>
> Where does the department head get his memoranda telling him what it is all about? We are not always neutral in our own affairs.
>
> The Court of Claims feels that this power is being abused and they see a lot of these things. We have either got to say a government contractor is at the mercy of the department or that the Court can decide these questions.

Counsel for the Government parried these questions by arguing that although the department head, like a Supreme Court judge, was a government employee, he had no financial interest in the outcome of the issue. The Moorman case (338 U.S. 924) was quoted as the authority for upholding the validity of the disputes clause.

Mr. Justice Black asked: "Where did they (the Court of Claims) find bad faith?"

The government counsel in answer stated that there was no finding of bad faith, except by inference, since the only findings were those of "arbitrary" and "capricious" conduct.

Mr. Justice Minton remarked to the attorney for the contractor: "You never made a request for a finding of bad faith and fraudulent conduct?"

The attorney answered that he had only made a request for a finding of "arbitrary" and "capricious" conduct implying bad faith.

Mr. Justice Black then stated: "That is going some, to find bad faith from gross negligence."

The above questions and answers show the divergence of opinions of the members of our highest court. The decision further emphasized this split. Mr. Justice Minton delivered the majority opinion, with which five justice concurred. Justices Douglas, Jackson, and Black dissented. Because of its great importance to those engaged in the building industry (and to those contracting with the government), the majority and minority opinions are here set out in full:

THE MAJORITY DECISION

"This Court is again called upon to determine the meaning of the 'finality clause' of a standard form of government contract. Respondents agreed to build a dam for the United States under a contract containing the usual 'Article 15.' That article provides that all disputes involving questions of fact shall be decided by the contracting officer, with the right of appeal to the head of the department 'whose decision shall be final and conclusive upon the parties thereto.' Dissatisfied with the resolution of various disputes by the department head, in this instance the Secretary of the Interior, respondents brought suit in the Court of Claims. That court reviewed their contentions, and in the one claim involved in this proceeding set aside the decision of the department head. 117 Ct. Cl. 92. Although there was some dispute below, the parties now agree that the question decided by the department head was a question of fact. We granted certiorari, 341 U.S. 924, to clarify the rule of this Court which created an exception to the conclusiveness of such administrative decision.

"The same Article 15 of a government contract was before this Court recently, and we held, after a review of the authorities, that such Article was valid. *Moorman v. United States,* 338 U.S. 457. Nor was the *Moorman* case one of first impression. Contracts, both governmental and private, have been before this Court in several cases in which provisions equivalent to Article 15 have been approved and enforced 'in the absence of fraud or such gross mistake as would necessarily imply bad faith, or a failure to exercise an honest judgment.' *Kihlberg v. United States,* 97 U.S. 398, 402; *Sweeney v. United States,* 109 U.S. 618, 620; *Martinsburg & P.R. Co. v. March,* 114 U.S. 549, 553; *Chicago, S F. & C. R. Co. v. Price,* 138 U.S. 185, 195.

"In *Ripley v. United States,* 223 U.S. 695, 704, gross mistake implying bad faith is equated to 'fraud.' Despite the fact that other words such as 'negligence,' 'incompetence,' 'capriciousness,' and 'arbitrary' have been used in the course of the opinions, this Court has consistently upheld the finality of the department head's decision unless it was founded on fraud, alleged and proved. So fraud is in essence the exception. By fraud we mean conscious wrongdoing, an intention to cheat or be dishonest. The decision of the department head, absent fraudulent conduct, must stand under the plain meaning of the contract.

"If the conclusiveness of the findings under Article 15 is to be set aside for fraud, fraud should be alleged and proved, as it is never presumed. *United States v. Colorado Anthracite Co.,* 225 U.S. 219, 226. In the case at bar, there was no allegation of fraud. There was no finding of fraud nor request for such a finding. The finding of the Court of Claims was that the decision of the department head was 'arbitrary,' 'capricious,' and 'grossly erroneous.' But these words are not the equivalent of fraud, the exception which this court has heretofore laid down and to which it now adheres without qualification.

"Respondents were not compelled or coerced into making the contract. It was a voluntary undertaking on their part. As competent parties they have contracted for the settlement of disputes in an arbitral manner. This, we have said in *Moorman,* Congress has left them free to do. *Moorman v. United States, supra,* at 462. The limitation upon this arbitral process is fraud, placed there by this Court. If the standard of fraud that we adhere to is too limited, that is a matter for Congress.

"Since there was no pleading of fraud, and no finding of fraud, and no request for such a finding, we are not disposed to remand the case for any further findings, as respondents urge. We assume that if the evidence had been sufficient to constitute fraud, the Court of Claims would have found. In the absence of such finding, the decision of the department head must stand as conclusive, and the judgment is reversed."

THE DISSENTING OPINIONS

Although the majority opinion of the Supreme Court of the United States becomes the law of the land, the two dissenting opinions are important because they enunciate with great force and vigor the arguments that could point to the need for legislative action.

Mr. Justice Douglas, with whom Mr. Justice Reed concurred, stated as follows:

"Law has reached its finest moments when it has freed man from the unlimited discretion of some ruler, some civil or military official, some bureaucrat. Where discretion is absolute, man has always suffered. At times it has been his property that has been invaded; at times, his privacy; at times, his liberty of movement;

at times, his freedom of thought; at times, his life. Absolute discretion is a ruthless master. It is more destructive of freedom than any of man's other inventions.

"The instant case reveals only a minor facet of the age-long struggle. The result reached by the Court can be rationalized or made plausible by casting it in terms of contract law; the parties need not have made this contract; those who contract with the Government must turn square corners; the parties will be left where their engagement brought them. And it may be that in this case the equities are with the Government, not with the contractor. But the rule we announce has wide application and a devastating effect. It makes a tyrant out of every contracting officer. He is granted the power of a tyrant even though he is stubborn, perverse, or captious. He is allowed the power of a tyrant even though he is incompetent or negligent. He has the power of life and death over a private business even though his decision is grossly erroneous. Power granted is seldom neglected.

"The principle of checks and balances is a healthy one. An official who is accountable will act more prudently. A citizen who has an appeal to a body independent of the controversy has protection against passion, obstinacy, irrational conduct, and incompetency of an official. The opinion by Judge Madden in this case expresses a revulsion to allowing one man an uncontrolled discretion over another's fiscal affairs. We should allow the Court of Claims, the agency close to these disputes, to reverse an official whose conduct is plainly out of bounds whether he is fraudulent, perverse, captious, incompetent, or just palpably wrong. The rule we announce makes government oppressive. The rule the Court of Claims espouses gives a citizen justice even against his government."

Mr. Justice Jackson, in a separate dissent, stated as follows:

"It is apparent that the Court of Claims, which deals with many such cases while we deal with a few, has reached a conclusion that contracting officers and heads of departments sometimes are abusing the power of deciding their own law suits, which these contract provisions give to them. It also is apparent that the Court of Claims does not believe that our decision in *United States v. Moorman,* 338 U.S. 457, completely closed the door to judicial relief from arbitrary action unless it also is fraudulent in the sense of 'conscious wrongdoing, an intention to cheat or be dishonest.' Nor could I have believed it.

"Granted that these contracts are legal, it should not follow that one who takes a public contract puts himself wholly in the power of contracting officers and department heads. When we recently repeated in *Moorman* that their decisions were 'conclusive, unless impeached on the ground of fraud, or *such gross mistake as necessarily implied bad faith,'* id., at 461 (emphasis supplied), I supposed that we meant that part of the reservation for which I have supplied emphasis. Today's decision seems not only to read that out of the Moorman decision, but also to add an exceedingly rigid meaning to the word 'fraud.'

"Undoubtedly contracting parties can agree to put decision of their disputes in the hands of one of them. But one who undertakes to act as a judge in his own case or, what amounts to the same thing, in the case of his own department, should be under some fiduciary obligation to the position which he assumes. He is not at liberty to make arbitrary or reckless use of his power, nor to disregard evidence, nor to shield his department from consequences of its own blunders, at the expense of contractors. He is somewhat in the position of the lawyer dealing with his client or the doctor with his patient, for the superiority of his position imposes restraints appropriate to the trust. Though the contractor may have covenanted to be satisfied with what his adversary renders to him, it must be true that he who bargains to be made judge of his own cause assumes an implied obligation to do justice. This does not mean that every petty disagreement should be readjudged, but that the courts should hold the administrative officers to the old but vanishing standard of good faith and care.

"I think that we should adhere to the rule that where the decision of the contracting officer or department head shows 'such gross mistake as necessarily to imply bad faith' there is a judicial remedy even if it has its origin in overzeal for the department, negligence of the deciding official, misrepresentations—however innocent—by subordinates, prejudice against the contractor, or other causes that fall short of actual corruption. Men are more often bribed by their loyalties and ambitions than by money. I still believe one should be allowed to have a judicial hearing before his business can be destroyed by administrative action, although the Court again thinks otherwise. Cf. *Ewing v. Mytinger,* 339 U.S. 594, 604."

What should the architect or engineer do about the *Wunderlich* case? It must be remembered that in *United States v. Moorman*, decided in 1950, the United States Supreme Court held that the arbiter's decision under a "final and conclusive" clause was determinative on questions involving the *interpretation* of the contract. (It is interesting to note, however, that if the architect or engineer draws or agrees to draw contracts for others, he has been held to be doing an illegal act, which may so taint the relationship with his client that he may lose his right to all compensation, as noted in the discussion of the Michigan *Sheill* case. The paradoxical conclusion seems to be that it is proper for him to act as judge—even on matters of law—but not as lawyer.) The case here discussed holds that his determination on questions of fact can be attacked only for actual fraud. Since the reasoning of the Court does not distinguish between government and private contracts, the architect, engineer, and the owner whom they represent should therefore carefully consider whether a similar clause should be inserted in each construction contract in which they are interested.

The "Architect's Decision" clauses most widely used are of course those contained in the AIA forms, each of which provides that the architect, in the first instance, is required to make decisions, but that all such decisions, except in matters relating to artistic effect, are subject to review by impartial arbitrators.

The General Conditions of the AIA standard form construction contract provides as follows:

> Art. 39. Architect's Decisions—The Architect shall, within a reasonable time, make decisions on all claims of the Owners or Contractor and on all other matters relating to the execution and progress of the work or the interpretation of the Contract Documents.
>
> The Architect's decisions, in matters relating to artistic effect, shall be final, if within the terms of the Contract Documents.
>
> Except as above or otherwise expressly provided in the Contract Documents, all the Architect's decisions are subject to arbitration.
>
> If, however, the Architect fails to render a decision within ten days after the parties have presented their evidence, either party may then demand arbitration. If the Architect renders a decision after arbitration proceedings have been initiated, such decision may be entered as evidence but shall not disturb or interrupt such proceedings except where such decision is acceptable to the parties concerned.

Art 40. Arbitration—All disputes, claims or questions subject to arbitration under this contract shall be submitted to arbitration in accordance with the provisions, then obtaining, of the Standard Form of Arbitration Procedure of The American Institute of Architects . . .

The AIA short form provides as follows:

Article 18. The Architect's Status—The Architect shall have general supervision of the work. He has authority to stop the work if necessary to insure its proper execution. He shall certify to the Owner when payments under the contract are due and the amounts to be paid. He shall make decisions on all claims of the Owner or Contractor. All his decisions are subject to arbitration.

Article 19. Arbitration—Any disagreement arising out of this contract or from the breach thereof, shall be submitted to arbitration and this agreement shall be specifically enforceable under the prevailing arbitration law, and judgment upon the award rendered may be entered in the highest court of the forum, state or federal, having jurisdiction. It is mutually agreed that the decision of the arbitrators shall be a condition precedent to any right of legal action that either party may have against the other.

The parties may agree upon one arbitrator; otherwise there shall be three, one named in writing by each party of this contract within five days after notice of arbitration is served by either party upon the other, and a third arbitrator selected by these two abritrators within five days thereafter. No one shall serve as an arbitrator who is in any way financially interested in this contract or in the affairs of either party thereto.

At the written request of either party, at any time prior to the complete appointment of arbitrators, as provided above, or in the event of any default or lapse in the proceeding, the arbitration shall be held under the Standard Form of Arbitration Procedure of The American Institute of Architects or of the Rules of the American Arbitration Association.

Certainly the holding of the *Wunderlich* case should be called to the attention of the owner, who should be given the opportunity of determining whether he should urge that the AIA clause be used or a clause making the architect's or engineer's decision "final and conclusive."

For the contractor, the "final and conclusive" clause now has grave implications. An "arbitrary," "capricious," or "grossly erroneous," architect's (or engineer's or other arbiter's) decision has expressly been held by the highest court of the land to be binding. From such a decision under these circumstances no appeal lies to any judicial or quasi-judicial body. On any substantial project the consequences could easily be financially ruinous ("power of life and death over a private business" and "his business can be destroyed by administrative action" are the phrases used by the Supreme Court). These may be the consequences, whether or not the contract is with the Government. This much is certain, that as the situation now exists in *all* federal government contracts the peril is present, because the "final and conclusive" clause is incorporated. It or a similar clause may be found in private, municipal, or state contracts. The ensuing risk should be carefully considered prior to embarking on a project where the clause will govern disputes between the parties.

In a contract between a private owner and contractor which provides that the architect shall be the final arbiter of any dispute, an ethical problem is presented. It is whether the architect, by the nature of his services, is so identified with the owner that, in fact, the owner is the judge of any dispute which arises between him and the contractor. From the contractor's point of view, a final and conclusive arbitration by the architect may make him subject to arbitrary or capricious decisions, or decisions not supported by substantial evidence.

However, where the contract between private owner and contractor provides for the final arbitration by the architect, the ethical considerations involved differ from the situation in which the contract between the government and the contractor provides that the government contracting officer shall be the final arbiter. In the first instance, the bargaining position of the contractor and private owner is on a much more equal basis than the respective bargaining positions of a contractor and the government. Consequently, if the contractor does not have confidence in the architect as a final arbiter, he is in a position to resist the inclusion of such a final arbitration clause in the contract. Further, the architect, in his capacity as arbiter, acts as a trustee and does not have the same identification with the owner that a government contracting officer has with the government.

The individual architect, in advising the owner in respect to the contract with a contractor, should present the question to the owner of whether it is desirous that the architect be made the final and conclusive arbiter of any dispute which may arise. The profession, however, should consider the ethical implications arising from the role of the architect as the final and conclusive arbitrator.

The validity of a contract between owner and contractor which stipulates that the decision of the architect with respect to all disputes shall be final and binding has been generally upheld. There is authority that has ruled that such provision is valid even if applied to a dispute involving the interpretation of the architect's plans and specifications.

The architect often assumes the role of umpire between owner, contractor and subcontractor. In undertaking to supervise construction of a project, he frequently determines questions and disputes relating to the performance of the building contract. The decision of the architect, however, may be challenged by the party who feels aggrieved, and the binding and conclusive nature of his decision will depend primarily upon the contract entered into between the parties to the dispute.

The rule has been well established by the courts that any stipulation in a building contract whereby the parties appoint an architect or engineer as the final arbiter between themselves, as to a matter connected with the performance of the contract, makes his decision conclusive on that matter. Despite this well-settled rule, courts are frequently called upon to determine whether, in a given case, the parties *did* intend to confer on the architect or engineer the authority to make a final decision.

Where the owner and contractor desire to make the architect's decision in respect to performance under the building contract binding upon them, it is important that their contract clearly authorize the architect to make such binding decisions. If the contract clearly furnishes such authority, the architect's decision cannot be attacked upon the merits, but can only be challenged upon such grounds as fraud, bad faith, or gross neglect. As an impartial arbiter authorized to make binding decisions, an architect is bound to act honestly and to exercise reasonable care. If he does so, his determination is conclusive on both parties and is not subject to review by the courts.

A case in the United States Court of Appeals (*Dyker Building Co. v. U.S.*, 182 F. 2d 85) clearly illustrates some of the factors which will defeat the conclusiveness of the decisions of an architect or engineer. In that case, a contract had been entered into between a contractor and a subcontractor, which contained the following provision:

> All quantities shall be computed by a disinterested, qualified professional engineer as may be mutually designated by both parties hereto, from data indicated on the contract drawings as prepared by the Alley Dwelling Authority.

Pursuant to this stipulation, an engineer was designated by the subcontractor to make certain computations, including a computation of borrow fill. The subcontractor took the position that a computation of the engineer was binding upon the contractor, but the court rejected this contention.

In its decision in the *Dyker* case, the United States Court of Appeals based its determination upon various grounds. The court found that the contract did not specifically provide that the engineer's computations were to be final. It further pointed out that the contractor had contended on the trial of the action that the engineer in question had not been "mutually designated," nor had his designation by the subcontractor as arbiter been accepted by the contractor. Lastly the court held that the computation relied upon by the subcontractor was not the engineer's final computation and that he had not intended it to be final.

When parties enter into a written agreement, all of their prior negotiations are merged into the written contract, which stands as the final expression of their intent. It is important, therefore, that in drawing a written contract the parties leave little to inference or conjecture. If it is their intention to select an arbiter who is an expert in the field, and by whose decision they are willing to abide, they should explicitly state such intention. The courts will not *imply* an agreement making the architect's decision binding. Thus, for example, in the *Dyker* case the trial court found that the engineer was merely regarded by the parties as an informed expert, and that since the contract did not expressly authorize him to make final determinations, the court would not imply such authority.

Generally the question of whether an architect has been mutually designated by the parties to a contract to act as arbiter, or has been accepted by the parties to a contract for that purpose, does not arise. In most instances, the designation of the architect to act as arbiter is set forth in the building contract. The fact that the architect is ordinarily employed by the owner does not disqualify him from acting in such capacity. In supervising construction of the project the architect acts on behalf of and as agent for the owner. As the arbiter charged with the task of determining disputes or specified questions relating to the contract, he acts for and binds both parties. Therefore, in acting in such dual capacity, both parties to the contract are entitled to his honest judgment and he must act impartially and in good faith in performing these duties.

The problem, however, of designating or accepting an arbiter may arise on the death, discharge, resignation, or other inability of the architect originally selected. The decisions of a substituted architect can only be binding if his mediation is accepted by both parties. The parties, therefore, in entering into a building contract, should consider whether it is advisable to insert a clause providing the means and method for replacement of the original designated architect.

The principle underlying the rule that an architect may not delegate his authority to make decisions binding upon the owner and contractor is that this authority is considered to be personal in nature. A specific obligation is imposed upon him to make his own decisions based upon his personal observation, investigation, and experience. Any attempt to delegate these responsibilities may be successfully resisted by the party who feels such delegation has prejudiced him.

Further, a decision by an arbitrator, to be binding, must be intended by him to be final. In the *Dyker* case, the computation of the engineer relied upon by the subcontractor was not in fact the engineer's final computation. The evidence disclosed that the engineer made various subsequent revisions due to mistakes and changes in methods of computing quantities.

Parties to a building contract often submit to the architect questions of account, measurement, or distance and this is proper even though these questions may be capable of mathematical ascertaining. The architect's determination is not necessarily predicated on the development of an actual controversy, but his computations, if final in nature, will be conclusive.

Architects authorized to issue certificates of performance or approve work that has been done cannot, after such issuance or approval, modify or revoke their decisions. The same principle would seem to apply to other decisions of an architect, made in his capacity as an arbiter of disputes arising under the building contract. However, if the architect's determination is not intended by him to be final, then he may amend or modify it.

To sum up—the decision of an architect on any matter as to performance which the parties have stipulated to submit to him is final when:

(1) The contract clearly provides that the architect's decision will be final and conclusive.

(2) Both parties to the contract agree upon a designated architect as arbiter, either in specific terms, or impliedly by their conduct.

(3) The architect acts honestly, in good faith, and with reasonable care in rendering his decision.

(4) The architect makes a decision which he intends to be final.

II

The New York Court of Appeals, the highest court of New York, has ruled in the case of *Board of Education of Union Free School, District No. 1 v. Barbaresi & Son, Inc.,* (4 N.Y. 2d 812) that a construction contract which provides for the final determination of all disputes between owner and contractor to be made by the architect is valid even though the dispute involves the construction and interpretation of the architect's own plans and specifications.

The dispute between the owner and the contractor concerned the installation of a certain type of ceiling in the auditorium of a school under construction. The general contractor contended that the installation was not his responsibility but was that of the electrical contractor and demanded arbitration of this issue under Article 39 of the General Conditions. The architect, however, ruled that his plans and specifications required installation of the ceiling by the general contractor, and the owner refused arbitration of the question under an express provision of the contract which stated that the architect shall "determine whether the . . . plans and specifications had been fully complied with by the contractor." The contract further provided that such determination "shall be final and binding upon the parties hereto."

The ruling that a construction contract may validly provide for the conclusive determination of all disputes between owner and contractor by the architect stems historically from a decision by the United States Supreme Court (*U.S.* v. *Moorman,* 328 U.S. 457). In that case, a contract between the United States Government and a contractor provided that the government's contracting officer was empowered to decide all questions of law and fact which might arise under the contract with a right to appeal to the head of the department, whose decision would be final and conclusive.

Following this rather harsh and sweeping decision, some courts attempted to soften its effect by construing the "Disputes Clause" contained in the government contract as excluding, for example, disputes which did not arise during the progress of the work or by finding that the contracting officer had not acted with impartiality or good faith. However, the effect of the *Moorman* decision was to place the federal government in a controlling position insofar as disputes between it and parties contracting with it were concerned.

Following the *Moorman* decision, the United States Supreme Court was called upon to determine the validity of a decision of a government contracting officer under a construction contract which provided that his decision would be "final and conclusive." This decision had been found by the Court of Claims to have been "arbitrary," "capricious," and "grossly erroneous." Despite the finding of the Court of Claims, the United States Supreme Court upheld the contracting officer's decision, ruling that such a determination could be set aside only on the ground of proved fraud (*United States* v. *Wunderlich,* 342 U.S. 98).

In discussing the *Wunderlich* case, we pointed out that the reasoning of the court did not distinguish between government and private contracts and one of the apparent conclusions that could be drawn is that an architect could validly and legally act as sole and conclusive arbiter of disputes arising in construction contracts between private individuals and contractors.

Congress, in 1954, adopted Public Law 356 which was directed at the "Disputes Clause" contained in Government contracts. This law was directed at the harsh result in the *Moorman* and *Wunderlich* cases. The statute provided in substance that no government contract should contain a provision making the decision of a goverment official final on a question of law and further provided that the decision of a contracting officer in respect to a question of fact shall not be final and conclusive if the same is fraudulent, capricious, arbitrary, so grossly erroneous as necessarily to imply bad faith, or is not supported by substantial evidence.

We have already pointed out that Public Law 356 did not apply to a contract between a private individual and a contractor which provided for a conclusive determination of disputes by the architect.

It has been suggested that there are many advantages implicit in increasing the role of the architect as an arbiter of disputes between an owner and contractor. An architect is certainly in a knowledgeable position and is qualified and competent to determine such disputes and his decisions can be speedily made and can be an effective tool in respect to the supervision of the project and of a contractor.

From the viewpoint of the architectural profession as whole, we have urged that it establish its leadership in the construction field by increasing its role wherever possible. As pointed out, the influence of the architect in respect to the preparation of the construction contract between the owner and the contractor affords an opportunity to this end. If the architect's role as the sole arbiter of disputes between the owner and the contractor is generally recognized and accepted, it would be an impressive step toward the establishment of the architect as the natural leader of the construction industry.

The legal validity of the role of the architect as the sole arbiter of disputes between the owner and the contractor, even where the dispute involves an interpretation of the architect's own plans and specifications, has been upheld. If there are ethical factors which require a limitation of the architect's role as sole arbiter of all such disputes then the profession should consider what limitation, if any should be placed upon this function.

The courts have given the "legal go-ahead" for the expansion of the architect's role as arbiter and it may be in the interests of the profession to take advantage of this fact—with due consideration to ethical problems involved.

MISCELLANEOUS DECISIONS

AGREEMENTS WITH OWNER

UNITED STATES. *Bush Building Co.* v. *City of Barbourville,* 155 F. Supp. 394 (D.C. Kentucky 1957). Although a contract for the construction of sewer lines in a city provided that an engineering firm was to decide every question relative to the fulfillment of the contract on the part of the contractor, in an action by the contractor against the city for an amount due under the contract, it was held that where the certificates issued by the engineers with reference to the completion of the job were made in violation of a contract provision requiring the engineer's decision to be fair and impartial, and were the results of such gross mistakes as to imply bad faith, the said certificates were not binding upon the city, and the city was justified in both refusing to accept the work as completed, and to pay the final estimates as submitted.

Davies v. *Kahn et al*, 251 F. 2d 324 (C.A. 4th-1958). In an action by a subcontractor instituted against the prime contractor for damages as a result of an allegedly illegal cancellation of the subcontract, the prime contractor defended on the grounds that the architect had not approved the subcontractor. The court held that in the absence of an express provision in the building contract requiring the architect's approval of the subcontractor, such requirement would not be implied. The court further ruled, in rejecting the prime contractor's contention that the architect had not approved the subcontractor's product, that the materials called for by the specifications were intended to be ordered by description and not by brand and that the architect's approval is only necessary when specifications call for a designated product "or approved equal." In the instant case, the goods of the subcontractor were offered not as a substitute, for a designated brand, but as compliance with the detailed description.

CALIFORNIA. *Crane* v. *City of Ukiah et al.* 110 Cal. App. 2d 640, 243 P.2d 582 (1952). The plaintiff general contractor agreed to construct a reservoir for the city within a fixed period of time and the individual defendant and the city entered into a contract whereby he was employed as consulting engineer to provide all necessary engineering services in connection with the construction of the reservoir. The general contractor, subsequently in consideration for an extension of time permit, agreed that the city should have the right to charge him for all or any part of the engineering and other charges accruing during the period of extension. The Court held that the defendant engineer was not such a third party beneficiary so as to entitle him to enforce an agreement between the city and plaintiff. The plaintiff therefore was permitted to recover from the city the amount of engineering charges deducted from the sum due plaintiff under the contract.

Stein v. *Drake,* 254 P. 2d 613 (1953). A clause in a building contract which provided that "all questions as to the rights and obligations of the parties arising under the terms of the contract, the plans and specifications are subject to arbitration" was held to be sufficiently enforceable and was irrevocable to the extent defined under the California statute. However, the Court reversed the decision of a lower Court, confirming the arbitrator's award, on the ground that it invaded the defendant's right first to have determined by a Court that a valid and enforceable contract existed.

Pancoast v. *Russel,* 307 P. 2d 719 (1957). Where contract between owner and architect provides for general supervision the court ruled in an action by the owner for breach of contract, that superficial supervision in connection with the inspection and approval of the contractor's work does not satisfy the architect's obligations under the contract, since it was his duty to secure workmanlike adherence to the building contract, and adequate performance on the part of the contractor.

KENTUCKY. *Ingram* v. *State Property and Building Commission,* 309 S.W. 2d 169 (1957). Where a contract between architect and owner specified the maximum fee to be received for all services, and the architect agreed to make changes and additions as might be requested, and further to provide all professional architectural, engineering and supervisory services required for the completion of the building, in a suit by the architect to recover compensation for alleged extras, it was held that the contract was clear and unambiguous, and that the alleged extras were within the scope of the contract, and were thus not compensable.

NEW YORK. *Brown et al.* v. *Mount Vernon Housing,* 279 App. Div. 794, 109 N.Y.S. 2d 392 (1952). The Appellate Division found that the housing authority could not be held liable for services rendered by the plaintiff where the resolutions of the authority specifically conditioned employment of architects upon approval of State Division of Housing, and such approval had not been obtained. Plaintiff architect agreed to submit to the defendant the preliminary plans for construction of dwelling units upon sites selected by the housing authority, and the services of plaintiff were accepted by defendant who refused to prepare formal contracts for submission to the State Division of Housing.

WASHINGTON. *Batcheller et al.* v. *Town of Westport,* 235 P. 2d 471 (1951). A consulting engineer sued a municipality to recover for engineering services rendered upon a contract of employment. Under a statute requiring the passage of municipal ordinance containing a plan or system for construction of a water system and the estimate of cost and method of payment; where such ordinance is passed on the advice of an architect or engineer, specifying the amount of funds to be made available for the payment of the project, the court declared that it becomes a part of the contract of employment and thus fixes the limits within which an architect or engineer must perform. The municipality was under no obligation to change the plan or system ordinance to comply with the shortcomings in his performance. While the plaintiffs failed to perform their contract, they did perform valuable services and the municipality may not retain such services without payment of reasonable compensation.

PART FOUR: *Rights and Liabilities of Architects, Engineers and Contractors*

Perhaps the most important right of an architect, engineer or contractor is the right to compensation. This right is based upon relatively well established and settled legal principles. The architect, engineer or contractor who seeks to recover his compensation for services rendered must establish a valid contract of employment, or a promise, either express or implied, to pay for his services, and substantial performance of that contract. If the contract is with a municipality or other public body, its validity may be measured by the statutory requirements governing public contracts. In general, however, the rules applying to the right to compensation are well defined.

There are other rights, however, some of which are subsidiary to the right to compensation, in connection with which the law is not uniformly established or is still evolving. Is an architect entitled to a lien on the real property of an owner who has not paid him for his plans and specifications if the project was never constructed? Does an architect have a property right in his plans after he has been paid for his services by the owner? May a critic defame the reputation or work of an architect or engineer without legal consequence? These questions and others similar in nature are subject to varying answers because of differing judicial opinion or divergent statutory enactment, and are sometimes dependent upon the provisions of the contract of employment. Since the right of the architect, engineer or contractor in relation to many facets of his practice are not clearly or adequately defined, a consideration of the legal conflicts in such areas is of special importance.

The area of potential liability of the architect, engineer or contractor is relatively great. Each has a direct responsibility to the client to perform with due care; but peculiar to these professions and businesses the result of their performance—the building project —is utilized by the public at large, by third parties. Consequently, negligent performance by the planner or the builder can cause injury or damage to third persons with whom they have no direct legal relationship.

Every contract made by an architect, engineer, or contractor impliedly contains the provision that he possesses sufficient knowledge, skill and ability to perform the services called for by the contract with reasonable competence and without negligence. Plans and specifications which result in inadequate supervision, delay, underestimation of cost, or the construction of a defective building, all subject the architect or engineer to liability for loss or extra expense occasioned the owner. Unworkmanlike methods, inferior materials, deviation from the architect's plans and specifications, and delay in construction, all subject the contractor to liability for loss or extra expense caused the owner thereby.

Liability, however, of the architect, engineer or contractor to third parties arising from injury caused by hazardous conditions resulting either from improper plans or improper construction may depend upon such factors as whether the building was accepted by the owner, whether the defects were latent or apparent, and whether the contractor had, or should have had knowledge of any inadequacies in the architect's or engineer's plans and specifications. The importance of these and other factors varies, dependent upon the jurisdiction involved, since the legal principles applicable in determining liability, as in the case of rights, are not uniformly established or defined. Recent developments in the law indicate a tendency to increase the area of the architect's and engineer's responsibility.

CHAPTER 15: *Property Right of Architect or Engineer in His Plans*

An architect or engineer has a common law copyright in plans and designs he has drawn, whereby he is entitled to the exclusive possession and use of his work until he publishes it. In the absence of a contract provision to the contrary, a client is entitled to plans and specifications which he has accepted and paid for. Registration of a plan or design by an architect or engineer in accordance with the terms of the Copyright Act protects him against infringement of his work even after it has been published.

To what extent does an architect have an exclusive right in the use of plans he has drawn, in the reproduction of these plans, or in the reproduction of a building originally constructed according to plans designed by him?

Can an architect, after preparing plans for and supervising the construction of a building and after having been paid for the work, prevent the owner from using these plans in the construction of other buildings?

Does he have any rights against third persons who reproduce in almost identical detail a building like one he has designed for a client?

Here we do not discuss the ethics of the situations involved, but will confine ourselves to the legal issues raised.

Two examples illustrate the type of situation which may arise. In one case an architect had drawn plans and specifications and supervised the construction of a unique residence for a client. Some months later he discovered that a house, copying in every respect the one he had designed, had been built in an adjoining state. On inquiry, he learned that the probabilities were that the contractor who had been employed to erect the building for which he had prepared plans had been requested by another person to construct a building like the original one; and the contractor, complying with this request, had constructed the second residence in exact conformity with the plans prepared for the first building.

Now for the second case: A hospital architect was associated with a consultant in preparing plans for a proposed hospital building. The working drawings were completed and the consultant received a complete set of plans. The hospital project then contemplated did not proceed, but the plans were submitted by the consultant to another architect who used them for another hospital in a different locality.

We will first consider the rights to ownership and use of plans as between owner and architect. Generally, the rights to the plans prepared by an architect for his client are provided for in the contract between the parties. The standard form of contract adopted by the AIA contains the following provision on this point: "Drawings and specifications, as instruments of service, are the property of the architect whether the work for which they are made be erected or not."

Under this stipulation the plans and specifications remain the property of the architect even after the building for which they are drawn is constructed and the architect has been paid for his services. The owner cannot resist the architect's demand for payment for his services on the ground that the architect has not delivered the plans to him. Even where the owner decides not to build, he must pay for the plans which the architect has prepared —and is entitled to keep.

In the absence of such an agreement between the client and architect, a somewhat different rule applies. An architect is ordinarily no longer the owner of the plans and specifications which he designs and which are furnished to and accepted and paid for by the owner. In such case, on acceptance of and payment for the plans, the owner is entitled to them. They become his property, and the architect cannot subsequently prevent the owner from using them in constructing another building. Nor does he have a right to receive additional compensation when they are used again, since he has already been paid for them under the original contract.

The fact that there may be a *custom* among architects that an architect is entitled to retain the plans which he prepares for a client is not necessarily conclusive on others outside the profession. A client is not bound by this practice, if at the time he entered into a contract with an architect he did not know of this custom and the contract did not include a provision covering it. He, therefore, cannot be compelled to pay the architect for his services in preparing the plans unless the plans are delivered to him, though he may have decided not to use them.

Apart from the question of ownership of plans on completion of his services, the architect is the owner of his plans before they have been accepted and paid for. As the product of his skill and ability, they are property for which he is entitled to be remunerated. The client cannot, therefore, by fraud or deception deprive the architect of the right to complete the contract while retaining the benefits of his work.

In one case an owner who represented to the architect that he was through with his services and did not intend to build, but in the meanwhile was secretly planning to use photographic copies of the architect's plans, was held guilty of fraud; and his misrepresentations in this regard vitiated any settlement made with the architect to his prejudice.

The architect's recovery under such circumstances was held not to be limited to payment for the reasonable value of the services he had performed, but included the profit he could have made if permitted to carry out the terms of the contract. Under the contract employing him to prepare plans for and supervise construction of the building, his loss was ascertained by allowing him the contract price less the costs and expenses he would have incurred in completing the contract.

The architect's right to be safeguarded against appropriation of his plans by other persons is protected by the common law of copyright. This is distinct from copyright secured under the Copyright Law (which will be considered subsequently) and operates independently of any statute. *The common law of copyright protects the architect's right in the design or plan which he has created only so long as he retains control of the work and until it is "published" (a term of art meaning some act which renders the work common property).* As a creator of a unique intellectual production the architect has a property right in any architectural plan he has designed and no copyright statute is required to protect him against use of the plan by anyone without his permission. As long as the plans and copies of the plans remain in his office, in his client's hands, and with others similarly situated, they are personal property, and no other person may, without his authorization, take them or use them without becoming liable to him for their use.

If the plans or copies of the plans are stolen, the architect may maintain an action to recover them. If they are lost, the court may grant him relief by barring the finder from using the plans without his consent. Should the plans fall into the hands of another architect who represents that they are his own and uses them in the construction of a building, there is little question that the architect who designed them has a legal remedy for such unauthorized use. However, where a client employs an architect to prepare plans for a building and the architect without his knowledge or consent, copies the plans of another architect, the employer is not responsible for his illegal act. As to the preparation of plans, the architect is said to be acting for himself as an independent contractor and not as an agent for whose wrongful act the owner would be liable.

A problem which arises more frequently is that regarding the architect's protection against copying of his plans once the building has been built.

As pointed out above, the architect is protected by common-law copyright against appropriation of his work so long as he retains control of his design or until he releases it for general and unrestricted "publication." Once the work has been "published," the architect no longer has an exclusive right either in the design or its reproduction. What amounts to unrestricted "publication" has from time to time been considered by the courts.

In an early case it was held that an architect had a common-law right of property in his design of a novel and artistic porch only *before* its "publication," by its application to a building which he erected. It would seem under this holding that once an architect's idea has been embodied in concrete form in a house that all the world can see, common-law copyright cannot prevent anyone from copying his idea.

It has also been held that the filing of plans with a building department amounts to a "publication" so as to terminate the architect's common-law copyright. What this means, so far as the right of other persons to copy the work is concerned, can perhaps best be illustrated by setting forth the fact situation in a case in which this principle is applied.

An architect had prepared plans and specifications for a residence and filed the plans with the building department to procure a building permit. A house was erected under his supervision according to his plans and he received compensation from his client for these services.

The defendant, a person who was not connected with either of the parties, liked the house and desired to have one built like it. He asked the architect how much it would cost for a duplicate of his plans and specifications, and on finding the figure named too high, he told the architect that he could get the same work for less money. He subsequently procured the services of another architect who prepared plans for a building which, when constructed, conformed substantially to that which the original architect had designed.

The architect then sued the owner of the second building to recover the value of the plans, claiming that they were copies of the plans and specifications filed by him with the building department. The court dismissed his complaint, stating that he had lost his common-law right of copyright by filing the plans with the building department. It emphasized that he had superintended the construction of a house under these plans and had been paid for the work. This, the court said, is as far as common-law right of copyright extends since the law protects him only in the first "publication" of his work. The court stated:

> When the architect has permitted the work to be filed in a public office as a step in furnishing the basis on which he is to receive compensation for his work, we are of opinion that . . . the plaintiff has published his work to the world and can have no exclusive right in the design or in its reproduction. This would seem to be especially true where the plans and specifications have been used in the construction of a building and the building has been exposed to the gaze of the public and has afforded to the plaintiff the full value of his services.

There was no evidence in the case that the defendant-owner or anyone acting in his behalf had copied the plans on file in the building department. It is doubtful, however, that had this been the case, the result would have been different, particularly since the court was of the opinion that all of the property rights in the plans, if they had any value as property after publication, belonged to the client for whom the architect had originally prepared the plans rather than to the architect himself.

In another case, where a house was built with the consent of an architect and according to his plans and was thereafter open to the public for inspection, the unrestricted exhibition of the house amounted to a publication and the architect's right to protection was extinguished. The facts in that case were that a magazine of national circulation had offered a prize for the best modernization of an old residence. A savings and loan association entered the competition by modernizing an old house in Kansas City and for this purpose employed an architect, paying him $250 for his plans. The house was thereafter advertised as being open for public inspection. Subsequently the plans were used by the defendant members of the association in erecting two other houses, and the architect sued them for unauthorized use of his plans.

The defendants, in their pleadings, admitted that they knew that the plans in question at all times remained the property of the plaintiff and entered into the contract with him in contemplation of this fact.

The question then arose whether in view of this understanding the defendants wrongfully appropriated and used the architect's plans. The court decided that the unrestricted exhibition to the public of the house with his consent was a "publication." It stated that if the idea itself was "published" with his consent he was not protected by a restrictive clause in the contract with the association. The court added that if there is an intention to render the work common property, then "publication" has incurred, and the intention of the author is not determined by what he says, but what he does.

Two other interesting points raised by the defendants were not considered by the court but it might be well to mention them here since they afford possible examples of a defense to a claim of infringement. The defendants alleged that the architect's plans were included with his consent in an article written for a national real estate journal and that this amounted to a "publication." They also alleged that exhibition of the plans at a "better homes show" sponsored by a city real estate association amounted again to a "publication" of the plans.

While that point was not decided by the court, it would appear that publication of the plans in magazines of wide circulation, or their unrestricted showing at an exhibition, or both, are such "publication" to the world as to render the work common property.

Whether a contractor who was originally employed to construct a building according to the architect's plans may later construct an identical building presents a somewhat different problem, since the contractor bears a fiduciary relationship to the architect. This relationship arises out of the previous contract employing him to construct the building, at which time he had full access to the plans. This question is, therefore, outside the scope of this discussion.

The contractor does, of course, have a right to the possession of the architect's plans while he is engaged under a contract with the owner to construct a building according to such plans. He is entitled to use the plans as long as they are necessary to the execution of the work. While he is engaged on the project, any unwarranted taking of the plans by the architect so as to deprive the contractor of their use constitutes a trespass for which the architect will be held liable even though he remains the owner of the plans.

Following completion of the work, however, the contractor has no further interest either to the possession or the use of the plans and, depending upon the contract between owner and architect, they become the property of the owner or remain that of the architect.

The architect's protection may be extended, however, if he registers his work under the Copyright Act. The Act then supersedes the common law and extends his protection. In effect, it permits the owner to release copies of his design provided he has stamped them with his brand.

The correct definition of a copyright is: the sole right of multiplying copies. Securing a statutory copyright means, therefore, that the copyrighted matter cannot be copied without the author's consent. The law permits the owner of copyrighted matter to print, reprint, publish, copy and sell the copyrighted matter. The owner has also the corollary right to execute and complete the copyrighted work, if it is a model or a design for a work of art.

Architectural plans may fall within either of two categories of work classified as copyrightable. One category [Sec. 5 (g)] includes "works of art, models or designs for works of art." This section is limited to inchoate works of art and would include models or designs of architects. Another category [Sec. 5 (i)] includes "drawings or plastic works of a scientific or technical character." Under Copyright Office Rules, architectural plans and designs for engineering works are included in this classification.

There is no section of the statute which specifically mentions completed architectural works. It is doubtful whether a building or other work of architecture may be copyrighted after it has been completed, as the law in England permits it to be. Authorities on the subject have expressed the opinion, however, that architects may obtain adequate protection against copying of a finished work if they copyright their models or designs.

What are the characteristics which a plan or design must have in order to be protected by copyright? A requirement insisted on by the courts, and considered implicit in the statute, is that works to be protected must be "original." The degree of originality may be very slight, nor must it necessarily be novel. It should not be confused with artistic merit, which is not required. What is required is independent thought and not a mere repetition or copying of the work of others.

All the essential elements of the design may be in common use. It is the arrangement or combination of the elements which makes for originality. In one case, where a design for a memorial had been copyrighted, it was contended by the person alleged to have infringed it that all of the essential elements were in common use prior to the copyright. The court regarded this as immaterial and stated that the combination of elements in the design and their plan or arrangement made the work original. Since the defendants had not shown any work similar to the design, or proved that anyone had produced a similar combination of elements, the argument that the work was not copyrightable failed.

With respect to the problem of originality, the court made the following general remarks:

> In truth, in literature, in science and in art, there are, and can be, few, if any, things, which, in an abstract sense, are strictly new and original throughout. It is a great mistake to suppose, because all the materials of a work or some parts of its plans and arrangements and modes of illustration may be found separately or in a different form, or in a different arrangement, in other distinct works, that therefore, if the plan or arrangement or combination of these materials in another work is new, or for the first time made, the author or compiler is not entitled to a copyright.

By the same token, the copyright law also protects *reproductions* of existing works in different adaptations, arrangements, or mediums of expression. The protection extends to the old and new matter in combination on the theory that the original work plus new matter constitutes new work. In one instance, a design of a miniature shrine was copyrighted, the principal elements of the design being taken from a shrine established by the Roman Catholic Church. While the various elements embodied in the design were symbols of worship and therefore deemed common property, the arrangement of these elements in an original fashion satisfied the criteria of originality and independent labor so as to permit copyright of the design.

It is important to remember that the copyright law does not protect ideas, but only the media or forms in which they are expressed. It is possible for an idea to be expressed in totally different manners, and it is these different manners of expressing it that are protected. This principle has received consistent expression by the courts but has been misunderstood by authors who have sought protection for ideas and systems rather than for their method of expression.

In the leading case on this subject, an author secured a copyright of a book explaining a system of bookkeeping with illustrations depicting the way the system should be used. The U.S. Supreme Court held that the copyright was not infringed by a book using the same plan as far as the result was concerned but with a different arrangement. The decision indicates that the author of the first book does not have a copyright in the idea of the book but only in the description of his idea. The rule has since been reiterated that no copyright exists in a plan or method of art, although it may in their decription.

A 1942 case on this point may serve to point up the difference between the right to be protected in an idea and the manner of expressing it. In that case, an engineer had procured a copyright of a drawing showing a novel bridge approach designed to unsnarl traffic congestion. He had presented his drawings before a Municipal Bridge Authority, which subsequently constructed a bridge approach similar to the engineer's design. The engineer then sued the Authority for infringement of his copyrighted drawing.

The court decided that the design had been conceived and executed from other sources of information, namely, a bridge already constructed in another locality. The court went on to say that even if the Authority had copied his idea, he could not recover for an infringement. His drawing showing a bridge approach would not prevent anyone from using and applying the system of traffic separation set forth in his design. Here again, the engineer's system of traffic separation embodied an idea and this idea anyone could utilize. Before an exclusive right can be obtained in an invention or discovery, the court stated, it must be subject to the examination of the patent office. The court compared the design with a book containing a system of shorthand. There is no copyrightable material in the system itself but the explanation of how to do it is copyrightable.

If the same idea can be expressed in different ways, similarity in composition between a copyrighted and un-copyrighted work does not necessarily lead to the conclusion that the one is a copy of the other. Furthermore, there are many figures and symbols which are not copyrightable since they are in the public domain—that is, available to everyone—such as political or religious symbols.

Whether a copyright has been infringed by the reproduction of another work without the copyright owner's consent is a question of fact. To begin with, there must be similarities in the two works. The problem is to determine whether the similarities are mere coincidence or are the result of plagiarism, for it often happens that a person has by independent thought and creative ability and labor produced a work of art that bears substantial resemblances to a work which has been registered as a copyright. The test of infringement, then, is whether an original independent production has been made or whether the work is merely a copy of the original registered work. A "copy" has been described as that which comes so near the original as to give every person seeing it the idea created by the original.

How much copying must there be to result in infringement? The general rule is that copying of some substantial or material portion of the copyrighted work will constitute infringement. Or, stated in another way, it means that it is not necessary that the whole work be copied but it is sufficient if so much is taken that the value of the original work is noticeably diminished or the labors of the author are substantially appropriated by another.

Whether an architect is protected against copying of uncopyrighted plans when they are published in a magazine, or other periodical which is itself copyrighted, has not been decided by the courts. However, the inference may be drawn from cases involving similar problems that the architect is not protected unless his individual contribution is copyrighted and is so labeled in the magazine.

A copyright notice in a periodical covers everything that is copyrightable in the work, provided that copyright in *all of the contents* belongs to the one whose name appears on the notice of copyright. If the publication does not have exclusive right to the article or design as owner, then separate notice is required in the part belonging to the contributor.

If the architect submits a plan to a magazine and the plan is accepted and paid for, the plan may become the property of the magazine, and reproduction of it by third persons would constitute infringement for which the magazine, not the author of the design, would have a remedy. If the architect remains the owner, then it would appear that to be protected against copying of his work he should procure a copyright of the work and place a notice of copyright on the design appearing in the periodical. The purpose of the notice is to warn the public against infringement and if it does not appear on each copy of the work reaching the public, the protection afforded by the copyright is lost.

It is clear, then, that an architect is not protected against copying of his work if he has not procured a copyright. The only way he can secure protection is to register his plan or design in accordance with the provisions of the Copyright Act. The degree of protection afforded by a copyright will necessarily depend on the individual situation.

CHAPTER 16: *Right to Mechanic's Lien*

The securing of a mechanic's lien upon the owner's property—to enforce compensation for architectural or engineering services—is a significant right that varies from state to state.

THE NECESSITY FOR LEGISLATION to protect architects is, of course, not confined to registration statutes. The need for exchanging and pooling information and for a "uniform" statute exists, for example, with respect to the architect's right to a "mechanic's lien" for the drawing of plans and specifications, as well as for supervision. His right to such a lien varies considerably in the fifty states. It may extend *only* to his services for supervision; or in some states, where he *also* supervised the construction, to plans and specifications; or in other states, to plans and specifications without the necessity for his having supervised the construction.

The right to any mechanic's lien is exclusively granted by way of statutory enactment. Such right did not exist at common law. An example of a statute providing for the filing of "mechanic's liens" by architects for their plans and specifications, as well as their supervision of construction, is found in *Compiled Laws of Colorado,* Section 6442(15). That statute reads as follows:

> Mechanics, material men, contractors, subcontractors, builders, and all persons of every class performing labor upon or furnishing materials to be used in the construction, alteration, addition to, or repair, either in whole or in part, of any building, mill, bridge, ditch, flume, aqueduct, reservoir, tunnel, fence, railroad, wagon road, tramway or any other structure or improvement, upon land, and *also architects, engineers, draughtsmen and artisans who have furnished designs, plans, plats, maps,*

specifications, drawings, estimates of cost, surveys or superintendence, or who have rendered other professional or skilled service, or bestowed labor in whole or in part, describing or illustrating, or superintending such structure, or work done or to be done, or any part connected therewith, shall have a lien upon the property upon which they have rendered service or bestowed labor or for which they have furnished materials or mining or milling machinery or other fixtures for the value of such services rendered or labor done or material furnished, whether at the instance of the owner, or of any other person acting by his authority or under him, as agent, contractor, or otherwise; for the work or labor done or services rendered or materials furnished, by each respectively, whether done or furnished or rendered at the instance of the owner of the building or other improvement, or his agent; and every contractor, architect, engineer, subcontractor, builder, agent or other person having charge of the construction, alteration, addition to, or repair, either in whole or in part, of any building or other improvement, as aforesaid, shall be held to be the agent of the owner for the purposes of this act. (pp. 1676-1677) (emphasis ours).

The above-quoted statute is not typical. A majority of the lien laws merely provide for the filing of mechanic's liens by "mechanics, material men, contractors, and builders," and where architects have not been named specifically as a group protected by the statute, the courts have held that they do not come within its coverage.

The decisions of the courts, in interpreting the statutes of the various states, may be classified into three distinct groups:

(1) The architect is permitted a lien for his plans and specifications, as well as for supervision of construction;

(2) The architect is permitted a lien for his plans and specifications only where he has also supervised construction;

(3) The architect is permitted a lien only with regard to supervision of construction and has no lien for the furnishing of plans and specifications.

Group 1:

Under statutes similar to the Colorado statute set forth above, the courts have held an architect entitled to a lien for his plans and specifications, as well as supervision of construction. The Supreme Court of Colorado, in *Park Lane Properties, Inc., et al* v. *Fisher, et al,* 5 P. 2d 577, set forth the rule as follows:

If we were to hold that the identical Fisher plans must have been used before their right of a lien attached they would not be given the full protection contemplated and created by the lien statute. Such ruling would afford opportunities for unscrupulous builders to defeat legitimate lien rights of architects. The services of the Fishers continued for over a year, and were largely evidenced by the plans, specifications, details and drawings submitted to Hooper and Janusch, Chicago architects, used by them in the preparation of, and partially incorporated in, the plans actually prepared and used in the construction of the building. Under such circumstances, it would be wholly inequitable and unjust to deny the Fishers a lien for such services which were proven and found to have been rendered upon the faith and credit of the real property and the improvement erected thereon.

A similar question was determined in the case of *Home Market Co.* v. *Fallis,* 72 Colo. 48, 209 P. 641, which is here controlling. There Fallis prepared for the lessee plans and specifications for the construction of the Home Public Market Building in Denver. His employment was terminated, but his plans were used in part by the architect of the assignee under whose plans and supervision the building was constructed. The judgment of the lower court that Fallis was entitled to a lien for the value of his services so rendered was affirmed. (p. 579)

It is interesting to note that here the plans and specifications were furnished by one group of architects to another, who then prepared the final plans which were used in the construction. Yet, the court allowed a lien to the original architect for his plans and specifications.

Group 2:

The courts of a majority of the states adhere to the rule that an architect is entitled to a lien for his plans and specifications and superintendence of construction only where such supervision is present. A typical example of a court decision adhering to this point of view may be found in *Beeson* v. *Overpack, et al,* 44 N.E. 2d 195, where the court stated:

The court, in reviewing the history of the mechanic's lien statutes of this state and the authorities of other jurisdictions on the subject, points out the purpose of such statutes in this language: "The mechanic's lien laws of America, in general, reveal the underlying motive of justice and equity in dedicating, primarily, buildings and the land on which they are erected to the payment of the labor and materials incorporated, and which have given to them an increased value. The purpose is to promote justice and honesty, and to prevent the inequity of an owner enjoying the fruits of the labor and materials furnished by others, without recompense." The definition of laborer as found in the Century Dictionary is also quoted in this opinion, a portion of which is: "one who labors with body or mind, or both."

This case when considered along with the phrase in the statute, "and all persons performing labor," strongly supports the contention of the appellant that his claim is lienable.

The labor and skill of an architect in drawing plans and specifications and in superintending the work upon a building or reparation thereof are a part of the expense of construction, and as an item of such expense, they enter into and help form the value of the building. We can conceive of no sound reason why the person who performs such labor and furnishes such skill should not receive the same protection as the carpenter, the mason, or other mechanics. In a case like the present, where the architect draws the plans, and uses them as his tools in the supervision of the work, we think he is entitled to a lien for the labor expended in the drawing of the plans and specifications and in the supervision of the construction. (pp. 197-198)

It should be emphasized that the supervision of construction by the architect under this decision is the underlying important factor by which the court grants the mechanic's lien to the architect.

Group 3:

The courts of a minority of our states differ from the views above set forth in that they have held an architect entitled only to a lien for his supervision of construction, but not for any plans or specifications which he may have furnished. A decision adhering to this point of view is *Palm Beach Bank & Trust Co. v. Lainhart, et al,* 95 So. 122, wherein the court stated:

As to the claim of E. A. Fonder, we think that the court was in error in designating him as an architect so far as his activities were regarded in relation to the buildings. He was employed not only to draw the plan for "Graham Circle," but he was employed as supervisor or superintendent of the construction and erection of the improvements. In that capacity he acted, not as architect, but as a kind of foreman in the erection of all the buildings and improvements. In so far as his claim rested upon that service he is entitled to a lien upon the property.

> That kind of work is differentiated from the services of an architect in drawing plans and specifications. Supervising the erection of a building and the selection of materials to be placed therein is often done by a skilled mechanic and is such labor as the statute contemplates shall be provided for in a lien upon the building or lands.

In some states adhering to this narrow construction of the lien law, one court has gone to the extreme of denying a mechanic's lien to an architect where he has supervised construction and prepared and furnished plans. The rationale of this decision was to the effect that although the architect was entitled to a lien for that portion relating to his supervision of construction, his agreement with the owner formed an indivisible contract. Therefore, since he was not entitled to a lien for his plans and specifications, and since the contract was an "entire one," the court held the architect was entitled to no lien at all.

The right of an architect to a mechanic's lien, where it exists, is an important adjunct in his perpetual battle to be paid adequately for services rendered. There is no reasonable argument that can be made for the architect being put in any worse position than the materials man or mechanic who renders work, labor, and services in construction. It is significant that a recent amendment in New York State with respect to the class of persons afforded the protection of the Lien Law extended its coverage to "landscape gardeners, nurserymen, or persons or corporations selling fruit or ornamental trees, roses, shrubbery, vines, and small fruits." If the architect is as diligent and organized as the landscape gardener, nurseryman, and fruit tree salesman, he too can become effective in a practical way —this time to assure himself of a lien law in each state that will aid him most effectively in collecting a fee justly earned.

II

May an architect file a mechanic's lien for *preliminary* drawings only?

The general rule is expressed as follows in *Architectural & Engineering Law,* Tomson (Reinhold 1951):

> Architects or engineers who prepare plans for and supervise the construction of buildings and other structures are generally entitled to a mechanic's lien under statutes which give a lien in

general terms for material and labor furnished in the erection of a building.

The mechanic's lien is purely statutory and is given to those who perform labor or furnish material in the improvement of real property. There has been much litigation as to whether an architect or engineer is entitled to protection under these acts. The courts have reached different conclusions, depending on the interpretation of a given statute, and the court's views as to the architect's or engineer's duties and the character of his work.

Architects have been given (or denied) mechanic's liens dependent on criteria such as the following:

Did the architect supervise construction?

Is the lien for supervision only?

Does the statute permit a lien for the preparation of plans without supervision?

Is a lien permitted for plans never used for construction?

A novel question was raised in New York, where an architect's services were engaged in connection with the proposed construction of four buildings and garages. He was later informed that the owners had decided to abandon the proposed project. The architect filed a lien in an amount representing the reasonable value of his services in preparing preliminary studies, plans, and drawings.

The owners filed a petition to vacate the lien, contending the preliminary studies and plans were insufficient to support a valid mechanic's lien under the New York Lien Law.

The applicable provision of the New York Lien Law, Section 2, Subdivision 4, reads as follows: "The term 'improvement' . . . shall also include the drawing by any architect or engineer or surveyor of any plans or specifications or survey, which are prepared for or used in connection with such improvement."

The Appellate Division of the Supreme Court of New York affirmed the architect's right to a lien and set an important precedent for other states which have similarly drawn Lien Laws.

Said the court, in *Matter of Bralus Corp.*, 282 App. Div. 959:

> Prior to 1916, an architect was not entitled to a mechanic's lien for services rendered solely in preparing plans. . . . By Chapter 507 of the Laws of 1916, Section 2 of the Lien Law was amended to permit a lien for the drawing of plans, even though no building was erected on the property. . . . By Chapter 608 of the Laws of 1934, Section 2 of the Lien Law was further amended by broadening the definition of the term "im-

provement" to include the drawing of plans "prepared for or used in connection with such improvement." The amendment must be deemed to have been intended to include the drawing of preliminary plans because work in drawing final plans was lienable prior to the amendment.

A dissenting opinion adopted the owner's argument that the statute did not contemplate preliminary studies and plans:

> Buildings are not erected on "preliminary" studies and "preliminary" plans. The statute must be strictly construed, and I believe it never was the intention of the Legislature to provide for "preliminary" service which, as such, could not be the basis for the improvement of the property.

The owners-appellants endeavored to distinguish earlier lower court cases where the architect's right to a lien was upheld by pointing out that in none of those cases was the plans referred to as "preliminary."

In one case, the plans were "filed" with the Building Department; in another case, the lien was in part for the drafting and preparation of "completed sketches"; in a third case, the services included "both preliminary and final" plans; and in still another case, the lien was for preparation of "working drawings."

The owners relied strongly upon a case where the architect's notice of lien was discharged. The notice of lien had stated the following:

> The labor performed was inspection, analysis, and recommendations as to alterations of the premises, 301 West 138th St., and the drawing up of preliminary sketches embodying the recommendations—financial analysis.

The Supreme Court, New York County, held in that case as follows:

> Such labor does not come within the category of "plans, specifications or survey," which are prepared for or used in connection with an improvement (Lien Law, Section 2), and cannot give any "right to a lien."

The Bralus case was appealed to the Court of Appeals, the highest court of New York, and that court affirmed the ruling that an architect was entitled to a lien for preliminaries, provided they could be characterized as "plans" as that term is understood in the building trades. The Court said:

> Respondent's mechanic's lien for making "drawings of preliminary plans" and allied architectural services which never became embodied in an erected structure should not summarily be dismissed on motion under subdivision (6) of section 19 of the Lien Law, upon the ground that they are not final plans. Mechanic's liens may be filed for materials furnished or labor performed "for the improvement of real property" (Lien Law, sec. 3). Subdivision 4 of section 2, as amended by chapter 608 of the Laws of 1934, defines "improvement" as including "the drawing by any architect or engineer or surveyor, of any plans or specifications or survey, which are prepared for or used in connection with such improvement." Nothing contained in this language disallows architects' plans which are preliminary in nature, provided that they have progressed to a point where they can be characterized as "plans" within the meaning of that term as it is used in the building trades. More than mere rough sketches is required in order to render lienable an architect's charges, but the term "preliminary plans" includes drawings which are sufficiently formal to be called plans, but which have been prepared to assist the owner in deciding whether he wants to have a building constructed according to such a design, or which leave some ultimate details to be selected and added later. (Matter of Bralus, 307 N.Y. 626)

Due to constant changes in the law and in light of the peculiarities of the law in each particular jurisdiction, the following questions pertaining to liens for architectural services should be considered:

(a) Does any right of lien exist under any circumstances in your state?

(b) Does the architect have a lien for supervision only in your state, whether or not he has drawn plans and specifications?

(c) Does the architect in your state have a lien for plans and specifications if he supervises construction?

(d) Does the architect in your state have a lien if he draws plans and specifications, but some other architect supervises construction?

(e) Does the architect in your state have a lien if he draws plans and specifications and construction proceeds, but his plans and specifications are changed, varied or abandoned?

(f) Does the architect in your state have a lien if construction does not proceed, but he has drawn complete working drawings and specifications?

(g) Does the architect in your state have a lien for preliminaries, sketches, or other work which does not involve actual drawing?

If it is your money that depends on the answers to these questions, the answers should be given by your lawyer, whose advice should be (because of the time elements involved) promptly obtained. Nor is it important that the attorney be a "specialist." Any competent attorney is in a position to advise an architect as to his rights in the state in which he practices.

CHAPTER 17: *Defamation of Architect or Engineer*

Defamatory architectural criticism will not be deemed libelous if it constitutes "fair comment."

UNTIL RECENTLY, THE CLASSIC approach of publications dealing with architecture was to praise the good and indict the bad by ignoring it. This concept is rapidly giving way to more aggressive architectural criticism. Thereby is raised the bugaboo of possible libel actions. Not only publications are concerned with the problems. The same or similar principles would control alleged slanderous statements made at forums, seminars, meetings, and the like. All this makes important the consideration of the law of defamation as it relates to architectural criticism.

Historically, the law of defamation has developed in a somewhat chaotic fashion. Although certain general principles in this field of law have been enunciated by the courts, there has been no unanimity in the application of these principles to particular, factual situations; and there is an area of disagreement among legal scholars in their approach to this field of law. There have been relatively few judicial determinations involving alleged defamation of architectural work or performance; consequently, legal precedent offers little guide to the proper application of these general principles to architectural criticism. To evaluate the appropriate rule that should be applied to criticism of architectural work, it is necessary to consider the development of the law of defamation as it relates to other fields of professional and artistic endeavor.

A statement which challenges the honesty, character, reputation, virtue, or integrity of an individual or subjects him to contempt, ridicule, or obloquy, or injures him in his business or occupation, is defamatory. Every defamatory statement, however, is not actionable. Under a doctrine known as "fair comment," defamatory statements within certain limits are privileged if they pertain to subjects which are inherently of interest to the public, or pertain to persons who have voluntarily offered themselves or their work for public consideration, review, and criticism. The public has a direct interest in government officials, candidates for elective office, administrators of public institutions, etc., as their activity directly affects the community health, safety, and welfare. Consequently, the "fair comment" doctrine applies to activities of these public men. The novelist, poet, playwright, and actress offer their services or product to the public and thus, in substance, invite criticism. Such criticism of a work of art or a performance may inferentially impeach the ability or capacity of the artist, but it is, nevertheless, privileged under the "fair comment" doctrine.

The rationale underlying the doctrine of "fair comment" is based upon the premise that a democratic society must be free to speak adversely of persons or matters involved with the public interest in order to safeguard and promote social, political, and cultural advancement. There are, however, limitations within which the privilege of "fair comment" must be exercised. In general, it has been held that critical comment must not attack the private reputation or character of an individual, unless the comment can be fairly drawn from true facts. It is also the general rule that the over-all competency of an artist may not be challenged but the privileged criticism limited rather to his incompetency in respect to a particular work or performance which is the direct subject matter of the criticism. The comment, to be privileged, must be based upon facts truly stated, and some courts have held that the comment inferred from the facts must be fair. It is also the prevailing rule that the comment must not be maliciously made, but offered for an honest purpose.

Many courts and writers have termed the doctrine of "fair comment" as a right rather than a privilege, and some legal scholars have contended that comment on a matter or person involved with the public interest should be privileged whether it is fair or is maliciously made. For example, in the well-known treatise, *Seelman on Libel and Slander,* it is stated that "criticism and comment should be defined as the right to publish libel, where that libel arises as an inference from the truly stated facts concerning matters clothed with a public interest." Undoubtedly, due to the importance in a free society of the expression of unfettered opinion where matters of public concern are involved, the tendency in the more recent judicial decisions has been to liberalize the area of "fair comment" and to limit the area of actionable libel.

In determining, then, the area of "fair comment" in respect to architectural work or performance, it is necessary to consider to what degree the public interest is involved. Architectural services are performed, as a rule, for a particular client, and in that respect, the architect can be compared to other professionals, such as attorneys or physicians. On the other hand, his work involves artistic expression, which is presented to the public upon the execution of his plans. The architectural work is thrust into public view and consciousness and becomes part of the environment in which the public lives and works. In this sense, architectural performance is comparable to that of an artist. It is generally recognized that criticism of a *public* building is privileged under the "fair comment" doctrine (*e.g., Bearce vs. Bass,* 88 Me. 521; *Dowling vs. Livingstone,* 108 Mich. 321). A public building in this sense refers to a building owned by a governmental division. It is clear that the public has an interest in such buildings, the cost of which are borne by the taxpayer. There is very little consideration given in legal texts to the application of the "fair comment" doctrine to architectural work other than public buildings. There would, however, appear to be no logical distinction, in this respect, between a public building, a building which the public utilizes, or a private residence. The public has an interest in all buildings and if there is a distinction, it is only one of degree.

The interest of the public in all types of structures is manifested in many different ways. The public's interest in the competency of the architect and his work is first indicated by the requirement in most states that the architect be duly licensed and registered. The plans of an architect must be filed and approval obtained before construction can be commenced. The municipality, through zoning laws and building ordinances, regulates the locality where the structure can be erected and regulates its height, setback, sanitary facilities, area, etc.

The power of the state or municipality to regulate the practice of architecture and to control, through its zoning and building laws, the architect's plans and specifications is based upon the police power of the government to safeguard the health, safety, and welfare of the community. This same health, safety, and welfare is involved whether the building in question is public or private. The public concern is with all structures, and there would be no justification for permitting a wider area of comment and criticism in respect to public buildings than to any other type.

The public interest in all buildings and architectural works is also manifested by the increasing importance of esthetic factors in zoning regulation and urban redevelopment. "Look alike" ordinances, minimum area restriction, and similar statutes evidence the public interest and concern with this subject. The United States Supreme Court in *Berman v. Parker*, 348 U.S. 26, recognized esthetic considerations as an integral part of the "public welfare" concept. The Court stated:

> The concept of the public welfare is broad and inclusive . . . the values it represents are spiritual as well as physical, aesthetic as well as monetary. It is within the power of the legislature to determine that the community should be beautiful as well as healthy, spacious, as well as clean, well balanced as well as carefully patrolled.

The validity of government regulation of construction, based upon esthetic factors in the interest of the general welfare, must be based upon the premise that the public has a direct, continuing, and vital interest in the design, appearance, and type of building that is constructed. It follows from this premise that the public must be free to criticize the esthetics or any other feature of a particular structure, within the rules laid down for "fair comment."

However, in at least one early New York case (N.Y. L.J. 2/1/27, Pg. 977, aff'd. 221 App. Div. 760) the court took the view that a graphic and sarcastic criticism pertaining to the design of an architectural work amounted to a personal censure of the architect and thus lay outside the protection afforded by the privilege of "fair comment." The criticism, which appeared in *The New Yorker* magazine, stated the following:

> Another disappointment on proud Fifth Avenue, at Forty-fourth Street, is the Delmonico Building, ... which causes older members of the profession wending their way luncheonward at the Century Club, to burst into tears. They do not look at the building itself. They can't. Every proportion appears to be unfortunate. The central tower, curiously set on no particular axis, has the grace of an overgrown grain elevator. Of

the detail one of the profession said "Isn't it curious how a simple element like a bandcourse or a molding can produce a feeling of nausea?"

The ruling of the court in the foregoing case to the effect that the criticism above quoted amounted to a personal censure of the architect has been much criticized, and there is doubt whether it would be followed today. Seelman, in his treatise on *Libel and Slander,* points out that it is difficult to understand how the comment described in this case, even though exaggerated, could be deemed an attack on the character and motive of the architect, and thus outside the scope of the "fair comment" privilege.

In another New York case (*Vosbury vs. Utica Daily Press Co.,* 183 App. Div. 769) it was held that a newspaper story was libelous which stated that the roof of a high school was in danger of falling; that the architect had been notified but had ignored the notification; and that these facts did not speak very well for those who designed and built the school. The decision of the Court was based upon the premise that the criticism in question charged the architect with general unskillfulness and general carelessness, and that such comment was not protected by the "fair comment" doctrine. A charge that an architect has disregarded possible danger to life and property, is, of course, of entirely different quality than criticism concerning the esthetics of a structure. Architectural criticism to be privileged under the "fair comment" doctrine must not charge the architect with general unskillfulness or negligence.

The fact, however, that architectural criticism is made in a sarcastic vein or with ridicule, does not exclude the application of the "fair comment" doctrine. Illustrative of this long established principle is an English case decided in 1827 (*Soane vs. Knight,* Moody & Malkins, 74), wherein the Court stated:

> This publication professes in substance to be a criticism on the architectural works of the plaintiff. On such works, as well as on literary productions, any man has a right to express his opinion, and however mistaken in point of taste that opinion may be, or however, unfavorable to the merits of the author or artist, the person entertaining it is not precluded by law from its fair, reasonable and temporate expression. It may be fairly and reasonably expressed, although through the medium of ridicule. . . .

The area of public interest justifying critical comment under the "fair comment" concept is ever-broadening. In a recent case in New York (157 N.Y.S. 2d, 209) a doctor who operated upon a member of the (then) Brooklyn Dodger baseball team claimed to have been slandered as a result of a statement which indicated that his fee was exorbitant, that the operation was probably unnecessary, and that he thought he was operating on the patient's bankroll rather than on his hand. In indicating the broad scope of public interest in respect to the privilege of "fair comment," the court stated:

> It is beyond dispute that the subject matter of defendant O'Malley's statement . . . is in the area of the public interest and, hence, subject to fair comment. The Brooklyn Dodgers and its players receive persistent national publicity and, on occasion, world-wide attention. Medical treatment of such players, especially in reference to their capacity to play, is likewise of general comment and interest.

If actions taken in respect to a baseball team are considered of sufficient public interest to justify defamatory statements under the doctrine of "fair comment," the public interest in architecture certainly justifies the widest area of privileged comment in this field. Public concern with architecture is such that the requirements of a free society demand the privilege of unfettered comment always provided the comment is based upon truly stated facts. The "fair comment" concept is entitled to the broadest application when applied to the field of architecture.

CHAPTER 18: *Negligent Performance*

An architect, engineer or contractor is liable to the owner for damages resulting from his negligence in performing architectural, engineering or building services.

THE LIABILITY OF AN ARCHITECT for malpractice does not differ essentially from that of a lawyer or physician. A state Supreme Court made this comparison in the following words:

> The responsibility resting on an architect is essentially the same as that which rests upon the lawyer to his client, or upon the physician to his patient, or which rests upon any one to another where such person pretends to possess some skill and ability in some special employment, and offers his services to the public on account of his fitness to act in the line of business for which he may be employed. The undertaking of an architect implies that he possesses skill and ability, including taste sufficient to enable him to perform the required services at least ordinarily and reasonably well, and that he will exercise and apply in the given case his skill and ability, his judgment and taste, reasonably and without neglect. But the undertaking does not imply or warrant a satisfactory result. It will be enough that any failure shall not be by the fault of the architect.

The legal yardstick which measures adequacy of the architect's performance, therefore, is based upon a determination as to whether the architect possessed and exercised that degree of skill and care which should be reasonably possessed and exercised in the profession. This determination is not made by architects but usually by a jury of twelve "good men and true." Thus, a judgment that an architect has been guilty of malpractice may, in the last analysis, depend almost as much upon the skill of the attorney representing him as upon the skill which he exercised in the performance of those acts which are claimed to have been negligently done.

It may be claimed that an architect was negligent in (1) the preparation of drawings, specifications, and plans; or (2) in supervising construction where it is his duty under the contract in force so to do. The consequences of negligent performance on the part of the architect may take the form of physically defective construction or a structure of depreciated value due to an impairment in utility or in appearance.

In deciding whether an architect was negligent in preparing plans and specifications, important factors to be considered are whether the architect provided for reasonable strength and proper materials for the structure. Further, the architect must be familiar with the new and improved techniques of his profession. The architect's plans must be reasonably adequate for the purpose for which they are intended. The architect, however, does not ensure the perfection of his work and he is not liable for an error in judgment, if he uses his best judgment. The question, even where the architect's plans are defective, is whether the architect exercised reasonable care and diligence in preparing them.

The line between an error of judgment and a negligent act is not clearly definable, and is often a fine one. For example, in a Washington case the question before the court was whether an architect had been negligent in the preparation of plans for a roof which subsequently collapsed under a load of snow, and whether he should have anticipated the possibility of that amount of snow. This and similar questions are factual, and therefore determined by a jury. It is also the duty of the architect not only to prepare proper plans but to furnish them without undue delay, as he will be accountable to the owner for any damages suffered where plans are not delivered at the time required.

Where, under the contract, it is the duty of the architect to supervise construction, he must exercise ordinary care and diligence in such supervision, and give attention to the work done by the contractor. Both the architect and the contractor may be liable to the owner for negligent work, and the owner may proceed against either or both. If there are defects in the construction that could only be determined by the exercise of *extraordinary* care and diligence, the architect will not be responsible. In considering what is ordinary or extraordinary care and attention, the courts are influenced by the usual and customary practices in the profession. For example, in a California case, defective concrete had been utilized in a structure. However, in adjudging the negligence of the architect, the court took into consideration the fact that the concrete had passed the usual 28-day test for determining strength.

The damages for which an architect will be held accountable are those which naturally and consequently flow from his negligent performance. If, due to defective plans, a building should collapse and injure a third party, the architect would be responsible to that third party for the damages suffered. However, where an owner maintains a defective structure and a third person is injured, the architect will not be liable, on the theory that it is the negligence of the owner in maintaining a defective structure which caused the injury, rather than the negligence of the architect.

The penalty for malpractice is loss of compensation for work performed and liability for damages caused by the negligence. It is an implied term of every contract between architect and owner that the architect will perform his duties thereunder with reasonable skill; therefore, negligent performance is a breach of the contract, and the owner is relieved of his obligation to compensate the architect for services rendered. The measure of damages utilized to determine the architect's responsibility for his negligence is the difference between the value of the structure as designed and constructed and the value it would have had, if the architect had not been negligent in all or part of his work. Where the defects in the building are not structural, the cost of correcting the defects which have been caused by the architect's negligence may be used in determining the difference between the value of the building as constructed, and the value which it would have had if it had been constructed properly. Where, however, the cost of correction is unreasonably out of proportion to the injuries suffered by the owner, the cost of repair may not be used as a measure. Consequently, where, due to architect's negligence, a different building has been constructed from the one desired by the owner but of no less value than the one desired, the owner has suffered (and may recover) only nominal damages.

The area of an architect's potential liability is large. Failure to possess and exercise reasonable skill may not only make him liable in damages to the owner, but he will be responsible for injuries suffered by third persons where the causal relationship between the negligence and the injury is established. The nature and adequacy of the architect's performance is a factual question dependent upon the circumstances of each situation. In litigation, the jury is the judge of facts and the architect must, therefore, convince the jury that in the performance of his professional duties he had acted with reasonable skill and diligence. It is, of course, obvious that the greater the care and attention on the part of the architect, the safer he will be from unfounded claims of malpractice and from adjudication, by laymen, of negligence. The extent of the architect's possible liability should make all the more clear the necessity of the architect to be provided with contract forms which will protect him as far as possible against avoidable liability and which will contain proper clauses referring his legal disputes to an arbitration tribunal of experts in the field.

II

In these days, when architects avail themselves of the services of structural, plumbing, heating, and lighting specialists, and every other known variety of specialist, it should be appropriate to determine how much reliance the architect can place on plans drawn for him by acknowledged experts and how much further reliance can be placed on specifications provided by reputable manufacturers. This of course becomes a matter of primary importance when the plans or specifications turn out to be inadequate—and the question of the architect's legal responsibility arises.

Discussions in terms of "reasonable skill and ability performed without neglect" may be of some help. More useful is a full exposition of the architect's duty, as is found in a case decided in New York in 1889 (*Hubert* v. *Aitken,* 2 N.Y. Supp. 711, 5 N.Y. Supp. 839, aff'd 123 N.Y. 655). There the precise question involved an architect's reliance on incorrect specifications supplied by a contractor for that then new-fangled device "steam heating." When the architect found it necessary to sue for his fee, the owner counterclaimed for damages. The court allowed the owner to deduct $1000 from the architect's fee with this interesting statement:

> The plaintiffs are architects of standing, who assume to be able to plan and superintend the construction of first-class apartment houses, to be heated by steam, and to be provided with every convenience demanded by the luxurious tastes of the day. They are not architects in a rural community, but in the first

city in America. Steam-heating is, as we all know, common, if not a necessity, in all apartment houses of large size, and of a high class. It is true that houses of this description are of recent introduction; but they are now a very important part of our system of economics, for in some of the new streets they are more numerous than private residences, or tenements of the kind that formerly were in vogue. The architect who undertakes to construct a house that is to be heated by steam is groping in the dark unless he knows how large a chimney is required. It is as necessary that the architect should know what is needed to make the steam-heating apparatus serviceable, as it is that he should know how sewer gas is to be kept out of the house.

No one would contend that at this day an architect could shelter himself behind the plumber, and excuse his ignorance of the ordinary appliances for sanitary ventilation by saying that he was not an expert in the trade of plumbing. He is an expert in carpentry, in cements, in mortar, in the strength of materials, in the act of constructing the walls, the floors, the stair cases, the roofs, and is in duty bound to possess reasonable skill and knowledge as to all these things; and when, in the progress of civilization, new conveniences are introduced to our homes, and become, not curious novelties, but the customary means of securing the comfort of the unpretentious citizen, why should not the architect be expected to possess the technical learning respecting them that is exacted of him with respect to other and older branches of his professional studies? It is not asking too much of the man who assumes that he is competent to build a house at a cost of more than $100,000 and to arrange that it shall be heated by steam, to insist that he shall know how to proportion his chimney to the boiler. It is not enough for him to say, "I asked the steamfitter," and then throw the consequences of any error that may be made upon the employer who engages him relying upon his skill. Responsibility cannot be shifted that way.

In the case of *Moneypenny v. Hartland* (twice reported, once in 1 Car. & P. 352, and then in 2 Car. & P. 378), it was held that if a surveyor be employed to erect a bridge and form the approaches to it, he is bound to ascertain for himself, by experiments, the nature of the soil, even though a person previously employed for that purpose by his employer has made such experiments, and has given him the result at his employer's request; and if the surveyor makes a low estimate, and thereby induces persons to subscribe for the execution of the work who would otherwise have declined it, and it turns out that, owing to his negligence and want of skill, such estimate is grossly incorrect, and that the work can be done, but at a much greater expense, he is not entitled to recover for his services.

The owner was not satisfied with the result and requested a reargument of this determination, urging that since the contract had not been performed entirely without fault that the architect should be entitled to nothing. In its determination that *this* argument was without merit, the court incidentally engaged in a useful discussion of the specific standard of care required of an architect in supervision. This, too, deserves extensive quotation:

> With regard to the plans, it appears that the contract was completely performed. Drawings for the whole building were furnished, and it was actually constructed in accordance therewith. After the building was finished, it was discovered that the chimney flues, connecting with the boiler flues, were not large enough for the purpose for which they were designed. These flues were not omitted from the plans; on the contrary, they were set down with the same fullness of detail as the other parts of the building. It cannot, therefore, be said that plaintiffs did not entirely perform their contract in this respect; they completely performed it, but they performed it negligently.
>
> Similar considerations apply to the other branch of the case. The learned counsel would not claim that an architect is bound to spend all his time at a building which is going up under his professional care so that no fraud or negligence can be committed by any of the contractors. The counsel would not contend that the architect is an insurer of the perfection of the mason work, the carpenter work, the plumbing, etc. He is bound only to exercise reasonable care, and to use reasonable powers of observation and detection, in the supervision of the structure. When, therefore, it appears that the architect has made frequent visits to the building, and in a general way has performed the duties called for by customs of his profession, the mere fact, for instance, that inferior brick have been used in places, does not establish, as a matter of law, that he has not entirely performed his contract. He might have directed at one of his visits that portions of the plumbing work be packed in wool; upon his next return to the building the pipes in question might have been covered with brick in the progress of the building. If he had inquired whether the wool-packing had been attended to, and had received an affirmative answer from the plumber and the bricklayer, I am of opinion that his duty as an architect, in the matter of the required protection of said pipes from the weather, would have been ended. Yet, under these very circum-

> stances, the packing might have been intentionally or carelessly omitted, in fraud upon both architect and owner, and could it still be claimed that the architect had not fully performed his work? The learned counsel for appellant is, in effect, asking us to hold that the defects of the character above named establish, as a matter of law, that plaintiffs have not completely performed their agreement.
>
> An architect is no more a mere overseer of foreman or watchman than he is a guarantor of a flawless building, and the only question that can arise in a case where general performance of duty is shown is whether, considering all the circumstances and peculiar facts involved, he has or has not been guilty of negligence. This is a question of fact and not of law.

The general principles have been restated many times since, but never with more clarity. The above quotations are as useful today as they were in 1889, and although the rule varies in its precise application from state to state, the case referred to is as much an excellent guide to the expressed rule of law now as then.

An architect or engineer may be held liable for injury to third persons as a result of plans or specifications which have resulted in the creation of hazardous conditions.

If an owner accepts a building which is so designed as to create a hazardous condition for third parties using it, can the architect be held liable in damages for injuries suffered by such third persons?

Whatever the law in other states, it is now the settled law of New York that an architect may be held liable for injury to third persons resulting from a hidden or latent defect in a structure caused by improper design or planning. The New York Court of Appeals in *Inman v. Binghamton Housing Authority,* 3 N.Y. 2d 137, has ruled that an architect will be liable for such defects, even if the owner has accepted the building. The court, however, overruled a lower court decision which had held the architect liable even where the defect in question was apparent.

In the *Inman* case—six years after the completion of construction —a two-year-old child fell off the stoop located at the rear entranceway to his apartment. Suit was instituted against the architect, the builder, and against the public housing authority which owned and operated the property.

The complaint against the architect alleged that the infant had sustained severe injury because the architect, in designing the apartment building, had created "hazardous and extremely dangerous conditions" in the stoop area, "well-knowing" that it would be used by infant children. The complaint further alleged that the architect furnished improper designs and plans because of the absence of a "protective railing, guard, or any device whatever to protect the occupants" and other persons from falling off the stoop; in designing a rear door which opens outwards to the porch in such a manner that anyone on the porch is "required to back precariously close to the edge"; and finally that the "step leading from the porch or stoop to the sidewalk" was "grossly inadequate" because it was located in the center of the porch and did not extend its entire length.

The architect contended that, since the accident occurred many years after the owner had accepted the building, he was not liable for injuries sustained by third persons with whom he had no contractual relationship. Both the Appellate Division (the lower court) and the Court of Appeals of New York ruled that an architect could be held liable for injury to third persons despite the lack of contractual relationship or "privity" between them. The Court of Appeals, however, in reversing the decision of the lower court further ruled that the architect could only be held liable for improper designs or plans after the acceptance by the owner if the hazardous or dangerous condition which he created was latent or concealed.

In considering the liability of an architect or builder to third persons, the court considered prior precedents which enunciated the rule that a manufacturer of something inherently dangerous is liable for injuries to remote users. The court said:

> The cases establish that the manufacturer of a machine or other article, "dangerous because of the way in which it functions, and patently so, owes to . . . [remote users] a duty merely to make it free from latent defects and concealed dangers." (*Campo v. Scofield,* 301 N.Y. 468, 471, 95 N.E. 2d 802, 803.) "We have not yet reached the state," we wrote in the Campo case, supra, 301 N.Y. at pages 472-473, 95 N.E. 2d at page 804, "where a manufacturer is under the duty of making a machine accident proof or foolproof." . . . Suffice it to note that, in cases dealing with a manufacturer's liability for injuries to remote users, the stress has always been upon the duty of guarding against *hidden*

defects and of giving notice of *concealed* dangers *(Cases cited).* In point of fact, several of the cases actually declare that a duty is owed, a liability is imposed, *only if* the defect or danger be not "known" or "patent" or discoverable "by a reasonable inspection." And, since the presence of a latent defect or a danger not generally known is precedent to the manufacturers' liability, the absence of such a recital in the complaint is fatal to the existence of a cause of action.

Examination of the pleading before us discloses its invalidity. It contains no allegation of any latent defect or concealed danger. It simply complains of (1) the absence of "a protective railing, guard or any device," (2) the arc made by the door when opened, and (3) the fact that the step did not extend full length of the stoop, all patently obvious defects, if, indeed, they are defects at all. From none of these recitals may it be said that the architects or the builder violated a duty owed to users of the stoop. Entirely lacking, to paraphrase what we said in the Campo case, supra, 301 N.Y. 468, 471, 95 N.E. 2d 802, is any suggestion that the structure possessed a latent defect or an unknown danger and, in the very nature of things, entirely lacking is any recital that the absence of a railing or other device was unknown or undiscoverable. As we have already indicated, such omissions are fatal.

The court further compared the type of defects considered in the decisions in which a remote user had recovered against a manufacturer to the facts of the case before it. The court stated:

Analysis of the decisions in which a remote user has recovered in tort, be it from a manufacturer, supplier or contractor, amply demonstrates how different the instant case is. Here, we have nothing like the sudden collapse of an imperfectly constructed scaffold, a defective automobile wheel or a faultily erected concrete ceiling (*Devlin v. Smith,* 89 N.Y. 470; *MacPherson v. Buick Motor Co.,* supra, 217 N.Y. 382, 111 N.E. 1050, L.R.A. 1916F, 696; *Adams v. White Construction Co.,* supra, 299 N.Y. 641, 87 N.E. 2d 52); nothing like the breaking of a poorly made handle on a coffee urn (*Hoenig v. Central Stamping Co.,* 273, N.Y. 485, 6 N.E. 2d 415); nothing like the explosion of a defectively manufactured soda bottle, aerated water bottle or coffee urn (*Smith v. Peerless Glass Co.,* 259 N.Y. 292, 181 N.E. 576; *Torgesen* v. *Schultz,* 192 N.Y. 156, 84 N.E. 956, 18 L.R.A., N.S., 726; *Statler v. George A. Ray Mfg. Co.,* 195 N.Y. 478, 88 N.E. 1063); nothing like the explosion of an electric transformer, improperly packed (*Rosebrock v. General Electric Co.*

236 N.Y. 227, 140 N.E. 571). In short, in the present case, we have nothing that is related to, or stems from, the existence of a latent fault or hidden danger in either design or construction. The complaint reveals a one-step stoop, two steps high along a part of its length, with no railing or other protective device around it, from which an apparently unattended child fell. Whatever the defect, it may not be said to have been latent, and, whatever the danger, it certainly was not hidden. That being so, it is evident that the requirements of the MacPherson-Buick rule have not been met; the complaint of the Inmans against the architects and the builder is without legal basis and was properly dismissed at Special Term.

In considering the liability of the architect and the contractor, the court in the *Inman* case applied the same standards and rules and thus dismissed the action against the contractor, as well as the architect. The liability, however, of a contractor is not always identical with that of an architect and to treat their legal position identically can lead to confusion. For example, in certain situations a contractor may be deemed to be free of responsibility because he has relied upon the plans and specifications of the architect (See 13 *American Law Reports* 2d, 195). Each factual situation must be separately considered. The conclusion to be drawn from the case discussed is that an architect may be held liable for latent defects in a building long after it was concluded. If at all possible his insurance should cover this contingency.

Architectural plans which violate building restrictions may constitute negligent performance and jeopardize the architect's right to compensation.

An architect who prepares plans and specifications for a building in ignorance or disregard of the applicable building restrictions may seriously jeopardize his right to compensation for his services. The courts have held that an architect is bound to know the statutory rules and regulations governing the use and erection of buildings. He must further know the building restrictions applicable to the specific lot on which the building he is planning is to be erected, if he is informed of the location. Should his plans violate the building restrictions in either regard he will not be entitled to recover from the owner the value of his services, and may be liable for the owner's damages. Some decisions will prove disturbing to those who are under the impression that the architect's responsibility or liability ends with the granting of a certificate of occupancy or its equivalent. A New York court confirmed the action of a municipality in revoking a certificate of occupancy some two years after it had been granted, after the premises had been used and after the owner had made investments in reliance upon the granting of the certificate. In part the court said:

> The petitioners although they could have done so, did not offer any proof at the hearings to show that the certificate of occupancy was lawfully applied for or that it was lawfully issued. They were content to rely solely upon the issuance of the certificate of occupancy as evidence of its validity. It is significant to observe that the petitioners did not know who actually filed Application No. 3453/1946 on their behalf. Both the petitioner . . . and his attorney disclaimed that they filed it. *The inference to be drawn from the attorney's statement is that petitioner's architect, . . . or someone in his behalf, filed it.* Petitioners did not offer any proof, however, as to the person who filed the application and as to its contents. The record also shows that it was the dishonest clerk who handled this application and made the entries in the docket book with respect thereto . . .
>
> Argument is also made by the petitioners that where an owner has acted in good faith upon the strength of a certificate of occupancy, he may not be deprived of the vested right of which he thus acquires. . . . Here, however, the certificate of occupancy was illegally issued and under such circumstances our courts have sustained the revocation of the permit or certificate of occupancy notwithstanding the fact that improvements or investments have been made on the strength of such illegal permit.

It seems quite clear that should an architect participate knowingly in the illegal granting of a certificate or permit, he forfeits his right to compensation for services rendered and, in addition, is subject to an action for damages to reimburse the owner for his costs.

An architect has certain duties and makes certain implied representations to those with whom he contracts to furnish architectural services. He implies that he possesses reasonable skill and ability;

that he has an adequate knowledge of the science of construction of buildings; that he will exercise reasonable care, judgment, and technical skill to see that the work is properly done. Further than that, he implies that the work when completed will be suitable and capable of being used for the purpose for which it was prepared. This will mean, among other things, that he undertakes to plan a building which can be lawfully built on the site intended by the owner.

As one court has pointed out:

> An architect is an expert in his particular line of work. He so holds himself and is employed because he is such. He is not only bound to know the character of materials necessary to the construction of a safe and durable building of the design required, but is bound to know also the building restrictions imposed by the law of the place where he is informed the building is to be erected.

The facts and decision in one of the leading cases on this subject are instructive about the extent to which such responsibility for knowledge of construction law has been imposed on the architect. In that case, the owner of a vacant lot in Seattle proposed to improve the lot by erecting an apartment building on it. He pointed out to the architect a six-story apartment building on an adjoining lot and requested a similar building. Before the plans were completed, the owner decided to increase the size of the building and directed plans to be drawn for an eight-story building. Following completion of the new plans bids were taken which exceeded the estimated cost considerably. The owner then decided to abandon the project and refused to pay for the architect's services.

The owner's defense to a suit by the architect to recover for his services was that the plans were useless to him since they violated city building ordinances. The plans as submitted provided for a smaller court area for light and air than required by the ordinance and failed to provide the necessary space for yard room. It was determined at the trial that to satisfy the statutory requirements would require a re-drawing of the entire set of plans. The architect was held not entitled to compensation for his services since he had failed to furnish plans for a building which could lawfully be built on the site chosen.

Nor was the architect relieved of responsibility by the fact that the owner desired a building similar to the apartment house on the adjoining lot, which violated the ordinances to the same extent as the building planned by the architect. The court stated:

> The rule might be otherwise, had the defendant (owner) known the fact and directed plans to be drawn in accordance therewith in spite of such knowledge. But the evidence makes it clear that he had no such knowledge and that a mere inspection of the building and the ordinances would not disclose the fact to a person not skilled in building construction. On the other hand, the plaintiff did know it, or ought to have known of it, and it was negligence on his part not to so inform the defendant before entering upon the work of drawing the plans.

If the architect is employed generally to prepare plans and specifications for a building of a given style and dimensions and is not informed where it is to be erected he may recover for his services even though the owner cannot lawfully build it on the plot he chooses.

The court, however, did permit the architect to recover for the initial plans drawn for the six-story building. The plans were incomplete at the time the defendant stopped work on them and it could not then be known with certainty whether they would have violated the ordinances or would have been otherwise defective when completed. Since the owner had stopped work on them, he could not escape payment for the work performed to that point.

This latter rule has been applied to other cases where work has been stopped on plans which in their incomplete state violate city or state laws. Where the architect agrees to revise the plans to conform to building restrictions, the owner is not justified in stopping work and refusing to pay the reasonable value of the services furnished up to that point.

In dealing with the cases involving plans violative of the building laws, courts have on occasion denied the architect recovery on the ground that his contract with the owner is unenforceable because it contemplates an unlawful end. In one case an architect was employed to draw plans for a motion picture theater. The building was to contain in addition to the theater several stores, dwellings, and a public bath house. The law relating to motion picture houses prohibited the use of any part of such building for dwelling or department store purposes and further imposed criminal penalties for its violation. The court held that a contract to plan and erect a building in violation of such law would be illegal and for that reason could not be enforced. In fixing responsibility, the court stated:

> All men are supposed to know the law, and further, one holding himself out as an architect is particularly charged

with knowledge of the statutory regulations and restrictions governing the erection and use of buildings; therefore, we must assume both the plaintiffs and the defendants knew that the uses to which the latter contemplated putting the proposed structure were forbidden under a criminal penalty by the statutes of Pennsylvania.

To what extent will an architect be charged with knowledge of the law relating to construction? The broad generalization found in the cases appear to set no definable limit to the scope of his inquiry into construction law. However the facts in these cases present a more limited picture permitting certain conclusions to be drawn.

It is apparent that when an architect draws plans and specifications for a building such as a theater, he must comply with the laws governing its construction and must make his work conform with the requirements pertaining to light, air space, exits, yardage area, etc.

But there is a larger area of zoning law which the cases have not touched. If he must know that a building is required to be set back 10 feet from the street, must he also know that a building in a certain neighborhood can be erected only on a plot containing a minimum of two acres? If he must know that a hotel building is required to have rooms of a certain size for each occupant, must he also know that a particular section is zoned to exclude hotels or other commercial establishments? These questions have not yet been directly considered.

A New York case seems to indicate that for certain types of zoning law the responsibility for compliance is solely that of the owner. In that case, an architect had been employed to draw plans for a theater. After the plans had been approved by the Building Department, it appeared that the zoning restrictions did not permit the erection of a theater on the site chosen. The owner opposed payment for architectural services performed on the ground that the building could not lawfully be built and that the contract was, therefore, unenforceable. The court permitted recovery stating that the contract was not primarily illegal although it would have become so if completed. The court further said that completion was rendered impossible through circumstances which were particularly the fault of the owner. The duty of the architect to know the zoning law was not directly raised or considered, but it is significant that he was permitted to recover for plans which could not be used on the site which the owner contemplated.

The courts may at some future date be compelled to draw more specific conclusions. Whatever the outcome, the foregoing cases amply demonstrate the principle that an architect will be well-advised to look into the law governing building restrictions, including zoning. It may also be advisable for the architect to require in his contract with the owner that the owner furnish him with a copy of the deed to the site on which construction is contemplated in order that the architect may check to ascertain if there are restrictive covenants of any kind upon the use of the property. Such precautionary measures will not only assure the architect that he will be paid for his services but also will save his client the cost of plans which he will be unable to use.

The right of a contractor to recover damages sustained because of the improper performance of another contractor may depend upon the terms of the owner's contract with each contractor.

Many contracts between owner and contractor (particularly contracts with governmental agencies) explicitly provide that each contractor employed on the project will co-operate with other contractors and co-ordinate his work with such other contractors. Two decisions by the United States Circuit Court of Appeals construing such a provision, one in New York and one in Mississippi, reached opposite conclusions as to the legal liability of one contractor to another contractor for improper performance.

The New York case (*Brotherton v. Merritt-Chapman & Scott Corp.*, 213 F. 2d 477) involved two contractors who had been awarded contracts with the United States to construct a portion of the buildings for a hospital. The contract with the government in each instance provided: "The contractor shall obtain all required licenses and permits. He shall be responsible for all damages to all persons that occur as a result of his fault or negligence in connection with the prosecution of the work."

The contract further provided:

> The government may award other contracts for additional work and the contractor shall fully co-operate with such other contractors and carefully fit his own work to that provided

under other contracts as may be directed by the contracting officer. The contractor shall not commit or permit any act which will interfere with the performance of work by any other contractor.

The plaintiff contended that the defendant, by unreasonably delaying the site preparation, and thereby making it impossible for the plaintiff to have access to the site on which the work was to be performed, had caused him great expense and increased costs. The court, however, took the position that the provisions of the contract above quoted were intended solely for the government's benefit, and not for the benefit of other contractors. The contractor in default would be responsible to the government, but not to another contractor who sustained damages because of such default.

The United States Circuit Court of Appeals in Mississippi, however, reached a contrary conclusion in a similar case (*M. T. Reed Const. Co. v. Virginia Metal Products Corp.*, 213 F. 2d 337). The plaintiff in that case had been awarded a contract by the Mississippi State Building Commission for the general construction of a library building for the University of Mississippi. The defendant had been awarded a contract by the Commission to furnish and install a metal section of steel book stacks. Another contractor was awarded a contract to install the plumbing and heating. Each contractor, in his agreement with the State Building Commission, specifically agreed to co-ordinate his work and to co-operate with each other contractor so as to facilitate and expedite the completion of the building. Performance was limited to 300 days.

The general contractor alleged that, due to the failure of the defendant to furnish and install expeditiously the steel book stacks and to co-ordinate his efforts with those of the plaintiff, he, the plaintiff, sustained substantial damages. The defendant contended that it only owed a duty to the owner and that the plaintiff was but an incidental beneficiary of the contract between the defendant and the State Building Commission and could not maintain an action for damages.

The court, in reversing the trial judge's dismissal of the suit, pointed out that the promise of each contractor to the owner that he would co-operate and co-ordinate his work with every other contractor was an inducement to each such other contractor to enter into his contract with the owner. In holding that the plaintiff was a direct beneficiary of the defendant's contract with the government and could maintain an action for damages, the court stated:

> Upon the facts . . . and under our interpretation of the written contract, we agree with appellant that it was a direct beneficiary of the contract of appellee with the state building commission, which obligated the appellee to co-operate with appellant and co-ordinate its work with that of appellant so as to enable both of them to complete their respective jobs on time. The building could not have been completed without such mutual obligation on the part of each of the contractors, and the obligation so to do was a part of the consideration that induced each of the contractors to undertake its particular job at the agreed price.

The negligence of one contractor can, and often does, cause hardship and damage to other contractors furnishing services on the same project. Under the present state of the law, a contractor cannot be certain that he will be permitted to maintain an action against another contractor who has caused him damage because of the latter's failure to perform properly, unless the owner's contract with each contractor specifically so provides. It is in the interest of the owner that such a provision be contained in his contract, as it would be further insurance of adequate and proper performance on the part of each contractor.

Faulty construction is not necessarily a result of negligent performance. Inadequate building codes or lack of other appropriate legislation may permit the creation of construction hazards.

On rare occasions there is dramatically demonstrated the vital service which the architect renders. Such an occasion may advance the architect's cause with more effect and with more impact than carefully planned public relations programs, extensively financed and pursued.

Such a situation occurred on May 9, 1955, when the temporary structural support of the New York Coliseum collapsed, causing the death of one laborer and injuring more than fifty.

The investigation into the cause of the collapse by the district attorney's office revealed the inadequacy of present Building Code Regulations and recommended a requirement that plans for temporary structures be drawn by a registered architect or engineer.

The district attorney's inquiry showed that metal jacks resting on 4″ ×4″ timbers were used to support the main floor where concrete was being poured. These timbers were braced horizontally, but there was little crossbracing and no bracing at all on the jacks. In the opinion of the district attorney's report, the temporary support was apparently designed only to sustain the dead load of reinforced concrete and collapsed under the thrust of pressures exerted by the activity of motorized buggies transporting cement, concrete-agitating machines, and other construction operations going on at the same time.

To pour the concrete, motorized buggies weighing about 3000 pounds fully loaded were used to transport fresh concrete to the main floor. When dumped, the concrete was spread and vibrated by concrete-agitating machines. Just before the collapse, there were about eight such buggies transporting concrete, several of which might dump their contents at the same time. In addition, other construction work in various phases was being speeded in order to meet the schedule on the project's completion.

The district attorney's report also found that the inspector assigned to the project by the Department of Housing & Buildings did not have an engineering background, but rather had been a bricklayer. It further reported that this inspector visited some 15 building sites each day in a wide city area and had last inspected the Coliseum site four days before the collapse.

The report concluded that the contractor had not been guilty of criminal negligence. It found that the applicable New York City Building Code and Charter provisions did not afford adequate protection to workmen and the public, in certain respects. The New York City Building Code presently provides that, in the pouring of concrete, "forms shall be substantially and sufficiently tight to prevent leakage of water; and shall be properly braced or tied together so as to maintain position and insure safety to workmen and passersby." It was recommended that this be changed to require that an engineer or architect design the temporary structure and that the plans be filed with the Department of Housing & Buildings to insure compliance by the builder.

The New York City Charter requires that the Inspector of Carpentry & Masonry shall have at least five years' experience as a mason, carpenter, architect, or engineer, at salaries ranging from $4200 to $4800. The report called for the presence of a properly compensated *engineer* to inspect projects which involve great quantities of reinforced concrete.

Although revision of building codes will provide an added safeguard, such revision is a long process and one which rarely reaches every community. In the meanwhile, there would seem to be a professional obligation on the part of architects and engineers to try to prevent such costly losses of life and property as occurred in the collapse of the New York Coliseum. Such an obligation depends on whether it is enough for the architect simply to design the structure, or whether he should also have a professional concern for the construction hazards created.

If the architectural profession is properly concerned with these hazards, then perhaps the immediate solution is to insist on a clause in builders' contracts requiring the use of professional services on the design of temporary supports. Such a clause would be an excellent stop-gap measure until such time as building codes are revised. And, if such a clause becomes a widespread and standard provision, it may even obviate the need for revision of existing regulations.

What is even more important, is that the public be made aware that the architectural profession is deeply concerned with the essential problems involved and that it, as well as the New York district attorney, is making and will make specific recommendations to the legislature, to those concerned with the drawing of contracts, to contractors' groups—to all those involved. In this way, the public will know that design of construction, the problems of construction, and construction itself, are the concern of the architect.

CHAPTER 19: *Underestimation of Cost*

An architect's estimate of costs, when it proves inaccurate, may jeopardize his compensation if it is attributable to want of skill or negligence on his part.

HAVE YOU HAD A CLIENT shake his finger under your nose and accuse you of having misled him as to the cost of the project? If this hasn't happened to you already, there is always the possibility that the immediate future may find you in this situation. Rising and fluctuating construction costs are a hazard not only to the prospective builder but also to the architect. The law provides severe penalties for *negligent* underestimates of costs or disregard of the client's express instructions as to cost limits. Facts in the case of *Eberhard v. Mehlman,* 60 A. 2d 540, are of such general interest in this respect that a direct quotation from the opinion is indicated. Both the Trial and Appellate courts held that the architect who was suing for his compensation was not entitled to a recovery for the drawings he prepared for the remodeling of a liquor store. The Appellate Court in unanimously holding for the client (defendants) and against the architect (plaintiff) said:

> From the stenographic transcript and from certain documents in the case there seems to have been no dispute that plaintiff was engaged to make the drawings and that his compensation was to be four percent of the estimated cost of the work covered thereby. The dispute centered around defendants' claim (which plaintiff denied) that they had made known to plaintiff before he undertook to prepare the drawings and also while such drawings were in course of preparation that they

> would not spend more than $8,000, or at the most $10,000 on the work, and that despite such knowledge he prepared drawings calling for a construction cost of $19,000 or $20,000. The principle error assigned is that there was no evidence to support the finding for defendants, because there was none to show that plaintiff had been given notice of the cost limitation we have just mentioned.
>
> There was testimony by defendants' contractor that before he took plaintiff to visit the premises he told him of the construction cost limitation which defendants had prescribed; that he repeated it to him after he took him there and introduced him to Defendant Mehlman and explained and discussed in detail the work to be done. Defendants' attorney testified that he repeated the prescribed cost limitation to plaintiff at a meeting between plaintiff, the owners, and the contractors, at which meeting plaintiff joined the contractors in expressing the opinion "that the cost of the proposed job should not exceed $10,000 and would seem likely to be approximately $8,000." There was also testimony by Defendant Mehlman that at the same meeting he emphasized in plaintiff's presence that $8,000 was all he could spend on the work. Clearly this testimony was ample to support the finding below.
>
> It is equally clear that the trial judge was not required to reject this testimony and accept plaintiff's statement that the cost of the work had never been discussed with him in advance or while he was preparing his drawings. The question of the weight of the evidence was for the trial judge and not for us to determine.

Although another judge or another jury could have found differently as to the facts, this decision is in accord with principles generally recognized in the law.

In every contract that provides for the services of an architect there is an implied condition that the architect possesses sufficient skill, ability, and taste to enable him to perform his duties properly under that contract. The legal standard which the architect must maintain in the performance of his profession calls for the possession and exercise of that skill and care which should be reasonably and ordinarily possessed and exercised by members of the profession. The architect, therefore, in undertaking to estimate costs holds himself out as having the ability and knowledge to estimate in advance, with reasonable accuracy, the cost of buildings planned and designed by him.

An architect would, of course, not be deprived of his compensation where plans were drawn calling for construction costs in excess of the architect's estimate, when the owner approved and accepted such plans, or where the architect is required to prepare plans in accordance with desires and specifications of the owner. *However, where the architect knows (or where knowledge may be imputed to him) that the owner wishes plans drawn that will call for a limited construction cost or where the contract between the parties specifically provides the same, the architect draws plans calling for a greater construction cost at the risk of losing his compensation and at the further risk of being held liable for any damages suffered by the owner.*

Municipalities and other governmental units enter into many contracts calling for architectural services. Many of these contracts provide that the plans to be drawn by the architect shall call for no greater construction cost than the amount of money appropriated for that purpose. There have been instances where architects have prepared plans that require construction costs greater than the sums appropriated by the legislative body in question. Courts have held that, under these circumstances, the architect may not recover the agreed price for the work he has performed or even on *quantum meruit* for these services.

One of the more interesting situations of this type arose in the City of New York, where an architect and the City negotiated a contract wherein it was stipulated that "the estimated cost . . . shall be well within the total appropriation," which in this instance was $500,000. But the architect in question drew plans which would have required a construction cost of $3,300,000, and the plans were approved by the president of the borough in which the project was to be constructed. The court, in denying the architect recovery for compensation for services rendered, held that the borough president, as well as the architect, was bound by the terms of the contract; and that the borough president could not waive these provisions even though the architect insisted that the public building, for the purpose for which it was to be used, could not have been built for the sum appropriated. Their expectation that further appropriations would be forthcoming was not legally justified. The court in this respect stated:

> It is argued that a public building, for the purpose that this was to be used, could not have been built for the sum appropriated, and, therefore, the parties were justified in believing that

> further sums would be appropriated. The difficulty with this argument is that we are required to prophesy the future action of the board of estimate or to exclude entirely the words referring to the appropriation. The contract may have been a foolish one for the parties to have made. We, however, are not required to make another one for them, but to interpret the contract they have made according to the language used by them.

Although loss of compensation for services rendered is of serious consequence to the architect for underestimating the cost of a proposed construction, a suit for damages instituted by the owner may have even more dire effect. In the same manner as a doctor or lawyer, an architect may be held responsible for any damages suffered by his employer resulting from malpractice on the part of the architect. If the architect fraudulently or negligently underestimates the cost of a structure to be built and in reliance upon such estimate the owner suffers damage, the owner may seek to compensate himself for such damage by legal action against the architect.

One of the leading cases of this type was litigated in Texas, *Capitol Hotel Co., Inc. v. Rittenberry,* 41 S.W. 2d 697. The architect and the owner in that case entered into a contract by the terms of which the architect agreed to furnish sketches, drawings, specifications; to superintend the work; and to audit all accounts in the construction of the hotel. The owner contended that the architect held himself out as proficient and experienced and having the ability to estimate the cost of buildings. The owner had informed the architect that he was proceeding in the construction of the hotel in reliance upon the architect's estimate of cost. The architect had estimated such cost at $340,000 and the owner had arranged to borrow that sum for construction. The hotel in question was to have from 150 to 160 guest rooms and the owner took the position that a reasonable return could be obtained on this investment only if the cost per guest room approximated $2,000. The actual cost of the material and labor for the hotel amounted to approximately $500,000, substantially more than the estimated cost. The Texas court held that if the owner could substantiate his contentions, he was entitled to recover his damages from the architect.

The measure of damages for negligent underestimation of costs is not uniform throughout the states. In the *Capitol Hotel Co., Inc.* case, the owner had sought to recover the difference between the cost of the building and the architect's estimated cost. This amounted to approximately $160,000. The court, however, held that the intrinsic value of the building in question had been enhanced by the expenditure of a greater sum than the estimated cost and therefore to permit the owner to recover this difference would afford him a greater relief than that to which he was entitled. The proper measure of damages as set forth by this court would be based upon a recovery that would give the owner a return on his investment equal to the return that he would have obtained if the actual cost of the building had been no greater than the estimated cost. There have been other legal determinations that have awarded damages based upon the difference between the actual and estimated cost of construction. However, in these instances there have been, in the damages, elements of fraud involved.

Loss of compensation or a legal suit for damages or both may be an architect's "reward" for misjudging the cost of a proposed structure for which he is engaged to draw plans. With a recent history of rising material and labor costs, estimates of cost are particularly hazardous. The architect must protect himself insofar as it is practicably possible. One such method would be to incorporate a specific provision in the contract of employment (more effective than provided in the standard American Institute of Architects form) that would prevent a disgruntled client from seizing on an early estimate as the basis of a law suit.

A more practical solution, however, would be for the architect to be as cautious as possible in giving estimates—to steel himself against underestimating "because construction costs are ridiculously high and should come down." Tell the client the sad news early! It may turn out to be an expensive mistake if you do not. If only for your peace of mind, make certain that your agreement covers you against litigious clients who find the project cost more than they anticipated—not an unusual situation today.

An architect who guarantees the cost of a building project is generally not entitled to compensation if his plans call for an expenditure in excess of such sum.

Does the American Institute of Architects Owner-Architect Agreement protect the architect from an owner's claim that the architect guaranteed a maximum cost of construction? The answer would appear to be "no," in view of a decision of an Illinois appellate court (and similar decisions in other jurisdictions) in which it was held that an owner may prove an oral promise by the architect that the project in question will not exceed a certain sum, even though the parties had entered into a written AIA contract for the furnishing of architectural services (*Spitz v. Brickhouse,* 3 Ill. App. 2d 536, 123 N.E. 2d 117).

This writer has previously pointed out the hazards to the architect of underestimating costs. Loss of compensation or a legal suit for damages for negligence may be the result if the architect misjudges the cost of a proposed structure for which he is engaged to draw plans. It was recommended that the contract of employment should be so worded as to prevent a disgruntled owner from seizing on an early estimate as the basis of a lawsuit, and it was urged that the architect be as cautious as possible in giving estimates.

The issue raised, however, in the Illinois case was not the liability of the architect for a negligent underestimation of costs; rather, the owner's defense was based upon a breach of an agreement by the architect under which, it was alleged, he undertook to furnish plans that could be executed within a particular price. In this case the architect and the owner entered into an AIA form contract for the furnishing of plans for the construction of a home. The owner agreed to pay the architect for his professional services a fee of 10% of the cost of the work, which was to be paid 25% upon the completion of preliminary studies, and an additional 50% during the period of preparation of specifications and working drawings. It was further provided that said payments were to be computed upon a "reasonable cost estimated upon such completed specifications and drawings, or if bids have been received, then computed upon the lowest bona fide bid or bids." The contract in respect to estimates further provided: "When requested to do so, the architect will furnish preliminary estimates on the cost of the work, but he does not guarantee the accuracy of such estimates."

The plaintiff prepared the plans and specifications and eventually bids were received. The lowest bid received was $39,000. The owner abandoned the project because of its cost and refused to pay the architect's fees. The architect instituted suit to collect his compensation.

The owner contended in the trial that he had informed the architect that the maximum amount he could afford for the house was $25,000 and that the architect agreed that the house would not cost in excess of that amount. The AIA form, as prepared by the architect, was signed without any changes, and the owner testified that, when he asked the architect what the contract meant, the architect said: "This is to keep you from changing horses in the middle of the stream."

The trial court ruled in favor of the owner and denied any compensation to the architect for services rendered because of his failure to furnish plans that could be executed for a cost of $25,000 or less. An appellate court affirmed this ruling.

It is a general principle of law that oral agreements, understandings, or conversations may not be introduced into evidence to vary or contradict the terms of a written agreement. The theory of this principle is that all prior negotiations are merged into the written contract. However, the court in the Illinois case permitted the owner to introduce testimony as to the alleged oral understanding relating to maximum cost, on the ground that this testimony did not vary or contradict the written agreement, but rather explained and completed it. The court said:

> The form contract in the instant case is silent as to the style of the house to be designed, the number of its rooms, its dimensions, the quantity and quality of the materials to be used in erecting it, and so on . . . There must be something outside the contract to determine these questions. The Architect must have had instructions outside the contract with which to undertake to comply, in the preparation of his plans . . . One of those instructions must have concerned the cost of the building . . . in the following—all involving similar or substantially identical AIA form contracts—parol evidence to prove an agreement as to maximum cost where the form contract was silent was held admissible. (*Citing cases*)
>
> Furthermore, to sustain plaintiff's contention that the cost is to be determined by the lowest bona fide bid, it would be necessary to hold that no matter how large the bid for doing the work, the Owner would be obligated to pay an architectural fee based on that amount.

The court further pointed out that since the architect furnished the contract form, it must be construed most strongly against him. The court, in this connection, said:

> There is nothing in the contract, nor anything in the circumstances of this case to buttress plaintiff's contention. Expres-

> sion of their intention could have been made clear. They provide the form contract. It is to be construed most strongly against them and any ambiguity resolved favorably to the defendant. . . .
>
> It was not error for the trial court to admit testimony to explain the ambiguities and any incomplete portions of the contract.

From this decision it would appear that proof of an alleged oral agreement guaranteeing the maximum cost of the house would have been excluded if the written contract had set forth in detail a description of the project including the quantity and quality of materials to be used. Such a procedure, however, may be neither practical nor realistic. An alternative method of protection would be to include an express provision in the contract between owner and architect (in addition to the proviso that the architect does not guarantee his estimate of costs) to the effect that the architect does not guarantee that the building can be constructed within any particular cost, estimate, or limitation.

This writer has recommended the following language:

> If requested by the Owner, the Architect will furnish preliminary estimates as to the cost of the Project. However, such estimates are not to be construed in any way as a representation, warranty, or agreement on the part of the Architect of the accuracy of such estimate or that the Project can be constructed for the amount thereof. The Architect's compensation under this contract shall in no way be affected by the correctness of such estimates.

Under the rationale of the cases discussed above, it would appear that such a clause would make it difficult for the owner to claim successfully an oral agreement by the architect pertaining to maximum cost.

CHAPTER 20: *Liability Insurance*

The protection afforded the architect or engineer by professional liability insurance will depend upon the scope of the policy secured.

ARCHITECTS HAVE BEEN DELUGED by letters, brochures and policies of companies offering professional liability insurance. An investigation reveals such a disparity in premium rates as to indicate that a disparity also exists in the coverage of the policies. It is, of course, important for an architect interested in purchasing professional liability insurance to read the policy itself in order to determine what coverage is actually obtained; for, even careful reading of the *literature* accompanying the policy may result in a misconception of the protection afforded. We have selected two typical policies for discussion which are designed to protect the architect against his "errors and omissions."

It should be pointed out that "errors and omissions" that may result in liability to the architect may be divided into three arbitrary classifications:

(1) Those resulting in physical injuries to persons or property (cracked walls, collapsed roofs, etc.).

(2) Those resulting in pecuniary loss to the owner other than that arising out of physical damage (total or partial lack of utility or esthetics of the structure; financial loss to the client as a result of negligent underestimates of cost, etc.).

(3) Damages to the client as a result of dishonest, fraudulent, criminal, or malicious acts, etc.

The last category is apparently exempted from coverage in *both* policies. Since a substantial number of the claims made would fall into the second as well as the first category, it is incumbent upon the architect to determine whether it is important for him to be covered in both categories. It should be kept in mind, of course, that coverage is directly related to the cost of insurance.

POLICY A

The lowest-cost policy by its terms covers "liability imposed upon him (the architect) by law for damages . . . because of bodily injury . . . sustained by any person or persons; and because of injury to or destruction of property, including the loss of use thereof, in direct consequence of any negligent act, error, or omission of the insured, in performance of professional services for others in the insured's profession as architect." Policy A apparently would furnish insurance only in the first category outlined above.

Reference to the brochure accompanying this policy, however, could very easily lead to an erroneous conclusion as to coverage. (We will not discuss at this time the interesting question as to whether the brochure, by its language, or statements by the broker in any way enlarges the coverage set forth in the policy itself.) If the apparent limitation of the language of the policy is kept in mind, it is difficult to understand statements in the brochure which was headed, "The Broadest Professional Liability Form Obtainable."

The text read, in part: "The Insurance Company agrees to pay on behalf of any insured architect all sums which he might be obliged to pay by law for loss to persons or property which is a consequence of negligence in performance of professional service."

"An architect who substantially underestimates, through lack of skill and care, the cost of a proposed structure, which representation is relied upon by the employer in entering in the contract and proceeding with construction, may not only forfeit his right to compensation, but may become liable to his employer for damages."

Policy A is *not* the "broadest form" obtainable; it does not agree to pay *all* sums; and it does *not* cover underestimates of cost.

In the same brochure, under the heading "Typical Court Cases Relating to Liability of Architects," six court cases are referred to. But the language of the policy seems to cover only three of the six cases as digested. These cases involve the collapse of a roof, a cracked wall and the death of a workman resulting from the collapse of the building. The other three cases, which are used to illustrate the possible and potential liability of an architect, as digested, are apparently not covered by the terms of Policy A concerning which the brochure was written. The purpose, therefore, of including them in the brochure is inexplicable.

One of the cases referred to in this brochure refers to the liability of an architect for fraud. By the express terms of Policy A, however, the company is not liable for fraud. In a second case referred to in the brochure an architect had negligently supervised the construction of a building resulting in a departure from the plans agreed upon. There was a variation in roof projection and construction in the front of the building as compared with the other three sides. This is regarded as an esthetic loss to the owner of the building and would not be covered by Policy A if it offers the architect protection only from injuries to person or property. The digest of a third case referred to in the brochure, which would not seem to be covered by the terms of Policy A, relates the situation in which an architect was held liable for failure to exercise reasonable taste. Once again, this is not an injury to person or property for which the policy would seem to protect the architect. It can readily be seen, therefore, that the statements and cases referred to in the brochure in question which do not limit their frame of reference to those situations where there is actual injury (as distinguished from damage) may cause a misconception as to the extent of coverage of Policy A.

It is also of interest to note under Policy A that the policy only applies to negligent acts, errors or omissions which occur during the period of the policy and that claims for damage must be instituted within five years after the end of such period. Also this policy may be cancelled by either party within *five days* after written notice.

Policy A also provides that if the insured has other insurance against a loss covered by this policy, the company shall only be liable for a proportionate share of such loss.

POLICY B

This policy agrees to indemnify the insured against any claim which may be made "by reason of any negligent act, error, or omission in or about the conduct of any business conducted by or on behalf of the firm in their professional capacity." This language, of course, is much broader in scope than the language of Policy A. There is no limitation of liability to errors or omissions which result in injury to person or property.

This language is broad enough to include the second as well as the first category heretofore discussed. However, by the terms of

Policy B, fraud, libel, slander, and other torts of this nature are specifically excluded.

It is a policy that is used by lawyers, doctors, and other professionals. Thus, the language contained therein affords a greater coverage and protection to the architect than a policy such as Policy A which was specifically designed for architectural liability. However, once again, it must be emphasized that Policy A is a low-cost policy presented as part of a planned group program. Policy B, on the other hand, calls for a much greater premium for its wider coverage.

There are, however, even under Policy B, certain provisions which weaken the protection of the architect. There is, for example, a deductible clause of $250.00 whereunder the insured bears the risk of any claim which does not exceed $250.00. Policy B may be cancelled by either party on giving ten days' notice of his intention to do so. Further, the company will be liable only for claims which are made against the insured during the subsistance of the policy. Under the terms of this policy, therefore, the insured architect might be prejudiced by the failure of the injured party to make a prompt claim.

It is important to the practicing architect in considering the purchase of professional liability insurance that he know exactly what he is buying and the extent of his protection. There should be *no reliance upon the literature* which is distributed to sell the various types of policies offered, although such literature may serve to emphasize the need and desirability of professional liability insurance. The only safe and sensible procedure is to study the policy itself to determine its exact coverage. It may well be that more than one type of policy may have to be purchased in order to afford the architect the extent of protection desired.

CHAPTER 21: *Specific Performance of Construction Contract*

The courts will not compel the specific performance of the contractor's, architect's or engineer's contract with the owner. Arbitration tribunals, however, may grant such relief.

IT IS THE RULE rather than the exception for a speculative builder to sell his house from a "model." The purchaser makes a down payment and usually makes periodic payments during the course of construction, which are not always matched by a correlative amount of performance on the part of the builder. What happens when the builder decides not to carry out his part of the bargain, and abandons the work? This may take the form of an obvious abandonment, or it may take the more subtle form of a slow-down. What can the buyer do? Can he, in the parlance of the courts, get specific performance of his contract? That is, can he get a judgment of the court requiring the builder to complete the building in accordance with the plans and specifications within a reasonable time? The answer is, unhappily, "probably not." It is unfortunate that more people purchasing a home under these circumstances do not understand the importance of investigating the reliability of a speculative builder. Not to do so is to make a speculator of the buyer, as well as the seller.

A New York case illustrates one court's attitude toward the problem of specific performance of construction contracts. The plaintiffs were purchasers of real property upon which the defendant was to erect a dwelling. The building constructed failed in many respects to comply with the plans and specifications, as required by the contract between the parties. The plaintiffs paid $1800 down on contract and claimed they were ready to pay the balance provided the builder finished the building in accordance with the plans. The relief sought by the plaintiffs was a judgment directing the defendant to remedy all defects and complete the building. The court refused to grant this relief, relying upon the "general" rule that on account of the great difficulty and, often, the impossibility attending a judicial superintendence and execution of performance, contracts for the erection or repair of buildings and the conduct of operations requiring time, special knowledge, skill, and personal supervision will not be specifically enforced (*Stern v. Freeport Acres, Inc.*, 107 N.Y.S. 2d 810).

The plaintiffs in the above case, although defeated in their attempt to obtain specific performance of the construction contract, were not without any legal remedy. The law affords a purchaser three distinct legal remedies:

(1) The purchaser is permitted to reject title and recover a judgment for his down-payment, with interest, and in furtherance of this, he is entitled to a purchaser's lien upon the real property for that amount.

(2) The purchaser may complete the building and bring action against the builder for the expense incurred.

(3) The purchaser may prove the difference in value between the building, as constructed, and as the plans provided, and obtain a corresponding abatement in the sales price.

The three remedies available to the purchaser, although compensating him to some degree for the builder's failure to complete the project, do not afford complete relief. A purchase of real property always has been considered by the courts as something special. It was for this reason that equity courts early developed the doctrine of specific performance of contracts for the purchase of real property on the theory that a money judgment alone would not adequately compensate for a breach of a contract to sell real property.

An exception to the rule that contracts for the purchase of real property may be specifically enforced exists, however, in the ruling found in the *Stern v. Freeport Acres, Inc.* case, which has been stated by the courts as follows:

> There is a class of special and exceptional contracts in which courts of equity refuse to exercise jurisdiction by way of specific performance. These are contracts having such terms and provisions that the court could not carry into effect its decree with-

out some personal supervision and oversight over the work to be done, extending over a considerable period of time, such as agreements to repair or build, to construct works, to build or carry on railways, mines and the like. (*Wharton v. Stoutenburgh,* 35 N.J. Eq. 266.)

The United States Supreme Court has also expressed itself in the following language:

> It must be liable to perpetual calls in the future for like enforcement of the contract, and it assumes, in this way, an endless duty, inappropriate to the functions of the Court, which is as ill-calculated to do this as it is to supervise and enforce a contract for building a house or building a railroad, both of which have in this country been declared to be outside of its proper functions, and not within its powers of specific performance. (*Texas & R.R. Co. v. Marshall,* 136 U.S. 393.)

The policy of completely rejecting the purchaser's plea for specific performance and relegating him to the law court for an action for money only, in many instances works a hardship upon the purchaser and in reality affords him inadequate relief. The alternative of allowing an abatement of the purchase price means that the purchaser becomes a reluctant builder—something he did not contemplate or desire when he signed the original contract. The other legal alternatives, *i.e.* the completion of the dwelling by the purchaser and his action for damages, or the rejection of title and an action for return of the purchase price, leave the purchaser with a money judgment which may be uncollectible because of the builder's insolvency.

For these reasons, therefore, some courts do permit specific performance of building contracts. Where the work to be performed by the defendant was for the benefit of land sold, conveyed, or leased by him to the plaintiff, these courts have found stronger equities in favor of specific performance of the contract. In *Zygmunt v. Avenue Realty Co.,* 108 N.J. Eq. 462, the defendant had sold a lot to the plaintiff but with a stipulation to construct a street and sidewalks in front of the lot within a year. The judge permitted evidence to be presented whereby the character of the sidewalks could be fixed. The following should be noted in his opinion granting specific performance:

> In cases involving building and construction contracts, the court usually weighs, on the one side, the difficulties of enforc-

> ing and supervising the execution of a decree, and on the other side of the balance, the importance of specific performance to complainant and the inadequacy of an action for damages. If the difficulties attendant upon enforcement are not impressive, and the actual performance of the contract seems of much moment to complainants, courts are apt to grant equitable relief. The court may decree performance of a contract for construction work on land of the defendant when the difficulty of enforcing and supervising the execution of the decree is not great and the work is essential to the use of complainant's adjoining land and damages are not an adequate remedy.
>
> But no contract is specifically enforced unless it be certain in all its part. . . . . The decree should be so exact that a defendant may not be in doubt with respect to his duty under the decree; he should not be left to guess what is required of him by the court.
>
> The importance of performance to complainants and the inadequacy of damages, are apparent. I cannot assume that complainants have sufficient funds to improve Orchard Street, and even if they are able to do so, an adequate remedy is not thereby indicated. . . . . Whether, after spending their money for this improvement, complainants could recover from defendant for the expense, is doubtful; there is no evidence concerning the financial standing of defendant. . . . A breach of contract which deprives one of the use of his land is a breach which cannot be adequately compensated by a judgment for damages.

The decision also serves as a guide to the owner or architect considering a contractor or builder. The owner particularly should understand that the lowest bid does not necessarily mean the lowest cost. He should understand how inadequate is an action for damages if the contractor does not properly perform. He should understand how important it is for the contract to be "certain in all its parts" so that neither the owner nor the contractor "should be left to guess what is required of him." He should know whether contractors considered by him "have sufficient funds," whether "they are able" to perform, whether if the contractor unjustifiably breaches his contract the owner can recover his damages—whether the contractor is good for a judgment. He should keep in mind that "a breach of contract which deprives one of the use of his land is a breach which cannot be adequately compensated by a judgment for damages."

Not until he understands all this should he choose his contractor.

II

Does an arbitration panel have the inherent power to compel the performance of a contract, or are its powers limited to awarding damages? This question is of importance to the architect, as agreements to arbitrate disputes are increasingly found in contracts between owner and architect and between owner and contractor. A decision of a New York Appellate court by majority opinion upheld the validity of an arbitration award which directed the specific performance of an employment contract (*Staklinski v. Pyramid Electric Co.*, 6 A.D. 2d 565).

The *Staklinski* case involved a contract between a corporation and its largest stockholder. Under this agreement, the corporation had hired the stockholder as its production manager for a term of years. The agreement provided that if the stockholder was "unable to substantially attend" to his duties for a period of three months, the board of directors of the corporation could, in its discretion, terminate the employment contract. The agreement also provided that "any controversy or claim arising out of or relating to this agreement" should be settled by arbitration.

Nine years before the agreement was to expire, the board of directors of the corporation adopted a resolution declaring the production manager unable to perform his duties because of disability. The production manager petitioned for arbitration, contending that he was not disabled and that the act of the board of directors was arbitrary. He requested the arbitration panel to declare the board's action null and void, and direct the board to perform the employment agreement by reinstating him.

A majority of the arbitrators with one dissenting, ruled that the petitioner was not disabled and that the action of the board of directors constituted an abuse of discretion. The arbitrators further ruled that the contract was still effective and directed the reinstatement of the petitioner.

On appeal to the courts, the board of directors of the corporation contended that reinstatement could not be compelled by the arbitration panel as the petitioner was a key executive in the corporation and, under statutory rule, corporate management is intrusted to the board of directors. They further contended that the award directing the reinstatement of the petitioner constituted an interference with the internal affairs of the corporation. The New York court, in rejecting these contentions, stated the following:

> The contention that upholding an award, which in effect means reinstatement of the petitioner, offends equity and the statutory rule entrusting corporate management to the directors is a most important one.
>
> This cannot be termed such interference with the corporate management by its Board of Directors as to constitute a violation of statutes applicable. . . . Nor does the provision for arbitration or any award made thereunder deprive the corporate board of its power to discharge its duties with respect to the corporate affairs, albeit like any contract it thereafter narrows the choices open to the corporation.

The corporate board of directors argued that if the dispute between it and the petitioner had been submitted to a court of equity, such court would have no power to order the performance of the contract of employment and the reinstatement of the petitioner to his position. The court, in answering this argument, asserted that the arbitration panel had greater power in this respect than a court of equity:

> Lastly, there is no rule of law limiting to money judgments the relief which an arbitrator may award, "even in cases where no equitable decree would be proper if the controversy between the parties were being determined by a court rather than by arbitrators." . . . It is urged that the nature of the award by the arbitrators and any judgment which confirms it presents problems of impossibility of enforcement. The fact that courts of equity have traditionally refused to grant equivalent specific performance in actions based on contracts is cited as proof of the difficulty. The fact of the matter is that much of equity jurisdiction and relief is patterned on the assumption of the test of the adequacy of the relief at law. This has undoubtedly influenced the areas where equitable relief is denied on other substantive grounds, such as is involved here. Hence, when there is an adequate remedy at law equity will the more quickly refrain from granting the extraordinary relief that has been historically associated with equity. But in the case of arbitration no distinction is made between these forms of relief the dichotomy of which is historically associated with the development of our courts. The granting of specific relief in arbitration does not depend upon the inadequacy of the remedy at law or anywhere else. As already pointed out, as embodied in the arbitra-

tion statute and as recognized in our highest court, arbitration may provide relief in circumstances and on conditions which even a court has no power to grant.

The dissenting judges were of the opinion that because the contract involved was one for personal services, specific performance could not be required by the arbitration tribunal. The dissent stated:

> Specifically, the problem here is whether a court must, on an application to confirm an arbitration award, enter a decree of specific performance of a contract for personal services where the court could not do so were an action brought on the contract. In our opinion, the statutory machinery for the enforcement of arbitrations awards contemplates the exercise of a judicial function and not a ministerial one. No judgment should issue from the court which contravenes deeply ingrained principles and rules of equity jurisprudence regarding the specific performance of contracts for personal service. It has long been settled that a court of equity will not decree specific enforcement of contracts for personal services. . . . That power, which courts have eschewed for two centuries, cannot be lightly given to arbitrators. The same conditions which have circumscribed the discretion of the chancery to award specific performance in such instances must be applied to arbitration awards. The established rule as to denial of specific performance of personal services contracts rested upon the difficulty of enforcing such decrees, the fact that the relationship in such contracts was a close personal one involving confidence and loyalty, and the refusal to decree any sort of involuntary servitude. . . . "It would be intolerable if a man could be compelled by a court of equity to serve another against his will, or if a man could be compelled to retain in his employ one he does not want; courts of equity exercise no such power and grant no such relief."

A rule that the parties to a contract for personal services may be compelled to specifically perform is of significance to the construction industry. A contract between owner and architect, consulting engineer and architect, owner and contractor, contractor and subcontractor, etc. all involve elements of personal service. In this area, then, arbitration procedure becomes a more potent weapon in the enforcement of contracts than court action.

MISCELLANEOUS DECISIONS

RIGHTS OF ARCHITECT, ENGINEER AND CONTRACTOR

UNITED STATES. (Ct. of App.) *Wildermuth et al. v. U.S.* 195 F. 2d 18 (1952). Plaintiff brought an action under the Tucker Act to recover additional compensation for architectural services rendered under a contract with the Federal Works Administrator. The contract provided that all disputes arising under the contract should be decided by an administrator whose decision should be final and conclusive on the parties. Upon the abandonment of the project the Commissioner of the Bureau of Community Facilities, who had taken over the functions of administrator, determined that the architects were entitled to a certain amount of compensation under the contract. The court held in the absence and failure to allege or prove fraud on the part of the Commissioner, the architects were not entitled to additional compensation.

COLORADO. *Medical Arts Building v. Ervin,* 257 P. 2d 969 (1953). In a suit to foreclose a mechanic's lien for services rendered by an architect under a contract to prepare plans and specifications for remodeling a building, the court held in favor of the architect where the contract was plain and unambiguous and contained no reference to a $75,000 cost limitation. It was further held that the architect was not liable for damages to the owner for expenditures beyond the expectations and financial ability of the owner in carrying out the plans.

FLORIDA. *Ungaro v. West Palm Beach Biltmore Apartments,* 61 So. 2d 642 (1952). An architect entered into a contract to draw plans and prepare specifications for a project and to secure a loan from the FHA as sponsor, and to make certain loans as working capital, if and when needed, for completion of the project. For these services he was to receive architectural fees and commissions. The court found that, in the absence of a surplus remaining after completion of the project, the sums owed did not become due and payable under the contract until the net revenue from the project should permit.

ILLINOIS. *Alden v. Stromsen,* 347 Ill. App. 439, 106 N.E. 2d 837 (1952). In a suit for engineering fees the defendant relying upon plaintiff's estimate as to the total cost of the engineering services rendered, which was approximately $1,175, the court in upholding a verdict for $4,746.82 declared it was within the province of the jury to determine whether or not additional services were involved and authorized and the nature, extent and value thereof.

INDIANA. *Baird v. Aluminum Seal Co., Inc.,* 105 N.E. 2d 825 (1952). In an action upon a note given as security for the performance of a building contract under which the plaintiff was given the right to declare forfeiture if the builder failed to procure FHA certificates by a certain date, the court held that, inasmuch as the plaintiff expressly waived its right to declare a forfeiture at the time it accrued, the right could not thereafter be asserted in the absence of reasonable and specific notice of intent to reassert it.

KENTUCKY. *Beech Creek Coal Co. v. Jones,* 262 S.W. 2d 174 (1953). A coal company was required to file certain maps and information to fulfil its statutory obligation and employed an engineer to make surveys and provide the maps and engineering data. Subsequent to the termination of employment, the coal company brought an action against the engineer for possession of field books, traverse calculation sheets, and base or hardback maps which the Engineer had made. The court held that, since the material was necessary in order to enable the coal company to fulfil its statutory obligation, such material was the property of the company, not the engineer, and the company was entitled to possession of it.

LOUISIANA. *Besson v. Oden,* 59 So. 2d 221 (1952). Owners found it necessary to move into building on the date of its completion and no objection was raised by the contractor. It was held that the occupancy of the building prior to complaint regarding certain defects was not such ratification and acceptance of the contractor's performance as to preclude the owners from complaining about the defects. Furthermore, the court held that, in the absence of specific evidence by the owner as to the cost of repairing the defective work, the contractor was entitled to the full contract price. The court deducted from that price the figure of $30, which the contractor himself had testified to as the estimated cost of repairing the defects.

Rosenthal v. Gauthier, 69 So. 2d 367 (1953). Where an architect furnished plans and specifications for a building whose cost of construction would exceed the cost limit contemplated, it was held that the architect was not entitled to his fee.

Bruno v. Gauthier, 70 So. 2d 693 (1954). An architect sued for the unpaid balance of his fee for preparing plans and specifications for the construction of a residence. It was held that he was entitled to recover the amount sued for, even though the parties' original agreement fixed a limit on the cost of construction, which limit was exceeded. The court's decision was based upon the fact that changes and additions requiring a larger expenditure were made and no objection had been registered to the plans ultimately furnished by the architect.

MICHIGAN. *Zannoth v. Booth Radio Station,* 333 Mich. 233, 52 N.W. 2d 678 (1952). The plaintiff architect was retained to draw plans for a radio studio and transmitter building. A cost limitation was imposed by the owner after the execution of the contract. The architect was held to be precluded from recovery for services in connection with the contract as there was a breach of his duty to make full disclosure to the owner when he proceeded to draw plans which he knew would far exceed the defendant's ability and willingness to pay and with knowledge that it was not within the owner's contemplation to erect such an expensive building.

The architect was entitled to compensation for his services prior to the imposition of cost limitation even though the contract was subsequently breached by his failure to stay within the cost limitation.

Plaintiff could not recover in *quantum meruit* for work done after the cost limitation was set, for the defendant received no benefit from work done during any of that time as the plans were drawn contrary to defendant's instructions and could not be used.

MINNESOTA. *Wick v. Murphy,* 54 N.W. 2d 805 (1952). In an action to foreclose a mechanic's lien for architectural services under a contract which provided that the compensation was to be based upon the total cost of construction, it was held that the architect's compensation could not be based on a rejected bid substantially in excess of the limitation placed by the owners on the cost of construction.

MISSISSIPPI. *Monroe v. Kimbrough Homes, Inc.,* 59 So. 2d 273. Action for breach of contract was brought arising from the fact that the contractor had made his bid and began construction on the basis of the foundation plans, without reference to floor plans which contained specifications irreconcilable with the foundation plans. The court held that under the contract the defendant had a duty to check all plans. It further held that the owners, in allowing the work to proceed upon the assurances by the contractor of later adjustment, had not waived their right to damages.

Greco v. Lutrich, 55 So. 2d 139 (1951). An architect agreed to furnish plans and specifications for the erecting of a commercial building to be used by defendant, who under the agreement paid a retainer fee which was to be credited upon total charge of three percent of the lowest and best contractor's bid received for the actual construction of the building. Plaintiff was permitted to bring an action within a reasonable time to recover three percent of the lowest bid less allowance already paid to him where the defendant did not let the contract at the bid stated or at any bid.

OHIO. *Burton, Inc. v. Durkee,* 106 N.E. 2d 313 (1951). The building contract was on a cost-plus-fee basis. Before the job was completed, a dispute arose as to the amount then due, and, because of the nonpayment of bills, the contractor refused to proceed further and withdrew from the job. It was held that, if the contractor's withdrawal was legally justified upon the facts, the owner was liable for the actual cost incurred to the date of the termination of the agreement, together with the fee provided for in the contract, if that was a definite amount, provided the contractor had not been guilty of malfeasance, extravagance, wastefulness, negligence, or laxity.

UTAH. *Parrish v. Tahtaras,* 318 P. 2d 642 (1957). Where the building costs, based upon the plans and specifications furnished by an architect, exceeded the owner's budget and where, despite the architect's agreement to modify such plans and specifications to conform to such budget limitations, the owner abandoned the project, it was held, in a suit brought by the architect to recover compensation from the owner, that the architect was entitled to recover the contract price for his services or their reasonable value.

WASHINGTON. *Hyak Lumber & Mill Work v. Cissell,* 244 P. 2d 253 (1952). In an action to foreclose a materialman's lien in which the plaintiff established that sales had been made to the defendant, but failed to show that the materials (1) actually went into the building for which they were furnished, or (2) were actually delivered upon the site for use in such building, the court, having refused to recognize the lien at the trial, denied a motion to reopen for further testimony by a carpenter to the effect that the carpenter had used the material on the home.

Jones v. Brisbin, 247 P. 2d 891 (1952). In a suit for services rendered where the architect offered advice, suggested changes, and furnished other services and the owner failed to reject the offered services but took the benefit of them under circumstances which would lead a reasonable man to believe they were offered for compensation, an implied contract arises and the architect is entitled to be compensated.

LIABILITIES OF ARCHITECT, ENGINEER AND CONTRACTOR

CALIFORNIA. *Raisch v. Sanitary Dist. No. 1 of Main County,* 240 P. 2nd 48 (1952). Plaintiffs brought an action to obtain an adjudication that an assessment of benefits for construction of a sewer system was invalid because of the interest of the engineer employed by the sanitary district in the contract and in the property within the district.

The court, although finding that the engineer accepted employment to subdivide property of the property owners within the district while employed by the district, determined that his action did not invalidate the assessment of benefits in the absence of an allegation by the plaintiffs of any specific misconduct by the engineer or of any discrimination in making assessments.

It was further found that the engineer was not a public officer and that he had no interest in what happened other than in performance of his duties so that the assessments were not void on the ground of the engineer's interest in the contracts as a quasi public officer. Finally it was determined that the engineer was not a party to the contract even though he was required by statute to sign the contract between the district and the contractor.

IDAHO. *Puget Sound National Bank of Tacoma v. C. B. Lauch Construction Co.,* 245 P. 2d 800 (1952). The siding to which a subcontractor applied paint was in a warped condition and the subcontractor knew that the two coats of paint called for in the specifications would be insufficient, considering the poor siding and the sunny climate. Nevertheless, the court said, "A contractor is required to follow the plans and specifications and when he does so, he cannot be held to guarantee that the work performed, as required by his contract, will be free from defects, or withstand reaction of the elements, or that the completed job will accomplish the purpose intended. He is only responsible for improper workmanship or other faults, or defects resulting from his failure to perform."

INDIANA. *Johnson-Johnson, Inc. v. Farah,* 108 N.E. 2d 638 (1952). In a mortgage foreclosure action in which the mortgagor counter-claimed for failure to complete construction, the court granted a new trial, saying that the award of substantial damages was improper in the absence of evidence of reasonable cost of completing construction or of the rental value for the period during which construction was unreasonably delayed.

ILLINOIS. *Wolters v. Venhaus,* 112 N.E. 2d 747 (1953). In a suit by a contractor to recover the balance due for construction of a house, the owner counter-claimed for damages resulting from defective workmanship and failure to comply with plans and specifications on the part of a subcontractor. The court held that, since the subcontractors had been paid in full on orders from the owner, who had a right under the contract to withhold fifteen percent of the price until acceptance, the general contractor was not liable for the default.

LOUISIANA. *Barraque v. Neff,* 202 La. 360, 11 So. 2d 697 (1942). Defendant architect was held liable for defective work when he substituted stucco for brick veneer in constructing the plaintiff's house and which necessitated the plaintiff reconstructing the walls, which had in the meantime become defective due to cracks and leaks. Plaintiff was granted recovery for the cost of repainting due to cracks and leaks and for the brick veneering.

MASSACHUSETTS. *Simpson Bros. Corp. v. Merrimac Chemical Co.* 248 Mass. 346, 142 N.E. 922 (1924). The approval of plans by the owner for an underground concrete tank for the storage of fuel oil, did not, as a matter of law, mean an unqualified acceptance and sanction of the plan in all its details, nor was it held to excuse the contractor, who had drawn the plans, from the exercise of ordinary and reasonable care in designing the structure and formulating his plans.

MICHIGAN. *Giffels & Vallet, Inc. v. Edw. C. Levy Co.,* 58 N.W. 2d 899 (1953). Suit was brought by an engineering-architectural firm for services rendered in connection with an enlargement of a corporation's plant and the corporation counterclaimed for alleged delay in furnishing drawings. The court held that the corporation had the burden of proving that the architectural firm was solely responsible for the delay and that it had failed to sustain this burden. The court added that, where both contracting parties contributed to a delay, neither can recover damages unless there is clear proof as to the apportionment of the delay and expenses attributable to each party.

MISSOURI. *Dysart-Cook Mule Co. v. Reed & Hechenlively,* 114 Mo. App. 296, 89 S.W. 591 (1905). Plaintiff employer was found to have been put to a greater expense in the construction of a mule barn than would have been necessary if the architect had drafted the plans according to agreed specifications. The plaintiff was entitled to recover of the defendants the amount of such expense.

MONTANA. *Garden City Floral Co., Inc. v. Hunt,* 255 P. 2d 352 (1953). A landowner sued a contractor for damages sustained when the wall of the landowner's building collapsed and fell into an adjoining excavation being made by the contractor for the landowner. The court held that although the landowner was required by the contract to employ a duly qualified architect to supervise the work, the requirement of full supervision did not extend to the method and means of doing the work, but was complied with by the employment of an architect to supervise the result. The fact that the architect's license had expired for nonpayment of his license fee was held not to affect his qualifications as a "duly qualified" architect in view of his years of experience.

NEW MEXICO. *Staley v. New,* 250 P. 2d 893 (1952). The owner's agent obtained plans and specifications for a radiant heating system and these were referred to in the building contract and became a part of it. The owner could not maintain an action for breach of contract and warranty against the general contractor and heating subcontractor for failure of the system to heat the house adequately, inasmuch as the contractor and subcontractor performed the work in accordance with the plans and specifications.

OHIO. *Sadler v. Bromberg,* 106 N.E. 2d 306 (1950). In an action for breach of contract to install certain tiling and fixtures, the court held that the measure of damages is not the difference in market value of the property immediately before and after the injury, but rather the cost of correction or completion of the work contracted for. The measure of damages is the money paid out to put the building in the condition it would have been in if the work had been well done.

OKLAHOMA. *Smith v. Goff,* 325 P. 2d 1061 (1958). Where the owner and architect entered into a written contract providing that the architect furnish complete architectural services for the construction of a residence, and the contract did not require the use of any designated materials, but merely required the architect to use his professional judgment, in an action by the owner against the architect for breach of contract, it was held that the architect was only required to exercise ordinary professional skill and diligence to conform to accepted standards (architectural); his contract did not guarantee perfect plans or satisfactory results, and the court would not overturn the jury's finding that the architect had exercised reasonable skill and diligence.

SOUTH CAROLINA. *Hill v. Polar Pantries,* 219 S.C. 263, 64 S.E. 2d. 885, 25 A.L.R.2d. 1080 (1951). In a suit for damages alleged to have been caused by a corporate defendant in furnishing unsuitable and defective plans and specifications for the installation of a frozen-food locker plant and in their failure to supervise the work properly, the court held that there was an implied warranty of the sufficiency of the plans and specifications for the contemplated purpose. The court reaffirmed the rule that where a person holds himself out as specially qualified to perform work of a particular character, there is an implied warranty that the work which he undertakes shall be of proper workmanship and reasonable fitness for its intended use.

VIRGINIA. *Surf Realty Corp. v. Standing,* 78 S.E. 2d 901 (1953). In a suit to enforce a mechanics' lien, in which the defendant claimed that the architect had promised but failed to complete the work by a specified date and that the supervision of construction had not been proper, the court found that the evidence did not sustain the contention that the architect promised completion of the building within a certain date, or that the design had been faulty. In doing so, the court said, at page 807: "An architect in the preparation of plans and drawings, owes to his employer the duty to exercise his skill and ability, his judgment and taste reasonably and without negligence . . . . in the absence of a special agreement, he is not liable for faults in construction resulting from defects in the plans because he does not imply or guarantee a perfect plan or a satisfactory result." Although affirming the judgment for enforcement of the mechanics' lien, the court found that evidence established that the defective work on the roof of the building had been done under plaintiff's supervision and that the architect had been negligent in failing to discover these defects.

PART FIVE: *Restrictions upon the Use of Property*

RESTRICTIONS upon the use of property are of direct interest and concern to the building industry. One such form of limitation is the restrictive covenant, "running with the land," which is imposed by the grantor or developer of the property. This type of covenant, in its most common form, is directed toward restricting subsequent owners from utilizing property to indulge their own taste without concern for its affect upon neighboring property values. In some instances, property has been subject to restrictive covenants not only to limit use, but also to limit ownership for the purpose of maintaining the "exclusive" character of the neighborhood. Insofar as such covenants are directed toward excluding members of particular racial, religious or ethnic groups from acquiring the property, they have been held unenforceable by the United States Supreme Court. In general, however, the effective application of restrictive covenants depends upon a number of factors, such as the efficiency of their enforcement.

Another approach to property-use restriction, and perhaps the most prevalent form thereof, is municipal zoning regulation. The exclusion of business and commercial operation from areas zoned for residential use and the requirement of minimum building area for residential occupancy are common municipal practices. The right of the municipality to limit or restrict the use of property is based upon its inherent "police power" to legislate in the interests of the health, safety, and general welfare of the community. On the other hand, individuals who have acquired a vested right in the use of their real property for a particular purpose may not be constitutionally deprived of that right. The conflicts thus created between these two concepts have been a source of extensive litigation, and the line between the power of the municipality and the rights of the individual is not one of clear delineation. However, where zoning ordinances have been applied to exclude churches, schools, and other similar institutional uses from residential zones, such application has generally been held void and unconstitutional.

Although the weight of judicial opinion has ruled that valid zoning regulation must bear direct relationship to the health, safety, and welfare of the community, esthetic factors have increasingly played a significant role in the adoption of such ordinances. Many suburban and rural communities faced with abnormal population growth have sought to put a brake on the unlimited construction of new homes in order to preserve community values and to maintain an economic balance. New residential construction has been limited by requiring a minimum plot area for residential construction, or by limiting the number of new homes that can be built in a particular area within a specified time. Although these legislative efforts to preserve a suburban or rural environment are based, for the most part, upon esthetic aims, the courts have increasingly given greater recognition to these factors in determining the validity of zoning laws.

CHAPTER 22: *Restrictive Covenants*

Covenants which restrict the use of real property to protect community esthetics are generally valid and enforceable if properly drawn and provided they do not discriminate on racial grounds.

COMMERCIALLY MINDED (yet well-intentioned) builders of homes in developments of varying sizes have attempted to reassure prospective purchasers that the neighborhoods they were buying into would not deteriorate in the foreseeable future. To accomplish this, they have set up restrictions in the deeds which "run with the land" and are designed to prevent any builder of the future from indulging his taste to the detriment of the neighborhood.

An interesting case involved Long Island's "University Gardens," a development which was advertised as "the most beautiful in this part of the United States." The advertisements further emphasized that future homes would be "in harmony with our scheme of affairs," 15 model homes having been completed to "show prospective purchasers of sites what type of construction is expected" and to assure "against inharmonious or bizarre styles of architecture in the community" and "annoying encroachments."

The deed designated the Board of Directors of the Property Owners' Association to enforce the admonition that "no dwelling house shall be erected upon any of said plots . . . except in harmony with the present standards of said development insofar as such standards are consistent and compatible with conditions as they exist at the time such erection . . . is contemplated." This restriction is remarkable for the fact that no hard and fast guide is stated (viz. no flat roof, minimum size, minimum plot, etc.). The yardstick is esthetic standards, to be reviewed at the time plans are filed.

To fortify its position in approving or rejecting plans, the Association engaged the services of a well-known architect who set up minimum standards for new construction, in conformity with the high standards current in the community.

One owner of a building plot, Schultz by name, was stubbornly determined to build the type of house that he desired and went forward with his construction despite disapproval of his plans. The Association then instituted suit to enforce its standards.

In this particular instance, the standard which was the subject of dispute was that of size. The University Gardens Property Owners' Association, Inc., had set as a desirable standard a minimum cubage of 29,250 cubic feet above grade. The majority of homes in this project exceeded that minimum. However, Mr. Schultz contended that the dwelling he planned would be in harmony with this standard of the development, because there were two other similarly detached houses in the immediate vicinity, which were smaller than his, and there were 10 row houses which were also smaller. The Association explained the 12 smaller houses by stating that they were on the perimeter of the development and served to hide other, less attractive homes outside the community.

Within a short time and by the end of the trial, Mr. Schultz succeeded in completing the construction of his home which totalled a cubic footage of 8,000 feet less than the minimum set by the Association as necessary for a dwelling to be in harmony with other homes in the development. The trial court came to the conclusion that the minimum size requirement was a reasonable one, in that this standard was not based on the larger homes in the development nor even on an average of the homes located there, but on one of the more modest homes which was used as a yardstick by the Association in its desire to facilitate more rapid development of the project. The trial court therefore ordered the owner to remove the structure within 30 days or to enlarge it to conform with the requirements of the Association, ruling: "As the court abhors waste and not because it believes the defendant had proven himself worthy of any sympathetic consideration, an opportunity will be given the defendant to satisfy the reasonable demands of the plaintiff by agreeing with the latter upon a suitable addition or enlargement of the present structure within 30 days after the service of a copy of the judgment to be entered herein. If the defendant remains adamant and shows no desire to enlarge the structure, then, if the building is still owned by him at the end of 30 days, it will be removed."

The owner appealed this decision and the higher court reversed the judgment of the court below. The Appellate Court refused to enforce the restrictive covenant, calling for the construction of a dwelling in harmony with the standards of the development, on the ground that the Association had been too slow to invoke the processes of the court so as to preserve the status quo. The court asserted that the inaction of the Association during the time elapsed between the commencement of construction on October 18, 1946 and the institution of suit on November 16, 1946 (during which time the dwelling was 50 percent completed) was inexcusable; and would not be countenanced in an action for injunctive relief.

The Appellate Court in this case (*University Gardens Property Owners' Association, Inc. v. Schultz,* 272 App. Div. 949) avoided a discussion of the validity and enforceability of the restrictive covenants. Since this case was not further appealed, the validity of the restrictive covenant calling merely for the erection of a dwelling "in harmony with the standards of the development" was not finally determined. However, assuming that this restriction is validly drawn so as to provide an adequate standard and guide, the important fact remains that this standard was circumvented by taking advantage of an "inexcusable delay" by the Association seeking to enforce it.

The Association had promptly informed the owner that his proposed plans were unsatisfactory and when notified of his defiance had promptly retained counsel. Only three weeks elapsed between the commencement of construction and the institution of suit. Despite the necessity of preparing and drawing the papers which are necessary to commence an action, the court nevertheless held this three-week period of time (perhaps also the Associations' failure to seek a temporary injunction during the litigation) was sufficient to bar the Association from the relief to which it might ordinarily be entitled. This case was followed by a case, *University Gardens Property Owners' Association, Inc. v. Crawford Homes, Inc.* 89 N.Y.S. 2d 258, in which the court held affirmatively that the restrictive covenant in question was "valid and enforceable." In that case it granted a temporary injunction since the Association had "moved with celerity" against Crawford Homes, Inc., which sought to circumvent the restrictions.

The importance of prompt action is again brought out in another New York case, *Sahm v. Poushter,* 187 Misc. 486. The property involved here was located in the City of Syracuse. The defendant was the owner of a tract of land which had a building restriction providing that no part of any building, except steps or bay windows and other similar projections, might be erected upon any part of the premises within 30 feet of the nearest line of the street on which it faced. The defendant's house was substantially in line with other neighboring houses. However, his dwelling was within 30 feet of the steet, whereas in the case of the other homes their porches or sun parlors projected within this distance. The plaintiff seeking the injunction was an individual and had not taken any action in reference to the defendant's house until after its completion. The court decided that since the defendant's house did not interfere with the plaintiff's view, light, and air, and because she had delayed in seeking relief and had seemingly acquiesced in the building of the defendant's dwelling, it would be oppressive to grant an injunction. However, a contrary conclusion was reached in another New York case entitled *McCain Realty Co., Inc. v. Aylesworth,* 128 Misc. 408, where the court did not believe that the conduct of the plaintiff, in failing to take action against other dwellings which were built in violation of a restrictive covenant, was sufficient to invalidate or waive his right to enforce the restrictive covenant against the defendant.

From the foregoing and other similar cases, no definite and clear-cut rule may be drawn to designate the point at which lack of action on the part of the person seeking to enforce or maintain esthetic or other standards will cause him to be deprived by the courts of his right to do so. The greater the cost and the greater the effort expended by the infringing builder before an attempt is made to stop the violation, the greater the reluctance of the courts to interfere with the *fait accompli.* The only safe course is to take immediate legal action when an owner has definitely committed himself to build in violation of a standard which it is desirable to maintain.

A municipality, in enforcing its zoning laws, is not in quite the same position as an individual seeking to enforce a restrictive covenant. As a rule, the courts will not permit the action or inaction of a municipal officer or employee to constitute an estoppel against a municipality or a waiver of its right to enforce its own laws. In another New York case entitled *Town of Clarkstown v. Hantman,* (N.Y. L. J. Apr. 9, 1948 p. 1328) a builder had erected, in an area zoned for 1-family dwellings, a 10-family dwelling. The town building inspector knew of the construction from the beginning and had even promised that a permit eventually would be issued. The court held that despite this inaction by an administrative officer, the municipality was entitled to an injunction, on the ground that the court will not recognize any attempt to condone, or afford immunity from a law violation.

Since no appeal was taken, the result of this determination was to restrict this 10-family dwelling to occupancy by 1 family only. Unless the zoning law is modified, this bizarre situation perhaps might be resolved by the removal of the building to an area zoned to permit its use for the purpose for which it was designed.

All this leads to the following conclusions:

(1) Community-wide "esthetic" restrictions in a deed, if properly drawn, are probably valid and enforceable.

(2) The community association must exercise eternal vigilance in promptly enforcing its restrictive covenants or run the risk of approving deviations by inaction, even temporary.

(3) Inactivity on the part of a governmental body or officer, as distinguished from a private body, may be prolonged and yet not excuse lack of compliance even when substantial hardship results to a builder.

II

The United States Supreme Court decisions, holding that it is an infringement of the United States Constitution for a state court to enforce racial restrictive covenants, have important implications for the practicing architect.

The restrictive covenant was first used to protect residential areas from commercial encroachment. Then racial restrictive covenants were drawn, aimed at the exclusion of Negroes, Mexicans, Jews and Indians (among others) from certain residential neighborhoods and developments. The racial covenant may take the form of prohibiting the *sale* of certain premises to certain classes of persons; or prohibiting the *use and occupancy* of such premises by such persons. Organizations interested in obtaining an unequivocal determination by the United States Supreme Court of the legality of these racial restrictive covenants were successful in having four companion cases considered together by that court.

One case, *Shelley v. Kraemer,* 334 US 1, arose in St. Louis, Missouri.

The racial restrictive covenant there prohibited *ownership and occupancy* by Negroes and was to run for 50 years, from 1911. In a second case, *McGhee v. Sipes,* 334 US 1, the restrictive covenant covered premises in Detroit, Michigan, and prohibited *use and occupancy* by non-Caucasians and was to run for 25 years, from 1934. The third and fourth cases, *Hurd v. Hodge* and *Urciolo v. Hodge,* 334 US 24, (both cases), arose in the District of Columbia and involved a restriction against *sale* of certain property to Negroes. The validity of these racial restrictions was in each case upheld by the lower courts, which required compliance with the restrictive covenants upon penalty of contempt of court. It was the contention of the various petitioners that the enforcement by state courts of these racial covenants was a violation of the Federal Constitution, in that this enforcement deprived the petitioners of property without due process of law and that the constitutional concept of equal protection of the law had been violated. In the Missouri and the District of Columbia cases, racial covenants restricted ownership as well as occupancy. In the Michigan case, the restriction was against occupancy only. Thus, in the latter situation, a Negro could own the residential property but could only rent it to white occupants and could not occupy it himself.

The position of the defendants in these cases was that since the racial restrictions involved were the result of agreements made by private parties, no constitutional privilege had been infringed. It was their contention that private conduct, however discriminatory or wrongful, is not forbidden by the Constitution and in fact any interference in this conduct would be an invasion of the fundamental right of freedom of contract. The plaintiffs, on the other hand, took the position that the freedom to purchase and use property, regardless of race or color, was a fundamental and basic freedom that was protected by the Constitution.

The Supreme Court in its decision held that the restrictive agreements standing alone could not be regarded as violative of the Constitution and that voluntary adherence to these would not be illegal. However, the Court declared that action by a state court to enforce such agreements was illegal and in violation of the Constitution. The Court stated: "Whatever else the framers (of the Constitution) sought to achieve, it is clear that the matter of primary concern was the establishment of equality in the enjoyment of basic civil and political rights and the preservation of those rights from discriminatory action on the part of the states based on considerations of race or color."

The Court thus stated the doctrine that the states may not constitutionally, through the agency of their courts, compel parties to live up to the terms of racial restrictive covenants even though such covenants as of and by themselves are not unconstitutional. This doctrine is consistent with the general and well-established rule of law that the states may not, through legislative action, restrict the ownership or use of property upon racial or similar ground.

Thus the state may not accomplish indirectly through the courts what it cannot constitutionally do directly through the legislature. The undisputed facts in the cases before the Supreme Court were that the petitioners were purchasers of properties upon which they desired to establish homes. The owners of the property were willing sellers. If it had not been for the interference of the state courts in actively intervening and enforcing the restrictive covenants, the petitioners would have been free to establish their homes. Thus the state in effect used its full powers to prevent the petitioners from enjoying ownership and the use of their property merely on the grounds of race and color. Affirmative and positive action of this sort by the courts of a state is an action of the state itself and, being discriminatory in nature, is forbidden a state under the express terms of the 14th Amendment to the Federal Constitution.

III

Can a public housing development discriminate against any group in its choice of tenants? We have just pointed out that a political entity such as the U.S. Government, a state, a city or the like, could not do so. It further was shown that courts were prohibited from enforcing racial restrictive covenants. Does this rule preclude discrimination by a housing development which had been given public tax benefits under a state redevelopment statute?

A New York case involves a housing development called Stuyvesant Town, constructed by the Metropolitan Life Insurance Company. There the issue was whether Stuyvesant Town, a private company, could discriminate against Negro tenants although it had been substantially aided by the City and State of New York in the financing of the development. By a four to three vote, the highest court in New York State held that a private corporation was free to discriminate in its choice of tenants even though it had been given substantial aid by the government before and during construction. (*Dorsey v. Stuyvesant Town Corp.*, 299 N.Y. 512).

Stuyvesant Town, which houses almost 25,000 persons, was

constructed in conformity with a contract between the City of New York and the Metropolitan Life Insurance Company, pursuant to a statute of New York State which concerned itself with the clearance, reconstruction, and rehabilitation of substandard and insanitary areas. Although Stuyvesant Town is a private corporation, it was built with the aid of the State and City of New York in that the real property upon which the project was built was obtained through the condemnation powers of the City and in that the development was entitled to receive certain tax exemptions.

The chief issue presented was whether the aid given by the State and City of New York to the project made its operation a "governmental" project and thus subject to the "equal protection of the law" provisions of the federal and state constitutions. The question was put by the court as follows:

> Upon that characteristic of the constitutional inhibition these parties have joined issue. Respondents contend that they are private companies beyond the reach of the constitutional restraint and free to select arbitrarily the tenants who will occupy Stuyvesant Town. Appellants insist that the avowed discrimination falls under the constitutional ban because they say it has been aided and made possible by the action of the State. The issue is decisive, for the policy of respondents could not be followed by a governmental body . . .
>
> Appellants here rely upon those cases in urging that we must characterize as governmental action the rental policy of Metropolitan and Stuyvesant. They point to the acknowledged contribution made by the government to the project—principally the tax exemption amounting to many millions of dollars, and aggregation of the land through use of the city's power of eminent domain and through exchange of bordering tracts for city streets which had been closed. Moreover, we are urged to consider the size of the project as in reality forming a large community within the city.

In determining, however, that Stuyvesant Town was free to choose its tenants in any way it saw fit, even if it discriminated, the majority opinion stated:

> Commissioner Robert Moses, active in the plan, stated publicly to the Governor and the Board of Estimate that if any requirement was imposed which deprived the landlord of the right to select its tenants, no private venture would go into the business. Certainly the general impression was created—

which Metropolitan did nothing to dispel—that Stuyvesant Town would not rent to Negroes. For that reason and others, unsuccessful attacks were made upon the desirability of the project. In the Board of Estimate at least three votes were cast against approval of the contract on the ground that exclusion on racial grounds would be practiced. The contract was finally approved without any provision regarding discrimination in the selection of tenants . . .

The State of New York has consciously and deliberately refrained from imposing any requirement of non-discrimination upon respondents as a condition to the granting of aid in the rehabilitation of substandard areas. Furthermore, it has deliberately refrained from declaring by legislation that the opportunity to purchase and lease real property without discrimination is a civil right. . . .

Tax exemption and power of eminent domain are freely given to many organizations which necessarily limit their benefits to a restricted group. It has not yet been held that the recipients are subject to the restraints of the Fourteenth Amendment . . .

To cite only a few examples: the merchant marine, air carriers, and farmers all receive substantial economic aid from our Federal Government and are subject to varying degrees of control in the public interest. Yet it has never been suggested that those and similar groups are subject to the restraints upon governmental action embodied in the Fifth Amendment similar to the restrictions of the Fourteenth . . .

We are agreed that the moral end advanced by appellants cannot justify the means through which it is sought to be attained. Respondents cannot be held to answer for their policy under the equal protection clauses of either Federal or State Constitution. The aid which the State has afforded to respondents and the control to which they are subject are not sufficient to transmute their conduct into State action under the constitutional provisions here in question.

Three of the judges of the New York State Court of Appeals came to an entirely opposite conclusion. The dissenting judges stated that the determination of the majority of the court—that the discrimination practiced had not been aided by the state, nor performed by private persons acting in a governmental capacity—was an argument without real substance. The dissenting judges stated:

The average citizen, aware of that truth but unschooled in legal niceties, will, I venture, find the decision which the court

> now makes extremely perplexing. While the Stuyvesant Town housing project was in blueprint and under construction, the public understood, and rightly, that it was an undertaking on which the State and the City of New York had bestowed the blessings and benefits of governmental powers. Now that the development is a reality, the public is told in effect that, because Metropolitan and Stuyvesant are private companies, they are not subject to the equal protection clause, and may, if they choose, discriminate against Negroes in selecting tenants. That conclusion strikes me as totally at odds with common understanding and not less so with the facts and circumstances disclosed by the record.

The minority of the court argued that the concept of "state action" is an expanding one and that the activities of the state and city governments in this case were of such a nature as to bring the operation of this project within the proscription of the federal and state constitutional provisions providing for equal protection under the law stating:

> As long as there is present the basic element, an exertion of governmental power in some form, as long as there is present something "more" than purely private conduct (see *Shelley v. Kramer*, supra, 334 U.S. 1, 13), the momentum of the principle carries it into areas once thought to be untouched by its direction.
>
> . . . the Fourteenth Amendment is no longer satisfied by a mechanical finding that the discriminatory conduct was not perpetrated by legislative, judicial, or executive officials of the State. The concept of "state action" has been vitalized and expanded; the definition of "private" conduct in this context has been tightened and restricted. When private individuals or groups move beyond "matters of merely private concern" and act in "matters of high public interest," the test is not, Mr. Justice Cardozo has written, whether they are "the representatives of the State in the strict sense in which an agent is the representative of his principal." The test is whether they are to be classified as representatives of the State to such an extent or in such a sense that the great restraints of the Constitution set limits to their action.

The minority of the court further felt that the act of New York City in entering into the contract with the Metropolitan Life Insurance Company, which did not specifically provide against discrimination, constituted governmental participation in illegal discrimination. Before the contract was executed this very question was raised and the intention of Stuyvesant Town not to rent to Negroes was made clear. Therefore, in accepting such a policy, said the minority judges, the government was actually participating in conduct which is not constitutionally sanctioned.

The minority opinion further referred to the provision of the New York State constitution which provides "no person shall be denied the equal protection of the laws of this state or any subdivision thereof." The dissenting judges argued that this provision did not refer to "state action" and was therefore broader in scope than the Fourteenth Amendment of the Constitution which prohibits discriminatory state action. The minority in its opinion stated:

> It is impossible to perceive or conjecture a benefit from the creation of a private barony in the heart of New York City, free of constitutional safeguards and devoted to undemocratic practices. It is impossible to balance the essence of democracy against fireproof buildings and well-kept lawns. Fortunately, the Constitutions, Federal and State, forbid our putting the former into the judicial scales just as they forbade the City officials from putting it upon the bargaining table. The mandate that there be equal protection of the laws, designed as a basic safeguard for all, binds us and respondents as well to put an end to this discrimination.

The points of view of the majority and minority opinions are stated at length because they reflect the fundamental disparity, well stated, between the conflicting points of view, that only the United States Supreme Court can determine.

The architect and builder will, even after such a definitive legal solution, still have to struggle with the sociological problem this decision points up.

The practical implications of this case are not to be dismissed lightly. Congress shortly afterwards provided for 1.5 billion dollars in loans and grants over five years for the rehabilitation of slum and substandard areas and for urban redevelopment. States will adopt or have adopted enabling legislation to take advantage of these subsidies. The right to select tenants without restriction or, contrariwise, the duty not to discriminate in the selection of tenants will have an important effect on the rate of development and the nature of the housing programs in the various states.

CHAPTER 23: *Zoning Ordinances and the "Police Power" of the Municipality*

The community's right to limit or prohibit certain uses of real property by zoning legislation —and the individual property owner's right to use his property without restriction—are conflicting concepts. The reasonableness of the zoning ordinance in relation to the health, safety, and welfare of the municipality is the standard which must be applied to determine the validity of zoning laws.

THE CONFLICT BETWEEN attempts by municipalities to zone and regulate use of property and the claims of property owners that their rights are being improperly invaded has been a continuing source of litigation. Illustrative decisions in New York have considered the following questions.

Can a property owner use an entire tract of his property for a use not permitted by a local zoning ordinance, where prior to the adoption of that ordinance only a portion of his tract was so used? Can a municipality regulate a use of property where a previous attempt by the municipality to prohibit such use by rezoning has been held to be an unconstitutional infringement of the rights of the property owner?

The New York Court of Appeals in the case of *Town of Somers v. Camarco,* 308 N.Y. 537, considered the constitutionality of a zoning ordinance in its application to the defendants who were in the sand-and-gravel business. Their property consisted of approximately 55 acres divided into two parcels. The defendants acquired title in 1943, and in 1944 commenced to utilize a portion of said property for the removal of sand and gravel. In 1945 a zoning ordinance was adopted by the town placing the defendants' property in a residential zone. The ordinance, however, provided for the continuance of nonconforming uses as follows:

> Any building, structure, or actual bona fide use, involving a substantial monetary investment, which shall exist at the time of the enactment of this ordinance may be continued, even though such building, structure, or use shall not conform with the provisions of this ordinance for the district in which it is located, provided such existing building, structure, or use shall have been constructed, altered, or used in conformity with other existing law.

In 1952 and in 1953, the zoning ordinance was amended to exclude any "natural products uses" from the protection afforded to other nonconforming uses. This change would have prohibited the use of the defendants' property as a sand-and-gravel pit. In determining the validity of these amendments as applied to the defendants, the Court of Appeals emphasized that they must be subject to the test of reasonableness "in order to afford stability to property owners who have existing nonconforming uses." In measuring the reasonableness, however, of a zoning ordinance, the court pointed out that this test was based on variable factors, such as density of population. The court said:

> In addition, the extent of the reasonable exercise of the police powers varies directly with the degree of the density of the population in the city, town, or village involved. An ordinance which might be considered as reasonable if enacted in New York City, would be considered as unreasonable if enacted in a smaller political subdivision. . . . A definition of reasonableness cannot be made for all occasions, and must, of necessity, be considered anew in the light of each problem presented.

The court concluded that the amendments to the zoning law prohibiting a nonconforming use for natural products unreasonably deprived the defendants of a "vested right" and were, therefore, unconstitutional.

In a dissenting opinion, a minority of the court argued that the zoning ordinance was unenforceable only in respect to that portion of the defendants' property which actually had been used for excavation of sand and gravel prior to the enactment of the ordinances in question. The dissent emphasized that the existing gravel pit comprised only a small portion of the total tract and that "the mere intention to excavate the remainder of the land did not amount to an existing use so as to entitle defendants to a nonconforming use encompassing and protecting their entire tract of 55 acres."

The dissenting judges were of the opinion that the decision of the court's majority was inconsistent with prior determinations. In an earlier case, *People v. Miller,* 304 N.Y. 105, the court of Appeals in a unanimous decision held that a zoning ordinance prohibiting the use of premises for harboring pigeons was validly applied to the defendant who had been using his premises for that purpose as a hobby prior to the adoption of the zoning ordinance. The rationale of the court in this case was that the property interest affected by the ordinance was too insubstantial to justify the continuation of a nonconforming use "in light of the objectives to be achieved by the enforcement of the provision." The court said:

> That being the rationale of our decisions, it follows, and the cases so hold, that the enforcement of a zoning regulation against a prior nonconforming use will be sustained where the resulting loss to the owner is relatively slight and insubstantial. . . . In this state, then, existing nonconforming uses will be permitted to continue, despite the enactment of a prohibitory zoning ordinance, if, and only if, enforcement of the ordinance would, by rendering valueless substantial improvements or businesses built up over the years, cause serious financial harm to the property owner. This rule, with its emphasis upon pecuniary and economic loss, is clearly inapplicable to a purely incidental use of property for recreational or amusement purposes only. Such an inconsequential use as that here involved—the harboring of pigeons as a hobby—does not amount to a "vested right," and depriving [defendant] of this pastime does not affect substantially [his] property rights . . . in the use of the premises, which are otherwise undisturbed and unimpaired.

In both cases discussed, a subsidiary question was raised as to whether the ordinances in question could be justified as an exercise of the town's police power in preventing the creation or maintenance of a nuisance. In the *Camarco* case, the majority opinion stated that it was unnecessary to determine the question of what may be a proper exercise of the town's police power so as to prevent the creation of a nuisance. The minority, however, in its opinion, concluded that it is a reasonable exercise of the town's police powers to limit the area which could be excavated by the sand and gravel company. In the *Miller* case, the court asserted that the ordinance in question might be justified as an exercise of the "police power" to prevent the maintenance of a nuisance.

II

It is well settled that a statute or ordinance which zoned a particular area for residential use would be unconstitutional if it also required, simultaneously with its enactment, the immediate termination of all nonresidential uses. However, the courts of some states have upheld the validity and constitutionality of zoning ordinances which require the termination of a prior nonconforming use or structure within a reasonable time after the adoption of the zoning ordinance. The Court of Appeals of New York, the State's highest court, by a sharply divided 4 to 3 decision has rendered a ruling on this point (*Harbison v. City of Buffalo,* 4 N.Y. 2d 553).

In the *Harbison* case, the petitioner owned real property in Buffalo, New York, on which he had been operating a cooperage business since 1924. This business, under local law, was classified as a "Junk Yard." At the time the business had been established, the street upon which it was located was unpaved, and there was a city dump and glue factory in the vicinity. In 1926, two years after the commencement of the cooperage business, the area was rezoned for residential use, but the petitioner continued his business as a prior nonconforming use.

In 1953, the zoning ordinance of the City of Buffalo was amended to provide in substance that certain nonconforming uses of structures or property located in a residential district must be discontinued within three years. "Junk Yards" were expressly covered by this amendment. In 1956, the City of Buffalo refused a license to the petitioner for the operation of his cooperage business on the ground that the three-year period in which the business was to be discontinued had expired. The owner petitioned the court for relief.

The lower court ruled in effect that the right of an owner of real property to continue a use which was lawful prior to the adoption of a zoning ordinance was perpetual. The New York Court of Appeals by majority opinion reversed the lower court, holding that a municipality might require the termination of a prior nonconforming use provided the time in which such termination was reasonable. The majority stated:

> In ascertaining the reasonable period during which an owner of property must be allowed to continue a nonconforming use, a balance must be found between social harm and private injury. We cannot say that a legislative body may not in any case, after consideration of the factors involved, conclude that the termination of a use after a period of time sufficient to allow a property owner an opportunity to amortize his investment and make other plans is a valid method of solving the problem.
>
> To enunciate a contrary rule would mean that the use of land for such purposes as a tennis court, an open air skating rink, a junk yard, or a parking lot—readily transferable to another site—at the date of the enactment of a zoning ordinance vests the owner thereof with the right to utilize the land in that manner in perpetuity, regardless of the changes in the neighborhood over the course of time. In the light of our ever-expanding urban communities, such a rule appears to us to constitute an unwarranted restriction upon the Legislature. . . .

In a vigorous opinion, the dissenting judges argued that the Buffalo ordinance resulted in a confiscation of the petitioner's property and constituted an infringement of basic individual rights for questionable objectives. The minority pointed out that the business was not a nuisance or injurious to the community, and that the residents who objected to this business purchased and moved into the neighborhood after the petitioner's business was in operation. The minority further asserted that the ordinance in question was, in reality, a retroactive zoning in the nature of urban redevelopment, and that this can only be constitutionally authorized by statutes which provided for just compensation for property appropriated. The dissenting opinion stated:

> Observing the vagaries of modern zoning, many a businessman (large or small) might properly hesitate to invest his life savings in a store or other commercial or industrial property knowing that his investment is liable to be expropriated after the enterprise has been successfully launched, if some pressure group succeeds in obtaining favorable action from a muncipal legislature. That is not in the public interest. Constitutional se-

> curity against such developments is infinitely more important to the public at large than the occasional presence of a nonconforming use, or the possibility that a nonconforming use may acquire some advantage by way of monopoly in the use of district. . . .
>
> The circumstance that this is a cooperage establishment or junk yard ought not to obscure that the principal of the decision applies to any kind of business which, due to lapse of time, has been overtaken by changes in the neighborhood. The principle of the decision applies equally to stores, shops, or service organizations which are retroactively legislated out of existence by the abolition of prior nonconforming uses. If petitioners' establishment is not secure against this kind of invasion, no one else's business is better protected. The neighbors or the officials of a municipality in one year may look askance at a junk or cooperage yard, and in another year may frown upon the conduct in a particular locality of any other type of commerce or industry. The people who moved into petitioners' vicinity and now find their business offensive may not be aware that the principle of this decision unsettles their own property rights, and that it may suddenly be used against them in unexpected ways if agitation arises to legislate them out of business. . . .

The minority, in discussing decisions of other states which have upheld similar statutes or ordinances, pointed out that these laws prescribe the same time limit for many different kinds of property and business use, and that there was no relationship between these "grace periods" and the type of structure or business involved. The dissent said:

> This theory to justify extinguishing nonconforming uses means less the more one thinks about it. It offers little more promise of ultimate success than the other theories which have been tried and abandoned. In the first place, the periods of time vary so widely in the cases which have been cited from different states where it has been tried and have so little relation to the useful lives of the structures, that this theory cannot be used to reconcile these discordant decisions. Moreover, the term "amortization" as thus employed, has not the same meaning which it carries in law or accounting. It is not even used by analogy. It is just a catch phrase, and the reasoning is reduced to argument by metaphor. Not only has no effort been made in the reported cases where this theory has been applied to determine what is the useful life of the structure, but almost all were decided under ordinances or statutes which prescribe the same

> time limit for many different kinds of improvements. This demonstrates that it is not attempted to measure the life of the particular building or type of building, and the word "amortization" is used as an empty shibboleth.

The conflict between individual rights and zoning objectives is most intense when the municipality attempts to prohibit a use or structure in existence at the time that the zoning ordinance is enacted. This conflict involves significant implications of a social, economic, and political nature. Consequently, as the law in this area evolves and develops, it warrants the closest scrutiny and consideration.

III

If a municipality may not lawfully zone property in order to prohibit a particular use, to what extent may that use be regulated? A municipality may not accomplish indirectly what it lawfully cannot do directly, but the line between prohibition and regulation of use is not always subject to clear definition.

It has been pointed out that the validity of zoning, when applied to a prior nonconforming use, depends in part upon the substantiality of the property interest of the owner in such use. However, it is clear that where the property interest of the owner in a prior nonconforming use is such that the municipality cannot constitutionally prohibit such use by means of zoning, it does not necessarily follow that the municipality is precluded from regulating that use.

In a New York case (*Town of Hempstead v. East Meadow Realty Corp.*, N.Y.L.J. Apr. 29, 1957, p. 13), the Town of Hempstead sought an injunction restricting the defendant from operating a sand and gravel business on property owned by the defendant. Under the local zoning law, excavation of sand and gravel was prohibited in the area in which the defendant's property was located.

The defendant's property consisted of a 38-acre tract which had been used for the sand and gravel business since 1927 whereas the zoning ordinance of the Town had been adopted in 1930. The defendant contended that the zoning ordinance was invalid, in so far as the Town sought to apply it to its property.

The court ruled that the defendant was entitled to use its premises for the excavation of sand and gravel, on the ground that a nonconforming use which existed prior to the adoption of the zoning ordinance is a vested right, of which the owner could not be constitutionally deprived.

Subsequent to this decision, the Town of Hempstead instituted a proceeding to enjoin the same defendant from continuing its mining operations, because of its failure to comply with a regulatory ordinance of the Town relating to sand removal and other excavations. This ordinance was adopted in 1945, and required persons engaged in excavation to immediately refill the excavation with clean, nonburnable fill during the course of their operations.

The defendant contended that the judgment in the earlier litigation, which permitted the continuance of the prior nonconforming use, constituted an adjudication of the issues raised by the Town in respect to the regulatory ordinance. The court, however, rejected this contention, pointing out that the zoning ordinance and the regulatory ordinance were two separate and distinct laws, and that it did not follow that the right to continue a use precluded regulation of that use. The court said:

> The earlier litigation and the present lawsuit are identical so far as parties plaintiff and defendant are concerned. However, the issues determined in the earlier litigation are not the same as those raised by the present lawsuit. In the former litigation the basic issue which was tried and determined was the existence or nonexistence of a nonconforming use under the zoning ordinance of the Town of Hempstead. That has been determined by a judgment which declares that the defendants do possess such a nonconforming use and that it entitles them to make such use of the entire 38 acres. The present suit is not concerned with the zoning ordinance at all. The ordinance which is involved in the present lawsuit is entirely separate and distinct from the zoning ordinance and is entitled "Sand Bank and Pit, Topsoil Removal and Other Excavations Ordinance of the Town of Hempstead." In this present action the town seeks to compel the defendants to comply with the provisions of that ordinance or to terminate its operation.

Under its "police powers" a municipality has the right to regulate the use of property in the interest of the health, safety, and welfare of the community. Unrestricted exercise of this power, however, could result in burdensome restrictions on the use of the property as would in effect prohibit such use. On the other hand the failure to exercise the power could result in the creation or continuance of a nuisance or the extension (as distinguished from preservation) of a prior nonconforming use.

Some of the difficulties implicit in the attempted regulation of the use of property is illustrated by the case of *Town of Somers v. Camarco* which has already been discussed. In that case the Town ordinance under judicial review not only regulated the method of excavating sand and gravel, but also limited the area that could be excavated to 5 acres.

The majority of the New York Court of Appeals ruled that the defendant had a vested right to excavate his entire tract of land of 55 acres based upon its use prior to the adoption of the ordinance. Consequently, it was unnecessary, the majority of the court asserted, to determine what was a proper exercise of the Town's "police powers."

The minority of the court, however, pointed out that the defendant had only utilized a portion of his property for excavation and therefore no vested right to excavate the entire tract was created by the prior limited use. Thus, the minority contended, a 5-acre limitation for excavation, as applied to the defendant's property, was a reasonable exercise of the Town's power to prevent the creation of a nuisance. The minority opinion stated:

> If the law were otherwise, if a single excavation in a given area of a large parcel of land were to create vested rights in the entire tract, a special privilege would be conferred upon sand and gravel operators, which is not recognized even in the case of substantial buildings and structures. Indeed, if the rationale at the court's decision were sound, a dog kennel run, a mink farm, or a piggery, existing on one acre of ground at the time of the passage of a zoning law prohibiting such use, could be extended without limit over the owner's entire tract, no matter how large its acreage. Yet such an expansion of a nonconforming use would, I venture, never be sanctioned, any more than would be the extension or an enlargement of a nonconforming building which might have involved an original investment of hundreds of thousands of dollars.

Undoubtedly, the attempts of municipalities to regulate the use of property, where they cannot rezone the same, will engender further and continuing litigation.

IV

Is the construction and exhibition of a developer's "model home" a business use of property in contravention of a residential-zoning use ordinance? The answer to this question is of considerable importance, for the use of model homes has become the chief method through which new homes are sold, particularly in large developments.

A decision in New York (*City of New York v. Jack Parker Associates, Inc.*, 5 Misc. 2d 633) held that the model homes, which were not located on the tract being developed, violated a zoning ordinance which restricted the property to one-family residences. This decision has been of concern to builders, because of its possible extension.

In this case, the builder was improving a tract of land on which approximately 678 homes were to be built. In order to promote the sale of these homes, the builder also erected four one-family dwellings, approximately one-half mile from the development in question. Across the street from the model homes, the builder maintained a sales office and a parking lot for potential purchasers, who were directed at the office to the models.

Permits for the erection of the model homes had been duly issued and, in the application for such permits, the builder had stated he was desirous of erecting "model homes." It was, of course, the intention of the builder to sell the model homes for residential use after they had served their purpose as models.

The model homes were connected by concrete walks; floodlights illuminated the homes at night; and each of the models contained furnishings with signs indicating the department stores which had supplied the items.

Due to the fact that hundreds of people, particularly on weekends, were visiting and inspecting the model homes, many complaints were received by the authorities from neighboring residents, and the builder was charged with violating the zoning law.

The model homes were located in an area defined as a residential district. The zoning law, in defining the buildings which could be constructed in a residence district, provided:

> In a residence district no building or buildings shall be erected other than a building or buildings arranged, intended, or designed exclusively for one or more of the following uses: (1) Dwellings, which except as hereinafter provided . . . shall include dwellings for one or more families and boarding houses, and also hotels which have 30 or more sleeping rooms, but shall not include motels. . . . (9) In a residence district, no building or premises shall be used for any other than a use above speci-

fied for which buildings may be erected and for the accessory uses customarily incident thereto. The term "accessory use" shall not include a business, nor shall it include any building or use not located on the same lot with the building or use to which it is accessory. . . .

The ordinance also provided that in the district in which the model homes were located, "no dwelling shall be erected or altered other than for occupancy for a single family."

The court, in granting an injunction enjoining the builder from using the homes in question as model homes, relied upon the word "exclusively" as contained in the zoning law. The court said:

> The language of the pertinent provisions of the Zoning Resolution is clear. Section 3 limits the erection and use of buildings in a residence district to those "arranged, intended or designed *exclusively*" for one or more of the uses specified, and then provides, in subdivision (9), that "no building or premises shall be used for any other than a use above specified," and customary accessory uses which shall not, however, include a business. By virtue of the further limitation contained in subdivision (a) of Section 16-C, it is clear that in the G-1 district in question only one-family dwellings arranged, intended or designed *exclusively* for use as such are permitted. While defendants' four model homes were intended eventually to be used as dwellings, they were erected primarily for use as an indispensable part of the defendants' business of selling hundreds of other homes to be erected at another location some five blocks away. In the opinion of this Court such a use violates the zoning resolution. This is true even though no actual sales or negotiations for sale took place in the model homes and even though no salesmen were present in the homes. By no stretch of the imagination can it be said that the model homes were being used as dwellings, much less exclusively so.

The opinion of the court in the New York case was based upon the fact that the model homes were not located on the tract which was being developed. If the use of a model home in one location to sell homes in another location is a business use, would it not as logically follow that model homes located on the very tract that was being developed would also constitute a business use? The New York court asserted that it would have arrived at a different determination if the model homes were located on the tract being developed. The court said:

> It does not follow, however, that enforcement of a zoning ordinance in the one case would require a like result in the other. Indeed, since it is common knowledge that the almost unvarying practice of builders today to sell homes by the use of sample or model homes, and since it is in the public interest to permit them so to do, this Court would arrive at a different determination if the model homes here involved had been erected on the tract sought to be developed. . . . Zoning ordinances must be reasonable and conducive to the public welfare. While they may be held so to be under one set of circumstances, the result may well be different under another. . . . In the opinion of this Court it is reasonable and in the public welfare to enforce this zoning resolution against the defendants.

The last point was not in issue in the case. It is a matter of conjecture what the result will be if the precise issue arises. It can be argued that the public welfare is affected adversely if model homes are permitted in residential areas wherever they are located. Other courts might reach the conclusion that if the use of homes as models for the sale of other homes in a different location is considered a business use, then model homes located on the tract which is being developed should also be so considered. On the other hand, they may follow the *obiter dictum* in the case discussed. If the scope of the New York decision is extended, the sales techniques of builders and developers will require extensive modification. In any event, the sequelae of the *Jack Parker* decision should be closely watched.

Zoning legislation which restricts an area to residential use may not validly be applied to exclude churches or schools from such area.

The mushrooming of suburban residential communities and the expansion of both public and private educational facilities has brought to the fore the issue whether zoning regulations can exclude public or private schools, or both, from a residential district.

Because public education is a governmental function of the state, the prevailing rule is that a locality or municipality cannot by zoning regulations validly exclude public schools from a residential zone or, for that matter, from any zone.

In the case, *Union Free School District of Hempstead v. The Vil-*

lage of Hewlett Bay Park (N. Y.) 198 Misc. 932, the court said the town could not prevent the construction of a public school within its borders, in the following language:

> As the plaintiff is an official body to whom the education of youth of the district has been entrusted by the State by special statute, I do not believe that the defendant village, whose territory is within the school district, may by the exercise of zoning powers conferred upon it by section 175 of the Village Law, defeat or obstruct the plaintiff in the performance of its State function.

May a zoning regulation permit *public* schools but exclude *private* schools from an area?

Until recently, the courts have struck down such regulations on the ground that they were capricious or arbitrary in distinguishing between public and private educational facilities. For example, in the leading case, *Catholic Bishop of Chicago v. Kingery* (Ill.), 20 N.E. 2d 583, the Court was squarely faced with the question. It stated the long-accepted rule that the exercise of the police power must bear a substantial relation to the public health, safety, morals, or welfare and held that the zoning ordinance which excluded only private schools was a capricious invasion of property rights and therefore unconstitutional. In this and similar cases the courts found no reasonable basis for distinguishing between the two types of schools, saying that both types would equally add to the congestion of the streets, bring crowds to athletic events, remove property from the tax rolls, etc. In all of these cases the nub of the decisions was that there was no substantial difference betwen public and private schools in relation to the object sought to be accomplished by the zoning ordinance and therefore, insofar as it prohibited the presence of a private school while allowing a public one, it was void.

Some later cases, however, have upheld the constitutionality of ordinances which permitted public and banned private schools in certain restricted areas. Thus, in the New York case, *In Re: Great Neck Community School,* in which the village ordinance permitted public schools in certain areas but excluded private schools except under certain conditions, a private school was denied a building permit to add a room to its facilities. The court stated with reference to the regulation that although a village cannot curtail the State's right to construct public schools, private schools have "something less in prerogatives" than public schools and the village may exclude them (140 N.Y.S. 2d 221).

The distinction was made more explicitly in the case, *State ex. rel. Wisconsin Lutheran High School Conference v. Sinar,* (Wis.) 65 N.W. 2d 43, in which a private nonprofit corporation sought to compel the city to issue a permit in order to construct a *private high school* in a residential zone in which only public schools and *private elementary schools* were permitted. The court dismissed the suit as follows:

> The subject of public education and the establishment and operation of public schools is a governmental function of the state. . . . In the performance of other governmental functions we do not restrict the behavior of persons or the use of property to the same extent that we do when only private interests are pursued and the fact that the standards are different commonly raises no suspicion that an illegal discrimination is thereby imposed or that the difference between muncipality and citizen is insufficient to support separate classifications. . . .
>
> However, we decide the present appeal on the narrower ground that tangible differences material to the classifications of the ordinance can be readily pointed out which sustain the distinction made by the ordinance between schools. To begin with, the term "public" is the antithesis of "private." The public school is not a private one. They serve different interests and are designed to do so. The private school is founded and maintained because it is different. Is that difference material to the purpose of zoning? In many respects the two schools perform like functions and in probably all respects concerning noise, traffic difficulties, and the other objectionable features already mentioned they stand on an equality, so that in several of the objects of zoning ordinances . . . the promotion of health, safety and morals . . . we may not say that the two schools differ. But when we come to "the promotion of the general welfare of the community," . . . "Ay, there's the rub." The public school has the same features objectionable to the surrounding area as a private one, but it has, also, a virtue which the other lacks, namely, that it is located to serve and does serve that area without discrimination. Whether the private school is sectarian or commercial, though it now complains of discrimination, in its service it discriminates and the public school does not. . . . The private school imposes on the community all the disadvantages of the public school but does not compensate the community in the same manner or to the same extent . . . we cannot say that such a distinc-

tion is arbitrary or unreasonable or that such discrimination between the two schools lacks foundation in a difference which bears a "fair, substantial, reasonable and just relation" to the promotion of the general welfare of the community, which is the statutory purpose of zoning laws in general and of the ordinance in question.

The court admitted that it had not found any decisions sustaining the distinction between schools in zoning cases and that the authority was, if anything, to the contrary. Nevertheless, it found support for its departure from the general line of decisions in other activities. It pointed out that an ordinance could properly distinguish between municipally owned and privately owned parks and playgrounds, on the ground that such areas for the common benefit of all the people are not to be compared with the lands used by private corporations. Finally, the court concluded that no unconstitutional or otherwise illegal discrimination existed in the ordinance which excluded private high schools and permitted public ones in the same residential area.

II

The courts have very often reversed the actions of administrative officials acting under zoning regulations which operated to exclude the erection of church buildings in residential districts. In the leading case of *State ex rel Synod of Ohio v. Joseph* (Ohio), 39 N.E. 2d 515, the ordinance restricted a district to single-family dwellings but provided that churches (among other public and semipublic buildings) could be erected by obtaining a special permit from the zoning commission and the village council. The special permit was denied and suit was brought to compel the authorities to issue it. In granting this relief, the court seriously questioned the constitutionality of any enactment which flatly prohibited the erection of churches in a residential district, but based its holding on the administrative application of the ordinance rather than on the constitutionality of the ordinance itself.

The authorities had sought to sustain their denial of the special permit on the grounds of public health, safety, morals, and welfare because of the increased noise, traffic congestion, parking difficulties, and the effect which a church structure would have on surrounding land values. The court, however, on the basis of the particular facts involved in the case, eliminated each of these factors in turn, and stated its conclusion as follows:

> We conclude that respondents' refusal to grant the permit to erect the church in the residential district so long as land was available in the business district was not authorized by the ordinance from which respondents derived their powers. And we further conclude that the administrative act of respondents in refusing a permit to erect a church in the residential district, there being no adequate showing that this exclusion of the church was in furtherance of the public health, safety, morals, or the public welfare, was arbitrary and unreasonable and in violation of realtor's rights under the State and Federal Constitutions.

The rationale of the relatively few cases on this aspect of zoning was simply and basically stated by the Supreme Court of Texas in *City of Sherman v. Simms,* 183 S.W. 2d 417, in these words: "To exclude churches from residential districts does not promote the health, the safety, the morals, or the general welfare of the community. . . ."

That rationale was contradicted in no uncertain terms in *Bishop* v. *City of Porterville* (California) 203P. 2d 823, where petitioner sought to compel the issuance of a permit to build a chapel and classrooms for religious worship and study in a single-family district. The court found that the zoning regulations had a substantial relation to the public health, safety, morals, and welfare in the following words:

> . . . since the city had power to zone the property herein affected, strictly for single-family dwellings, there was no abuse of the power in prohibiting the erection and construction of church buildings therein. It is a matter of common knowledge that people in considerable numbers assemble in churches and that parking and traffic problems exist where crowds gather. This would be true particularly in areas limited to single-family dwellings. There necessarily is an appreciable amount of noise connected with the conduct of church and "youth activities." These and many other factors may well enter into the determination of the legislative body in drawing the lines between districts, a determination primarily the province of the city.
>
> A single-family residence may be much more desirable when not in an apartment-house neighborhood or adjacent to a public building such as a church. The municipal legislative body may require that church buildings be erected to conform to health

> and safety regulations as provided in its building code and we see no reason to hold that churches may be erected in a single-family residential area when a duplex, triplex, or other multiple dwelling can lawfully be excluded therefrom. The provision in the ordinance for a single-family residential area affords an opportunity and inducement for the acquisition and occupation of private homes where the owners thereof may live in camparative peace, comfort and quiet. Such a zoning regulation bears a substantial relation to the public health, safety, morals, and general welfare because it tends to promote and perpetuate the American home and protect its civic and social values.

The court dismissed the petition on the ground that it failed to state a cause of action and the appeal from this decision was dismissed by the United States Supreme Court for want of a substantial federal question (338 U.S. 805).

III

May a municipality which permits the construction of churches within a residential zone nevertheless refuse authority for such construction at a particular site within the residential area?

In previous discussion the right of a municipality to exclude churches or private schools from residential areas was examined. It was pointed out that the courts had consistently struck down zoning regulations which attempted to distinguish between public and private educational facilities, or which sought to exclude churches from residential districts. However, as we also showed, a few decisions departed from precedent and distinguished between the right of public and private institutions to construct non-residential buildings in a residential zone.

If those departures from precedent were the beginning of a trend, that trend—in New York, at least—was abruptly halted by two decisions of the New York Court of Appeals, the highest court of New York. The court, in reaffirming the principle that a municipal ordinance may not be construed so that it would in any manner interfere with the free exercise of religious worship, rejected the attempts of municipalities to limit or restrict the sites on which churches could be constructed. (*Matter of Diocese of Rochester* v. *Planning Board of Town of Brighton,* 1 N.Y. 2d 508; *Matter of Community Synagogue* v. *Incorporated Village of Sands Point,* 1 N.Y. 2d 445.)

In both of the cases referred to above, the zoning ordinances of the respective communities involved did not prohibit the erection of churches in residential areas, but required the church or organization to obtain a permit from a planning board. The planning board in each case refused a permit, contending that a place of worship on the respective sites would (1) depreciate the value of the property in the neighborhood, and (2) be detrimental to the neighborhood and the residents thereof; and (3), it was held that there were other sites which would be more suitable for the erection of a church. In each case, the Court of Appeals rejected these contentions as valid considerations.

In the *Rochester* case, in answer to the assertion that the construction would be detrimental to the neighborhood and change its character, the court stated:

> This, in effect, is a declaration by the Board that a proposed church and school, such as we have here, could only be built in an outlying area. . . . Thus, the Diocese is forced to locate in an undeveloped section of the Town without being able to adequately serve the territorial need of its parishioners, hoping that people of the Catholic faith will move near it. I know of no rule of law which requires that churches may only be established in sparsely settled areas. On the contrary, as was said in *O'Brien* v. *City of Chicago,* (347 Ill. App. 45) "wherever the souls of men are found, there the House of God belongs." . . .
>
> Noise and other inconveniences have been held to be insufficient grounds upon which to deny a permit to a church [*State ex rel Synod of Ohio* v. *Joseph* (Ohio) (*supra*)] or a parochial school [*Archbishop of Oregon* v. *Baker* (*supra*)].

In regard to the contention that the value of property in the neighborhood would be depreciated, the court stated: "Moreover, in view of the high purposes and the moral value of these institutions, mere pecuniary loss to a few persons should not bar their erection and use."

In the *Sands Point* case, the court reiterated the general rule that churches may not be wholly excluded from residential areas, by stating:

> The text writers agree that churches and schools should be allowed in Class A residential areas which are usually the quietest and least congested areas of a town. . . . It is well established in this country that a zoning ordinance may not wholly exclude a church or synagogue from any residential district. Such a provision is stricken on the ground that it bears no substantial re-

lation to the public health, safety, morals, peace or general welfare of the community. . . . An ordinance will also be stricken if it attempts to exclude private or parochial schools from any residential area where public schools are permitted.

However, in the *Sands Point* case, the planning board argued that its objection was only to the "precise spot" in question and that there were many other sites in the residential zones on which a church could be more suitably erected. The court asserted that if the municipality had the power to bar a particular site, then it would follow it had the power to select the appropriate site, and concluded that it had neither.

While many may be tempted to think that the solution offered by the intervenor is excellent, when one thinks it through, one realizes that if the municipality has the unfettered power to say that the "precise spot" selected is not the right one, the municipality has the power to say eventually which is the proper "precise spot." That, we can all see, is the wrong solution. The men and women who left Scrooby for Leyden and eventually came to Plymouth in order to worship God where they wished and in their own way must have thought they had terminated the interference of public authorities with the exercise of religion. We think that we should accept the fact that we are the successors of "We, The People" of the Preamble to the United States Constitution and that we may not permit a municipal ordinance to be so construed that it would appear in any manner to interfere with the "free exercise and enjoyment of religious profession and worship."

In still a third case which followed the two cases discussed above (*Matter of Garden City Jewish Center,* 2 Misc. 2d 1009), a New York lower court was called upon to consider the refusal of a planning board to issue a permit for the construction of a synagogue. The contention of the planning board in this case was that the parking facilities available at the site in question might not be adequate for the future expansion of the contemplated church. The court, in rejecting this argument, said:

The evidence in the record establishes that at the present time the off-street parking provision is sufficient. As to the future, the board may not require excess parking facilities now to take care of all future growth. . . . To hold now that provision for the unforeseeable future must be made would restrict the freedom of worship by denying the right to establish a church, not because the facilities are presently inadequate or unsuitable but because they may become so with the passage of time.

The unrestricted right to construct churches or private schools may conflict with some of the goals and aims of zoning regulation. However, it is the weight of judicial opinion that the principle of freedom from interference in religious worship outweighs the public policy considerations underlying the principles of zoning.

A use which is prohibited by a zoning ordinance may be performed by the municipality itself, if functioning in a governmental capacity.

Can a municipality, in effect, violate its own zoning ordinance? After zoning an area for residential use, may a muncipality then, in disregard of its own ordinance, use a part of such area for nonresidential purposes? These are the questions presented in a case decided by the Supreme Court of the State of New York (*Nehrbas* v. *Incorporated Village of Lloyds Harbor,* 147 N.Y.S. 2d 738).

In 1950, the Incorporated Village of Lloyd Harbor adopted a zoning ordinance restricting the entire village to private residential use on minimum plots of two acres. This 1950 ordinance changed the previous zoning by completely eliminating business use in the village. In 1953 the plaintiff, Nehrbas, purchased eight acres of property within the village and erected a home, which cost, together with improvements to the land, in excess of $80,000. The following year the village acquired a two-acre parcel diagonally opposite to the property of Nehrbas. It was the intention of the village to alter a barn located on the parcel and to use the building for various municipal purposes. Nehrbas instituted a legal action to restrain the village from such action.

The court held that it was unlawful for the village to use the building for the storage and maintenance of garbage and highway repair trucks and other vehicles, but ruled that the village had the legal right to use the premises as offices for the village, as a meeting place for the village trustees, and as a courtroom for the use of the village police justice.

In permitting the limited violation by the village of its own zoning ordinance, the court distinguished between municipal functions which it termed private or proprietary and municipal functions which it classified as public or governmental. The court stated that the collection and disposal of garbage and the maintenance and repair of highways were private or proprietary functions on the part of the municipality and that, therefore, such uses fell within the restriction of the village's zoning ordinance. On the other hand, it was the opinion of the court that the use of the premises as offices of the village and as a courtroom were public or governmental functions to which the zoning ordinance did not apply.

There would seem to be no clear-cut distinction between those municipal functions classified as governmental and those classified as private. The village, in its argument before the court, relied on a previous decision of another New York court (*Stiger* v. *Village of Hewlett Bay Park,* 129 N.Y.S. 2d 38) in which a municipality was permitted to lease land in a residentially zoned area for the purpose of erecting a garage for the storage of village trucks and equipment which were used in connection with the care of the streets. In this case, the court ruled that the use of the garage was an exercise of a governmental or public function and that, consequently, the village would be unrestricted by its own zoning ordinance.

The inconsistency in these two decisions is difficult of explanation, unless consideration is given to the differing practical factors raised in each of the cases. In the *Nehrbas* case, there was evidence that the proposed use of the premises would result in a substantial diminution in the value of surrounding homes. Further, in that case, the court emphasized that the village was motivated by the fact that the premises sought to be used could be purchased for an advantageous price and that the village had other available sites on which to construct premises for the proposed uses. In the *Stiger* case, however, the court found that the neighboring residences would sustain no damages as a consequence of the proposed use by the village, and that the village had no other area available for the intended use. Differing pragmatic considerations, therefore, led to different conclusions in the two decisions.

Due to shifting and rapid increases in population, many communities throughout our country have been faced with additional and unexpected responsibilities. Under these circumstances, the apparent tendency of the courts to give great weight to practical considerations when determining the right of a municipality to violate its own zoning is understandable. In still another New York case (*Hewlett* v. *Town of Hempstead,* 133 N.Y.S. 2d 690), the court frankly stated the necessity of giving weight to practical factors in determining the legitimacy of the use of property by the municipality.

In that case, the town had amended its zoning ordinances in order to authorize the erection of an incinerator in an area zoned as a residential district. The court was faced with the fact that the weight of precedent, through application of the "governmental-proprietary" test, held the collection and disposal of garbage to be a private or proprietary function. If the court had strictly applied this test, it would have been compelled to hold that it was unlawful for the village to put the property to the use sought. The court, however, took into account the pressing need of the community and ruled that under existing circumstances the operation of an incinerator was a governmental, rather than private, function of the town:

> . . . Yet the conditions which exist in a closely-knit, fast-growing township such as the Town of Hempstead, have made it imperative that the Town provide for the disposal of refuse and garbage. It is a matter of public health that offal and garbage be disposed of scientifically and efficiently. Burial of refuse and open dump disposal is no longer permissible and the capital to be supplied for the erection of a large incinerator has become a public responsibility. It is perhaps true that in some places the public disposal of waste is optional, but in the Town of Hempstead with its present population and closely developed territory, it is no longer an optional matter. In such a circumstance, the incineration of garbage is not a proprietary but rather a governmental function. Without it, the community in its present form cannot continue to exist without risk to the general health of its inhabitants.

The concept underlying zoning is the promotion and protection of public welfare and safety by the limitation of property use. The violation or disregard by a municipality of zoning laws previously adopted may be necessary, but is, at the same time, self-defeating. In the wake of rapid municipal expansion and its accompanying pressures for the furnishing of vital services, it will be of interest to see how far the courts will go in departing from established precedent in permitting municipalities to disregard their own zoning.

Since the responsibility for designing a building in accordance with existing ordinances rests on the architect, this again emphasizes the importance of placing the burden on the owner's attorney in doubtful cases when any question arises as to the propriety of the program contemplated for a particular site.

The facts and circumstances will determine whether a builder has acquired that type of "vested right" which will preclude the application of a zoning ordinance change to the project which he intends to construct.

An architect retained by a builder who commences construction despite the imminence of changes in the zoning laws should inform his client that he acts at his peril. The builder is in a particularly hazardous position where the work is begun before he has obtained a building permit covering the entire structure. A case in New York (*Riverdale Community Planning Assn.* v. *Crinnion,* 133 N.Y.S. 2d 706) highlights this problem.

In the Riverdale case, the builder acquired title to certain property in early 1953, intending to erect an apartment house. The apartment was to be erected in the Riverdale area of New York City, which was at that time predominantly a one-family residential section. He engaged architects and engineers, proceeded to make test borings and made a topographical survey of the site.

In November 1953 the Planning Commission of New York City held hearings for the purpose of amending the zoning ordinance to prohibit the further erection of apartment houses. In December 1953 the builder was granted an excavation permit; and in early January 1954 he was issued a foundation permit. These permits authorized work to begin, pending issuance of a building permit for the entire structure, which would have been issued upon final approval of all plans. The proposed zoning change prohibiting the further construction of apartment dwellings was adopted and became effective on January 14, 1954.

Between the time the builder had obtained an excavation permit and a foundation permit and the date the change in the zoning law became effective, the builder had completely excavated the property but had not poured foundation concrete or done any other foundation work in any substantial degree. The question presented to the court was whether the change in the zoning law applied to the project in question, thereby prohibiting its completion or whether the builder had such a "vested right" in the project that the change in the zoning law could not be constitutionally applied.

The court ruled that the builder could not proceed because the work which had been performed prior to the change in the zoning ordinance did not represent a substantial part of the structure and therefore did not create a "vested right."

The court, in its decision, was influenced not only by the fact that the builder had not obtained a final building permit at the time of the change in the law, but also by the fact that he had not completed the foundation. The court stated:

> . . . even if it be held that all the claimed excavation work had been done, it cannot be held that any part of the foundation work was completed, as no concrete had been poured . . . The builder is, therefore, not in the position of having substantially performed to the extent allowable under the permits held. Without substantially completing the foundations it cannot be held that any substantial part of these structures of approximately ten-story apartment houses with connecting garage had been built.

The courts will often consider surrounding circumstances in determining whether a builder has that type of "vested right" which will preclude the applicability of a zoning ordinance change to the project which he is constructing. Some courts will consider as a factor the expenses incurred by the builder prior to the change in the zoning ordinance. However, the courts look with suspicion upon the claim of hardship by a builder where he has incurred expenses despite his knowledge of the imminence of a change in the zoning laws.

In a Connecticut case (*Graham Corp.* v. *Board of Zoning Appeals, Town of Greenwich,* 140 Conn. 1) the builder, despite opposition of adjacent land owners, succeeded in obtaining an excavation permit and foundation permit for the construction of a building. Within two days, with the use of power shovels, the builder excavated the land and poured concrete footings. The adjacent land owners appealed the issuance of the permits on the third day following their issuance. The builder contended that, by excavating the land and by pouring concrete footings, he had obtained a "vested right" in the project which would preclude the adjacent land owners from questioning the propriety of the issuance of the permits. The builder further asserted that he had incurred great expense in commencing the work and that it would be inequitable to withdraw the permits.

The court rejected the argument of the builder, ruling that the building was not substantially in the course of construction and, therefore, no "vested right" of the builder had been created. The court, in pointing out that the expenditure of the builder was hurriedly incurred over a two-day period when he knew that the issuance of the permits would be challenged, stated:

> When, then, the foundation permit was issued under date of October 27, the plaintiff doubtless expected, in view of its past experience, that the opposition would seek a review of the inspector's action; anything which the plaintiff accomplished on Saturday and Sunday, October 27 and 28, in excavating the land with the use of power shovels and in pouring concrete footings did not bring the building to the point where it was "substantially in the course of construction," as mentioned in the rule. Nor does the hurried incurring of expenditures on the two days mentioned commend itself to any equitable consideration. The difficulty in which the plaintiff finds itself on this matter of expense was one of its own deliberate choice.

The foregoing cases are illustrative of the dangers of proceeding with construction where there are strong pressures for a change in the zoning law and such a change is imminent. Commencement of construction without the issuance of a building permit is particularly risky, even though excavation and foundation permits have been obtained. A builder cannot always protect himself from a change in the zoning law by commencing or continuing construction as quickly and as fast as possible prior to such change. Whether he may continue with the construction will depend upon whether a "vested right" to do so has been created, and the existence of such a right is a question of factual determination which differs in each situation.

II

What effect does a change of zone have upon a property owner who has filed plans for a structure whose "use" would be prohibited under the new law?

In an interesting case, *Kunz* v. *Hill, Jr.*, 128 N.Y.S. 2d 680, the court had before it for determination the following situation:

(a) On *August 4, 1953* the Town Board of Yorktown, New York, adopted a resolution recommending the rezoning of several areas, and then referred this resolution to the Planning Board.

(b) On *August 7, 1953* the Planning Board recommended the adoption of the zoning law revision to the Town Board.

(c) On *August 11, 1953* at a regular meeting of the Town Board, a resolution was passed providing for a public hearing on the matter.

(d) On *August 12, 1953* the plans and application in question were filed.

(e) On *August 13, 1953* the notice of public hearing was duly advertised.

(f) On *August 28, 1953* the public hearing was held, the revision passed and adopted.

This schedule indicates that *following* the Planning Board's action but *before* the adoption of the zoning change, the owner filed his application for a building permit to allow him to erect a retail store or professional offices on a site, which was, under the Town Board's resolution, in an area to be re-zoned from business to residential. The building inspector, aware of the proposed revision of the zoning law, did not pass upon petitioner's application. The court was requested to direct the inspector to issue the permit to petitioner on the grounds that the erection of a business structure was still permissible at the time of the filing of the application for a building permit.

In denying the petition and dismissing the proceedings, the court went on to answer these questions:

(1) *What is the power of a building inspector with regard to the granting or denial of a building permit?*

"Ordinarily the issuance of a building permit is purely an administrative act, and the person charged with issuing the same must follow the literal provisions of the zoning ordinance. The granting or withholding of a building permit is not a matter of arbitrary discretion. If the applicant complies with the valid requirements of the building zone ordinance or building code of the municipality, he is entitled to his permit as a matter of right."

(2) *Will the courts review the actions of the building inspector?*

"It is universally true that courts are zealous not to interfere with administrative discretion in denial of building permits, except for unreasonable arbitrary, discriminatory, or unlawful conduct on the part of the duly authorized administrative officer."

(3) *Can a permit, once issued, be revoked?*

"It is well established, too, that building permits duly issued may, nevertheless, be specifically or in effect revoked by subsequent changes of law or ordinances. There are abundant authorities governing instances where a building permit has been issued but no work has been commenced, or has progressed to a substantial degree prior to the enactment of an amendatory ordinance prohibiting the use for which the permit was originally issued. In such cases it has been held that no vested rights have been acquired."

(4) *Suppose construction has already begun?*

"Similarly, there are authorities holding that a property owner may acquire vested rights by reason of having changed his position by performing substantial work, or by incurring expense and obligations in pursuance of the building permit, prior to the enactment of the amendatory ordinance prohibiting the use."

(5) *Can a property owner acquire a "vested right" by commencing construction immediately after filing his application but prior to the issuance of a permit?*

"It is apparent that the use to which petitioners seek to put their property is no longer permitted under the Building Zone Ordinance (of the Town of North Hempstead). Petitioners claim, however, that if the permit had been issued promptly, they would by this time have acquired a vested right which could not be taken away by legislative amendment of the ordinance. That may be, but the fact of the matter is that petitioners have not acquired any vested rights since no permit has been issued. Any obligations incurred by them or money spent without a permit cannot give rise to a vested right.

"The contractual obligations assumed by respondent after filing his application for a building permit and prior to the issuance thereof, were not such acts as to vest any rights which could not be defeated by the subsequent amendment of the local ordinance.

"Quite apart from the above collated authorities, each case must be analyzed and determined on its own peculiar facts and circumstances. Here there is entirely no foundation for any claim of bad faith, willful delay or hindrance by the town authorities. The machinery for modification of the zoning ordinance was already in operation at the time petitioner filed his application for a building permit on August 12, 1953. The undisputed facts and circumstances negatives any finding of a deliberate design or policy of delay by the municipal authorities to frustrate petitioner on his application. Petitioner could not, and did not, acquire any vested right to the building permit by winning the race in filing his application prior to the effective date of the amendment to the ordinance, but subsequent to the unequivocal acts on the part of the municipal authorities evidencing an intention to amend the zoning ordinance."

The lesson: To protect a "use" of unimproved land it is necessary to obtain a building permit and incur "expense and obligations" or perform "substantial work."

Flexibility in the application of zoning legislation to prevent a serious injustice or hardship is provided by a Board of Zoning Appeals which may vary the application of the zoning ordinance within statutory limits.

The field of zoning legislation is relatively new and is understandably suffering from growing pains. A discussion of some basic applicable rules is therefore useful. In each state there has been created a body called a Board of Zoning Appeals (in some states it is referred to as either a Board of Adjustment or a Board of Review), whose primary function is to weigh and evaluate questions of fact relating to the use of property within its jurisdiction.

The powers of the Board are circumscribed and confined within the framework of the law governing zoning. Its basic consideration is in the maintenance of such a system of zoning as will best serve the interests of the community as a whole.

A New York Court, in *Van Auken v. Kimmey*, 141 Misc. 105, 252 N.Y.S. 329, expressed the considerations of the Board of Appeals as follows:

> Zoning ordinances are not intended to be and cannot long continue to be mere straitjackets to be applied and held rigid by pure bureaucratic authority. The letter of the ordinance must yield, in instances of extreme hardship, and according to conditions of irrepressible growth and development. Properly administered, zoning ordinances do not destroy but add to values; arbitrarily administered or adopted, without regard to the proper limits of police power, they can become instruments of hardship and tyranny which can only be relieved by multitudinous applications to the court. The final determination of the proper application of the rules as adopted ought not to be left to the final determination of an administrative officer, but a citizen aggrieved should have opportunity to appeal to a quasi judicial body with power to view and study the situation, whose determination, in the absence of bad faith or abuse of discretion, would rarely be disturbed upon review by a court.

The function of the Board is, therefore, to provide a measure of flexibility in the application of general rules imposed for the public welfare and to interpose when the circumstances indicate that a serious injustice would be done by an exercise of the general rule and it should grant relief in those cases where justice requires it.

The Board may be called upon from time to time to interpret various provisions of an ordinance, as well as consider applications for exceptions as specifically provided for in the ordinance.

By far the greatest portion of the Board's time is in the granting of variances. The difference between a variance and an exception is that, in the former, it is necessary for the applicant to show hardship, while in the latter, it is not.

The Board, in considering whether a variance should be granted, weighs the particular hardship against the equities, that is to say, the modification or adjustment must be in harmony with the general purpose of the ordinance and must not interfere with the rights of other property owners.

Any general hardship which may develop by reason of a zoning ordinance cannot be relieved by the Board, which is an administrative agency carrying out policies within the framework of the definite standards as prescribed by the ordinance. The Board, not being a legislative body, may only remedy a special hardship upon a showing that the restriction will cause the particular individual a hardship, with respect to a specific parcel of property, that it is special, peculiar, and unique.

The mere fact that an applicant will suffer financial hardship is, standing alone, insufficient grounds for the granting of a variance. A property owner's objection that his property cannot be put to its most profitable use or that the value of the land has depreciated, are not considered the proper criteria in determining "unnecessary hardship" (*Welton v. Hamilton,* 344 Ill. 82, 176 N.E. 333).

The hardship must not be caused by acts of the applicant. For example, in *Cohen v. Rosedale,* 120 Misc. 416, 199 N.Y. S.4, 206 A.D. 681, 199 N.Y.S. 916, aff'd. 211 A.D. 812, 206 N.Y.S. 893, the court denied relief to a property owner who began to erect a building in violation of a restrictive covenant in the deed, even though erection had begun prior to the adoption of the zoning ordinance which prohibited the erection of such buildings.

In some instances, the variance will be denied even where there was a peculiar hardship established. If the Board ascertains that the granting of a variance will cause injury to other properties or adversely affect the essential character of the neighborhood, it will deny relief.

The authority to vary the provisions of the ordinance must, for the most part, be sparingly exercised. Any departure from the provisions must be prompted by substantial compelling reasons. Once the Board exceeds its properly delegated powers, it is, in effect, exercising legislative functions under the guise of a variance.

The Boards today are recognized as being absolutely necessary for the safe operation of a zoning plan. As the court, in *Van Auken v. Kimmey, supra,* declared:

> It is the safety valve of the zoning plan. A zoning ordinance, like a steam boiler, will sooner or later blow up if there is no safety valve. Where there is a functioning Board of Appeals to which every aggrieved applicant for a permit may resort, litigation automatically assumes the form of a court review of the discretion of the board, instead of out and out attacks on the constitutionality of specific instances of regulation. . . . Where there is no Board of Appeals, instances are sure to arise which the courts must under the law declare unreasonable and arbitrary and therefore void.

II

In recent years, a practice has been employed by cities, towns, and villages which constitutes a serious encroachment upon the powers of a Board. This practice consists of the granting by local governing bodies of certain "special permits" or "use permits" to property owners.

Such action by a governing body is in many (if not most) instances unauthorized and improper. The State of New York has, as do all states, zoning-enabling acts which empower the cities and local governing bodies to enact zoning ordinances and appoint boards of zoning appeals. The enabling acts in New York do not delegate to the governing or legislative body the power to grant variances or grant administratively "special or use permits." Under the New York acts, it is the chief purpose and function of the board to grant or deny variances and their determinations are always subject to judicial review.

It is manifestly clear that when the local governing body grants a "use permit" for a use not permitted by the zoning ordinance, it is, in effect, amending the ordinance as to that particular parcel of property. Such action is legislative rather than administrative. As the local body is acting in a legislative capacity, there can be no summary review by a court.

The New York Court of Appeals in *Matter of Neddo* v. *Schrade,* 270 N.Y. 97, determined that the adoption of a resolution by the City Council of the City of Saratoga Springs transferring real property from a partially restricted to an unrestricted zone was not subject to judicial review. In labeling the action legislation, the court declared as follows:

> The setting up of a Board of Appeals and the exercise by it of its limited statutory authority does not detract from the legislative power remaining in the City Council to amend, alter or change the lines of the zones. When application is made to this latter power, we find instances where the City Council grants relief through legislative power reserved to it, even though a Board of Appeals may be functioning with concurrent power pursuant to a grant to the Board of statutory power. (p. 102)

There is no question of the power of the local governing body to amend from time to time its zoning ordinance, as to any or all properties. Such amendments, however, should encompass the same considerations and requirements that were applicable when the original ordinance was enacted. The Village Law of the State of New York (Section 177) prescribes that a zoning ordinance must deal with zoning the village "in accordance with a comprehensive" plan applying to the entire village. It must be designed to do the following things:

> . . . lessen congestion in the streets; to secure safety from fire, panic and other dangers; to promote health and the general welfare; to provide adequate light and air; to prevent the overcrowding of land; to avoid undue concentration of population; to facilitate the adequate provision of transportation, water, sewerage, schools, parks and other public requirements. Such regulations shall be made with reasonable consideration, among other things, as to the character of the district and its peculiar suitability for particular uses, and with a view of conserving the value of buildings and encouraging the most appropriate use of land throughout such municipality.

Thus, when a governing body grants a "use permit," it is amending the ordinance without following its own comprehensive plan, and such legislation is not calculated to effect the stated purposes and objectives contained in the enabling act of the state. Such action in many instances is actually a form of legislative discrimination against other parcels of property similarly situated. The property owners affected by such action are deprived of their court review which would be their right if the matter had been before the Board of Zoning Appeals. The granting of "use permits" constitutes, therefore, little more than a circumvention or usurpation by the municipal body of jurisdiction expressly reserved by the enabling statute to the board.

The courts have viewed critically, in some instances, the practice of local bodies granting "special uses." In *Village of South Orange* v. *Hiller,* 92 N.J. Eq. 505, the court held invalid an ordinance that provided for granting of "special permits" by the Board of Trustees of the Village, after a hearing, to the property owners.

The court, in recognizing the discriminatory nature of the provision which could not apply to all citizens alike throughout the district, said as follows: "Discretionary powers reserved to the trustees to give to one and to withhold from another the privilege of violating the ordinance is not conferred by the enabling act, and is without legal effect and is void."

The courts have been unalterably opposed to piecemeal zoning and have consistently advocated zoning acts containing a comprehensive plan for the development of a community. Such a view was aptly stated in *Chapman* v. *Troy,* 241 Ala. 637, as follows: "A single ordinance laying off a small portion of the city as a residence district, taking no account of other areas equally residential in character and so far as appears without any comprehensive plan with a view to the general welfare of the inhabitants of the city as a whole, is not permissible. Piecemeal ordinances are not favored."

In order to be effective, zoning must, of necessity, be in accordance with a comprehensive plan, so as to insure proper development and use of a given community.

CHAPTER 24: *Esthetics as a Factor in Zoning Regulation*

Esthetics are an increasingly important—often indirect—factor in judicial determination of the validity of zoning legislation.

THE SUPREME COURT has spoken in *Berman* v. *Parker,* 348 U.S. 26—and by its decision established a landmark in community planning. Consider these quotes:

> * * * Miserable and disreputable housing conditions may do more than spread disease and crime and immorality. They may also suffocate the spirit by reducing the people who live there to the status of cattle. They may indeed make living an almost insufferable burden. They may also be an ugly sore, a blight on the community which robs it of charm, which makes it a place from which men turn. The misery of housing may despoil a community as an open sewer may ruin a river.
>
> We do not sit to determine whether a particular housing project is or is not desirable. The concept of the public welfare is broad and inclusive. See *Day-Brite Lighting, Inc.* v. *Missouri,* 342 US 421, 424, 96 L. Ed. 469, 472, 72 S. Ct. 405. The values it represents are spiritual as well as physical, aesthetic as well as monetary. It is within the power of the legislature to determine that the community should be beautiful as well as healthy, spacious as well as clean, well-balanced as well as carefully patrolled. In the present case, the Congress and its authorized agencies have made determinations that take into account a wide variety of values. It is not for us to reappraise them. If those who govern the District of Columbia decide that the

Nation's capital should be beautiful as well as sanitary, there is nothing in the Fifth Amendment that stands in the way.
* * * The particular uses to be made of the land in the project were determined with regard to the needs of the particular community. The experts concluded that if the community were to be healthy, if it were not to revert again to a blighted or slum area, as though possessed by a congenital disease, the area must be planned as a whole. It was not enough, they believed, to remove existing buildings that were insanitary or unsightly. It was important to redesign the whole area so as to eliminate the conditions that cause slums—the overcrowding of dwellings, the lack of parks, the lack of adequate streets and alleys, the absence of recreational areas, the lack of light and air, the presence of outmoded street patterns. It was believed that the piecemeal approach, the removal of individual structures that were offensive, would be only a palliative. The entire area needed redesigning so that a balanced, integrated plan could be developed for the region, including not only new homes but also schools, churches, parks, streets, and shopping centers. In this way it was hoped that the cycle of decay of the area could be controlled and the birth of future slums prevented. Cf. *Gohld Realty Co.* v. *Hartford,* 141 Conn. 135, 141—144, 104 A2d 365, 368-370; *Hunter* v. *Norfolk Redevelopment & Housing Authority,* 195 Va 326, 338-339, 78 SE2d 893, 900-901. Such diversification in future use is plainly relevant to the maintenance of the desired housing standards and therefore within congressional power.

The decision in *Berman* v. *Parker* is a significant addition to the law of slum clearance and community redevelopment. This case approved the condemnation of *inoffensive* property located in a slum area which was being condemned and redeveloped. The decision is important not only for what it decides, but also for the aesthetic grounds on which the decision partly rests.

The case involved the constitutionality of the District of Columbia Redevelopment Act of 1945. This act established an agency with power to redevelop slum areas in Washington, D. C., into planned communities on a co-ordinated basis for the entire territory.

The *Berman* case arose when the owner of a department store located in a slum area objected to the taking of his property on the ground that it was not slum housing. The property was commercial, not residential, and it was in good condition. Therefore, the owner argued, it would be unconstitutional to condemn his property when it was not contributing to slum conditions.

On the other hand, the agency argued that Congress had authorized it to replan the entire area to eliminate slum-causing factors. This required the planning of balanced communities. The agency argued it could not do its job properly if it was not allowed to condemn every building and reconstruct the whole area.

The Court held that the property could constitutionally be taken even if it did not then contribute to slum conditions. It said that Congress could determine that "the community should be beautiful as well as healthy, spacious as well as clean, well-balanced as well as carefully patrolled."

The decision noted that property might be taken for redevelopment which "standing by itself is innocuous and unoffending. But we have said enough to indicate that it is the need of the area as a whole which Congress and its agencies are evaluating. If owner after owner were permitted to resist these redevelopment programs on the ground that his particular property was not being used against the public interest, integrated plans for redevelopment would suffer greatly."

By its decision in *Berman* v. *Parker* the Supreme Court recognized the validity and importance of the Congressional mandate for "comprehensive and co-ordinated planning of the whole territory." In doing so, it has made possible the redevelopment of entire communities within our cities into areas consistent with present-day thinking about the planning and integration of residential and business structures.

Such planning and integration has done much to develop the suburban areas around our larger cities into attractive, balanced, self-contained communities. However, partly because of the legal uncertainty which existed prior to this decision, the need of the inveterate city dweller for similar developments has gone almost unheeded. The *Berman* case puts an end to that uncertainty and so clears another obstacle from the path of "comprehensive and co-ordinated planning."

It is important to note that the decision was based partly on esthetic considerations which up to then the courts had generally refused to recognize. The Court considered the validity of intangible factors in the vigorous words quoted at the beginning of this essay; and the importance of that language lies in the Court's recognition of esthetic considerations as an integral part of the "public welfare." Traditionally, the courts would not allow esthetic reasons to be the sole basis for zoning regulations, let alone condemnation of property. As a result, communities that wished to preserve their appearance or attractiveness had to invent other criteria to achieve their purposes. Zoning regulations were therefore phrased in terms of restrictions on "maximum height" or "minimum area" or "number of inhabitants." Although their purpose was really esthetic, the courts held them valid on the ground that they were necessary for the public safety to minimize fire hazards. However, such zoning regulations were usually held invalid whenever the esthetic purposes did not appear to be auxiliary to some long-recognized standard of public health, safety, or morals.

Even before the *Berman* case, however, a few bold courts recognized the importance of esthetic considerations. A Texas Court of Civil Appeals found that esthetic standards may properly be used in zoning because they "tend to conserve the value of property." The New York Court of Appeals has stated that esthetic considerations are "not wholly without weight." But even in such incidents, the courts betrayed a reluctance toward giving full legal status to esthetic values and usually phrased decisions in terms of property values instead of human values.

Why did it take the courts so long to arrive at the language in the *Berman* case? Because the judicial branch is in a very real sense the guardian of individual freedom, including the freedom of individual taste and esthetic judgment. There is a danger that legislatively-inspired esthetics might be reduced to the lowest common denominator, as well as stifle creative architecture and personal taste. Although that danger is always present, it is not a sufficient reason to deny esthetics its legitimate place. The language in the *Berman* case gives such a place to esthetic considerations.

Although the *Berman* case does not hold that esthetic considerations can be the sole basis of zoning regulations or redevelopment statutes, it is a significant step in that direction. Inherent in the Supreme Court's language is an appreciation of the role the architect must play in planning for the public welfare. The ultimate impact of the *Berman* case cannot yet be measured. Nevertheless, esthetic values in commercial and residential housing can be expected to play a greater role in future legislation. Finally, when such legislation is enacted, the *Berman* case may come to be reflected in an increased public demand for attractive communities in which to live and work.

Again I wish to point out that in all of this the architect is the *professional*—the expert best qualified for leadership in this field. This leadership he must assume—or the profession, as a profession, fails.

Minimum plot areas for residential construction, and prohibition against "look-alike" homes, are two examples of zoning regulation which are based in part upon esthetic considerations.

How far may a municipality go in limiting the minimum area upon which a residence may be constructed? This is a question which will assume increasing importance as a result of expanding activity in residential housing developments. There are a few cases in the United States which have touched upon the problem, but they by no means express uniformity in viewpoint.

Generally speaking, a municipality has the right to restrict the use of property in the exercise of its inherent police power. But such restriction must be reasonable and based upon the protection of the health, morals, and safety of the community. A zoning law may not be validly adopted where its only purpose is esthetic, or artistic, or where its intent is to protect the value of large estates against the influx of persons with modest incomes.

The Appellate Division of the New York Supreme Court was called upon to determine the validity of a zoning ordinance which prescribed a minimum area of two acres for plots upon which residences were to be constructed. (*Dilliard et ano. v. Village of North Hills*, 276 App. Div. 969). The court upheld the validity of this ordinance on the ground that it was neither unreasonable nor arbitrary.

The Village of North Hills is a residential community on Long Island in New York, containing, for the most part, homes of substantial character. The total number of property owners is 52, of whom 32 are resident property owners. The area of the Village is 1500 acres having an assessed valuation of $4,270,600.

There had not been any unusual real estate activity within the village at the time the suit was instituted. All of the property owners held at least two acres, with the exception of one who owned 1.9 acres on the outskirts of the village. He, however, had other adjoining property which was outside the incorporated village. The unincorporated area outside the village contained home developments on plots ranging from 8500 square feet to 15,000 square feet. Neighboring villages had developments on plots ranging from 12,000 square feet to one-half acre.

The plaintiffs purchased for $40,000 approximately 48 acres of land in the Village of North Hills. Two two-acre plots were sold by the plaintiffs for the sum of $22,000. It was their desire to subdivide the balance of their property into plots containing 10,000 square feet.

In their suit against the Village of North Hills, the plaintiffs contended that the two-acre restriction was unreasonable, discriminatory, and confiscatory, and that their property could be profitably used only by sub-division into plots with a minimum area of 10,000 square feet. Such a restriction, they argued, had no substantial relation to the public health, morals, safety or welfare, its purpose being to protect the real estate values of the large estates in the village.

The village, on the other hand, argued that any regulation which permits persons to live in a country environment, free from congestion and noise, is a valid one in that the health of the residents of the community is benefited thereby. The village made the further argument that the voiding of the two-acre restriction would increase the economic burden upon the then residents of the village in that the greater density of population would call for greater municipal facilities.

The Appellate Court rejected the contentions of the plaintiffs, and in upholding the validity of the two-acre restriction, stated: "In the light of the location and character of the village, it was within defendant's legislative province to determine, in the absence of proof of superior public need, that the two-acre restriction is justifiable as an elastic application of police power. . . ."

In the absence of proof that the public welfare of the residents was not enhanced by the restriction, the court determined that it would let the restriction stand.

A similar decision was reached by the Massachusetts Supreme Court in upholding a zoning law which restricted construction in the residential district to plots of at least one acre. The court in that case found that the town in question was particularly available for residential purposes because of its nearness to Boston, and was suitable for those "who desire the advantages of quiet and beauty of rural surroundings." The court further found that a one-acre restriction protected the health, safety, and welfare of the community by preventing noise, congestion, and overcrowding, and by permitting adequate air, sunshine, rest, and relaxation. In the opinion of the court these factors were sufficient to justify the ordinance and to prevent the court from substituting its judgment for that of the town legislature.

Yet many decisions in other cases pertaining to certain restrictive zoning have declared such restrictions invalid. It has been held that a zoning regulation which provided that more than 14 families could not be accommodated on an acre of land was invalid and unreasonable if applied to flats. It has also been held that a zoning ordinance regulating the density of population by limiting the use of property in a residence zone to 36 families per acre was invalid. Still other decisions have declared invalid regulations describing the minimum width of side and rear yards where no relationship was found to exist between such regulations and the health, morals, and general welfare of the community.

The reasonableness of any restriction upon use or size depends upon the nature, location, and characteristics of each individual community. The upholding of a one- or two-acre restriction for one community would not, of necessity, be a precedent for the validity of such an ordinance in another community.

There is an indistinct point at which an acreage restriction is no longer substantially related to health and welfare, but becomes arbitrary and unreasonable. Just where this point is reached and where the line should be drawn must be determined by the courts in each individual case. The only conclusion that can be ventured at this time is that the extent to which a municipality may go in limiting acreage upon which a residence may be constructed is indefinite and uncertain.

To discuss a two-acre or a one-acre or even a substantially smaller acreage restriction in terms of "health and welfare" is obvious sophistry. Such restriction can pragmatically be justified only on the ground of esthetics—whatever words the courts use. Until that word finds its place alongside "health and welfare," the validity of ordinances will be judged by the last phrase alone—even if its distortion beyond recognition is required to justify the results.

II

Esthetics (in a zoning ordinance) and property rights squared off against each other in a New York case, with esthetics the apparent victor. An appellate court of New York, by a divided opinion, upheld a zoning ordinance which required a minimum of two acres for a single family residence (*Levitt* v. *The Incorporated Village of Sands Point*, 6 A.D. 2d 701). This decision reversed a lower court determination that the ordinance was unconstitutional because it was apparently based upon esthetic factors only and could not be justified on the ground of public health, safety, morals, or general welfare.

The Village of Sands Point had originally been zoned to provide for a minimum of one acre for residential construction. The zoning ordinance was amended in 1954 to divide the village into two districts entitled "A" and "B." The residence "A" district was four times the size of the residence "B" district and the ordinance provided for a two-acre minimum in the residence "A" district.

The zoning ordinance was challenged by a property owner who intended to develop property which he had purchased prior to the amendment for one-acre residential sites and which was located in District "A." The village contended that there was a demand for more spacious living and that it was within its power to preserve to the greatest possible extent the existing character of the village by providing the two-acre minimum plot restriction. The lower court, however, pointed out that there was no showing that two-acre zoning was necessary to provide adequate light or air or that there was an undue concentration of population in the area. Consequently, it concluded the statute was unreasonable because its apparent purpose had no direct relationship to public health, safety, or welfare.

On appeal, however, the Appellate Court refused to declare the ordinance unconstitutional and further emphasized that the statute provides that the Village Board of Appeals, within certain limitations, may grant a variance based upon the general character of neighboring property. The majority opinion stated:

> The amended complaint alleged, *inter alia*, that the amended ordinance was unreasonable and confiscatory because there was on the westerly side of Middle Neck Road, directly opposite to respondents' property, land developed with small single-family residences on plots having a maximum area of 7500 square feet, and there was, south of respondents' property and a short distance therefrom, land improved with a multiple low-cost housing project. The amended ordinance provides that the village board of appeals may within stated limitations grant

variances of the provisions thereof which respondents complain of "where the general character of the land in the immediate vicinity is such that residences have been erected on lots of less than two (2) acres." The record discloses that the variances authorized, if granted, would be sufficient to permit respondents to develop their property in accordance with their plans.

. . . It is our opinion that in view of the provisions of the amended ordinance which permit a variance to be granted under the circumstances complained of in the amended complaint, it has not been established that there has been any deprivation of respondents' property rights which would permit a determination that the ordinance is unconstitutional as confiscatory. Concededly, respondents have not applied for, nor have they been refused, such a variance with respect to any of their property. . . .

A minority of the Appellate Court, however, in a dissenting opinion agreed with the opinion of the lower court stating that two-acre zoning bears no relation to public health, morals, safety, or general welfare. The dissenting judges said:

After respondents purchased in 1951 a 127-acre tract of land for the purpose of subdividing it into then permissible one-acre plots, the village zoning ordinance was amended in 1954 to require that a residential building plot have a minimum area of two acres. This amendment resulted in a depreciation of the value of respondents' property of $1000 an acre (according to appellants) and $2500 an acre (according to respondents). We agree with the learned official referee that two-acre zoning in this village bears no relation to public health, morals, safety, or general welfare, that it would retard the growth and development of the village, that it is not necessary to provide adequate light and air, and that there is no threat of overcrowding or of overconcentration of population. Respondents' property will necessarily remain unimproved and unproductive, and a source of expense to the owners. In the absence of some showing that the property can be put to a profitable use within a reasonable time so that temporary hardship may ultimately be compensated (and there was no such proof here), the burden placed on the owner is in the nature of confiscation.

The number of municipal zoning ordinances based, at least in part, upon esthetic factors is constantly increasing. The courts in many instances have construed zoning regulations which involve esthetic considerations as justifiable on the ground of the public health, safety, morals or welfare. Implicit in the majority decision of the New York Appellate Court is a reluctance to substitute its judgment for that of the municipality as to the reasonableness and necessity of an acreage restriction in respect to the welfare of the community. If this attitude is extended, esthetic considerations in matters of zoning will become increasingly significant.

III

How can a municipality legally insist upon an esthetic approach to zoning? This writer will not discus esthetics as such! Parenthetically it should be pointed out, however, that there must be considered by the realistic community planner, in addition to the architects' different and often divergent esthetic concepts, the concepts held by laymen, whose views often conform to no principle expressed by any highly regarded architectural expert. (See Scarsdale Ordinance discussed below.)

Population increase and expanding housing activity in suburban areas have prompted many communities to enact zoning laws regulating the character of residential development. Such zoning constitutes an attempt by these communities to preserve for their residents the advantages of a distinctive and attractive rural environment.

The courts have traditionally looked upon zoning restrictions as a permitted exercise of the police power only where they tend to promote the "public health, morals, and safety." The rule has been well established that the police power cannot be validly exercised where its purpose is esthetic or artistic, yet compelling public pressure has been exerted both upon the legislatures and courts to approve zoning laws, the enactment of which has been motivated by esthetic considerations. The courts have not resisted this demand entirely and recent decisions tend to uphold such legislation. Nevertheless, the time-honored legal criteria have caused the courts considerable difficulty in rationalizing decisions, when they have approved in principle the endeavor of communities to promote esthetic and property values and have found their application reasonable. Decisions written in terms of health, morals and safety concepts bear no immediate relation to the objectives of present day zoning legislation.

The insistence of residential dwellers that esthetic and property values are important and should be recognized has already compelled a few legislatures and courts to approach the issue more candidly and realistically.

A law enacted by the legislative authority of a New York village illustrates the effective pressure which public demand can bring to bear on the legislative authority to enact a law to promote esthetic and artistic development of residential construction in the community. The Village of Scarsdale has enacted a law designed to prohibit the construction of homes that look alike in the same residential neighborhood. Uniformity in the exterior design and appearance of neighboring dwellings, the law states, "adversely affects the desirability of immediate and neighboring areas for residence purposes and by so doing impairs the benefits of occupancy of existing property in such areas, impairs the stability and value of both improved and unimproved real property in such areas, prevents the most appropriate use of such real property, prevents the most appropriate development of such areas, produces degeneration of residential property in such areas with attendant deterioration of conditions affecting the health, safety, and morals of the inhabitants thereof, deprives the municipality of tax revenue which it otherwise could receive and destroys a proper balance in relationship between the taxable value of real property in such areas and the cost of the municipal services provided therefor."

The indicia of such uniformity are detailed in Section 2 of the law, set forth below:

> Section 2. Except as provided in this local law, no building permit shall be issued under the Building Code of the Village for the erection of any building for occupancy as a dwelling for one or two families if it is like or substantially like any neighboring building, as hereinafter defined, then in existence or for which a building permit has been issued, in more than three of the following six respects:
>
> (1) Height of the main roof ridge, or, in the case of a building with a flat roof, the highest point of the roof beams, above the elevation of the first floor;
>
> (2) Height of the main roof ridge above the top of the plate (all flat roofs shall be deemed identical in this dimension);
>
> (3) Length of the main roof ridge, or in the case of a building with a flat roof, length of the main roof;
>
> (4) Width between outside walls at the ends of the building measured under the main roof at right angles to the length thereof;
>
> (5) Relative location of windows in the front elevations

with respect to each other and with respect to any door, chimney, porch or attached garage in the same elevation;

(6) In the front elevation, both (a) relative location with respect to each other of garage, if attached, porch, if any, and the remainder of the building, and (b) either (i) height of any portion of the building located outside the limits of the main roof, measured from the elevation of the first floor to the roof ridge, or, in the case of a flat roof, the highest point of the roof beams, or (ii) width of said portion of the building if it has a gable in the front elevation, otherwise length of said roof ridge or said flat roof in the front elevation.

Buildings shall be deemed to be like each other in any dimension with respect to which the differences between them is not more than two feet. Buildings between which the only difference in relative location of elements is end to end or side to side reversal of elements shall be deemed to be like each other in relative location of such elements. In relation to the premises with respect to which the permit is sought, a building shall be deemed to be a neighboring building if the lot upon which it or any part of it has been or will be erected is any one of the following lots, as shown on the tax map of the Village:

(a) Any lot on the street upon which the building to be erected on said premises would front which is the first or the second lot next along said street in either direction from said premises, without regard to intervening street lines;

(b) Any lot any part of the street line frontage of which is across said street from said premises or from a lot referred to in subparagraph (a) of this section;

(c) Any lot any part of the street line frontage of which faces the end of, and is within the width of, said street, if there are less than two lots between said premises and the end of said street;

(d) Any lot on another street which adjoins said premises on such other street; or

(e) Any lot any part of the street line frontage of which is across such other street from said premises or from a lot referred to in subparagraph (d) of this section; provided, however, that, notwithstanding any of the foregoing provisions of this section, no building shall be deemed to be a neighboring building in relation to said premises if its rear elevation faces the street upon which the building to be erected on said premises would front.

Provision is made for review of the denial of a permit by the Building Inspector by appeal to a Building Board, composed of three residents of the community, at least one of whom is to be an architect.

Whether the above ordinance will be upheld if its validity is attacked in a law suit is not now determinable. The law undoubtedly contemplates a far-reaching exercise of the police power. No substantially similar enactment from which a comparison could be drawn has yet been before the courts. However, a review of some of the legal criteria used in zoning cases furnishes a mass of precedent opposed to the recognition of a law, the enactment of which is motivated by esthetic considerations.

The law is well settled that the police power cannot be exercised for purely esthetic or artistic purposes. The rule has been stated thus: "While the promotion of esthetic or artistic considerations is a proper object of governmental care, these considerations alone will not justify, as an exercise of the police power, a radical restriction of the right of the owner of property to use his property in an ordinary and beneficial way."

A Michigan court has expressed a similar attitude (*Senefsky* v. *Huntington Woods,* 307 Mich. 728, 12 N.W. 2d 387). In that case the court denied the validity of a zoning provision which prescribed a minimum floor area of 1,300 square feet for any proposed building to be constructed in a given subdivision. Concerning testimony given at the trial to the effect that the moving consideration for the passage of the ordinance was the promotion of property value of persons who already lived in the section, the court said: "Esthetics may be an incident but cannot be the moving factor in enforcing police power restrictions. Likewise, it may be said that preservation or enhancing the values of their property in a given zone may be an incident but cannot be the moving factor."

The courts have not only ruled out esthetics as a proper consideration, but have also expressed concern that zoning laws must promote the "public health, safety, and morals." The liberal application of such a criterion has probably resulted in the invalidation of ordinances which have benefited the community though induced by esthetic considerations. The Michigan court specifically stated that the zoning ordinance in no way promoted or protected in the subdivision the health, safety, morals or welfare.

A similar attitude is illustrated in a Maryland case (*Byrne* v. *Maryland Realty Co.,* 129 Md. 202, 98 Atl. 547) which involved a zoning law providing that within a defined section of Baltimore no dwellings could be erected unless constructed as separate and unattached buildings and located 20-feet apart, if of frame construction, and 10-feet apart, if of stone or brick construction. A real estate corporation proposed to improve a lot in this section by constructing semi-detached two-story brick dwellings, with a distance of eight feet between each pair of houses. The court found there would be nothing inherently dangerous to the public safety or the public health in properly constructed semi-detached brick houses. It agreed that the proposed housing development would undoubtedly depreciate to some extent the value of some property but the court decided that neither it nor the legislature had power to prevent the construction. It stated: "The Act does not relate to the police power and its enforcement would deprive the appellee of property rights guaranteed by the Constitution, which cannot be invaded for purely esthetic purposes under the guise of police power."

IV

Some courts are coming to recognize and respect the esthetic features of municipal zoning, and they have been groping toward more appropriately phrased legal acceptance of these objectives. A few courts have recognized the inadequacy of the old formulas and have already treated the problem more candidly. Two cases decided in New York courts have specifically approved community endeavor to preserve esthetic values, and have determined that they promote the general welfare.

In *Gignoux* v. *Village of Kings Point,* 85 N.Y.S. 2d 675, action was instituted by certain property owners to have declared void a zoning ordinance providing that in two designated resident districts no building should be erected to accommodate more than one family for each 20,000 square feet or 40,000 square feet of land, respectively.

The Village of Kings Point is located in a distinctive setting and is the most northerly of a group of nine villages, most of which are small in area and population. In various sections of the village may be found developments containing many beautiful and expensive homes. The court stressed the fact that the Village of Kings Point is unique in the sense that its governing authorities have endeavored to make it available for residential purposes only, and the village depends entirely upon adjacent villages for its business, school, and church needs. In view of this objective, which the court approved, the sole question before it was whether the zoning regulations under attack were unreasonable or arbitrary in their character and operation. According to the court, zoning serves a twofold purpose: "It should protect districts already established. It should control developments in a manner that is reasonable and for the best interests of the municipality in a comprehensive manner, which would aid in the development of new areas."

In deciding that the zoning regulations were neither arbitrary nor unreasonable, the court stated that the plaintiffs had not proved that if the ordinance were enforced the resulting restrictions would preclude the use of their property for any purposes to which it was reasonably adapted. In approving the ordinance, as promoting the general welfare, the court reasoned as follows:

> The beauty of a residential neighborhood tends to the comfort and happiness of the people of the community. It tends to promote the general welfare, adds to the attractiveness of the community and living conditions therein and to the value of residential property therein located.
>
> Real property located in a village does not have to conform in zoning restrictions with other villages. If the inhabitants of a village desire to make the real property therein available for residential purposes only, so that its beauty and rustic character may be preserved and increased and such zoning may be accomplished without arbitrary and confiscatory action, such a village should be sustained in its attempt to secure the village from the noise and traffic, the danger from fire, a better opportunity for rest and relaxation and safety for children.
>
> The Court is not convinced that the action of the zoning authority was arbitrary or unreasonable. In fact, it finds just the opposite. The Court is convinced that the zoning had a definite bearing upon the general welfare.

The tenor of the court's opinion may be interpreted as an approval of this "attempt by the zoning authorities not only to preserve the exclusive, high-class, and rural aspects of the community, but also to insure a further development of the land within the village along the lines of the present development."

Another case illustrates zoning regulations involving the validity of an ordinance regulating space to be devoted to livable areas in dwellings (*Matter of Flower Hill Bldg. Corp.* 199 Misc. 344). A builder had been denied a permit for a proposed building because the plans contemplated a livable floor area considerably smaller than the "1800 square feet" required by the zoning ordinance.

The builder sought an order directing issuance of the permit and maintained that "the livable floor area" restriction lacked a reasonable relationship to the promotion of public health, safety and welfare. The court decided that the power conferred upon villages to regulate and restrict the size of buildings determined the right of the municipality to make such a regulation. It emphasized however that there should be a less narrow approach to the problem. The court explained that the growing population trend to the suburbs was influenced by the desire of urban dwellers for improved living conditions in rural areas. These conditions they were now seeking to maintain by legislation. It examined the real purpose of the State law enabling villages to regulate community developments and said:

> . . . the intendment of the state was to exert its police power by setting up local legislative means for the adoption of ordinances which would encourage better living for its inhabitants and protect them when established in their abodes against invasion of their neighborhood by other activities, and buildings by their nature out of harmony with the established order.

It referred specifically to that portion of the Enabling Act which required that consideration be given to "the most desirable use for which the land of each district may be adapted, the peculiar suitability for a particular use of a district, the conservation of property values and the direction of building development, in accordance with a well considered plan."

Concerning the above expression of purpose the court said:

> The broad objectives of the state zoning legislation should receive the fullest endorsement and co-operation of the court to the end that the objectives hoped for be achieved. Those objectives are a sustained effort by the state to serve the vital interests of humanity. . . . I find that regulating livable floor areas in dwellings is only giving effect to the intent and spirit of the Enabling Act.

Whether in this particular instance the village authorities exceeded their statutory discretion by providing an 1800-square-feet restriction, the court held to be a question of fact to be determined only upon a trial of that issue.

The fact that these courts have appraised zoning objectives more realistically does not insure that future restrictions will be uniformly upheld. Each locality must be considered individually when effect is sought to be given to zoning legislation. It is on this basis that the *Flower Hill* case is distinguished from the decision of the Michigan courts discussed above, which had held invalid a similar provision regulating livable floor area. While the Michigan court was preoccupied with health and safety concepts, on the facts it might have reached the same conclusion had its own approach altered. The court was strongly influenced by the fact that a substantial number of dwellings already located in the area had not complied with the ordinance and that there were a large number of vacant lots, the use of which would have been materially restricted by the ordinance.

The validity of building restrictions will continue to be judged by considering them in connection with the character and circumstances of each individual locality. However, the value of these New York cases lies in their forthright consideration of the problem and in the abandonment of inappropriate phraseology. The new approach bridges the gap between non-legal conclusions and strained legal rationalizations for such conclusions. It encourages a direct handling of the problem and does not confuse the real issue or controversy. It furnishes a more appropriate basis for consideration of zoning ordinances designed to promote attractive housing development.

As esthetic factors gain increasing acceptance as a foundation for zoning regulation, the architectural profession must play a greater role in community planning and in the establishment of appropriate esthetic standards.

The tendency has been to incorporate in a building or zoning ordinance a rigid set of rules intended to be applicable to all building projects. Lately, an interesting variation has begun to appear. Under these zoning laws a commission, or similar body, has been set up to determine, among other things, the esthetics of a building project at the time the building project is contemplated.

An excellent example of this device is found in New York City, where the pressure of finding industrial sites has directed some companies into residential areas. An additional advantage in such a site stems from the fact that a project in such an area has immediately available a ready pool of labor. The difficulties inherent in placing an industrial plant in a residential area are readily apparent. How New York City solved this problem is intriguing.

In 1943, New York City adopted a zoning resolution permitting the erection of certain types of industrial plants in residential areas. Art. 2, Sec. 3 (10) of the resolution provided for the submission to the New York City Planning Commission of a site plan, and general building plans showing design, location, uses, structures and open spaces of project. The resolution listed the type of project permitted (administrative offices and industrial laboratory projects), and restricted the size of plots, the height of buildings, the distance between buildings and required conformity to all applicable laws and regulations relating to construction, operation and maintenance.[1] The City Planning Commission was then to consider the

[1] "Landscaped administrative offices and industrial laboratory projects, consistent with and designed to promote and benefit the value and use of property in residence districts or in areas which are predominantly residential although partly lying in less restricted districts. Such use may be permitted only if approved in accordance with the following terms and conditions:

"(a) Every project authorized under this subsection (10) shall occupy a plot of not less than ten acres, of which not more than 25 percent shall be occupied by buildings and structures and not less than 25 percent shall consist of a landscaped park area to which the public shall have access subject to a reasonable restriction. The aggregate floor area of the buildings and structures shall not exceed one-half of the area of the plot.

"The minimum distance between any two buildings or structures shall be not less than 20 feet. All buildings and structures shall be erected and arranged in a manner which will provide adequate light and air at least equivalent to the requirements of this resolution. The height of any building or structure shall not exceed 50 feet, and within such limits shall be that best suited to the architectural design and arrangement of all the buildings, notwithstanding the provisions of Article III of this resolution. The location and design of all buildings and structures on the plot shall be consistent with the predominantly residential character of the district. The uses provided for in this subsection (10) shall in no instance include the trades, industries and uses procribed by section 4(a) and 4(b) of this resolution.

"(b) Upon presentation to the City Planning Commission of a site plan and general building plans, showing the design, location and uses of buildings, structures and open spaces of a project within a residence district or in an area predominantly residential although partly lying in less restricted districts, the commission may, after public notice and hearing, and subject to appropriate conditions and safeguards, by resolution certify that the construction, operation and maintenance of such a project is consistent with the use of property in such district or districts and is designed to promote, enhance and benefit the value and use of such property and may, thereupon,

merits of each contemplated project individually in the light of promoting and benefiting the use and value of property in the area.

Only one concern took advantage of this resolution. In August of 1943, Sylvania Electric Products, Inc. of New York made an application for the erection of a research, developmental, and administrative center in a residential zone. The project presented by Sylvania comprehended the initial utilization of two buildings then occupying the site in Little Neck, Queens, and the subsequent erection of five administration and industrial laboratory buildings, a garage, and club house. The site contained 28.5 acres, of which seven acres were set aside as a park area for use by the general public. The total floor area of the entire project was 429,104 square feet, or 36 percent of the net area of the site. The plan further provided for parking areas (approximately 500 cars) and for landscaping and developing of the entire area so as to create "a pleasing appearance to the community, an attractive setting for the buildings and a general atmosphere of a high-grade technical institute . . . The architecture will be a modified Georgian style depending upon project wings and ells and varying roof treatment to break up otherwise long building masses. Modified classic entrance porticoes and varying treatment of the fenestration together with low connecting

---

approve such plan of a project. Such resolution of the City Planning Commission, together with the plan of a project shall be filed with the Secretary of the Board of Estimate within five (5) days after its adoption. Unless the Board of Estimate shall disapprove such resolution by a majority vote within thirty days from the date of filing, it shall thereupon take effect, except that in case a protest against a proposed resolution shall have theretofore been presented, duly signed and acknowledged by the owners of 20 percent or more of the area of the land immediately adjacent extending 100 feet from said plot, or by the owners of 20 percent or more of the area of land directly opposite thereto extending 100 feet from the street frontage of such opposite land, such resolution shall not be effective unless approved by the Board of Estimate by unanimous vote of the entire Board.

"(c) All buildings and structures authorized and established under the provisions of this subsection (10) shall conform to all applicable laws and regulations relating to construction, operation and maintenance.

"(d) No modification, variance or change in the general location, layout and character of the project as shown on the plan as approved shall be permitted except when approved in acordance with the procedure set forth in subdivision (b) of this subsection (10), provided that upon abandonment of a particular project authorized under this subsection (10) the land and the structures thereon may be used without such approval for any other lawful purpose permissible within the district or districts in which the project is located."

colonnades and arcades will create an intimate college campus effect, suitable to a highly restricted residential neighborhood."

The project was to contain complete facilities for research and development in lighting, communication and electronics, as well as general administration and sales offices for the concern. Manufacturing was strictly limited and the ultimate number of employees upon completion of the project was not to exceed 2,000. The City Planning Commission, after considering the merits of this application by Sylvania by resolution dated September 22, 1943, approved the contemplated project.

It will be noted that the original resolution made no provision for the erection of any type of manufacturing plant. In 1950 this was remedied by the insertion of the words "and light Industrial Plants" into Art. 2, Sec. 3(10), which dealt with the types of projects which might be erected. In November of 1950, under the then-amended resolution, the Bulova Watch Company, Inc. filed an application for the erection of a light industrial plant in a residential area.

The Bulova project, in Jackson Heights, Queens, was prepared with the problem of esthetics kept foremost in mind. The application provided for the erection of a three-story building on a site area of approximately 24 acres, a plot coverage of 15%. Six acres were reserved for landscaped park area, for public use. The floor area of the building was to be 390,000 square feet. There were also provisions for a parking area to accommodate not less than 500 cars. The entire area, including the plant building, interior roadways and walks, park areas and automobile parking area was to be landscaped, developed and maintained, "in such a way as to create a suitable and attractive appearance." The application further stated that the three-story building would be used as central headquarters and plant for Bulova Watch Company. More specifically the activities would include administration and sales offices, advertising, personnel administration, product research and development, general engineering, quality control and metallurgic development, production of watch parts, assembly of watch movements, shipping, and the production of tools and dies for watch parts manufacturing. This light manufacturing would be permitted under the amended resolution. It was also estimated that the number of employees to be accommodated on this project would not exceed 2,000. There were also provisions for the building of the new streets, the widening of existing streets, and the deeding of these to the city.

The City Planning Commission, in its resolution approving the Bulova application, on December 27, 1950, stated:

> The Commission was impressed by the Community Campus plan, but the effectuation of any such plan is not practical at this time because of the numerous interests and agencies involved. It is obvious that the proposed plan would require expenditures far in excess of sums now available for such purposes. However, development of the Bulova project would not preclude the subsequent use of other land in the vicinity for public purposes. It would appear that the Bulova project could be integrated with a larger community plan without adversely affecting the over-all objectives of the latter. The Commission is hopeful that, so far as practical, schools, parks and other needed facilities in this area may be provided in conformity with such an integrated plan.

The results of these two projects alone may be listed as follows:

(1) New York City gathered increased revenues by their real estate tax on the greater assessed valuation of these two large projects, as opposed to lower assessed residences.

(2) Employment was provided for residents of neighboring communities close to their homes.

(3) The City was given a large area for public parks—the *Bulova* site provides playgrounds, swimming pool, comfort station, baseball, basketball and football fields available to the public.

II

During the past few years municipalities, faced with expanding housing activity in suburban areas, have enacted zoning laws regulating the character of residential development. These enactments were an attempt to preserve for the residents the advantages of a distinctive and attractive rural environment. Some legislation has concerned itself exclusively with the promotion of esthetic and artistic development of new residential construction in the community. We have previously discussed the law enacted by the Village of Scarsdale (New York State), by which the Village sought to eliminate "look-alike" homes, using indicia of uniformity rigidly set forth in its ordinance. The enforcement of the law was left in the hands of the building inspector with a review of his determination, by an appeal to a Building Board, composed of three residents, at least one of whom was to be an architect.

On February 15, 1952, the Village of Garden City (New York State) enacted legislation aimed at the accomplishment of this same purpose, but by a procedure providing flexibility in its operation.

The Garden City local law, as did the Scarsdale law, lists the indicia of similarity, but with a great deal less rigidity and employs a novel approach. The law provides for *initial* consideration of any application by a Board of Review, created under Section 2, which reads in part as follows:

> There is hereby created a Board of Review, consisting of five members, who shall serve without compensation. All members of said Board shall be residents of the Village of Garden City and shall be persons deemed by the Board of Trustees to be qualified by reason of training, experience, or civic interest, and by reason of sound judgment, to determine the effects of a proposed building, group of buildings, or a plan of building development on the desirability, property values, and development of surrounding areas and on the development of the village as a whole.

In effect, what is provided for, by this statute, is a fresh consideration of the "esthetics" of each building, as it is proposed. This procedure is similar to that employed by The City of New York, for the erection of light-industry projects in residential areas. The Board of Review, in disapproving any application, may specify modifications in design of the building or buildings that will be adequate to render them acceptable under the provisions of the law. Other procedural devices which operate to the benefit of the applicant are:

(1) the Building Inspector must refer an applicant to the Board of Review within three days;

(2) the Board of Review must disapprove an application within eighteen days, or else must issue a permit; and

(3) any party aggrieved has a right of appeal to the Board of Zoning Appeals.

The legislation leaves to the Board of Review a great deal of discretion. The indicia of similarity are flexible, and the Board of Review is granted the authority to vary (to a degree) other legislation in this same field. Section 7 of the law reads, in part:

> With the purpose of encouraging the most appropriate use of land throughout the Village, the Board of Review may vary the minimum floor area requirements set forth in Zoning Ordinance No. 29 of the Village, as amended, so as to reduce said

requirements by not more than ten percent, if, by reason of greater lot frontages or areas or side yard widths or less percentage of lot coverage by building area than are specified by said zoning ordinance or by reason of the provision of public or common open space as a part of the development or exceptionally skillful lot arrangement and site design, the result of said variation will be in harmony with the character of the neighborhood.

For the lawyer, the Garden City zoning law presents some very interesting questions as to its enforceability, legality, and constitutionality. For the architect, it raises a further interesting question as to how effective it will prove to be in the application of "esthetic" considerations to community planning.

III

May a community prohibit the erection of new homes having modern architectural design where the predominant architectural style of existing homes is traditional? This question was presented to a New Jersey court and answered in the negative (*Hankins* v. *Borough of Rockleigh,* 55 N.J. Super. 132, 150 A. 2d 63). However, the court ruled that architectural standards can be validly regulated by the municipality if the general welfare is directly and clearly involved.

The development of "esthetic zoning" has been slow and its validity often questioned. The Hankins case is illustrative of both the difficulties involved in establishment of "esthetic zoning" and the increasing acceptance of the concept.

Rockleigh, New Jersey, is a community with a population of approximately 150 people. There were 37 residences in the community, 80 per cent of which were over 50 years of age. The architectural style of these homes was "Dutch Colonial," "Early American," "Victorian," and "Farmhouse American." The plaintiffs were owners of a tract of land in the community and filed plans for the construction of a home. Subsequent to the filing of such plans, an ordinance was adopted by the municipality providing as follows:

> The architectural design of all new houses and other buildings in the Borough of Rockleigh, or old houses or buildings that may be renovated or reconstructed, shall be subject to the approval of the Planning Board and of the Mayor and Council of the Borough of Rockleigh. Such design may be Early Ameri-

> can, or of other architectural style conforming with the existing residential architecture and with the rural surroundings in the Borough, and acceptable to the Planning Board and to the Mayor and the Council of the Borough of Rockleigh.

This ordinance was amended in 1948 to prohibit flat roofs.

The plans filed by the plaintiffs called for a two-story home with extensive use of glass and with a flat roof. The location of the home was at least 4,000 feet from the nearest neighboring home. These plans were rejected by the Mayor and Borough Council on the grounds they were violative of the zoning ordinances.

The plaintiffs contended that the ordinances under which the Mayor and Council acted were unconstitutional and were not based upon reasonable standards and specifications. The municipality, on the other hand, contended that the ordinances were a valid exercise of the police power relating to the general welfare of the community. In this connection, the town asserted that a zoning ordinance whose purpose is to conserve the value of property is reasonable and not arbitrary. In describing the purpose of the ordinances, the court stated:

> It thus becomes very obvious that the ordinances in question are adopted for esthetic reasons and are an attempt to control the architectural style of homes in the community, despite the fact there have been more modern touches in the new buildings recently erected and a lack of strict application as to others in the community. The desire of the officials is an attempt to preserve in the community types of homes similar to their own and their neighbors'.

The court pointed out that under the earlier law of New Jersey, no ordinance which attempted to regulate esthetics in construction was considered valid. The court, however, emphasized that "esthetic zoning" has been more sympathetically treated in later years "but with the qualification that it has been approved on grounds other than esthetics alone." The court gave as an example of this change in approach, the so-called "look alike" ordinances. These ordinances, the court said, "have primarily dealt with minor changes in the façades of the buildings and have not required any great expense on the part of the builder *nor have they gone as far as our case where complete architectural standards come into question.*"

The court, in its opinion, however, recognized that regulation limited merely to the question of uniformity and avoiding the over-all issue of architectural standards is considered, in many quarters, as superficial. In this respect a nationally known architect was quoted as follows:

> No-look-alike legislation fails to achieve proper results and is only superficial. The design of a residential neighborhood requires a much more positive attack going beyond the façade of a building; variety in building does play a part, but unless governed by significant underlying principles, little or nothing is achieved. . . . A competent board of people can do better than regulate uniformity if armed with legislation that goes to the heart of the matter, which is esthetics.

The court concluded that the regulation of construction in the establishment of architectural standards is valid and legal provided there is a definite relationship to the general welfare. It further concluded, however, that such relationship did not exist in respect to the ordinance before it. The court stated:

> While I am firmly of the opinion that the regulation of building by the setting up of architectural standards is valid and legal, yet under the present status of the law, we cannot say that it may be the regulation of esthetics alone but must be liberally construed on the basis of the general welfare and bear a relationship to the general welfare in some definite way. I have given a great deal of consideration to the ordinances in question and the testimony before me. I cannot support the contention of the municipality under the facts of the instant case. . . . There is no showing before me that earlier ordinance bears relation to the general welfare of the community . . . the only testimony before the Court was that the governing body wanted to keep the town as it was. This is not a proper relation to the general welfare nor do their past actions support their position.

As stated by United States Supreme Court (*Berman v. Parker*), "the concept of the public welfare is broad and inclusive. The values it represents are spiritual as well as physical, esthetic as well as monetary." The case discussed illustrates the dangers inherent in attempted regulation and on the plus side, the motivation, confused as it is, toward "esthetic zoning."

MISCELLANEOUS DECISIONS

ENFORCEMENT OF ZONING LAW

NEW YORK. *City of Yonkers v. Rentways,* 304 N.Y. 499, 109 N.E. 2d 597 (1952). A garage located in a commercial zone had rear doors which opened on to a lot owned by the garage keeper in a residential zone. Although contrary to the municipal zoning law, the rear entrance was used for many years as a means of ingress and egress to the garage. Later, a permit was issued authorizing the addition of a second story to the garage. The New York Court of Appeals held that the municipality was not estopped, either by the issuance of the building permit or by laches, from enforcing the zoning law many years later. Nor was the garage owner entitled to assert a vested right in his use of the residentially located lot when such use, although continuing for many years, did not commence before the effective date of the applicable zoning ordinance.

TEXAS. *Davis v. City of Abilene,* 250 S.W. 2d 685 (1952). The city building inspector had knowledge at the time of granting the permit that the precise location and intended use of the building to be erected was in violation of the zoning ordinance then in effect, and the city failed to appeal from the granting of the permit within the time allotted. Nevertheless, it was held that the lot owners were charged with notice of the provisions of the ordinance, and therefore could not rely on the action of the city's employee to raise an estoppel, nor could they assert vested rights even though the construction of the building was eighty percent complete.

INDEX OF CASES

UNITED STATES

GENERAL INDEX

APPENDIX: *Contract and Miscellaneous Forms*

CONTRACT FORMS ARE USEFUL TOOLS and serve an imporant function in the building industry. They establish recognized and accepted patterns of obligation and performance on the part of all parties to the form documents, and thereby tend to avoid tedious negotiation and disagreements between the contracting parties at the time the formal agreement is prepared.

The standard contract documents of the American Institute of Architects have great prestige in the construction industry and enjoy wide use. It must be emphasized, however, that these documents—or *any* forms—should not be used without consideration of the necessity for their adaption and modification in order to cover adequately the particular and special conditions of each project. Forms serve a significant and helpful function unless used by rote and without thought.

Collected in this section are the latest editions of the contract documents and legal forms of the American Institute of Architects which relate to the Owner-Architect agreement and the Construction Contract. These include tne Owner-Architect agreements which provide for varying methods of compensation, Owner-Contractor agreement based upon stipulated sum, Owner-Contract agreement based upon cost-plus fee, short form for small construction contracts, General Conditions of the construction contract, bid bond, performance bond and labor and material payment bond, and agreement between Contractor and Sub-contractor. Also included is a form agreement between Architect and Engineer prepared by the author and editor. In order to condense the forms, the authors have taken the liberty in some instances of reducing the amount of blank space or blank lines on the pages.

A.I.A. DOCUMENT NO. B-121

(Formerly Form B102) 1958 Edition

THE STANDARD FORM OF AGREEMENT BETWEEN OWNER AND ARCHITECT

Issued by The American Institute of Architects for use when a percentage of the cost of the work forms the basis of payment, and engineers' fees are included in the architect's compensation.

THIS AGREEMENT made as of the ....

day of .... in the year Nineteen Hundred and ....

by and between ....

.... hereinafter called the Owner, and

....

.... hereinafter called the Architect,

WITNESSETH, that whereas the Owner intends to erect ....

....

....

.... hereinafter called the Project.

NOW, THEREFORE, the Owner and the Architect for the considerations hereinafter named, agree as follows:

A The Architect agrees to perform, for the above-named Project, professional services as hereinafter set forth.

B The Owner agrees to pay the Architect for such services a fee of .... per cent of the construction cost of the Project, with other payments and reimbursements as hereinafter provided, the said percentage being hereinafter called the Basic Rate. ....

....

....

....

A.I.A. DOCUMENT NO. B-121

(Formerly Form B102) 1958 Edition

C The parties hereto further agree to the following conditions:

1 THE ARCHITECT'S SERVICES

The Architect's professional services consist of the necessary conferences, the preparation of preliminary studies, working drawings, specifications, large scale and full size detail drawings, for architectural, structural, plumbing, heating, electrical, and other mechanical work; assistance in the drafting of forms of proposals and contracts; the issuance of Certificates for Payment; the keeping of accounts and the general administration of the construction contracts.

2 REIMBURSEMENTS

The Owner is to reimburse the Architect the costs of transportation and living incurred by him and his assistants while traveling in discharge of duties connected with the Project, the cost of all reproductions of drawings, the cost of any special consultants other than for normal plumbing, heating, electrical, and other mechanical work, and other disbursements on his account approved by the Owner.

3 SEPARATE CONTRACTS

The Basic Rate applies to work let under a single contract. For any portions of the Project let under separate contracts, on account of extra service thereby required, the rate shall be four per cent greater, and if substantially all the Project is so let the higher rate shall apply to the entire Project; but there shall be no such increase on the plumbing, heating, electrical and other mechanical work or on any contracts in connection with which the Owner reimburses special consultants' fees to the Architect, or for articles not designed by the Architect but purchased under his direction.

4 EXTRA SERVICES AND SPECIAL CASES

If the Architect is caused extra drafting or other expense due to changes ordered by the Owner, or due to the delinquency or insolvency of the Owner or Contractor, or as a result of damage by fire, he shall be equitably paid for such extra expense and the service involved.

Work let on any cost-plus basis shall be the subject of a special charge in accord with the special service required.

If any work designed or specified by the Architect is abandoned or suspended, in whole or in part, the Architect is to be paid for the service rendered on account of it.

5 PAYMENTS

Payments to the Architect on account of his fee shall be made as follows, subject to the provisions of Article 4:

Upon completion of the preliminary studies, a sum equal to 25% of the basic rate computed upon a reasonable estimated cost.

During the period of preparation of specifications and general working drawings, monthly payments aggregating at the completion thereof, a sum sufficient to increase payments to 75% of the rate or rates of commission arising from this Agreement, computed upon a reasonable cost estimated on such completed specifications and drawings, or if bids have been received, then computed upon the lowest bona fide bid or bids.

From time to time during the execution of work and in proportion to the amount of service rendered by the Architect, payments shall be made until the aggregate of all payments made on account of the Architect's compensation under this Article, but not including any covered by the provisions of Article 4, shall be a sum equal to the rate or rates of commission arising from this Agreement, computed upon the final cost of the Project.

Payments to the Architect, other than those on his compensation, fall due from time to time as his work is done or as costs are incurred.

No deductions shall be made from the Architect's compensation on account of penalty, liquidated damages, or other sums withheld from payments to contractors.

6 INFORMATION FURNISHED BY OWNER

The Owner shall, so far as the work under this Agreement may require, furnish the Architect with the following information: A complete and accurate survey of the building site, giving the grades and lines of streets, pavements, and adjoining properties; the rights, restrictions, easements, boundaries, and contours of the building site, and full information as to sewer, water, gas and electrical service. The Owner is to pay for borings or test pits and for chemical, mechanical, or other tests when required.

The Owner shall provide all legal advice and services required for the operation.

7 GENERAL ADMINISTRATION

The Architect will endeavor by general administration of the construction contracts to guard the Owner against defects and deficiencies in the work of contractors, but he does not guarantee the performance of their contracts. The general administration of the Architect is to be distinguished from the continuous on-site inspection of a Project Inspector.

When authorized by the Owner, a Project Inspector acceptable to both Owner and Architect shall be engaged by the Architect at a salary satisfactory to the Owner and paid by the Owner, upon presentation of the Architect's monthly statements.

8 PRELIMINARY ESTIMATES

When requested to do so the Architect will furnish preliminary estimates on the cost of the Project, but he does not guarantee such estimates.

9 CONSTRUCTION COST OF THE PROJECT

The construction cost of the Project, as herein referred to, means the cost to the Owner, but such cost shall not include any Architect's or special consultants' fees or reimbursements or the cost of a Project Inspector.

When labor or material is furnished by the Owner below its market cost, the cost of the work shall be computed upon such market cost.

10 OWNERSHIP OF DOCUMENTS

Drawings and specifications as instruments of service are the property of the Architect whether the work for which they are made be executed or not, and are not to be used on other work except by agreement with the Architect.

A.I.A. DOCUMENT NO. B-121

(Formerly Form B102) 1958 Edition

11 SUCCESSORS AND ASSIGNMENTS

The Owner and the Architect, each binds himself, his partners, successors, legal representatives, and assigns to the other party to this Agreement, and to the partners, successors, legal representatives and assigns of such other party in respect to all covenants of this Agreement.

Except as above, neither the Owner nor the Architect shall assign, sublet or transfer his interest in this Agreement without written consent of the other.

12 ARBITRATION

Arbitration of all questions in dispute under this Agreement shall be at the choice of either party and shall be in accordance with the provisions, then obtaining, of the Standard Form of Arbitration Procedure of The American Institute of Architects. This Agreement shall be specifically enforceable under the prevailing arbitration law and judgment upon the award rendered may be entered in the court of the forum, state or federal, having jurisdiction. The decision of the arbitrators shall be a condition precedent to the right of any legal action.

IN WITNESS WHEREOF the parties hereto have made and executed this Agreement, the day and year first above written.

Owner	Architect ....
....	....
....	....
....	....

A.I.A. DOCUMENT NO. B-101

(Formerly Form A-102) 1958 Edition

THE STANDARD FORM OF AGREEMENT BETWEEN OWNER AND ARCHITECT

Issued by The American Institute of Architects for use when a percentage of the cost of the work forms the basis of payment, and engineers' fees are reimbursed to architect by owner.

THIS AGREEMENT made as of the ....

day of .... in the year Nineteen Hundred and ....

by and between ....

.... hereinafter called the Owner, and

....

.... hereinafter called the Architect,

WITNESSETH, that whereas the Owner intends to erect ....

....

....

.... hereinafter called the Project.

NOW, THEREFORE, the Owner and the Architect, for the considerations hereinafter named, agree as follows:

A The Architect agrees to perform, for the above-named Project, professional services as hereinafter set forth.

B The Owner agrees to pay the Architect for such services a fee of .... per cent of the construction cost of the Project, with other payments and reimbursements as hereinafter provided, the said percentage being hereinafter called the Basic Rate. ....

....

....

....

A.I.A. DOCUMENT NO. B-101

(Formerly Form A-102) 1958 Edition

The parties hereto further agree to the following conditions:

1 THE ARCHITECT'S SERVICES

The Architect's professional services consist of the necessary conferences, the preparation of preliminary studies, working drawings, specifications, large scale and full size detail drawings, for architectural, structural, plumbing, heating, electrical, and other mechanical work; assistance in the drafting of forms of proposals and contracts; the issuance of Certificates for Payment; the keeping of accounts, and the general administration of the construction contracts.

2 REIMBURSEMENTS

The Owner is to reimburse the Architect the costs of transportation and living incurred by him and his assistants while traveling in discharge of duties connected with the Project, the cost of all reproductions of drawings, the cost of the services of engineers for normal plumbing, heating, electrical, and other mechanical work and of special consultants, and other disbursements on his account approved by the Owner.

3 SEPARATE CONTRACTS

The Basic Rate applies to work let under a single contract. For any portions of the Project let under separate contracts, on account of extra service thereby required, the rate shall be four per cent greater, and if substantially all the Project is so let the higher rate shall apply to the entire Project; but there shall be no such increase on the plumbing, heating, electrical and other mechanical work or on any contracts in connection with which the Owner reimburses special consultants' fees to the Architect, or for articles not designed by the Architect but purchased under his direction.

4 EXTRA SERVICES AND SPECIAL CASES

If the Architect is caused extra drafting or other expense due to changes ordered by the Owner, or due to the delinquency or insolvency of the Owner or Contractor, or as a result of damage by fire, he shall be equitably paid for such extra expense and the service involved.

Work let on any cost-plus basis shall be the subject of a special charge in accord with the special service required.

If any work designed or specified by the Architect is abandoned or suspended, in whole or in part, the Architect is to be paid for the service rendered on account of it.

5 PAYMENTS

Payments to the Architect on account of his fee shall be made as follows, subject to the provisions of Article 4:

Upon completion of the preliminary studies, a sum equal to 25% of the basic rate computed upon a reasonable estimated cost.

During the period of preparation of specifications and general working drawings, monthly payments aggregating at the completion thereof, a sum sufficient to increase payments to 75% of the rate or rates of commission arising from this Agreement, computed upon a reasonable cost estimated on such completed specifications and drawings, or if bids have been received, then computed upon the lowest bona fide bid or bids.

From time to time during the execution of work and in proportion to the amount of service rendered by the Architect, payments shall be made until the aggregate of all payments made on account of the Architect's compensation under this Article, but not including any covered by the provisions of Article 4, shall be a sum equal to the rate or rates of commission arising from this agreement, computed upon the final cost of the Project.

Payments to the Architect, other than those on his compensation, fall due from time to time as his work is done or as costs are incurred.

No deductions shall be made from the Architects' compensation on account of penalty, liquidated damages, or other sums withheld from payments to contractors.

6 INFORMATION FURNISHED BY OWNER

The Owner shall, so far as the work under this Agreement may require, furnish the Architect with the following information: A complete and accurate survey of the building site, giving the grades and lines of streets, pavements, and adjoining properties; the rights, restrictions, easements, boundaries, and contours of the building site, and full information as to sewer, water, gas and electrical service. The Owner is to pay for borings or test pits and for chemical, mechanical, or other tests when required.

The Owner shall provide all legal advice and services required for the operation.

7 GENERAL ADMINISTRATION

The Architect will endeavor by general administration of the construction contracts to guard the Owner against defects and deficiencies in the work of contractors, but he does not guarantee the performance of their contracts. The general administration of the Architect is to be distinguished from the continuous on-site inspection of a Project Inspector.

When authorized by the Owner, a Project Inspector acceptable to both Owner and Architect shall be engaged by the Architect at a salary satisfactory to the Owner and paid by the Owner, upon presentation of the Architect's monthly statements.

8 PRELIMINARY ESTIMATES

When requested to do so the Architect will furnish preliminary estimates on the cost of the Project, but he does not guarantee such estimates.

9 CONSTRUCTION COST OF THE PROJECT

The construction cost of the Project, as herein referred to, means the cost to the Owner, but such cost shall not include any Architect's or Engineers' or special consultants' fees or reimbursements or the cost of a Project Inspector.

When labor or material is furnished by the Owner below its market cost, the cost of the work shall be computed upon such market cost.

10 OWNERSHIP OF DOCUMENTS

Drawings and specifications as instruments of service are the property of the Architect whether the work for which they are made be executed or not, and are not to be used on other work except by agreement with the Architect.

A.I.A. DOCUMENT NO. B-101

(Formerly Form A-102) 1958 Edition

11 SUCCESSORS AND ASSIGNMENTS

The Owner and the Architect, each binds himself, his partners, successors, legal representatives, and assigns to the other party to this Agreement, and to the partners, successors, legal representatives and assigns of such other party in respect to all covenants of this Agreement.

Except as above, neither the Owner nor the Architect shall assign, sublet or transfer his interest in this Agreement without written consent of the other.

12 ARBITRATION

Arbitration of all questions in dispute under this Agreement shall be at the choice of either party and shall be in accordance with the provisions, then obtaining, of the Standard Form of Arbitration Procedure of The American Institute of Architects. This Agreement shall be specifically enforceable under the prevailing arbitration law and judgment upon the award rendered may be entered in the court of the forum, state or federal, having jurisdiction. The decision of the arbitrators shall be a condition precedent to the right of any legal action.

IN WITNESS WHEREOF the parties hereto have made and executed this Agreement the day and year first above written.

Owner .... Architect ....

....

....

....

....

A.I.A. DOCUMENT NO. B-131

(1958 Edition)

A STANDARD FORM OF AGREEMENT BETWEEN OWNER AND ARCHITECT

On a Percentage Basis Including Engineering Services

THIS AGREEMENT made as of the ....

day of .... in the year Nineteen Hundred and ....

by and between ....

....

.... hereinafter called the Owner, and

....

.... hereinafter called the Architect,

WITNESSETH, that whereas the Owner intends to..

....

....

.... hereinafter called the Project.

NOW, THEREFORE, the Owner and the Architect for the considerations hereinafter set forth agree as follows:

A The Architect agrees to perform professional services for the above Project as hereinafter set forth.

B The Owner agrees to pay the Architect as compensation for his services:

1) For his basic services .... (%) of the project construction cost, hereinafter referred to as the Basic Rate, the work to be let under a single lump sum contract. For work let on a cost-plus-fee basis, increase the Basic Rate to .... per cent (%).

A.I.A. DOCUMENT NO. B-131
(1958 Edition)

For work let under separate contracts, increase the Basic Rate to .... per cent (%).

2) For extra services defined in Article II hereinafter, the Owner agrees to pay the Architect ....

.... ( ) times the Direct Personnel Expense as defined in Article V hereinafter including principals' time at .... ($) per hour.

3) Reimbursable expense as defined hereinafter in Article V to the amount expended.

C The parties hereto further agree to the following conditions:

I BASIC SERVICES OF THE ARCHITECT

1 *Schematic Design Phase*

a) The Architect shall consult with the Owner to ascertain the requirements of the Project and shall confirm such requirements to the Owner.

b) He shall prepare schematic design studies leading to a recommended solution together with a general description of the Project for approval by the Owner.

c) He shall submit to the Owner a statement of the probable project construction cost based on current area, volume or other unit costs.

2 *Design Development Phase*

a) The Architect shall prepare from the approved schematic design studies, the design development documents consisting of plans, elevations and other drawings, and outline specifications, to fix and illustrate the size and character of the entire Project in its essentials as to kinds of materials, type of structure, mechanical, and electrical systems and such other work as may be required.

b) He shall submit to the Owner a further statement of the probable project construction cost and, if authorized, obtain a semi-detailed estimate of such cost.

3 *Construction Documents Phase*

a) The Architect shall prepare from the approved design development documents, working drawings and specifications setting forth in detail and prescribing the work to be done, and the materials, workmanship, finishes, and equipment required for the architectural, structural, mechanical, electrical, service-connected equipment, and site work, and the necessary bidding information, General Conditions of the Contract, and Supplementary General Conditions of the Contract, and shall assist in the drafting of proposal and contract forms.

b. He shall keep the Owner informed of any adjustments to previous statements of the probable project construction cost indicated by changes in scope, requirements or market conditions.

4 *Construction Phase*

a) The Architect shall assist the Owner in obtaining proposals from contractors, and in awarding and preparing construction contracts.

b) He shall keep the Owner informed of the progress of construction; check and approve schedules and shop drawings for compliance with design; maintain construction accounts; prepare change orders; examine contractors' Applications for Payment; issue Certificates for Payment in amounts approved by him; provide general administration of the construction contracts, including periodic inspections at the site; determine date of substantial completion; make final inspection of the Project; assemble written guarantees required of the contractors; and issue the final Certificate for Payment.

c) He shall endeavor to guard the Owner against defects and deficiencies in the work of contractors, but he does not guarantee contractors' performance under their contracts.

d) If recommended by the Architect and approved by

A.I.A. DOCUMENT NO. B-131

(1958 Edition)

the Owner, a full-time Project Inspector will be selected, employed, and directed by the Architect.

II EXTRA SERVICES OF THE ARCHITECT

The following services, if performed due to unusual circumstances, cause the Architect extra expense, and shall be paid for by the Owner as a Multiple of Direct Personnel Expense:

1 Making planning surveys and special analyses of the Owner's needs to clairfy requirements of the Project when requested by the Owner.

2 Making measured drawings of existing construction when required for planning additions or alterations thereto.

3 Revising previously approved drawings or specifications to accomplish changes ordered by the Owner.

4 Preparing documents for alternate bids and change orders requested by the Owner.

5 Supervising the replacement of any work damaged by fire or other cause during construction.

6 Arranging for the work to proceed should the contractor default due to delinquency or insolvency.

7 Providing prolonged contract administration and inspection of construction should the construction contract time be exceeded by more than 25% due to no fault of the Architect.

8 Preparing as-built drawings showing construction changes in the work and final locations of mechanical service lines and outlets, if requested by the Owner.

9 Making an inspection of the Project prior to expiration of the guarantee period and reporting observed discrepancies under guarantees provided by the construction contracts, if requested by the Owner.

III THE OWNER'S RESPONSIBILITIES

1 The Owner shall provide full information as to his requirements for the Project.

2 He shall designate, when necessary, representatives authorized to act in his behalf. He shall examine documents submitted by the Architect and render decisions pertaining thereto promptly, to avoid unreasonable delay in the progress of the Architect's work. He shall observe the procedure of issuing orders to contractors only through the Architect.

3 He shall furnish or direct the Architect to obtain at the Owner's expense, a certified survey of the site, giving, as required, grades and lines of streets, alleys, pavements, and adjoining property; rights of way, restrictions, easements, encroachments, zoning, deed restrictions, boundaries, and contours of the building site; locations, dimensions, and complete data pertaining to existing buildings, other improvements and trees; full information as to available service and utility lines both public and private; and test borings and pits necessary for determining subsoil conditions.

4 He shall pay for structural, chemical, mechanical, soil mechanics or other tests and reports if required.

5 He shall arrange and pay for such legal and auditing services as may be required for the Project.

IV PROJECT CONSTRUCTION COST

1 Project construction cost as herein referred to means the total cost of all work designed or specified by the Architect, but does not include any payments made to the Architect or consultants.

2 Project construction cost shall be based upon one of the following sources with precedence in the order listed:
a) Lowest acceptable bona fide Contractor's proposal received for any or all portions of the Project.
b) Estimate of project construction cost as defined in paragraph 4 below.
c) The Architect's latest statement of probable project construction cost based on current area, volume or other unit costs.

3 When labor or material is furnished by the Owner, the project construction cost shall include such labor and material at current market cost.

4 If a fixed limit of project construction cost is stated herein, or if otherwise authorized by the Owner, estimates of the project construction cost prepared in semi-detailed or detailed form by an experienced estimator will be secured by the Architect during the Design Development or Construction Documents Phase.

5 If the estimated project construction cost or the lowest bona fide proposal is in excess of any limit stated herein, the Owner shall give written approval of an increase in the limit, or he shall cooperate in revising the project scope or quality, or both, to reduce the cost as required.

5 Since the Architect has no control over the cost of labor and materials, or competitive bidding, he does not guarantee the accuracy of any statements of probable construction cost.

V THE ARCHITECT'S EXPENSE

1 Direct Personnel Expense includes that of principals and employees engaged on the Project including architects, engineers, designers, job captains, draftsmen, specification writers, typists and inspectors, in consultation, research, designing, producing drawings, specifications and other documents pertaining to the Project, and inspecting construction of the Project. Employees' time shall be at their regular rates of pay.

2 Reimbursable Expense includes actual expenditures made by the Architect in the interest of the Project for the following incidental expenses.
a) Expense of transportation and living of principals and employees when traveling in connection with the Project; long distance calls and telegrams; reproduction of drawings and specifications, excluding copies for Architect's office use and duplicate sets at each phase for the Owner's review and approval; and fees paid for securing approval of authorities having jurisdiction over the Project.
b) If authorized in advance by the Owner, the expense of Project Inspector, overtime work requiring higher than regular rates, semi-detailed and detailed estimates of project construction cost, perspectives or models for the Owner's use.
c) If their employment is authorized in advance by the Owner, fees of special consultants, for other than the normal structural, mechanical and electrical engineering services.

VI PAYMENTS TO THE ARCHITECT

1 Payments on account of the Architect's basic services shall be as follows:
a) A primary payment of 5 per cent of the compensation for basic services, payable upon the execution of the Agreement, is the minimum payment under the Agreement.
b) Subsequent payments shall be made monthly in pro-

A.I.A. DOCUMENT NO. B-131

(1958 Edition)

portion to services performed to increase the compensation for basic services to the following percentages at the completion of each phase of the work:

1 Schematic Design Phase.................. 15%
2 Design Development Phase.............. 35%
3 Construction Documents Phase........... 75%
4 Receipt of Bids 80%
5 Construction Phase......................100%

2 Payments for extra services of the Architect as defined in Article II above, and for Reimbursable Expense as defined in Article V, paragraph 2, shall be made monthly upon presentation of Architect's detailed invoice.

3 No deduction shall be made from the Architect's compensation on account of penalty, liquidated damages, or other sums withheld from payments to contractors.

4 If any work designed or specified by the Architect during any phase of service is abandoned or suspended in whole or in part, the Architect is to be paid for the service performed on account of it prior to receipt of written notice from the Owner of such abandonment or suspension, together with reimbursements then due and any terminal expense resulting from abandonment or suspension for more than three months.

VII ACCOUNTING RECORDS OF THE ARCHITECT

Records of the Architect's Direct Personnel, Consultant, and Reimbursable Expense pertaining to this Project and records of accounts between the Owner and contractor shall be kept on a generally recognized accounting basis and shall be available to the Owner or his authorized representative at mutually convenient times.

VIII TERMINATION OF AGREEMENT

This Agreement may be terminated by either party upon seven days' written notice should the other party fail substantially to perform in accordance with its terms through no fault of the other. In the event of termination, due to the fault of others than the Architect, the Architect shall be paid for services performed to termination date, including reimbursements then due, plus terminal expense.

IX OWNERSHIP OF DOCUMENTS

Drawings and specifications as instruments of service are the property of the Architect whether the Project for which they are made be executed or not. They are not to be used on other projects except by agreement in writing.

X ARBITRATION

Arbitration of all questions in dispute under this Agreement shall be at the choice of either party and shall be in accordance with the provisions, then obtaining, of the Standard Form of Arbitration Procedure of The American Institute of Architects. This Agreement shall be specifically enforceable under the prevailing arbitration law and judgment upon the award rendered may be entered in the court of the forum, state or federal, having jurisdiction. The decision of the arbitrators shall be a condition precedent to the right of any legal action.

XI SUCCESSORS AND ASSIGNS

The Owner and the Architect each binds himself, his partners, successors, assigns and legal representatives to the other party to this Agreement and to the partners, successors, assigns and legal representatives of such other party in respect of all covenants of this Agreement. Neither the Owner nor the Architect shall assign, sublet or transfer his interest in this Agreement without the written consent of the other.

IN WITNESS WHEREOF the parties hereto have made and executed this Agreement, the day and year first above written.

Owner .... Architect...

....

....

....

....

A.I.A. DOCUMENT NO. B-211
(1958 Edition)

A STANDARD FORM OF AGREEMENT BETWEEN OWNER AND ARCHITECT

On Basis of a Multiple of Direct Personnel Expense

THIS AGREEMENT made as of the ....

day of .... in the year Nineteen Hundred and ....

by and between ....

....

.... hereinafter called the Owner, and

....

.... hereinafter called the Architect,

WITNESSETH, that whereas the Owner intends to ....

....

....

.... hereinafter called the Project.

NOW, THEREFORE, the Owner and the Architect for the considerations hereinafter set forth agree as follows:

A The Architect agrees to perform professional services for the above Project as hereinafter set forth.

B The Owner agrees to pay the Architect as compensation for his services:

1) A sum equal to .... ( ) times the Direct Personnel Expense as defined hereinafter in Article IV, including principals' time at .... ($) per hour.

A.I.A. DOCUMENT NO. B-211
(1958 Edition)

2) A sum equal to .... ( ) times the expenses of consultants for structural, mechanical and electrical engineering, and other specialized work and equipment.

3) Reimbursable Expense as defined hereinafter in Article IV to the amount expended.

4) A primary payment of .... ($) payable upon the execution of the Agreement as defined in Article V.

C The parties hereto further agree to the following conditions:

I SERVICES OF THE ARCHITECT

1 *Schematic Design Phase*

a) The Architect shall consult with the Owner and, if required, prepare analyses and planning surveys to ascertain the requirements of the Project, and shall confirm such requirements to the Owner.
b) He shall make measured drawings of existing work or buildings as required for the development of drawings.
c) He shall prepare schematic design studies leading to a recommended solution together with a general description of the Project for approval by the Owner.
d) He shall submit to the Owner a statement of the probable project construction cost based on current area, volume or other unit costs.

2 *Design Development Phase*

a) The Architect shall prepare from the approved schematic design studies, the design development documents consisting of plans, elevations and other drawings, and outline specifications, to fix and illustrate the size and character of the entire Project in its essentials as to kinds of materials, type of structure, mechanical and electrical systems and such other work as may be required.
b) He shall submit to the Owner a further statement of the probable project construction cost and, if authorized by the Owner, obtain a semi-detailed estimate of such cost.

3 *Construction Documents Phase*

a) The Architect shall prepare from the approved design development documents, working drawings and specifications setting forth in detail and prescribing the work to be done, and the materials, workmanship, finishes and equipment required for the architectural, structural, mechanical, electrical, service-connected equipment and site work, and the necessary bidding information, General Conditions of the Contract and Supplementary General Conditions of the Contract, and shall assist in the drafting of proposal and contract forms.

b) He shall keep the Owner informed of any adjustments to previous statements of the probable project construction cost indicated by changes in scope, requirements, or market conditions.

4. *Construction Phase*

a) The Architect shall assist the Owner in obtaining proposals from contractors, and in awarding and preparing construction contracts.

b) He shall keep the Owner informed of the progress of construction; check and approve schedules and shop drawings for compliance with design; maintain construction accounts; prepare change orders; examine contractors' Applications for Payment; issue Certificates for Payment in amounts approved by him; provide general administration of the construction contracts including periodic inspections at the site; determine date of substantial completion; make final inspection of the Project; assemble written guarantees required of the contractors; and issue the final Certificate for Payment.

c) He shall endeavor to guard the Owner against defects

A.I.A. DOCUMENT NO. B-211

(1958 Edition)

and deficiencies in the work of contractors, but he does not guarantee contractors' performance under their contracts.

d) If recommended by the Architect and approved by the Owner, a full-time Project Inspector will be selected, employed, and directed by the Architect.

e) He shall supervise the replacement of any work damaged by fire or other cause during construction.

f) He shall arrange for the work to proceed should the contractor default due to delinquency or insolvency.

g) He shall prepare as-built drawings showing construction changes in the work and final locations of mechanical service lines and outlets, if requested by the Owner.

h) He shall make an inspection of the Project prior to expiration of the guarantee period and report observed discrepancies under guarantees provided by the construction contracts, if requested by the Owner.

II THE OWNER'S RESPONSIBILITIES

1 The Owner shall provide full information as to his requirements for the Project.

2 He shall designate, when necessary, representatives authorized to act in his behalf. He shall examine documents submitted by the Architect and render decisions pertaining thereto promptly, to avoid unreasonable delay in the progress of the Architect's work. He shall observe the procedure of issuing orders to contractors only through the Architect.

3 He shall furnish, or direct the Architect to obtain at the Owner's expense, a certified survey of the site, giving, as required, grades and lines of streets, alleys, pavements, and adjoining property; rights of way, restrictions, easements, encroachments, zoning, deed restrictions, boundaries, and contours of the building site; locations, dimensions, and complete data pertaining to existing buildings, other improvements and trees; full information as to available service and utility lines, both public and private; and test borings and pits necessary for determining subsoil conditions.

4 He shall pay for structural, chemical, mechanical, soil mechanics or other tests and reports if required.

5 He shall arrange and pay for such legal and auditing services as may be required for the Project.

III PROJECT CONSTRUCTION COST

1 Project construction cost as herein referred to means the total cost of all work designed or specified by the Architect, but does not include any payments made to the Architect or consultants.

2 When labor or material is furnished by the Owner, the project construction cost shall include such labor and material at current market cost.

3 If a fixed limit of project construction cost is stated herein, or if otherwise authorized by the Owner, estimates of the project construction cost prepared in semi-detailed or detailed form by an experienced estimator will be secured by the Architect during the Design Development or Construction Documents Phase.

4 If the estimated project construction cost or the lowest bona fide proposal is in excess of any limit stated herein, the Owner shall give written approval of an increase in the limit, or he shall cooperate in revising the project scope or quality, or both, to reduce the cost as required.

5 Since the Architect has no control over the cost of labor and materials, or competitive bidding, he does not guarantee the accuracy of any statements of probable construction cost.

IV THE ARCHITECT'S EXPENSE

1 Direct Personnel Expense includes that of principals and employees engaged on the Project including architects, engineers, designers, job captains, draftsmen, specification writers, typists and inspectors, in consultation, research, designing, producing drawings, specifications and other documents pertaining to the Project, and inspecting construction of the Project. Employees' time shall be at their regular rates of pay.

2 Expense of consultants shall include expenses and fees for structural, mechanical and electrical engineering and for other specialized work and equipment.

3 Reimbursable Expense includes actual expenditures made by the Architect in the interest of the Project for the following incidental expenses:

a) Expense of transportation and living of principals and employees when traveling in connection with the Project; long distance calls and telegrams; reproduction of drawings and specifications, excluding duplicate sets at each phase for the Owner's review and approval; and fees paid for securing approval of authorities having jurisdiction over the Project.

b) If authorized in advance by the Owner, overtime work requiring higher than regular rates, semi-detailed or detailed estimates of project construction cost, perspectives or models and other incidental expenditures.

V PAYMENTS TO THE ARCHITECT

1 The primary payment provided for above in B, 4 payable upon the execution of the Agreement, is the minimum payment under the Agreement, and shall be credited to the Owner's account at the time of final accounting.

2 Payments for Direct Personnel Expense, Consultants and Reimbursable Expense shall be made monthly upon presentation of Architect's detailed invoice.

3 No deduction shall be made from the Architect's compensation on account of penalty, liquidated damages, or other sums withheld from payments to contractors.

4 If the Project is abandoned or suspended for more than three months, the Architect is to be paid for the services performed on account of it prior to receipt of written notice from the Owner of such abandonment or suspension, together with any terminal expense.

VI ACCOUNTING RECORDS OF THE ARCHITECT

Records of the Architect's Direct Personnel, Consultant, and Reimbursable Expense pertaining to this Project and records of accounts between the Owner and contractor shall be kept on a generally recognized accounting basis and shall be available to the Owner or his authorized representative at mutually convenient times.

VII TERMINATION OF AGREEMENT

This Agreement may be terminated by either party upon seven days' written notice should the other party fail substantially to perform in accordance with its terms through

A.I.A. DOCUMENT NO. B-211

(1958 Edition)

no fault of the other. In the event of termination due to the fault of others than the Architect, the Architect shall be paid for services performed to termination date, including reimbursements then due, plus terminal expense.

VIII OWNERSHIP OF DOCUMENTS

Drawings and specifications as instruments of service are the property of the Architect whether the Project for which they are made be executed or not. They are not to be used on other projects except by agreement in writing.

IX ARBITRATION

Arbitration of all questions in dispute under this Agreement shall be at the choice of either party and shall be in accordance with the provisions, then obtaining, of the Standard Form of Arbitration Procedure of The American Institute of Architects. This Agreement shall be specifically enforceable under the prevailing arbitration law and judgment upon the award rendered may be entered in the court of the forum, state or federal, having jurisdiction. The decision of the arbitrators shall be a condition precedent to the right of any legal action.

X SUCCESSORS AND ASSIGNS

The Owner and the Architect each binds himself, his partners, successors, assigns and legal representatives to the other party to this Agreement and to the partners, successors, assigns and legal representatives of such other party in respect of all covenants of this Agreement. Neither the Owner nor the Architect shall assign, sublet or transfer his interest in this Agreement without the written consent of the other.

IN WITNESS WHEREOF the parties hereto have made and executed this Agreement, the day and year first above written.

Owner .... Architect ....

....

....

....

....

A.I.A. DOCUMENT NO. B-311

(1958 Edition)

A STANDARD FORM OF AGREEMENT BETWEEN OWNER AND ARCHITECT

On Basis of a Professional Fee Plus Expense

THIS AGREEMENT made as of the ....

day of .... in the year Nineteen Hundred and ....

by and between ....

.... hereinafter called the Owner, and

....

.... hereinafter called the Architect,

WITNESSETH, that whereas the Owner intends to ....

....

....

.... hereinafter called the Project.

NOW, THEREFORE, the Owner and the Architect for the considerations hereinafter set forth agree as follows:

A The Architect agrees to perform professional services for the above Project as hereinafter set forth.

B The Owner agrees to pay the Architect as compensation for his services:

1) A Professional Fee ....

....

If the scope of the Project is changed materially, the Professional Fee shall be changed in the same proportion.

A.I.A. DOCUMENT NO. B-311

(1958 Edition)

2) A sum equal to .... ( ) times the Direct Personnel Expense

as defined hereinafter in Article IV, including principal's time at .... ($) per hour.

3) A sum equal to .... ( ) times the expenses of consultants for structural, mechanical and electrical engineering, and other specialized work and equipment.

4) Reimbursable Expense as defined hereinafter in Article IV to the amount expended.

C The parties hereto further agree to the following conditions:

I SERVICES OF THE ARCHITECT

1 *Schematic Design Phase*

a) The Architect shall consult with the Owner and, if required, prepare analyses and planning surveys to ascertain the requirements of the Project, and shall confirm such requirements to the Owner.
b) He shall make measured drawings of existing work or buildings as required for the development of drawings.
c) He shall prepare schematic design studies leading to a recommended solution together with a general description of the Project for approval by the Owner.
d. He shall submit to the Owner a statement of the probable project construction cost based on current area, volume or other unit costs.

2 *Design Development Phase*

a) The Architect shall prepare from the approved schematic design studies, the design development documents consisting of plans, elevations and other drawings, and outline specifications, to fix and illustrate the size and character of the entire Project in its essentials as to kinds of materials, type of structure, mechanical and electrical systems and such other work as may be required.
b) He shall submit to the Owner a further statement of the probable project construction cost and, if authorized by the Owner, obtain a semi-detailed estimate of such cost.

3 *Construction Documents Phase*

a) The Architect shall prepare from the approved design development documents, working drawings and specifications setting forth in detail and prescribing the work to be done, and the materials, workmanship, finishes and equipment required for the architectural, structural, mechanical, electrical, service-connected equipment and site work, and the necessary bidding information, General Conditions of the Contract and Supplementary General Conditions of the Contract, and shall assist in the drafting of proposal and contract forms.
b) He shall keep the Owner informed of any adjustments to previous statements of the probable project construction cost indicated by changes in scope, requirements, or market conditions.

4. *Construction Phase*

a) The Architect shall assist the Owner in obtaining proposals from contractors, and in awarding and preparing construction contracts.
b) He shall keep the Owner informed of the progress of construction; check and approve schedules and shop drawings for compliance with design; maintain construction accounts; prepare change orders; examine contractors' Applications for Payment; issue Certificates for Payment in amounts approved by him; provide general administration of the construction contracts including periodic inspections at the site; determine date of substantial completion; make final inspection of the Project; assemble written guarantees required of the contractors; and issue the final Certificate for Payment.
c) He shall endeavor to guard the Owner against defects and deficiencies in the work of contractors, but he does not guarantee contractors' performance under their contracts.

A.I.A. DOCUMENT NO. B-311

(1958 Edition)

d) If recommended by the Architect and approved by the Owner, a full-time Project Inspector will be selected, employed, and directed by the Architect.

e) He shall supervise the replacement of any work damaged by fire or other cause during construction.

f) He shall arrange for the work to proceed should the contractor default due to delinquency or insolvency.

g) He shall prepare as-built drawings showing construction changes in the work and final locations of mechanical service lines and outlets, if requested by the Owner.

h) He shall make an inspection of the Project prior to expiration of the guarantee period and report observed discrepancies under guarantees provided by the construction contracts, if requested by the Owner.

II THE OWNER'S RESPONSIBILITIES

1 The Owner shall provide full information as to his requirements for the Project.

2 He shall designate, when necessary, representatives authorized to act in his behalf. He shall examine documents submitted by the Architect and render decisions pertaining thereto promptly, to avoid unreasonable delay in the progress of the Architect's work. He shall observe the procedure of issuing orders to contractors only through the Architect.

3 He shall furnish, or direct the Architect to obtain at the Owner's expense, a certified survey of the site, giving, as required, grades and lines of streets, alleys, pavements, and adjoining property; rights of way, restrictions, easements, encroachments, zoning, deed restrictions, boundaries, and contours of the building site; locations, dimensions, and complete data pertaining to existing buildings, other improvements and trees; full information as to available service and utility lines, both public and private; and test borings and pits necessary for determining subsoil conditions.

4 He shall pay for structural, chemical, mechanical, soil mechanics or other tests and reports if required.

5 He shall arrange and pay for such legal and auditing services as may be required for the Project.

III PROJECT CONSTRUCTION COST

1 Project construction cost as herein referred to means the total cost of all work designed or specified by the Architect, but does not include any payments made to the Architect or consultants.

2 Project construction cost shall be based upon one of the following sources with precedence in the order listed:
a) Lowest acceptable bona fide Contractor's proposal received for any or all portions of the Project.
b) Estimate of project construction cost as defined in paragraph 4 below.
c) The Architect's latest statement of probable project construction cost based on current area, volume or other unit costs.

3 When labor or material is furnished by the Owner, the project construction cost shall include such labor and material at current market cost.

4 If a fixed limit of project construction cost is stated herein, or if otherwise authorized by the Owner, estimates of the project construction cost prepared in semi-detailed or detailed form by an experienced estimator will be secured by the Architect during the Design Development and Construction Documents Phase.

5) If the estimated project construction cost or the lowest bona fide proposal is in excess of any limit stated herein, the Owner shall give written approval of an increase in the limit, or he shall cooperate in revising the project scope or quality, or both, to reduce the cost as required.

6 Since the Architect has no control over the cost of labor and materials, or competitive bidding, he does not gurantee the accuracy of any statements of probable construction cost.

IV THE ARCHITECT'S EXPENSE

1 Direct Personnel Expense includes that of principals and employees engaged on the Project including architects, engineers, designers, job captains, draftsmen, specification writers, typists and inspectors, in consultation, research, designing, producing drawings, specifications and other documents pertaining to the Project, and inspecting construction of the Project. Employees' time shall be at their regular rates of pay.

2 Expense of consultants shall include expenses and fees for structural, mechanical and electrical engineering and for other specialized work and equipment.

3 Reimbursable Expense includes actual expenditures made by the Architect in the interest of the Project for the following incidental expenses:

a) Expense of transportation and living of principals and employees when traveling in connection with the Project; long distance calls and telegrams; reproduction of drawings and specifications, excluding duplicate sets at each phase for the Owner's review and approval; and fees paid for securing approval of authorities having jurisdiction over the Project.

b) If authorized in advance by the Owner, overtime work requiring higher than regular rates, semi-detailed or detailed estimates of project construction cost, perspectives or models and other incidental expenditures.

V PAYMENTS TO THE ARCHITECT

1 Payments on account of the Architect's Professional Fee shall be as follows:

a) A primary payment of 10 per cent of the Professional Fee, payable upon the execution of the Agreement, is the minimum payment under this Agreement.

b) Subsequent payments of the Professional Fee shall be made monthly in proportion to services performed to increase the total payments on account of the Professional Fee to the following percentages at the completion of each phase:

1 Schematic Design Phase 15%
2 Design Development Phase 35%
3 Construction Documents Phase 75%
4 Receipt of Bids 80%
5 Construction Phase 100%

2 Payments for Direct Personnel Expense, Consultants and Reimbursable Expense shall be made monthly upon presentation of Architect's detailed invoice.

3 No deduction shall be made from the Architect's compensation on account of penalty, liquidated damages, or other sums withheld from payments to contractors.

4 If any work designed or specified by the Architect during any phase of service is abandoned or suspended in whole or in part, the Architect is to be paid for the service performed on account of it prior to receipt of written notice from the Owner of such abandonment or suspension, together with reimbursements then due and any terminal expense resulting from abandonment or suspension for more than three months.

A.I.A. DOCUMENT NO. B-311

(1958 Edition)

VI ACCOUNTING RECORDS OF THE ARCHITECT

Records of the Architect's Direct Personnel, Consultant, and Reimbursable Expense pertaining to this Project and records of accounts between the Owner and contractor shall be kept on a generally recognized accounting basis and shall be available to the Owner or his authorized representative at mutually convenient times.

VII TERMINATION OF AGREEMENT

This Agreement may be terminated by either party upon seven days' written notice should the other party fail substantially to perform in accordance with its terms through no fault of the other. In the event of termination due to the fault of others than the Architect, the Architect shall be paid for services performed to termination date, including reimbursements then due, plus terminal expense.

VIII OWNERSHIP OF DOCUMENTS

Drawings and specifications as instruments of service are the property of the Architect whether the Project for which they are made be executed or not. They are not to be used on other projects except by agreement in writing.

IX ARBITRATION

Arbitration of all questions in dispute under this Agreement shall be at the choice of either party and shall be in accordance with the provisions, then obtaining, of the Standard Form of Arbitration Procedure of The American Institute of Architects. This Agreement shall be specifically enforceable under the prevailing arbitration law and judgment upon the award rendered may be entered in the court of the forum, state or federal, having jurisdiction. The decision of the arbitrators shall be a condition precedent to the right of any legal action.

X SUCCESSORS AND ASSIGNS

The Owner and the Architect each binds himself, his partners, successors, assigns and legal representatives to the other party to this Agreement and to the partners, successors, assigns and legal representatives of such other party in respect of all covenants of this Agreement. Neither the Owner nor the Architect shall assign, sublet or transfer his interest in this Agreement without the written consent of the other.

IN WITNESS WHEREOF the parties hereto have made and executed this Agreement, the day and year first above written.

Owner .... Architect ....

A.I.A. DOCUMENT NO. B-321

(Formerly Form 103) 1958 Edition

A FORM OF AGREEMENT BETWEEN OWNER AND ARCHITECT

Issued by The American Institute of Architects for use with the Fee-Plus-Expense System

THIS AGREEMENT made as of the ....

day of .... in the year Nineteen Hundred and ....

by and between ....

.... hereinafter called the Owner, and

....

.... hereinafter called the Architect,

WITNESSETH, that whereas the Owner intends to erect ....

....

....

...., hereinafter called the Project,

NOW, THEREFORE, the Owner and the Architect, for the considerations hereinafter named, agree as follows:

A The Architect agrees to perform for the above-named Project, professional services as hereinafter set forth.

B The Owner agrees to pay the Architect the sum of .... dollars

($.........................) as his fee, of which .... dollars ($.........................)

is to be payed in .... equal installments monthly beginning ...., the balance to be paid on issuance of final certificate; and to reimburse the Architect monthly all costs incurred by him in the performance of his duties hereunder as hereinafter more fully set forth.

A.I.A. DOCUMENT NO. B-321

(Formerly Form 103) 1958 Edition

The parties hereto further agree to the following conditions:

1 THE ARCHITECT'S SERVICES

The Architect's professional services consist of the necessary conferences, the preparation of preliminary studies, working drawings, specifications, large scale and full size detail drawings, for architectural, structural, plumbing, heating, electrical, and other mechanical work; assistance in the drafting of forms of proposals and contracts; the issuance of Certificates for Payment; the keeping of accounts, and the general administration of the construction contracts.

2 THE ARCHITECT'S FEE

The fee payable by the Owner to the Architect for his personal professional services shall be named elsewhere in this Agreement.

In case of the abandonment or suspension of the Project or of any part or parts thereof, the Architect is to be paid in proportion to the services rendered on account of it up to the time of its abandonment or suspension, such proportion being 25% upon completion of preliminary sketches and 75% upon completion of working drawings and specifications.

If the scope of the Project or the manner of its execution is materially changed subsequent to the signing of the Agreement, the fee shall be adjusted to fit the new conditions.

If additional personal service of the Architect is made necessary by the delinquency or insolvency of either the Owner or the Contractor, or as a result of damage by fire, he shall be equitably paid by the Owner for such extra service.

3 THE ARCHITECT'S EXPENSE

The Architect shall maintain an efficient and accurate cost-keeping system as to all costs incurred by him, in connection with the subject of this Agreement, and his accounts, at all reasonable times, shall be open to the inspection of the Owner or his authorized representatives.

The costs referred to in this Article comprise the following items:

a) The sums paid for drafting, including verification of shop drawings, for specification writing and for general administration of the construction contract.

b) The sums paid to structural, mechanical, electrical, sanitary or other engineers.

c) The sums paid for incidental expenses such as costs of transportation or living incurred by the Architect or his assistants while traveling in discharge of duties connected with the Project, costs of reproducing drawings, printing or mimeographing the specifications, models, telegrams, long distance telephone calls, legal advise, expressage, etc.

d) A proportion of the indirect expenses of the Architect's office, commonly called "Overhead," representing items that cannot be apportioned in detail to this work, such as rent, light, heat, stenographer's services, postage, drafting materials, telephone, accounting, business administration, etc.

It is agreed that the charge for such general expenses shall be .... per cent of item (a) of this Article.

4 PAYMENTS

On or about the first day of each month, the Architect shall present to the Owner a detailed statement of the payment due on account of the fee and the costs referred to in Article 3, and the Owner shall pay the Architect the amount thereof.

5 INFORMATION FURNISHED BY OWNER

The Owner shall, so far as the work under this Agreement may require, furnish the Architect with the following information: A complete and accurate survey of the building site, giving the grades and lines of streets, pavements, and adjoining properties; the rights, restrictions, easements, boundaries, and contours of the building site, and full information as to sewer, water, gas and electrical service. The Owner is to pay for borings or test pits and for chemical, mechanical, or other tests when required.

The Owner shall provide all legal advice and services required for the operation.

6 GENERAL ADMINISTRATION

The Architect will endeavor by general administration of the construction contracts to guard the Owner against defects and deficiencies, but he does not guarantee the performance of their contracts. The general administration of the Architect is to be distinguished from the continuous on-site inspection of a Project Inspector.

When authorized by the Owner, a Project Inspector acceptable to both Owner and Architect shall be engaged by the Architect at a salary satisfactory to the Owner and paid by the Owner, upon presentation of the Architect's monthly statements.

7 PRELIMINARY ESTIMATES

When requested to do so the Architect will furnish preliminary estimates on the cost of the Project, but he does not guarantee such estimates.

8 OWNERSHIP OF DOCUMENTS

Drawings and specifications as instruments of service are the property of the Architect whether the work for which they are made be executed or not, and are not to be used on other work except by agreement with the Architect.

9 SUCCESSORS AND ASSIGNMENTS

The Owner and the Architect, each binds himself, his partners, successors, legal representatives, and assigns to the other party to this Agreement, and to the partners, successors, legal representatives, and assigns of such other party in respect to all covenants of this Agreement.

A.I.A. DOCUMENT NO. B-321

(Formerly Form 103) 1958 Edition

Except as above, neither the Owner nor the Architect shall assign, sublet or transfer his interest in this Agreement without the written consent of the other.

10 ARBITRATION

Arbitration of all questions in dispute under this Agreement shall be at the choice of either party and shall be in accordance with the provisions, then obtaining, of the Standard Form of Arbitration Procedure of The American Institute of Architects. This Agreement shall be specifically enforceable under the prevailing arbitration law and judgment upon the award rendered may be entered in the court of the forum, state or federal, having jurisdiction. The decision of the arbitrators shall be a condition precedent to the right of any legal action.

IN WITNESS WHEREOF the parties hereto have made and executed this Agreement, the day and year first above written.

Owner ....

....

....

....

Architect ....

....

....

....

A.I.A. DOCUMENT NO. A-101
(Formerly Form A1) 1958 Edition

THE STANDARD FORM OF AGREEMENT BETWEEN CONTRACTOR AND OWNER FOR CONSTRUCTION OF BUILDINGS

Issued by The American Institute of Architects
for use when a Stipulated Sum Forms the Basis of Payment

Approved by THE ASSOCIATED GENERAL CONTRACTORS OF AMERICA; THE CONTRACTING PLASTERERS' AND LATHERS' INTERNATIONAL ASSOCIATION; COUNCIL OF MECHANICAL SPECIALTY CONTRACTING INDUSTRIES, INC.; THE NATIONAL BUILDING GRANITE QUARRIES ASSOCIATION, INC.; THE NATIONAL ELECTRICAL CONTRACTORS ASSOCIATION; THE PAINTING AND DECORATING CONTRACTORS OF AMERICA, AND THE PRODUCERS' COUNCIL, INC.*

This form is to be used only with the standard general conditions of the contract for construction of buildings.

THIS AGREEMENT made the ....

day of .... in the year Nineteen Hundred and ....

by and between ....

.... hereinafter called the Contractor, and ....

.... hereinafter called the Owner,

WITNESSETH, that the Contractor and the Owner for the considerations hereinafter named agree as follows:

ARTICLE 1. SCOPE OF THE WORK

The Contractor shall furnish all of the materials and perform all of the work shown on the Drawings and described in the Specifications entitled ....

....

(Here insert the caption descriptive of the work as used on the Drawings and in the other Contract Documents)

prepared by ....
acting as and in these Contract Documents entitled the Architect; and shall do everything required by this Agreement, the General Conditions of the Contract, the Specifications and the Drawings.

* Formal approval, which has been given previous editions, has not yet been received from all of these organizations.

A.I.A. DOCUMENT NO. A-101

(Formerly Form A1) 1958 Edition

ARTICLE 2. TIME OF COMPLETION

The work to be performed under this Contract shall be commenced ....

and shall be substantially completed ....

(Here insert stipulation as to liquidated damages, if any.)

ARTICLE 3. THE CONTRACT SUM

The Owner shall pay the Contractor for the performance of the Contract, subject to additions and deductions provided therein, in current funds as follows: ....

(State here the lump sum amount, unit prices, or both, as desired in individual cases.)

....

Where the quantities originally contemplated are so changed that application of the agreed unit price to the quantity of work performed is shown to create a hardship to the Owner or the Contractor, there shall be an equitable adjustment of the Contract to prevent such hardship.

AGREEMENT BETWEEN CONTRACTOR AND OWNER.

Sixth Edition / Five pages / Page 2.

A.I.A. DOCUMENT NO. A-101

(Formerly Form A1) 1958 Edition

ARTICLE 4. PROGRESS PAYMENTS

The Owner shall make payments on account of the Contract as provided therein, as follows:

On or about the .... day of each month .... per cent of the value, based on the Contract prices of labor and materials incorporated in the work and of materials suitably stored at the site thereof up to the .... day of that month, as estimated by the Architect, less the aggregate of previous payments; and upon substantial completion of the entire work, a sum sufficient to increase the total payments to .... per cent of the Contract price ....

(Insert here any provision made for limiting or reducing the amount retained after the work reaches a certain stage of completion.)

ARTICLE 5. ACCEPTANCE AND FINAL PAYMENT

Final payment shall be due .... days after substantial completion of the work provided the work be then fully completed and the contract fully performed.

Upon receipt of written notice that the work is ready for final inspection and acceptance, the Architect shall promptly make such inspection, and when he finds the work acceptable under the Contract and the Contract fully performed he shall promptly issue a final certificate, over his own signature, stating that the work provided for in this Contract has been completed and is accepted by him under the terms and conditions thereof, and that the entire balance found to be due the Contractor, and noted in said final certificate, is due and payable.

Before issuance of final certificate the Contractor shall submit evidence satisfactory to the Architect that all payrolls, material bills, and other indebtedness connected with the work have been paid.

If after the work has been substantially completed, full completion thereof is materially delayed through no fault of the Contractor, and the Architect so certifies, the Owner shall, upon certificate of the Architect, and without terminating the Contract, make payment of the balance due for that portion of the work fully completed and accepted. Such payment shall be made under the terms and conditions governing final payment, except that it shall not constitute a waiver of claims.

A.I.A. DOCUMENT NO. A-101

(Formerly Form A1) 1958 Edition

ARTICLE 6. THE CONTRACT DOCUMENTS

The General Conditions of the Contract, the Specifications and the Drawings, together with this Agreement, form the Contract, and they are as fully a part of the Contract as if hereto attached or herein repeated. The following is an enumeration of the Specifications and Drawings:

AGREEMENT BETWEEN CONTRACTOR AND OWNER.

Sixth Edition / Five pages / Page 4.

A.I.A. DOCUMENT NO. A-101

(Formerly Form A1) 1958 Edition

IN WITNESS WHEREOF the parties hereto have executed this Agreement, the day and year first above written.

A.I.A. DOCUMENT NO. A-111

(Formerly Form 105) 1958 Edition

A FORM OF AGREEMENT BETWEEN CONTRACTOR AND OWNER

Issued by The American Institute of Architects for use when the cost of the work plus a fee forms the basis of payment

This form is to be used only with The Institute's standard general conditions of the Contract, 1958 edition, and it should not be used without careful study of its accompanying "Circular of Information."

THIS AGREEMENT made the ....

day of .... in the year nineteen hundred and ....

by and between ....

.... hereinafter called the Contractor, and

.... hereinafter called the Owner,

WITNESSETH, that whereas the Owner intends to erect ....

....

....

NOW, THEREFORE, the Contractor and the Owner, for the considerations hereinafter named, agree as follows:

ARTICLE 1. THE WORK TO BE DONE AND THE DOCUMENTS FORMING THE CONTRACT.
The Contractor agrees to provide all the labor and materials and to do all things necessary for the proper

construction and completion of the work shown and described on Drawings bearing the title ....

....

and numbered ....

and in Specifications bearing the same title, the pages of which are numbered ....

....

A.I.A. DOCUMENT NO. A-111
(Formerly Form 105) 1958 Edition

The said Drawings and Specifications and the General Conditions of the Contract consisting of Articles numbered one to ....
together with this Agreement, constitute the Contract; the Drawings, Specifications and General Conditions being as fully a part thereof and hereof as if hereto attached or herein repeated. If anything in the said General Conditions is inconsistent with this Agreement, the Agreement shall govern.

The said documents have been prepared by ....
....
therein and hereinafter called the Architect.

ARTICLE 2. CHANGES IN THE WORK.

The Owner, through the Architect, may from time to time, by written instructions or drawings issued to the Contractor, make changes in the above-named Drawings and Specifications, issue additional instructions, require additional work or direct the omission of work previously ordered, and the provisions of this contract shall apply to all such changes, modifications and additions with the same effect as if they were embodied in the original Drawings and Specifications. Since the cost of all such changes is to merge in the final cost of the work, Articles 15 and 16 of the General Conditions of the Contract are annulled, unless elsewhere especially made applicable.

ARTICLE 3. THE CONTRACTOR'S DUTIES AND STATUS.

The Contractor recognizes the relations of trust and confidence established between him and the Owner by this Agreement. He covenants with the Owner to furnish his best skill and judgment and to cooperate with the Architect in forwarding the interests of the Owner. He agrees to furnish efficient business administration and superintendence and to use every effort to keep upon the work at all times an adequate supply of workmen and materials, and to secure its execution in the best and soundest way and in the most expeditious and economical manner consistent with the interests of the Owner.

ARTICLE 4. FEE FOR SERVICES.

In consideration of the performance of the contract, the Owner agrees to pay the Contractor, in current funds as compensation for his services hereunder .... ($........................)

which shall be paid as follows: ....
....

ARTICLE 5. COSTS TO BE REIMBURSED

The Owner agrees to reimburse the Contractor in current funds all costs necessarily incurred for the proper execution of the work and paid directly by the Contractor, such costs to include the following items, and to be at rates not higher than the standard paid in the locality of the work except with prior consent of the Owner;

(*a*) All labor directly on the Contractor's pay roll, including social security and old age benefit taxes and other taxes related thereto.

(*b*) Salaries of Contractor's Employees stationed at the field office, in whatever capacity employed. Employees engaged, at shops or on the road, in expediting the production or transportation of material, shall be considered as stationed at the field office and their salaries paid for such part of their time as is employed on this work.

(*c*) The proportion of transportation, traveling and hotel expenses of the Contractor or of his officers or employees incurred in discharge of duties connected with this work.

Agreement between Contractor and Owner
Cost Plus Fee Basis / Five pages / Page 2

A.I.A. DOCUMENT NO. A-111

(Formerly Form 105) 1958 Edition

(*d*) All expenses incurred for transportation to and from the work of the force required for its prosecution.

(*e*) Permit fees, royalties, damages for infringement of patents, and costs of defending suits therefor and for deposits lost for causes other than the Contractor's negligence.

(*f*) Losses and expenses, not compensated by insurance or otherwise, sustained by the Contractor in connection with the work, provided they have resulted from causes other than the fault or neglect of the Contractor. Such losses shall include settlements made with the written consent and approval of the Owner. No such losses and expenses shall be included in the cost of the work for the purpose of determining the Contractor's fee, but if, after a loss from fire, flood or similar cause not due to the fault or neglect of the Contractor, he be put in charge of reconstruction, he shall be paid for his services a fee proportionate to that named in Article 4 hereof.

(*g*) Minor expenses, such as telegrams, telephone service, expressage, and similar petty cash items.

(*h*) Cost of hand tools, not owned by the workmen, canvas and tarpaulins, consumed in the prosecution of the work, and depreciation on such tools, canvas and tarpaulins used but not consumed and which shall remain the property of the Contractor.

(*i*) Materials, supplies, equipment and transportation required for the proper execution of the work, which shall include all temporary structures and their maintenance, including sales and other taxes related thereto.

(*j*) The amounts of all sub-contracts.

(*k*) Premiums on all bonds and insurance policies called for under the Contract.

(*l*) Rentals of all construction plant or parts thereof, whether rented from the Contractor or others, in accordance with rental agreements approved by the Architect. Transportation of said construction plant, costs of loading and unloading, cost of installation, dismantling and removal thereof and minor repairs and replacements during its use on the work—all in accordance with the terms of the said rental agreements.

ARTICLE 6. COSTS NOT TO BE REIMBURSED.

Reimbursement of expenses to the Contractor shall not include any of the following:

(*a*) Salary of the Contractor, if an individual, or salary of any member of the Contractor, if a firm, or salary of any officer of the Contractor, if a corporation.

(*b*) Salary of any person employed, during the execution of the work, in the main office or in any regularly established branch office of the Contractor.

(*c*) Overhead or general expenses of any kind, except as these may be expressly included in Article 5.

(*d*) Interest on capital employed either in plant or in expenditures on the work, except as may be expressly included in Article 5.

....

....

....

ARTICLE 7. DISCOUNTS, REBATES, REFUNDS.

All cash discounts shall accrue to the Contractor unless the Owner deposits funds with the Contractor with which to make payments, in which case the cash discounts shall accrue to the Owner. All trade discounts, rebates and refunds, and all returns from sale of surplus materials and equipment shall accrue to the Owner, and the Contractor shall make provisions so that they can be secured.

ARTICLE 8. CONTRACTOR'S FINANCIAL RESPONSIBILITY.

Any cost due to the negligence of the Contractor or anyone directly employed by him, either for the making good of defective work, disposal of material wrongly supplied, making good of damage to property, or excess costs for material or labor, or otherwise, shall be borne by the Contractor, and the Owner may withhold money due the Contractor to cover any such cost already paid by him as part of the cost of the work.

This article supersedes the provisions of Articles 13, 19 and 20 of the General Conditions of the Contract so far as they are inconsistent herewith.

ARTICLE 9. SUB-CONTRACTS.

All portions of the work that the Contractor's organization has not been accustomed to perform or that the Owner may direct, shall be executed under sub-contracts unless otherwise directed by the Owner. The Contractor shall ask for bids from sub-contractors approved by the Architect and shall deliver such bids to him, or the Architect shall procure such bids himself, and in either case the Architect shall determine, with the advice of the Contractor and subject to the approval of the Owner, the award and amount of the accepted bid. Such work shall be contracted for with such approved bidders in accordance with the terms of this agreement and the General Conditions of the Contract which conditions shall, for the purposes of such contracts, stand as printed or written and not be subject to the modifications set forth herein.

The Contractor, being fully responsible for the general management of the building operation, shall have full directing authority over the execution of the sub-contracts.

If the Owner lets any portions of the work under separate contracts the separate Contractors shall not only cooperate with each other and with the Contractor as provided in Article 35 of the General Conditions of the Contract, but they shall conform to all directions of the Contractor in regard to the progress of the work.

ARTICLE 10. TITLE TO THE WORK

The title of all work completed and in course of construction and of all materials on account of which any payment has been made, shall be in the Owner.

ARTICLE 11. ACCOUNTING, INSPECTION, AUDIT.

The Contractor shall check all materials and labor entering into the work and shall keep such full and detailed accounts as may be necessary to proper financial management under this Agreement and the system shall be such as is satisfactory to the Architect or to an auditor appointed by the Owner. The Architect, the auditor and their timekeepers and clerks shall be afforded access to the work and to all the Contractor's books, records, correspondence, instructions, drawings, receipts, vouchers, memoranda, etc., relating to this contract, and the Contractor shall preserve all such records for a period of two years after the final payment hereunder.

ARTICLE 12. APPLICATIONS FOR PAYMENT.

The Contractor shall, between the first and seventh of each month, deliver to the Architect a statement, sworn to if required, showing in detail and as completely as possible all moneys paid out by him on account of the cost of the work during the previous month for which he is to be reimbursed under Article 5 hereof, with original pay rolls for labor, checked and approved by a person satisfactory to the Architect, and all receipted bills.

The provisions of this Article supersede those of Article 24 of the General Conditions of the Contract.

ARTICLE 13. CERTIFICATES OF PAYMENT.

The Architect shall check the Contractor's statements of moneys due, called for in Article 12, and shall promptly issue certificates to the Owner for all such as he approves, which certificates shall be payable on issuance.

The provisions of this Article supersede the first paragraph of Article 25 of the General Conditions of the Contract.

A.I.A. DOCUMENT NO. A-111

(Formerly Form 105) 1958 Edition

ARTICLE 14. DISBURSEMENTS.

Should the Contractor neglect or refuse to pay, within five days after it falls due, any bill legitimately incurred by him hereunder (and for which he is to be reimbursed under Article 5) the Owner, after giving the Contractor twenty-four hours' written notice of his intention so to do, shall have the right to pay such bill directly, in which event such payment shall not, for the purpose either of reimbursement or of calculating the Contractor's fee, be included in the cost of the work.

ARTICLE 15. TERMINATION OF CONTRACT.

(The provisions of this Article supersede all of Article 22 of the General Conditions of the Contract except the first sentence.)

If the Owner should terminate the contract under the first sentence of Article 22 of the General Conditions of the Contract, he shall reimburse the Contractor for the balance of all payments made by him under Article 5, plus a fee computed upon the cost of the work to date at the rate of percentage named in Article 4 hereof, or if the Contractor's fee be stated as a fixed sum, the Owner shall pay the Contractor such an amount as will increase the payments on account of his fee to a sum which bears the same ratio to the said fixed sum as the cost of the work at the time of termination bears to a reasonable estimated cost of the work completed, and the Owner shall also pay to the Contractor fair compensation, either by purchase or rental, at the election of the Owner, for any equipment retained. In case of such termination of the contract the Owner shall further assume and become liable for all obligations, commitments and unliquidated claims that the Contractor may have theretofore, in good faith, undertaken or incurred in connection with said work and the Contractor shall, as a condition of receiving the payments mentioned in this Article, execute and deliver all such papers and take all such steps, including the legal assignment of his contractual rights, as the Owner may require for the purpose of fully vesting in him the rights and benefits of the Contractor under such obligations or commitments.

The Contractor and the Owner for themselves, their successors, executors, administrators and assigns hereby agree to the full performance of the covenants herein contained.

IN WITNESS WHEREOF they have executed this agreement the day and year first above written.

....

....

Agreement between Contractor and Owner
Cost Plus Fee Basis / Five pages / Page 5

A.I.A. DOCUMENT NO. A-201
(Formerly Form A2) 1958 Edition
Revised Printing, 1959

THE AMERICAN INSTITUTE OF ARCHITECTS

THE GENERAL CONDITIONS OF THE CONTRACT FOR THE CONSTRUCTION OF BUILDINGS

The Standard Form of General Conditions, 1958 Edition, has received the approval of THE ASSOCIATED GENERAL CONTRACTORS OF AMERICA; THE CONTRACTING PLASTERERS' AND LATHERS' INTERNATIONAL ASSOCIATION; COUNCIL OF MECHANICAL SPECIALTY CONTRACTING INDUSTRIES, INC.; THE NATIONAL BUILDING GRANITE QUARRIES ASSOCIATION, INC.; THE NATIONAL ELECTRICAL CONTRACTORS ASSOCIATION; THE PAINTING AND DECORATING CONTRACTORS OF AMERICA; AND THE PRODUCERS' COUNCIL, INC.*

INDEX TO THE ARTICLES

* Formal approval, which has been given previous editions, has not yet been received from all of these organizations.

A.I.A. DOCUMENT NO. A-201

(Formerly Form A2) 1958 Edition

ARTICLE 1

DEFINITIONS

a) The Contract Documents consist of the Agreement, the General Conditions of the Contract, the Supplementary General Conditions, the Drawings and Specifications, including all modifications thereof incorporated in the documents before their execution. These form the Contract.

b) The Owner, the Contractor and the Architect are those mentioned as such in the Agreement. They are treated throughout the Contract Documents as if each were of the singular number and masculine gender.

c) The term Subcontractor, as employed herein, includes only those having a direct contract with the Contractor and it includes one who furnishes material worked to a special design according to the plans or specifications of this work, but does not include one who merely furnishes material not so worked.

d) Written notice shall be deemed to have been duly served if delivered in person to the individual or to a member of the firm or to an officer of the corporation for whom it is intended, or if delivered at or sent by registered mail to the last business address known to him who gives the notice.

e) The term "work" of the Contractor or Subcontractor includes labor or materials or both.

f) All time limits stated in the Contract Documents are of the essence of the Contract.

g) The law of the place of building shall govern the construction of this Contract.

ARTICLE 2

EXECUTION, CORRELATION AND INTENT OF DOCUMENTS

The Contract Documents shall be signed in duplicate by the Owner and the Contractor. In case either the Owner or Contractor or both fail to sign the General Conditions, Drawings or Specifications, the Architect shall identify them.

The Contract Documents are complementary, and what is called for by any one shall be as binding as if called for by all. The intention of the documents is to include all labor and materials, equipment and transportation necessary for the proper execution of the work. Materials or work described in words which so applied have a well-known technical or trade meaning shall be held to refer to such recognized standards.

It is not intended, that work not covered under any heading, section, branch, class or trade of the specifications, shall be supplied unless it is shown on drawings or is reasonably inferable therefrom as being necessary to produce the intended results.

ARTICLE 3

DETAIL DRAWINGS AND INSTRUCTIONS

The Architect shall furnish with reasonable promptness, additional instructions by means of drawings or otherwise, necessary for the proper execution of the work. All such drawings and instructions shall be consistent with the Contract Documents, true developments thereof, and reasonably inferable therefrom.

The work shall be executed in conformity therewith and the Contractor shall do no work without proper drawings and instructions.

Immediately after being awarded the contract the Contractor shall prepare a estimated Progress Schedule and submit same for Architect's approval. It shall indicate the dates for the starting and completion of the various stages of construction.

ARTICLE 4

COPIES FURNISHED

Unless otherwise provided in the Contract Documents the Contractor will be furnished, free of charge, all copies of drawings and specifications reasonably necessary for the execution of the work.

ARTICLE 5

SHOP DRAWINGS

The Contractor shall check and verify all field measurements and shall submit with such promptness as to cause no delay in his own work or in that of any other Contractor, three copies, checked and approved by him, of all shop or setting drawings and schedules required for the work of the various trades, and the Architect shall pass upon them with reasonable promptness, making desired corrections, including all necessary corrections relating to design and artistic effect. The Contractor shall make any corrections required by the Architect, file with him two corrected copies and furnish such other copies as may be needed. The Architect's approval of such drawings or schedules shall not relieve the Contractor from responsibility for deviations from drawings or specifications, unless he has in writing called the Architect's attention to such deviations at the time of submission, and secured his written approval, nor shall it relieve him from responsibility for errors in shop drawings or schedules.

ARTICLE 6

DRAWINGS AND SPECIFICATIONS ON THE WORK

The Contractor shall keep one copy of all drawings and specifications on the work, in good order, available to the Architect and to his representative.

ARTICLE 7

OWNERSHIP OF DRAWINGS

All drawings, specifications and copies thereof furnished by the Architect are his property. They are not to be used on other work, and, with the exception of the signed Contract set, are to be returned to him on request, at the completion of the work.

GENERAL CONDITIONS. 1958 EDITION.
Ten pages / Page 2

A.I.A. DOCUMENT NO. A-310

(1958 Edition)

ARTICLE 8

SAMPLES

The Contractor shall furnish for approval all samples as directed. The work shall be in accordance with approved samples.

ARTICLE 9

MATERIALS, APPLIANCES, EMPLOYEES

Unless otherwise stipulated, the Contractor shall provide and pay for all materials, labor, water, tools, equipment, light, power, transportation and other facilities necessary for the execution and completion of the work.

Unless otherwise specified all materials shall be new and both workmanship and materials shall be of good quality. The Contractor shall, if required, furnish satisfactory evidence as to the kind and quality of materials.

The Contractor shall at all times enforce strict discipline and good order among his employees, and shall not employ on the work any unfit person or anyone not skilled in the work assigned to him.

ARTICLE 10

ROYALTIES AND PATENTS

The Contractor shall pay all royalties and license fees. He shall defend all suits or claims for infringement of any patent rights and shall save the Owner harmless from loss on account thereof, except that the Owner shall be responsible for all such loss when a particular process or the product of a particular manufacturer or manufacturers is specified, but if the Contractor has information that the process or article specified is an infringement of a patent, he shall be responsible for such loss unless he promptly gives such information to the Architect or Owner.

ARTICLE 11

SURVEYS, PERMITS, LAWS AND REGULATIONS

The Owner shall furnish all surveys unless otherwise specified.

Permits and licenses necessary for the prosecution of the work shall be secured and paid for by the Contractor. Easements for permanent structures or permanent changes in existing facilities shall be secured and paid for by the Owner, unless otherwise specified.

The Contractor shall give all notices and comply with all laws, ordinances, rules and regulations bearing on the conduct of the work as drawn and specified. If the Contractor observes that the drawings and specifications are at variance therewith, he shall promptly notify the Architect in writing and any necessary changes shall be adjusted as provided in the Contract for changes in the work. If the Contractor performs any work knowing it to be contrary to such laws, ordinances, rules and regulations, and without such notice to the Architect, he shall bear all costs arising therefrom.

Wherever the law of the place of building requires a sales, consumer, use, or other similar tax, the Contractor shall pay such tax.

ARTICLE 12

PROTECTION OF WORK AND PROPERTY

The Contractor shall continuously maintain adequate protection of all his work from damage and shall protect the Owner's property from injury or loss arising in connection with this Contract. He shall make good any such damage, injury or loss, except such as may be directly due to errors in the Contract Documents or caused by agents or employees of the Owner, or due to causes beyond the Contractor's control and not to his fault or negligence. He shall adequately protect adjacent property as provided by law and the Contract Documents.

The Contractor shall take all necessary precautions for the safety of employees on the work, and shall comply with all applicable provisions of Federal, State, and Municipal safety laws and building codes to prevent accidents or injury to persons on, about or adjacent to the premises where the work is being performed. He shall erect and properly maintain at all times, as required by the conditions and progress of the work, all necessary safeguards for the protection of workmen and the public and shall post danger signs warning against the hazards created by such features of construction as protruding nails, hoists, well holes, elevator hatchways, scaffolding, window openings, stairways and falling materials; and he shall designate a responsible member of his organization on the work, whose duty shall be the prevention of accidents. The name and position of any person so designated shall be reported to the Architect by the Contractor.

In an emergency affecting the safety of life or of the work or of adjoining property, the Contractor, without special instruction or authorization from the Architect or Owner, is hereby permitted to act, at his discretion, to prevent such threatened loss or injury, and he shall so act, without appeal, if so authorized or instructed. Any compensation, claimed by the Contractor on account of emergency work, shall be determined by agreement or Arbitration.

ARTICLE 13

INSPECTION OF WORK

The Architect and his representatives shall at all times have access to the work wherever it is in preparation or progress and the Contractor shall provide proper facilities for such access and for inspection.

If the specifications, the Architect's instructions, laws, ordinances or any public authority require any work to be specially tested or approved, the Contractor shall give the Architect timely notice of its readiness for inspection, and if the inspection is by another authority than the Architect, of the date fixed for such inspection, required certificates of inspection being secured by the Contractor. Inspections by the Architect shall be promptly made, and where practicable at the source of supply. If any work should be covered up without approval or consent of the Architect, it must, if required by the Architect, be uncovered for examination at the Contractor's expense.

Re-examination of questioned work may be ordered by the Architect and if so ordered the work must be uncovered by the Contractor. If such work be found in accordance with the Contract Documents the Owner shall pay the cost of re-examination and replacement. If such work be found not in accordance with the Contract Documents the Contractor shall pay such cost, unless it be found that the defect in the work was caused by a Contractor employed as provided in Article 35, and in that event the Owner shall pay such cost.

ARTICLE 14

SUPERINTENDENCE: SUPERVISION

The Contractor shall keep on his work, during its progress, a competent superintendent and any necessary assistants, all satisfactory to the Architect. The superintendent shall not be changed except with the consent of the Architect, unless the superintendent proves to be unsatisfactory to the Contractor and ceases to be in his employ. The superintendent shall represent the Contractor in his absence and all directions given to him shall be as binding as if given to the Contractor. Important directions shall be confirmed in writing to the Contractor. Other directions shall be so confirmed on written request in each case.

The Contractor shall give efficient supervision to the work, using his best skill and attention. He shall carefully study and compare all drawings, specifications and other instructions and shall at once report to the Architect any error, inconsistency or omission which he may discover, but he shall not be liable to the Owner for any damage resulting from any errors or deficiencies in the contract documents or other instructions by the architect.

ARTICLE 15

CHANGES IN THE WORK

The Owner, without invalidating the Contract, may order extra work or make changes by altering, adding to or deducting from the work, the Contract Sum being adjusted accordingly. All such work shall be executed under the conditions of the original contract except that any claim for extension of time caused thereby shall be adjusted at the time of ordering such change.

In giving instructions, the Architect shall have authority to make minor changes in the work, not involving extra cost, and not inconsistent with the purposes of the building, but otherwise, except in an emergency endangering life or property, no extra work or change shall be made unless in pursuance of a written order from the Owner signed or countersigned by the Architect, or a written order from the Architect stating that the Owner has authorized the extra work or change, and no claim for an addition to the contract sum shall be valid unless so ordered.

The value of any such extra work or change shall be determined in one or more of the following ways:

a) By estimate and acceptance in a lump sum.

b) By unit prices named in the contract or subsequently agreed upon.

c) By cost and percentage or by cost and a fixed fee.

If none of the above methods is agreed upon, the Contractor, provided he receives an order as above, shall proceed with the work. In such case and also under case (c), he shall keep and present in such form as the Architect may direct, a correct account of the cost, together with vouchers. In any case, the Architect shall certify to the amount, including reasonable allowance for overhead and profit, due to the Contractor. Pending final determination of value, payments on account of changes shall be made on the Architect's certificate.

Should conditions encountered below the surface of the ground be at variance with the conditions indicated by the drawings and specifications the contract sum shall be equitably adjusted upon claim by either party made within a reasonable time after the first observance of the conditions.

ARTICLE 16

CLAIMS FOR EXTRA COST

If the Contractor claims that any instructions by drawings or otherwise involve extra cost under this contract, he shall give the Architect written notice thereof within a reasonable time after the receipt of such instructions, and in any event before proceeding to execute the work, except in emergency endangering life or property, and the procedure shall then be as provided for changes in the work. No such claim shall be valid unless so made.

ARTICLE 17

DEDUCTIONS FOR UNCORRECTED WORK

If the Architect and Owner deem it inexpedient to correct work injured or done not in accordance with the Contract, an equitable deduction from the contract price shall be made therefor.

ARTICLE 18

DELAYS AND EXTENSION OF TIME

If the Contractor be delayed at any time in the progress of the work by any act or neglect of the Owner or the Architect, or of any employee of either, or by any separate Contractor employed by the Owner, or by changes ordered in the work, or by strikes, lockouts, fire, unusual delay in transportation, unavoidable casualties or any causes beyond the Contractor's control, or by delay authorized by the Architect pending arbitration, or by any cause which the Architect shall decide to justify the delay, then the time of completion shall be extended for such reasonable time as the Architect may decide.

No such extension shall be made for delay occurring more than seven days before claim therefor is made in writing to the Architect. In the case of a continuing cause of delay, only one claim is necessary.

If no schedule or agreement stating the dates upon which drawings shall be furnished is made, then no claim for delay shall be allowed on account of failure to furnish drawings until two weeks after demand for such drawings and not then unless such claim be reasonable.

This article does not exclude the recovery of damages for delay by either party under other provisions in the contract documents.

ARTICLE 19

CORRECTION OF WORK BEFORE FINAL PAYMENT

The Contractor shall promptly remove from the premises all work condemned by the Architect as failing to conform to the Contract, whether incorporated or not, and the Contractor shall promptly replace and re-execute his own work in accordance with the Contract and without expense to the Owner and shall bear the expense of making good all work of other contractors destroyed or damaged by such removal or replacement.

If the Contractor does not remove such condemned work within a reasonable time, fixed by written notice, the Owner may remove it and may store the material at the expense of the Contractor. If the Contractor does not pay the expenses of such removal within ten days' time thereafter, the Owner may, upon ten days' written notice, sell such materials at auction or at private sale and shall account for the net proceeds thereof, after deducting all the costs and expenses that should have been borne by the Contractor.

ARTICLE 20

CORRECTION OF WORK AFTER FINAL PAYMENT

The Contractor shall remedy any defects due to faulty materials or workmanship and pay for any damage to other work resulting therefrom, which shall appear within a period of one year from the date of final payment, or from the date of the Owner's substantial usage or occupancy of the project, whichever is earlier, and in accordance with the terms of any special guarantees provided in the contract. Neither the foregoing nor any provision in the contract documents, nor any special guarantee time limit, shall be held to limit the Contractor's liability for defects, to less than the legal limit of liability in accordance with the law of the place of building. The Owner shall give notice of observed defects with reasonable promptness. All questions arising under this Article shall be decided by the Architect subject to arbitration, notwithstanding final payment.

ARTICLE 21

THE OWNER'S RIGHT TO DO WORK

If the Contractor should neglect to prosecute the work properly or fail to perform any provision of this contract, the Owner, after three days' written notice to the Contractor may, without prejudice to any other remedy he may have, make good such deficiencies and may deduct the cost thereof from the payment then or thereafter due the Contractor, provided, however, that the Architect shall approve both such action and the amount charged to the Contractor.

ARTICLE 22

OWNER'S RIGHT TO TERMINATE CONTRACT

If the Contractor should be adjudged a bankrupt, or if he should make a general assignment for the benefit of his creditors, or if a receiver should be appointed on account of his insolvency, or if he should persistently or repeatedly refuse or should fail, except in cases for which extension of time is provided, to supply enough properly skilled workmen or proper materials, or if he should fail to make prompt payment to subcontractors or for material or labor, or persistently disregard laws, ordinances or the instructions of the Architect, or otherwise be guilty of a substantial violation of any provision of the contract, then the Owner, upon the certificate of the Architect that sufficient cause exists to justify such action, may, without prejudice to any other right or remedy and after giving the Contractor, and his surety if any, seven days' written notice, terminate the employment of the Contractor and take possession of the premises and of all materials, tools and appliances thereon and finish the work by whatever method he may deem expedient. In such case the Contractor shall not be entitled to receive any further payment until the work is finished. If the unpaid balance of the contract price shall exceed the expense of finishing the work including compensation for additional architectural, managerial and administrative services, such excess shall be paid to the Contractor. If such expense shall exceed such unpaid balance, the Contractor shall pay the difference to the Owner. The expense incurred by the Owner as herein provided, and the damage incurred through the Contractor's default, shall be certified by the Architect.

ARTICLE 23

THE CONTRACTOR'S RIGHT TO STOP WORK OR TERMINATE CONTRACT

If the work should be stopped under an order of any court, or other public authority, for a period of thirty days, through no act or fault of the Contractor or of anyone employed by him, then the Contractor may, upon seven days' written notice to the Owner and the Architect, terminate this Contract and recover from the Owner payment for all work executed and any proven loss sustained upon any plant or materials and reasonable profit and damages.

Should the Architect fail to issue any certificate for payment, through no fault of the Contractor, within seven days after the Contractor's formal request for payment or if the Owner should fail to pay to the Contractor within seven days of its maturity and presenta-

A.I.A. DOCUMENT NO. A-201

(Formerly Form A2) 1958 Edition

tion, any sum certified by the Architect or awarded by arbitrators, then the Contractor may, upon seven days' written notice to the Owner and the Architect, stop the work or terminate this Contract as set out in the preceding paragraph.

ARTICLE 24

APPLICATIONS FOR PAYMENTS

At least ten days before each payment falls due, the Contractor shall submit to the Architect an itemized application for payment, supported to the extent required by the Architect by receipts or other vouchers, showing payments for materials and labor, payments to subcontractors and such other evidence of the Contractor's right to payment as the Architect may direct.

If payments are made on valuation of work done, the Contractor shall, before the first application, submit to the Architect a schedule of values of the various parts of the work, including quantities, aggregating the total sum of the contract, divided so as to facilitate payments to subcontractors in accordance with Article 37(e), made out in such form as the Architect and the Contractor may agree upon, and, if required, supported by such evidence as to its correctness as the Architect may direct. This schedule, when approved by the Architect, shall be used as a basis for certificates for payment, unless it be found to be in error. In applying for payments, the Contractor shall submit a statement based upon this schedule.

If payments are made on account of materials not incorporated in the work but delivered and suitably stored at the site, or at some other location agreed upon in writing, such payments shall be conditioned upon submission by the Contractor of bills of sale or such other procedure as will establish the Owner's title to such material or otherwise adequately protect the Owner's interest including applicable insurance.

ARTICLE 25

CERTIFICATES FOR PAYMENTS

If the Contractor has made application for payment as above, the Architect shall, not later than the date when each payment falls due, issue a certificate for payment to the Contractor for such amount as he decides to be properly due, or state in writing his reasons for withholding a certificate.

No certificate issued nor payment made to the Contractor, nor partial or entire use or occupancy of the work by the Owner, shall be an acceptance of any work or materials not in accordance with this contract. The making and acceptance of the final payment shall constitute a waiver of all claims by the Owner, other than those arising from unsettled liens, from faulty work appearing after final payment or from requirement of drawings or specifications, and of all claims by the Contractor, except those previously made and still unsettled.

Should the Owner fail to pay the sum named in any certificate for payment issued by the Architect or in any award by arbitration, upon demand when due, the Contractor shall receive, in addition to the sum named in the certificate, interest thereon at the legal rate in force at the place of building.

ARTICLE 26

PAYMENTS WITHHELD

The Architect may withhold or, on account of subsequently discovered evidence, nullify the whole or a part of any certificate to such extent as may be necessary to protect the Owner from loss on account of:

a) Defective work not remedied.

b) Claims filed or reasonable evidence indicating probable filing of claims.

c) Failure of the Contractor to make payments properly to subcontractors or for material or labor.

d) A reasonable doubt that the contract can be completed for the balance then unpaid.

e) Damage to another Contractor.

When the above grounds are removed payment shall be made for amounts withheld because of them.

ARTICLE 27

CONTRACTOR'S LIABILITY INSURANCE

The Contractor shall maintain such insurance as will protect him from claims under workmen's compensation acts and other employee benefits acts, from claims for damages because of bodily injury, including death, and from claims for damages to property which may arise both out of and during operations under this Contract, whether such operations be by himself or by any subcontractor or anyone directly or indirectly employed by either of them. This insurance shall be written for not less than any limits of liability specified as part of this Contract. Certificates of such insurance shall be filed with the Owner and Architect.

ARTICLE 28

OWNER'S LIABILITY INSURANCE

The Owner shall be responsible for and at his option may maintain such insurance as will protect him from his contingent liability to others for damages because of bodily injury, including death, which may arise from operations under this contract, and any other liability for damages which the Contractor is required to insure under any provision of this contract.

ARTICLE 29

FIRE INSURANCE WITH EXTENDED COVERAGE

Unless otherwise provided, the Owner shall effect and maintain fire insurance with extended coverage upon the entire structure on which the work of this contract is to be done to one hundred per cent of the insurable value thereof, including items of labor and materials connected therewith whether in or adjacent to the structure insured, materials in place or to be used as part of the permanent construction including surplus materials, shanties, protective fences, bridges, temporary structures, miscellaneous materials and supplies incident to the work, and such scaffoldings, stagings, towers, forms, and equipment as are not owned or rented by the contractor, the cost of which is included in the cost of the work. EXCLUSIONS: This insurance does not cover any tools owned by mechanics, any tools, equipment, scaffolding, staging, towers, and forms owned or rented by the Contractor, the capital value of which is not included in the cost of the work, or any cook shanties, bunk houses or other structures erected for housing the workmen. The loss, if any, is to be made adjustable with and payable to the Owner as Trustee for the insureds and contractors and subcontractors as their interests may appear, except in such cases as may require payment of all or a proportion of said insurance to be made to a mortgagee as his interests may appear.

Certificates of such insurance shall be filed with the Contractor if he so requires. If the Owner fails to effect or maintain insurance as above and so notifies the Contractor, the Contractor may insure his own interests and that of the subcontractors and charge the cost thereof to the Owner. If the Contractor is damaged by failure of the Owner to maintain such insurance or to so notify the Contractor, he may recover as stipulated in the contract for recovery of damages. If other special insurance not herein provided for is required by the Contractor, the Owner shall effect such insurance at the Contractor's expense by appropriate riders to his fire insurance policy. The Owner, Contractor, and all subcontractors waive all rights, each against the others, for damages caused by fire or other perils covered by insurance provided for under the terms of this contract, except such rights as they may have to the proceeds of insurance held by the Owner as Trustee.

The Owner shall be responsible for and at his option may insure against loss of use of his existing property, due to fire or otherwise, however caused. If required in writing by any party in interest, the Owner as Trustee shall, upon the occurrence of loss, give bond for the proper performance of his duties. He shall deposit any money received from insurance in an account separate from all his other funds and he shall distribute it in accordance with such agreement as the parties in interest may reach, or under an award of arbitrators appointed, one by the Owner, another by joint action of the other parties in interest, all other procedure being as provided elsewhere in the contract for arbitration. If after loss no special agreement is made, replacement of injured work shall be ordered and executed as provided for changes in the work.

The Trustee shall have power to adjust and settle any loss with the insurers unless one of the Contractors interested shall object in writing within three working days of the occurrence of loss, and thereupon arbitrators shall be chosen as above. The Trustee shall in that case make settlement with the insurers in accordance with the directions of such arbitrators, who shall also, if distribution by arbitration is required, direct such distribution.

ARTICLE 30

GUARANTY BONDS

The Owner shall have the right, prior to the signing of the Contract, to require the Contractor to furnish bond covering the faithful performance of the Contract and the payment of all obligations arising thereunder, in such form as the Owner may prescribe and with such sureties as he may approve. If such bond is required by instructions given previous to the submission of bids, the premium shall be paid by the Contractor; if subsequent thereto, it shall be paid by the Owner.

ARTICLE 31

DAMAGES

Should either party to this Contract suffer damages because of any wrongful act or neglect of the other party or of anyone employed by him, claim shall be made in writing to the party liable within a reasonable time of the first observance of such damage and not later than the final payment, except as expressly stipulated otherwise in the case of faulty work or materials, and shall be adjusted by agreement or arbitration.

ARTICLE 32

LIENS

Neither the final payment nor any part of the retained percentage shall become due until the Contractor, if required, shall deliver to the Owner a complete release of all liens arising out of this Contract, or receipts in full in lieu thereof and, if required in either case, an affidavit that so far as he has knowledge or information the releases and receipts include all the labor and material for which a lien could be filed; but the Contractor may, if any subcontractor refuses to furnish a release or receipt in full, furnish a bond satisfactory to the Owner, to indemnify him against any lien. If any lien remains unsatisfied after all payments are made, the Contractor shall refund to the Owner all moneys that the latter may be compelled to pay in discharging such a lien, including all costs and a reasonable attorney's fee.

ARTICLE 33

ASSIGNMENT

Neither party to the Contract shall assign the Contract or sublet it as a whole without the written consent of the other, nor shall the Contractor assign any moneys due or to become due to him hereunder, without the previous written consent of the Owner.

ARTICLE 34

MUTUAL RESPONSIBILITY OF CONTRACTORS

Should the Contractor cause damage to any separate contractor on the work the Contractor agrees, upon due notice, to settle with such contractor by agreement or arbitration, if he will so settle. If such separate contractor sues the Owner on account of any damage alleged to have been so sustained, the Owner shall notify the Contractor, who shall defend such proceedings at the Owner's expense and, if any judgment against the Owner arise therefrom, the Contractor shall pay or satisfy it and pay all costs incurred by the Owner.

ARTICLE 35

SEPARATE CONTRACTS

The Owner reserves the right to let other contracts in connection with this work under similar General Conditions. The Contractor shall afford other contractors reasonable opportunity for the introduction and storage of their materials and the execution of their work, and shall properly connect and coordinate his work with theirs.

If any part of the Contractor's work depends for proper execution or results upon the work of any other contractor, the Contractor shall inspect and promptly report to the Architect any defects in such work that render it unsuitable for such proper execution and results. His failure so to inspect and report shall constitute an acceptance of the other contractor's work as fit and proper for the reception of his work, except as to defects which may develop in the other contractor's work after the execution of his work.

To insure the proper execution of his subsequent work the Contractor shall measure work already in place and shall at once report to the Architect any discrepancy between the executed work and the drawings.

ARTICLE 36

SUBCONTRACTS

As soon as practicable and before awarding any subcontracts, the Contractor shall notify the Architect in writing of the names of the subcontractors proposed for the principal parts of the work, and for such other parts as the Architect may direct, and shall not employ any to whom the Architect may have a reasonable objection.

If before or after the execution of the Contract, the Contractor has submitted a list of subcontractors which has been approved by the Architect, and the change of any subcontractor on such list is required by the Owner after such approval, the contract price shall be increased or decreased by the difference in cost occasioned by such change.

The Contractor shall not be required to employ any subcontractor against whom he has a reasonable objection.

The Architect shall, on request, furnish to any subcontractor, wherever practicable, evidence of the amounts certified on his account.

The Contractor agrees that he is as fully responsible to the Owner for the acts and omissions of his subcontractors and of persons either directly or indirectly employed by them, as he is for the acts and ommissions of persons directly employed by him.

Nothing contained in the contract documents shall create any contractual relation between any subcontractor and the Owner.

ARTICLE 37

RELATIONS OF CONTRACTOR AND SUBCONTRACTOR

The Contractor agrees to bind every Subcontractor and every Subcontractor agrees to be bound by the terms of the Agreement, the General Conditions of the Contract, the Supplementary General Conditions, the Drawings and Specifications as far as applicable to his work, including the following provisions of this article, unless specifically noted to the contrary in a subcontract approved in writing as adequate by the Owner or Architect.

The Subcontractor agrees—

a) To be bound to the Contractor by the terms of the Agreement, General Conditions of the Contract, the Supplementary General Conditions, the Drawings and Specifications, and to assume toward him all the obligations and responsibilities that he, by those documents, assumes toward the Owner.

b) To submit to the Contractor applications for payment in such reasonable time as to enable the Contractor to apply for payment under Article 24 of the General Conditions.

c) To make all claims for extras, for extensions of time and for damages for delays or otherwise, to the Contractor in the manner provided in the General Conditions of the Contract and the Supplementary General Conditions for like claims by the Contractor upon the Owner, except that the time for making claims for extra cost is one week.

The Contractor agrees—

d) To be bound to the Subcontractor by all the obligations that the Owner assumes to the Contractor under the Agreement, General Conditions of the Contract, the Supplementary General Conditions, the Drawings and Specifications, and by all the provisions thereof affording remedies and redress to the Contractor from the Owner.

e) To pay the Subcontractor, upon the payment of certificates, if issued under the schedule of values described in Article 24 of the General Conditions, the amount allowed to the Contractor on account of the Subcontractor's work to the extent of the Subcontractor's interest therein.

f) To pay the Subcontractor, upon the payment of certificates, if issued otherwise than as in (e), so that at all times his total payments shall be as large in proportion to the value of the work done by him as the total amount certified to the Contractor is to the value of the work done by him.

g) To pay the Subcontractor to such extent as may be provided by the Contract Documents or the subcontract. if either of these provides for earlier or larger payments than the above.

h) To pay the Subcontractor on demand for his work or materials as far as executed and fixed in place, less the retained percentage, at the time the certificate should issue, even though the Architect fails to issue it for any cause not the fault of the Subcontractor.

j) To pay the Subcontractor a just share of any fire insurance money received by him, the Contractor, under Article 29 of the General Conditions.

k) To make no demand for liquidated damages or penalty for delay in any sum in excess of such amount as may be specifically named in the subcontract.

l) That no claim for services rendered or materials furnished by the Contractor to the Subcontractor shall be valid unless written notice thereof is given by the Contractor to the Subcontractor during the first ten days of the calendar month following that in which the claim originated.

m) To give the Subcontractor an opportunity to be present and to submit evidence in any arbitration involving his rights.

n) To name as arbitrator under arbitration proceedings as provided in the General Conditions the person nominated by the Subcontractor, if the sole cause of dispute is the work, materials, rights or responsibilities of the Subcontractor; or, if of the Subcontractor and any other subcontractor jointly, to name as such arbitrator the person upon whom they agree.

The Contractor and the Subcontractor agree that—

o) In the matter of arbitration, their rights and obligations and all procedure shall be analogous to those set forth in this contract; provided, however, that a decision by the Architect shall not be a condition precedent to arbitration.

Nothing in this article shall create any obligation on the part of the Owner to pay or to see to the payment of any sums to any subcontractor.

ARTICLE 38

ARCHITECT'S STATUS

The Architect shall have general supervision and direction of the work. He is the agent of the Owner only to the extent provided in the Contract Documents and when in special instances he is authorized by the Owner so to act, and in such instances he shall, upon request, show the Contractor written authority. He has authority to stop the work whenever such stoppage may be necessary to insure the proper execution of the Contract.

As the Architect is, in the first instance, the interpreter of the conditions of the Contract and the judge of its performance, he shall side neither with the Owner nor with the Contractor, but shall use his powers under the contract to enforce its faithful performance by both.

In case of the termination of the employment of the Architect, the Owner shall appoint a capable and reputable Architect against whom the Contractor makes no reasonable objection, whose status under the contract shall be that of the former Architect; any dispute in connection with such appointment shall be subject to arbitration.

ARTICLE 39

ARCHITECT'S DECISIONS

The Architect shall, within a reasonable time, make decisions on all claims of the Owner or Contractor and on all other matters relating to the execution and progress of the work or the interpretation of the Contract Documents.

The Architect's decisions, in matters relating to artistic effect, shall be final, if within the terms of the Contract Documents.

Except as above or as otherwise expressly provided in the Contract Documents, all the Architect's decisions are subject to arbitration.

If, however, the Architect fails to render a decision within ten days after the parties have presented their evidence, either party may then demand arbitration. If the Architect renders a decision after arbitration proceedings have been initiated, such decision may be entered as evidence but shall not disturb or interrupt such proceedings except where such decision is acceptable to the parties concerned.

ARTICLE 40

ARBITRATION

All disputes, claims or questions subject to arbitration under this contract shall be submitted to arbitration in accordance with the provisions, then obtaining, of the Standard Form of Arbitration Procedure of The American Institute of Architects, and this agreement shall be specifically enforceable under the prevailing arbitration law, and judgment upon the award rendered may be entered in the court of the forum, state or federal, having jurisdiction. It is mutually agreed that the decision of the arbitrators shall be a condition precedent to any right of legal action that either party may have against the other.

The Contractor shall not cause a delay of the work during any arbitration proceedings, except by agreement with the Owner.

Notice of the demand for arbitration of a dispute shall be filed in writing with the other party to the contract, and a copy filed with the Architect. The demand for arbitration shall be made within a reasonable time after the dispute has arisen; in no case, however, shall the demand be made later than the time of final payment, except as otherwise expressly stipulated in the contract.

The arbitrators, if they deem that the case requires it, are authorized to award to the party whose contention is sustained, such sums as they or a majority of them shall deem proper to compensate him for the time and expense incident to the proceeding and, if the arbitration was demanded without reasonable cause, they may also award damages for delay. The arbitrators shall fix their own compensation, unless otherwise provided by agreement, and shall assess the costs and charges of the proceedings upon either or both parties.

A.I.A. DOCUMENT NO. A-201

(Formerly Form A2) 1958 Edition

ARTICLE 41

CASH ALLOWANCES

The Contractor shall include in the contract sum all allowances named in the Contract Documents and shall cause the work so covered to be done by such contractors and for such sums as the Architect may direct, the contract sum being adjusted in conformity therewith. The Contractor declares that the contract sum includes such sums for expenses and profit on account of cash allowances as he deems proper. No demand for expenses or profit other than those included in the contract sum shall be allowed. The Contractor shall not be required to employ for any such work persons against whom he has a reasonable objection.

ARTICLE 42

USE OF PREMISES

The Contractor shall confine his apparatus, the storage of materials and the operations of his workmen to limits indicated by law, ordinances, permits or directions of the Architect and shall not unreasonably encumber the premises with his materials.

The Contractor shall not load or permit any part of the structure to be loaded with a weight that will endanger its safety.

The Contractor shall enforce the Architect's instructions regarding signs, advertisements, fires and smoking.

ARTICLE 43

CUTTING, PATCHING

The Contractor shall do all cutting, fitting or patching of his work that may be required to make its several parts come together properly and fit it to receive or be received by work of other contractors shown upon, or reasonably implied by, the Drawings and Specifications for the completed structure, and he shall make good after them as the Architect may direct.

Any cost caused by defective or ill-timed work shall be borne by the party responsible therefor.

The Contractor shall not endanger any work by cutting, excavating or otherwise altering the work and shall not cut or alter the work of any other contractor save with the consent of the Architect.

ARTICLE 44

CLEANING UP

The Contractor shall at all times keep the premises free from accumulations of waste materials or rubbish caused by his employees or work, and at the completion of the work he shall remove all his rubbish from and about the building and all his tools, scaffolding and surplus materials and shall leave his work "broom-clean" or its equivalent, unless more exactly specified. In case of dispute the Owner may remove the rubbish and charge the cost to the several contractors as the Architect shall determine to be just.

A.I.A. DOCUMENT NO. A-107

(Formerly 307) Revised Printing 1959

A. I. A. SHORT FORM FOR SMALL CONSTRUCTION CONTRACTS

AGREEMENT AND GENERAL CONDITIONS BETWEEN CONTRACTOR AND OWNER

Issued by The American Institute of Architects for use only when the proposed work is simple in character, small in cost, and when a stipulated sum forms the basis of payment. For other contracts the Institute issues the standard form of agreement between Contractor and Owner for construction of buildings and the standard general conditions in connection therewith for use when a stipulated sum forms the basis for payment.

THIS AGREEMENT made the ....

day of .... in the year Nineteen Hundred and ....

by and between ....

....

.... hereinafter called the Contractor, and

....

.... hereinafter called the Owner.

WITNESSETH, That the Contractor and the Owner for the considerations hereinafter named agree as follows:

ARTICLE 1. SCOPE OF THE WORK—The Contractor shall furnish all of the material and perform all of the work for .... as shown on the drawings and described in the specifications entitled ....

....

prepared by .... Architect

all in accordance with the terms of the contract documents.

ARTICLE 2. TIME OF COMPLETION—The work shall be substantially completed ....

....

ARTICLE 3. CONTRACT SUM—The Owner shall pay the Contractor for the performance of the contract subject to the additions and deductions provided therein in current funds, the sum of ....

.... dollars. ($..

A.I.A. DOCUMENT NO. A-107

(Formerly 307) Revised Printing 1959

ARTICLE 4. PROGRESS PAYMENTS—The Owner shall make payments on account of the contract, upon requisition by the Contractor, as follows:

ARTICLE 5. ACCEPTANCE AND FINAL PAYMENT—Final payment shall be due ______________ days after completion of the work, provided the contract be then fully performed, subject to the provisions of Article 16 of the General Conditions.

ARTICLE 6. CONTRACT DOCUMENTS—Contract Documents are as noted in Article 1 of the General Conditions. The following is an enumeration of the drawings and specifications:

GENERAL CONDITIONS

ARTICLE 1

CONTRACT DOCUMENTS

The contract includes the AGREEMENT and its GENERAL CONDITIONS the DRAWINGS, and the SPECIFICATIONS. Two or more copies of each, as required, shall be signed by both parties and one signed copy of each retained by each party.

The intent of these documents is to include all labor, materials, appliances and services of every kind necessary for the proper execution of the work, and the terms and conditions of payment therefor.

The documents are to be considered as one, and whatever is called for by any one of the documents shall be as binding as if called for by all.

ARTICLE 2

SAMPLES

The Contractor shall furnish for approval all samples as directed. The work shall be in accordance with approved samples.

ARTICLE 3

MATERIALS, APPLIANCES, EMPLOYEES

Except as otherwise noted, the Contractor shall provide and pay for all materials, labor, tools, water, power and other items necessary to complete the work.

Unless otherwise specified, all materials shall be new, and both workmanship and materials shall be of good quality.

All workmen and sub-contractors shall be skilled in their trades.

ARTICLE 4

ROYALTIES AND PATENTS

The Contractor shall pay all royalties and license fees. He shall defend all suits or claims for infringement of any patent rights and shall save the Owner harmless from loss on account thereof.

ARTICLE 5

SURVEYS, PERMITS, AND REGULATIONS

The Owner shall furnish all surveys unless otherwise specified. Permits and licenses necessary for the prosecution of the work shall be secured and paid for by the Contractor. Easements for permanent structures or permanent changes in existing facilities shall be secured and paid for by the Owner, unless otherwise specified. The Contractor shall comply with all laws and regulations bearing on the conduct of the work and shall notify the Owner if the drawings and specifications are at variance therewith.

ARTICLE 6

PROTECTION OF WORK, PROPERTY, AND PERSONS

The Contractor shall adequately protect the work, adjacent property and the public and shall be responsible for any damage or injury due to his act or neglect.

A.I.A. DOCUMENT NO. A-107

(Formerly 307) Revised Printing 1959

ARTICLE 7

INSPECTION OF WORK

The Contractor shall permit and facilitate inspection of the work by the Owner and his agents and public authorities at all times.

ARTICLE 8

CHANGES IN THE WORK

The Owner may order changes in the work, the Contract Sum being adjusted accordingly. All such orders and adjustments shall be in writing. Claims by the Contractor for extra cost must be made in writing before executing the work involved.

ARTICLE 9

CORRECTION OF WORK

The Contractor shall re-execute any work that fails to conform to the requirements of the contract and that appears during the progress of the work, and shall remedy any defects due to faulty materials or workmanship which appear within a period of one year from the date of completion of the contract. The provisions of this article apply to work done by subcontractors as well as to work done by direct employees of the Contractor.

ARTICLE 10

OWNER'S RIGHT TO TERMINATE THE CONTRACT

Should the Contractor neglect to prosecute the work properly, or fail to perform any provision of the contract, the Owner, after seven days' written notice to the Contractor, and his surety if any may, without prejudice to any other remedy he may have, make good the deficiencies and may deduct the cost thereof from the payment then or thereafter due the contractor or, at his option, may terminate the contract and take possession of all materials, tools, and appliances and finish the work by such means as he sees fit, and if the unpaid balance of the contract price exceeds the expense of finishing the work, such excess shall be paid to the Contractor, but if such expense exceeds such unpaid balance, the Contractor shall pay the difference to the Owner.

ARTICLE 11

CONTRACTOR'S RIGHT TO TERMINATE CONTRACT

Should the work be stopped by any public authority for a period of thirty days or more, through no fault of the Contractor, or should the work be stopped through act or neglect of the Owner for a period of seven days, or should the Owner fail to pay the Contractor any payment within seven days after it is due, then the Contractor upon seven days' written notice to the Owner, may stop work or terminate the contract and recover from he Owner payment for all work executed and any loss sustained and reasonable profit and damages.

ARTICLE 12

PAYMENTS

Payments shall be made as provided in the Agreement. The making and acceptance of the final payment shall constitute a waiver of all claims by the Owner, other than those arising from unsettled liens or from faulty work appearing thereafter, as provided for in Article 9, and of all claims by the Contractor except any previously made and still unsettled. Payments otherwise due may be withheld on account of defective work not remedied, liens filed, damage by the Contractor to others not adjusted, or failure to make payments properly to subcontractors or for material or labor.

ARTICLE 13

CONTRACTOR'S LIABILITY INSURANCE

The Contractor shall maintain such insurance as will protect him from claims under workmen's compensation acts and other employee benefits and from claims for damages because of bodily injury, including death, and from claims for damages to property which may arise both out of and during operations under this contract, whether such operations be by himself or by any subcontractor or anyone directly or indirectly employed by either of them. This insurance shall be written for not less than any limits of liability specified as part of this contract. Certificates of such insurance shall be filed with the Owner and architect.

ARTICLE 14

OWNER'S LIABILITY INSURANCE

The Owner shall be responsible for and at his option may maintain such insurance as will protect him from his contingent liability to others for damages because of bodily injury, including death, which may arise from operations under this contract, and any other liability for damages which the Contractor is required to insure under any provision of this contract.

ARTICLE 15

FIRE-INSURANCE WITH EXTENDED COVERAGE

The Owner shall effect and maintain fire insurance with extended coverage upon the entire structure on which the work of this contract is to be done to one hundred per cent of the insurable value thereof, including items of labor and materials connected therewith whether in or adjacent to the structure insured, materials in place or to be used as part of the permanent construction including surplus materials, shanties, protective fences, bridges, temporary structures, miscellaneous materials and supplies incident to the work, and such scaffoldings, stagings, towers, forms, and equipment as are not owned or rented by the contractor, the cost of which is included in the cost of the work. EXCLUSIONS: The insurance does not cover any tools owned by mechanics, any tools, equipment, scaffolding staging, towers, and forms owned or rented by the Contractor, the capital value of which is not included in the cost of the work, or any cook shanties, bunk houses or other structures erected for housing the workmen. The loss, if any, is to be made adjustable with and payable to the Owner as Trustee for the insureds and contractors and subcontractors as their interests may appear, except in such cases as may require payment of all or a proportion of said insurance to be made to a mortgagee as his interests may appear.

Certificates of such insurance shall be filed with the Contractor if he so requires. If the Owner fails to effect or maintain insurance as above and so notifies the Contractor, the Contractor may insure his own interests and that of the subcontractors and charge the cost thereof to the Owner. If the Contractor is damaged by failure of the Owner to maintain such insurance or to so notify the Contractor, he may recover as stipulated in the contract for recovery of damages. If other special insurance not herein provided for is required by the Contractor, the Owner shall effect such insurance at the Contractor's expense by appropriate riders to his fire insurance policy. The Owner, Contractor, and all subcontractors waive all rights, each against the others, for damages caused by fire or other perils covered by insurance provided for under the terms of this contract, except such rights as they may have to the proceeds of insurance held by the Owner as Trustee.

A.I.A. DOCUMENT NO. A-107

(Formerly 307) Revised Printing 1959

The Owner shall be responsible for and at his option may insure against loss of use of his existing property, due to fire or otherwise, however caused.

If required in writing by any party in interest, the Owner as Trustee shall, upon the occurrence of loss, give bond for the proper performance of his duties. He shall deposit any money received from insurance in an account separate from all his other funds and he shall distribute it in accordance with such agreement as the parties in interest may reach or under an award of arbitrators appointed, one by the Owner, another by joint action of the other parties in interest, all other procedure being as provided elsewhere in the contract for arbitration. If after loss no special agreement is made, replacement of injured work shall be ordered and executed as provided for changes in the work.

The Trustee shall have power to adjust and settle any loss with the insurers unless one of the Contractors interested shall object in writing within three working days of the occurrence of loss, and thereupon arbitrators shall be chosen as above. The Trustee shall in that case make settlement with the insurers in accordance with the directions of such arbitrators, who shall also, if distribution by arbitration is required, direct such distribution.

ARTICLE 16

LIENS

The final payment shall not be due until the Contractor has delivered to the Owner a complete release of all liens arising out of this contract, or receipts in full covering all labor and materials for which a lien could be filed, or a bond satisfactory to the Owner indemnifying him against any lien.

ARTICLE 17

SEPARATE CONTRACTS

The Owner has the right to let other contracts in connection with the work and the Contractor shall properly cooperate with any such other contractors.

ARTICLE 18

THE ARCHITECT'S STATUS

The Architect shall have general supervision of the work. He has authority to stop the work if necessary to insure its proper execution. He shall certify to the Owner when payments under the contract are due and the amounts to be paid. He shall make decisions on all claims of the Owner or Contractor. All his decisions are subject to arbitration.

ARTICLE 19

ARBITRATION

Any disagreement arising out of this contract or from the breach thereof shall be submitted to arbitration, and judgment upon the award rendered may be entered in the court of the forum, state or federal, having jurisdiction. It is mutually agreed that the decision of the arbitrators shall be a condition precedent to any right of legal action that either party may have against the other. The arbitration shall be held under the Standard Form of Arbitration Procedure of The American Institute of Architects or under the Rules of the American Arbitration Association.

ARTICLE 20

CLEANING UP

The Contractor shall keep the premises free from accumulation of waste material and rubbish and at the completion of the work he shall remove from the premises all rubbish, implements and surplus materials and leave the building broom-clean.

IN WITNESS WHEREOF the parties hereto executed this Agreement, the day and year first above written.

Contractor ....

Owner ....

A.I.A. DOCUMENT NO. A-310
(1958 Edition)

BID BOND

This document approved and issued by The American Institute of Architects
1735 New York Avenue, N. W., Washington 6, D. C.

KNOW ALL MEN BY THESE PRESENTS,

That we, ...

.... (hereinafter called the "Principal"),

as Principal, and the ....

...., of ....,

a corporation duly organized under the laws of the State of ....,

(Hereinafter called the "Surety"), as Surety, are held and firmly bound unto ....

....

.... (Hereinafter called the "Obligee"),

in the sum of .... Dollars

($), for the payment of which sum well and truly to be made, the said Principal and the said Surety, bind ourselves, our heirs, executors, administrators, successors and assigns, jointly and severally, firmly by these presents.

WHEREAS, the Principal has submitted a bid for ....

....

....

....

A.I.A. DOCUMENT NO. A-310

(1958 Edition)

NOW, THEREFORE, if the Obligee shall accept the bid of the Principal and the Principal shall enter into a contract with the Obligee in accordance with the terms of such bid, and give such bond or bonds as may be specified in the bidding or contract documents with good and sufficient surety for the faithful performance of such contract and for the prompt payment of labor and material furnished in the prosecution thereof, or in the event of the failure of the Principal to enter such contract and give such bond or bonds, if the Principal shall pay to the Obligee the difference not to exceed the penalty hereof between the amount specified in said bid and such larger amount for which the Obligee may in good faith contract with another party to perform the work covered by said bid, then this obligation shall be null and void, otherwise to remain in full force and effect.

Signed and sealed this .... day of .... A.D. 195.....,

.... (Seal)

(Principal)

....

....

(Title)

.... (Seal)

(Surety)

....

....

(Title)

A.I.A. DOCUMENT NO. A-311

(Formerly Form 107) 1968 Edition

PERFORMANCE BOND

This document approved and issued by The American Institute of Architects
1735 New York Avenue, N. W., Washington 6, D. C.

KNOW ALL MEN BY THESE PRESENTS:

That ....,
(Here insert the name and address or legal title of the Contractor)

....

as Principal, hereinafter called Contractor, and ....

....,
(Here insert the legal title of Surety)

....

as Surety, hereinafter called Surety, are held and firmly bound unto ....

....,
(Here insert the name and address or legal title of the Owner)
as Obligee, hereinafter called Owner, in the amount of ....

.... Dollars ($..................),
for the payment whereof Contractor and Surety bind themselves, their heirs, executors, administrators, successors and assigns, jointly and severally, firmly by these presents.

WHEREAS, Contractor has by written agreement dated ....

entered into a contract with Owner for ....

....

....

in accordance with drawings and specifications prepared by ....

....
(Here insert full name and title)
which contract is by reference made a part hereof, and is hereinafter referred to as the Contract.

A.I.A. DOCUMENT NO. A-311

(Formerly Form 107) 1958 Edition

NOW, THEREFORE, THE CONDITION OF THIS OBLIGATION is such that, if Contractor shall promptly and faithfully perform said contract, then this obligation shall be null and void; otherwise it shall remain in full force and effect.

The Surety hereby waives notice of any alteration or extension of time made by the Owner.

Whenever Contractor shall be, and declared by Owner to be in default under the Contract, the Owner having performed Owner's obligations thereunder, the Surety may promptly remedy the default, or shall promptly

1) Complete the Contract in accordance with its terms and conditions, or

2) Obtain a bid or bids for submission to Owner for completing the Contract in accordance with its terms and conditions, and upon determination by Owner and Surety of the lowest responsible bidder, arrange for a contract between such bidder and Owner, and make available as work progresses (even though there should be a default or a succession of defaults under the contract or contracts of completion arranged under this paragraph) sufficient funds to pay the cost of completion less the balance of the contract price; but not exceeding, including other costs and damages for which the Surety may be liable hereunder, the amount set forth in the first paragraph hereof. The term "balance of the contract price," as used in this paragraph, shall mean the total amount payable by Owner to Contractor under the Contract and any amendments thereto, less the amount properly paid by Owner to Contractor.

Any suit under this bond must be instituted before the expiration of two (2) years from the date on which final payment under the contract falls due.

No right of action shall accrue on this bond to or for the use of any person or corporation other than the Owner named herein or the heirs, executors, administrators or successors of Owner.

Signed and sealed this ....day of .... A.D. 195.......

IN THE PRESENCE OF:

.... { .... *(Principal)* (Seal)

.... *(Title)*

.... { .... *(Surety)* (Seal)

.... *(Title)*

A.I.A. DOCUMENT NO. A-311

(Formerly Form 107) 1958 Edition

LABOR AND MATERIAL PAYMENT BOND

This document approved and issued by The American Institute of Architects
1735 New York Avenue, N. W., Washington 6, D. C.

Note: This bond is issued simultaneously with another bond in favor of the owner conditioned for the full and faithful performance of the contract.

KNOW ALL MEN BY THESE PRESENTS:

That ....,
(Here insert the name and address or legal title of the Contractor)

....

as Principal, hereinafter called Principal, and ....

....
(Here insert the legal title of Surety)

....

as Surety, hereinafter called Surety, are held and firmly bound unto ....

....,
(Here insert the name and address or legal title of the Owner)

as Obligee, hereinafter called Owner, for the use and benefit of claimants as hereinbelow defined, in the amount of .... Dollars ($..............................),
(Here insert a sum equal to at least one-half of the contract price)
for the payment whereof Principal and Surety bind themselves, their heirs, executors, administrators, successors and assigns, jointly and severally, firmly by these presents.

WHEREAS, Principal has by written agreement dated ....

entered into a contract with Owner for ....

....

....

in accordance with drawings and specifications prepared by ....

....
(Here insert full name and title)
which contract is by reference made a part hereof, and is hereinafter referred to as the Contract.

A.I.A. DOCUMENT NO. A-311

(Formerly Form 107) 1958 Edition

NOW, THEREFORE, THE CONDITION OF THIS OBLIGATION is such that if the Principal shall promptly make payment to all claimants as hereinafter defined, for all labor and material used or reasonably required for use in the performance of the Contract, then this obligation shall be void; otherwise it shall remain in full force and effect, subject, however, to the following conditions:

1. A claimant is defined as one having a direct contract with the Principal or with a subcontractor of the Principal for labor, material, or both, used or reasonably required for use in the performance of the contract, labor and material being construed to include that part of water, gas, power, light, heat, oil, gasoline, telephone service or rental of equipment directly applicable to the Contract.

2. The above named Principal and Surety hereby jointly and severally agree with the Owner that every claimant as herein defined, who has not been paid in full before the expiration of a period of ninety (90) days after the date on which the last of such claimant's work or labor was done or performed, or materials were furnished by such claimant, may sue on this bond for the use of such claimant, prosecute the suit to final judgment for such sum or sums as may be justly due claimant, and have execution thereon. The Owner shall not be liable for the payment of any costs or expenses of any such suit.

3. No suit or action shall be commenced hereunder by any claimant.

a) Unless claimant, other than one having a direct contract with the Principal, shall have given written notice to any two of the following: The Principal, the Owner, or the Surety above named, within ninety (90) days after such claimant did or performed the last of the work or labor, or furnished the last of the materials for which said claim is made, stating with substantial accuracy the amount claimed and the name of the party to whom the materials were furnished, or for whom the work or labor was done or performed. Such notice shall be served by mailing the same by registered mail or certified mail, postage prepaid, in an envelope addressed to the Principal, Owner or Surety, at any place where an office is regularly maintained for the transaction of business, or served in any manner in which legal process may be served in the state in which the aforesaid project is located, save that such service need not be made by a public officer.

b) After the expiration of one (1) year following the date on which Principal ceased work on said Contract, it being understood, however, that if any limitation embodied in this bond is prohibited by any law controlling the construction hereof such limitation shall be deemed to be amended so as to be equal to the minimum period of limitation permitted by such law.

c) Other than in a state court of competent jurisdiction in and for the county or other political subdivision of the state in which the project, or any part thereof, is situated, or in the United States District Court for the district in which the project, or any part thereof, is situated, and not elsewhere.

4. The amount of this bond shall be reduced by and to the extent of any payment or payments made in good faith hereunder, inclusive of the payment by Surety of mechanics' liens which may be filed of record against said improvement, whether or not claim for the amount of such lien be presented under and against this bond.

Signed and sealed this ....day of .... A.D. 195........

IN THE PRESENCE OF:

.... (Principal) (Seal)

.... (Title)

.... (Surety) (Seal)

.... (Title)

A.I.A. DOCUMENT NO. A-401

(Formerly Form C1) 1958 Edition

STANDARD FORM OF SUBCONTRACT

For use in connection with the 1958 edition of the Standard Form of Agreement and General Conditions of the Contract

Approved by THE ASSOCIATED GENERAL CONTRACTORS OF AMERICA; THE CONTRACTING PLASTERERS' AND LATHERS' INTERNATIONAL ASSN.; COUNCIL OF MECHANICAL SPECIALTY CONTRACTING INDUSTRIES, INC.; THE HEATING, PIPING AND AIR CONDITIONING CONTRACTORS NATIONAL ASSN.; THE NATIONAL ASSOCIATION OF ORNAMENTAL METAL MANUFACTURERS; THE NATIONAL BUILDING GRANITE QUARRIES ASSN., INC.; THE NATIONAL ELECTRICAL CONTRACTORS ASSN.; THE PAINTING AND DECORATING CONTRACTORS OF AMERICA, AND THE PRODUCERS' COUNCIL, INC.*

THIS AGREEMENT made this ....

day of .... in the year Nineteen Hundred and ....

by and between ....

.... hereinafter called the Subcontractor and

.... hereinafter called the Contractor.

WITNESSETH, That the Subcontractor and Contractor for the consideration hereinafter named agree as follows:

SECTION 1. The Subcontractor agrees to furnish all material and perform all work as described in Section 2 hereof for ....

(Here name the kind of building.)

....

for .... hereinafter called the Owner,

(Here insert the name of the Owner.)

at ....

(Here insert the location of the work.)

in accordance with the General Conditions of the Contract between the Owner and the Contractor and in accordance with Supplementary General Conditions, the Drawings and the Specifications prepared by

.... hereinafter called the Architect, all of which General Conditions, Drawings and Specifications, signed by the parties thereto or identified by the

* Formal approval, which has been given previous editions, has not yet been received from all of these organizations.

A.I.A. DOCUMENT NO. A-401

(Formerly Form C1) 1958 Edition

Architect, form a part of a Contract between the Contractor and the Owner dated, ...

.... 19, ..., and hereby become a part of this Contract.

SECTION 2. The Subcontractor and the Contractor agree that the materials to be furnished and work to be done by the Subcontractor are ....
(Here insert a precise description of the work, preferably by reference to the numbers of the Drawings and the pages of the Specifications.)

....

SECTION 3. The Subcontractor agrees to complete the several portions and the whole of the work herein sublet by the time or times following: ....
(Here insert the date or dates and if there be liquidated damages state them.)

....

SECTION 4. The Contractor agrees to pay the Subcontractor for the performance of his work the sum of .... ($..............................)

in current funds, subject to additions and deductions for changes as may be agreed upon, and to make payments on account thereof in accordance with Section 5 hereof.

....

A.I.A. DOCUMENT NO. A-401

(Formerly Form C1) 1958 Edition

SECTION 4. (Continued)

....

....

....

....

....

....

....

SECTION 5. The Contractor and Subcontractor agree to be bound by the terms of the Agreement, the General Conditions, Drawings and Specifications as far as applicable to this subcontract, and also by the following provisions:

The Subcontractor agrees—

a) To be bound to the Contractor by the terms of the Agreement, General Conditions of the Contract, the Supplementary General Conditions, the Drawings and Specifications, and to assume toward him all the obligations and responsibilities that he, by those documents, assumes toward the Owner.

b) To submit to the Contractor applications for payment in such reasonable time as to enable the Contractor to apply for payment under Article 24 of the General Conditions.

c) To make all claims for extras, for extensions of time and for damage for delays or otherwise, to the Contractor in the manner provided in the General Conditions of the Contract and Supplementary General Conditions for like claims by the Contractor upon the Owner, except that the time for making claims for extra cost is one week.

The Contractor agrees—

d) To be bound to the Subcontractor by all the obligations that the Owner assumes to the Contractor under the Agreement, General Conditions of the Contract, the Supplementary General Conditions, the Drawings and Specifications, and by all the provisions thereof affording remedies and redress to the Contractor from the Owner.

e) To pay the Subcontractor, upon the payment of certificates, if issued under the schedule of values described in Article 24 of the General Conditions, the amount allowed to the Contractor on account of the Subcontractor's work to the extent of the Subcontractor's interest therein.

f) To pay the Subcontractor, upon the payment of certificates, if issued otherwise than as in (e), so that at all times his total payments shall be as large in proportion to the value of the work done by him as the total amount certified to the Contractor is to the value of the work done by him.

g) To pay the Subcontractor to such extent as may be provided by the Contract Documents or the subcontract, if either of these provide for earlier or larger payments than the above.

h) To pay the Subcontractor on demand for his work or materials as far as executed and fixed in place, less the retained percentage, at the time the certificate should issue, even though the Architect fails to issue it for any cause not the fault of the Subcontractor.

j) To pay the Subcontractor a just share of any fire insurance money received by him, the Contractor, under Article 29 of the General Conditions.

k) To make no demand for liquidated damages or penalty for delay in any sum in excess of such amount as may be specifically named in the subcontract.

l) That no claim for services rendered or materials furnished by the Contractor to the Subcontractor shall be valid unless written notice thereof is given by the Contractor to the Subcontractor during the first ten days of the calendar month following that in which the claim originated.

m) To give the Subcontractor an opportunity to be present and to submit evidence in any arbitration involving his rights.

n) To name as arbitrator under arbitration proceeding as provided in the General Conditions the person nominated by the Subcontractor, if the sole cause of dispute is the work, materials, rights or responsibilities of the Subcontractor; or if, of the Subcontractor and any other subcontractor jointly, to name as such arbitrator the person upon whom they agree.

The Contractor and the Subcontractor agree that—

o) In the matter of arbitration, their rights and obligations and all procedure shall be analogous to those set forth in this Contract.

Nothing in this article shall create any obligation on the part of the Owner to pay or to see to the payment of any sums to any Subcontractor.

A.I.A. DOCUMENT NO. A-401

(Formerly Form C1) 1958 Edition

SECTION 6.

....

....

....

....

....

....

....

AGREEMENT BETWEEN

.... *Subcontractor*

.... *Contractor*

.... *Owner*

.... *Architect*

Contract Price $....................................

IN WITNESS WHEREOF the parties hereto have executed this Agreement, the day and year first above written.

....

....

....

FORM OF AGREEMENT BETWEEN ARCHITECT & ENGINEER

THIS AGREEMENT made the ....

day of ...., in the year Nineteen Hundred and ....,

by and between ....

....(hereinafter called the "Architect"), and

....(hereinafter called the "Engineer").

WITNESSETH:

The Architect and the Engineer, for the considerations hereinafter named, agree as follows:

1. The engineer will furnish mechanical engineering services, under the direction and control of the Architect, in connection with a project for which the Architect holds the prime contracts with ....

...., Owner.

2. A description of the Project and its scope, as contained in the said prime contract, is annexed hereto, marked Exhibit "1" and made a part hereof.

3. The Engineer will provide the Project complete mechanical engineering services, including, but not by way of limitation, the following:

(a) Conferences by the Engineer and by members of his staff with Architect, Owner, or others, as may be required throughout duration of contract.

(b) Inspection of site and obtaining of any information necessary to the Engineer's work.

(c) Preliminary estimates of construction and operating costs.

(d) Schematic design.

(e) Outline specifications.

(f) Studies as may be needed to justify choice of material, equipment, or system.

(g) Notification to Architect of all mechanical equipment space and clearance requirements as a guide to preliminary architectural plans.

(h) Notification of Architect's office as to any unusual conditions affecting overall design and likely to cause difficulties of any sort.

(i) Complete design calculations and working drawings in pencil on tracing paper.

(j) Complete specifications in triplicate, including adequate performance clauses and provision for testing all equipment before acceptance so as to assure a complete and properly operating system.

(k) Checking and coordination of all drawings and specifications prepared by the Engineer.

(l) Obtaining of final budget estimates.

(m) Composite or reflected ceiling drawings showing all mechanical trades superimposed (if requested).

(n) Obtaining of all approvals on the Engineer's work as may be required by law.

(o) Aid in preparing and letting of mechanical contracts.

(p) Checking of shop drawings.

(q) Visits to site for inspection purposes as often as may be requested or needed, but not to exceed .... visits during the construction period.

(r) Final inspection and report, including statements on results of operating tests a required by specifications.

(s) Operating manual for major equipment.

(t) As-built drawings.

4. It is expressly understood and agreed that the Engineer will be bound by all the terms of the prime contract between the Owner and Architect that may apply to the Engineer's work.

5. The Engineer's fee for his work under this contract will be as follows: ....

....

6. Anything to the contrary contained herein notwithstanding, it is expressly understood and agreed that the Architect will not be obligated to pay the Engineer any fee, or other compensation, unless and until the Architect has received from the Owner under his prime contract compensation for the services rendered by the Engineer, and in no event shall the Architect be obliged to make payments to the Engineer in such a manner that the Engineer will receive a larger proportion in relation

to his gross fee than the Architect has received from the Owner in relation to the Architect's gross fee.

7. Except as provided in Paragraph "6" hereof, the Engineer's fee will be due and payable within seven (7) days after the Architect has received his fee from the Owner covering the Engineer's services.

8. The Engineer will be reimbursed at cost on receipt of receipt of properly itemized and receipted vouchers for:

Transportation and living expenses incurred by the Engineer, or his representatives, while travelling out of town in discharge of duties connected with the work.

Reproductions of working drawings required for bidding and constructing purposes.

Fees paid in connection with obtaining approvals required by law.

Fees paid to special consultants or other expenditures but only when the Engineer has obtained prior written approval from the Architect.

The Architect shall not be obligated to reimburse the Engineer the items set forth in this paragraph, unless and until the Architect has received reimbursements from the Owner under his prime contract for these items.

9. In the event the Owner abandons or suspends the Project, and/or the Architect's contract with the Owner is terminated, this contract shall be terminated and the Engineer's fee for services performed to the date of termination will be a pro rata amount in proportion to the extent of services rendered.

10. The Engineer will be paid .... times his technical payroll involved for:

(a) Major changes in the Engineer's working drawings and specifications after approval of said drawings and specifications, provided the Architect has requested such changes in writing, and further provided that the Engineer has notified the Architect in advance of the probable cost of such changes.

The Engineer will not be entitled to any extra compensation for changes which are necessary because of the Engineer's error, negligence or omissions.

(b) Any other services beyond the scope of this agreement as may be required by the Architect in writing and performed by the Engineer.

11. Payroll costs as referred to herein mean the actual technical net payroll applicable to this Project as evidenced by time cards, and including payroll taxes, but excluding any increment for overtime unless on prior written approval, and excluding any increment for holidays, vacations, sick leave, bonuses or profit sharing. Clerical time and the time of any principal shall not be changed unless on prior written approval. The Engineer's records are to be accurately kept and open at reasonable times for inspection by the Architect or the Owner.

12. The Architect will provide the Engineer with all available information, but the Engineer will be responsible for insuring that he has all information needed for his work.

13. The Engineer's services are to be performed in a first-class professional manner and with expedition. The Engineer shall be liable to the Architect for any damages which the Architect might sustain because of the Engineer's failure to meet this standard.

If any litigation, or other controversy, arises involving the Engineer's work, the Engineer will assume the responsibility therefor, and the Engineer will hold the Architect harmless against any claim for damages by the Owner, or any other person, arising out of the Engineer's work.

14. On completion of the Engineer's work, he will turn over to the Architect either the original tracings and calculations, or a complete set of transparencies of them. It is agreed that this material will not be used on other work without the Engineer's consent.

15. The Engineer agrees to have his preliminary work completed by .... and his working drawings and specifications complete by ....

16. Any dispute arising between the parties to this agreement, or involving the interpretation of the terms of this agreement, or any breach thereof, shall be submitted to and determined by arbitration before the American Arbitration Association in the city of ...., in accordance with the rules then obtaining of said Association and the laws of the State of ....

All notices with respect to the demand for arbitration, the conduct of the arbitration, and the enforcement of the arbitration award shall be deemed sufficient if served by registered mail addressed by one party to the other at the addresses set forth herein.

17. This agreement is binding on the partners, successors, executors, administrators and assigns of both parties, and neither party shall assign, sub-let or transfer his interest in this agreement without the written consent of the other.

IN WITNESS WHEREOF, the parties hereto have hereunto set their hands and seals the day and year first above written.

.... Architect

.... Engineer